MARVEL

WOMEN
OF MARVEL

Read more and listen at MARVEL.COM/VOICES.

WOMEN OF MARVEL #1

INTRODUCTION by LOUISE SIMONSON

START HERE

"MANI"

MARIKO TAMAKI // writer
PEACH MOMOKO // artist & colorist

"OPERATION SPYGLASS"

ELSA SJUNNESON // writer
NAOMI FRANQUIZ // artist
BRITTANY PEER // colorist

"SHE'S GOT THE LOOK"

MARIKO TAMAKI // writer
NINA VAKUEVA // artist & colorist

"CRETACEOUS FLIRTATIOUS"

NATASHA ALTERICI // writer
JOANNA ESTEP // artist
IRMA KNIIVILA // colorist

"GOOD HAIR"

MARIKO TAMAKI // writer
RACHAEL STOTT // artist
RACHELLE ROSENBERG // colorist

"SATURDAY MORNING IN HARLEM"

ANNE TOOLE // writer
KEI ZAMA // artist
RUTH REDMOND // colorist

"WILD RHINO CHASE"

NADIA SHAMMAS // writer
SKYLAR PATRIDGE // artist
TRÍONA FARRELL // colorist

"WATER WHEN NEEDS WATERING"

MARIKO TAMAKI // writer
MARIKA CRESTA // artist
RACHELLE ROSENBERG // colorist

"GIVE A CAT A BONE..."

SOPHIE CAMPBELL // writer
ELEONORA CARLINI // artist
TRÍONA FARRELL // colorist

"THE GODDESS OF DEATH SLEEPS TONIGHT"

MARIKO TAMAKI // writer
JUNE BRIGMAN // penciller
ROY RICHARDSON // inker
RACHELLE ROSENBERG // colorist

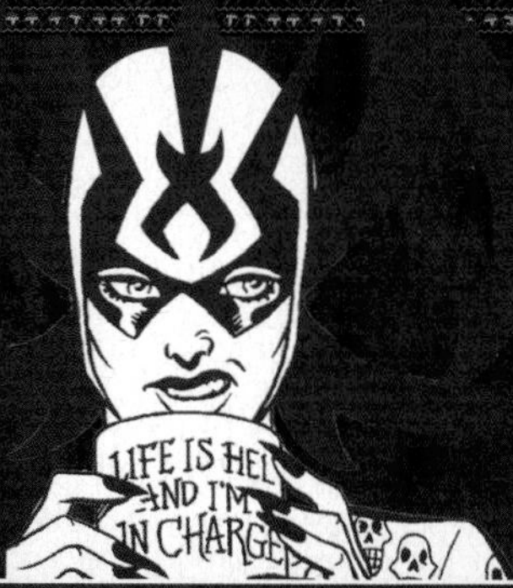

LIFE IS HEL
AND I'M
IN CHARGE

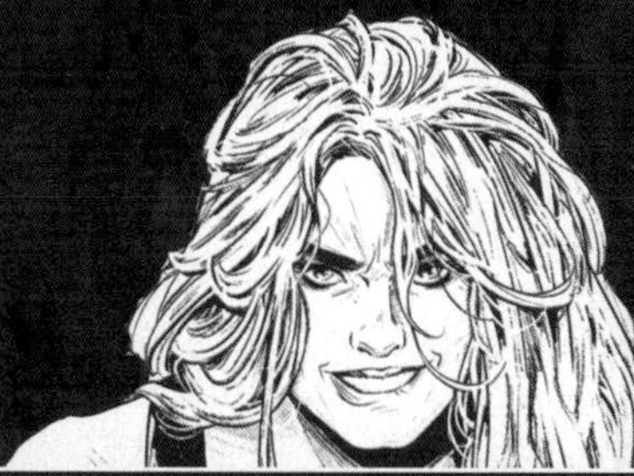

"DATE NIGHT"

ZORAIDA CÓRDOVA // writer
MARIA FRÖHLICH // artist
RACHELLE ROSENBERG // colorist

"POWER POSE: SPOTLIGHTING WOMEN OF COLOR IN THE MARVEL UNIVERSE"

by ANGÉLIQUE ROCHÉ

letterer VC's ARIANA MAHER
cover art SARA PICHELLI & MATTIA IACONO
consulting editor ANGÉLIQUE ROCHÉ
editor SARAH BRUNSTAD

MARVEL'S VOICES #1

"PUNISHMENT"

ROXANE GAY // writer
BRITTNEY L. WILLIAMS // artist
RACHELLE ROSENBERG // colorist

GIRL COMICS #1-3

INTRODUCTIONS
COLLEEN COOVER // writer, artist, colorist & letterer

letterer VC's TRAVIS LANHAM
cover art RYAN BENJAMIN & ANTHONY WASHINGTON
editor CHRIS ROBINSON

"MORITAT"

G. WILLOW WILSON // writer
MING DOYLE // artist
CRIS PETER // colorist
KATHLEEN MARINACCIO // letterer

"VENUS"

TRINA ROBBINS // writer
STEPHANIE BUSCEMA // artist & colorist
KRISTYN FERRETTI // letterer

CONTINUE

CONTINUE ⬇

"A BRIEF RENDEZVOUS"
VALERIE D'ORAZIO // writer
NIKKI COOK // artist
ELIZABETH DISMANG BREITWEISER // colorist
KRISTYN FERRETTI // letterer

"SHOP DOG"
LUCY KNISLEY //
writer, artist, colorist & letterer

"CLOCKWORK NIGHTMARE"
ROBIN FURTH // writer
AGNES GARBOWSKA // artist & colorist
KRISTYN FERRETTI // letterer

"HEAD SPACE"
DEVIN GRAYSON // writer
EMMA RÍOS // artist
BARBARA CIARDO // colorist
KATHLEEN MARINACCIO // letterer

"DOGGED PURSUIT"
JILL THOMPSON // writer, artist & colorist
KATHLEEN MARINACCIO // letterer

"GOOD TO BE LUCKY"
KATHRYN IMMONEN // writer
COLLEEN COOVER // artist & letterer
ELIZABETH DISMANG BREITWEISER // colorist

"DOOM <3'S SUE!"
STEPHANIE BUSCEMA // writer, artist & colorist
KATHLEEN MARINACCIO // letterer

"DO YOU EVER?"
FAITH ERIN HICKS // writer, artist & letterer
CRIS PETER // colorist

"AD VICE"
ABBY DENSON // writer
EMMA VIECELI // artist
EMILY WARREN // colorist
KRISTYN FERRETTI // letterer

"RONDEAU"
CHRISTINE BOYLAN // writer
CYNTHIA MARTIN // artist
JUNE CHUNG // colorist
KATHLEEN MARINACCIO // letterer

"THE JOB"
LOUISE SIMONSON // writer
JUNE BRIGMAN // penciller
REBECCA BUCHMAN // inker
RONDA PATTISON // colorist
KATHLEEN MARINACCIO // letterer

"THINGS THAT NEVER CHANGE"
MARJORIE LIU // writer
SARA PICHELLI // artist
RACHELLE ROSENBERG // colorist
KATHLEEN MARINACCIO // letterer

WOMEN OF MARVEL. Contains material originally published in magazine form as WOMEN OF MARVEL (2021) #1, MARVEL'S VOICES (2020) #1 and GIRL COMICS (2010) #1-3. First printing 2021. ISBN 978-1-302-93419-4. Published by MARVEL WORLDWIDE, INC., a subsidiary of MARVEL ENTERTAINMENT, LLC. OFFICE OF PUBLICATION: 1290 Avenue of the Americas, New York, NY 10104. © 2021 MARVEL No similarity between any of the names, characters, persons, and/or institutions in this book with those of any living or dead person or institution is intended, and any such similarity which may exist is purely coincidental. **Printed in Canada.** KEVIN FEIGE, Chief Creative Officer; DAN BUCKLEY, President, Marvel Entertainment; JOE QUESADA, EVP & Creative Director; DAVID BOGART, Associate Publisher & SVP of Talent Affairs; TOM BREVOORT, VP, Executive Editor; NICK LOWE, Executive Editor, VP of Content, Digital Publishing; DAVID GABRIEL, VP of Print & Digital Publishing; JEFF YOUNGQUIST, VP of Production & Special Projects; ALEX MORALES, Director of Publishing Operations; DAN EDINGTON, Managing Editor; RICKEY PURDIN, Director of Talent Relations; JENNIFER GRÜNWALD, Senior Editor, Special Projects; SUSAN CRESPI, Production Manager; STAN LEE, Chairman Emeritus. For information regarding advertising in Marvel Comics or on Marvel.com, please contact Vit DeBellis, Custom Solutions & Integrated Advertising Manager, at vdebellis@marvel.com. For Marvel subscription inquiries, please call 888-511-5480. **Manufactured between 12/31/2021 and 2/1/2022 by SOLISCO PRINTERS, SCOTT, QC, CANADA.**

"A MOVING EXPERIENCE"
LEA HERNANDEZ // *writer, artist, colorist & letterer*

"BLINDSPOT"
ANN NOCENTI // *writer*
MOLLY CRABAPPLE // *artist & colorist*
STAR ST. GERMAIN // *letterer*

"MIXOLOGY AT TERATO GENA'S"
CARLA SPEED McNEIL // *writer, artist & letterer*
RONDA PATTISON // *colorist*

"CHAOS THEORY"
KELLY SUE DeCONNICK // *writer*
ADRIANA MELO // *penciller*
MARIAH BENES // *inker*
CRIS PETER // *colorist*
KATHLEEN MARINACCIO // *letterer*

cover art AMANDA CONNER & LAURA MARTIN (#1),
JILL THOMPSON (#2), JO CHEN (#3)
assistant editors SANA AMANAT & RACHEL PINNELAS
associate editor LAUREN SANKOVITCH
editors JEANINE SCHAEFER with LAUREN SANKOVITCH
special thanks to SPRING HOTELING

WOMEN OF MARVEL TPB

" FINDING MYSELF AMONG THE PANELS"
by LORRAINE CINK

"MARVEL, OUR UNIVERSE"
by SANA AMANAT & JUDITH STEPHENS

"THE WOMEN OF MARVEL LOCKER ROOM"
by MacKENZIE CADENHEAD

ASKED & ANSWERED WITH THE WOMEN OF MARVEL:
KRISTEN ANDERSON-LOPEZ
PEACH MOMOKO
GUGU MBATHA-RAW & WUNMI MOSAKU
CATE SHORTLAND

SUPER VISIBLE Q&A WITH
MARGARET STOHL & JUDITH STEPHENS

collection cover art EMA LUPACCHINO & RACHELLE ROSENBERG

consulting editor ANGÉLIQUE ROCHÉ
collection editor JENNIFER GRÜNWALD
assistant editor DANIEL KIRCHHOFFER
assistant managing editor MAIA LOY
associate manager, talent relations LISA MONTALBANO
associate editor, special projects SARAH SINGER

associate manager, digital assets JOE HOCHSTEIN
vp production & special projects JEFF YOUNGQUIST
research JESS HARROLD
book designer STACIE ZUCKER
svp print, sales & marketing DAVID GABRIEL
editor in chief C.B. CEBULSKI

special thanks to SARAH AMOS, BRAD BARTON, BRENDON BIGLEY, LAUREN BISOM, JOHN CERILLI,
TIMOTHY CHENG, HALEY CONATSER, ADRI COWAN, TIM DILLON, CHRISTINE DINH, JILL DuBOFF,
JASMINE ESTRADA, JAMIE FREVELE, ZACHARY GOLDBERG, BRANDON GRUGLE, CHRISTINA HARRINGTON,
KIRAN HEFA, TAMARA KRINSKY, JEN LAI, JASON LATORRE, ALEX LOPEZ, JENNIFER MANEL, BEN MORSE,
EMILY NEWCOMEN, MIKE PASCUILLO, RYAN PENAGOS, ALANA PERI, ELLIE PYLE, ISABEL ROBERTSON,
LARISSA ROSEN, JEANINE SCHAEFER, WALT SCHWENK, REBECCA SEIDEL, MARY STEVENS,
PERCIA VERLIN, STEPHEN WACKER, BEN WHITMORE & ALEXIS WILLIAMS

END HERE

MARVEL, OUR UNIVERSE

by JUDITH STEPHENS & SANA AMANAT
Co-Creators of the *Women of Marvel* Podcast

When we were early on in our careers at Marvel, we were working on a book called *Girl Comics*, a collection of stories and editorials written, drawn, colored, and edited by women. For the women working on that book, it was a lovely celebration of those often overlooked in our industry and a reminder that we were not in it alone. Because, for many of us, the comics industry had become a place dominated and led by men. What was illuminating about that experience though was the rich history we discovered about the comics industry and the women at Marvel. Women like Violet Barclay and Ruth Atkinson who were the first artists at the company, and the silent giants like Marie Severin and Flo Steinberg who were as much among the founding pillars of this company as Stan Lee and Jack Kirby were. The truth is that women and nonbinary folks have always been here at Marvel, and now, over eighty years later, they're embedded in the very fabric of what this company has become.

Though we may not have always been super visible, we have existed every step of the way, reshaping not just the story of comics, its characters, and the story of Marvel as a company, but how the world honors our identities and perspectives. From the early artists and inkers of the Timely Comics days to the first women in the Marvel offices, from the first credited woman writers and editors to the first woman executives, women have been blazing the path, opening doors and building a bigger and more inclusive table for decades. While so many of these incredible women will never have their names in lights, their (our) names are endless. Through the years, our presence has grown in numbers, our voices more prominent in every aspect of Marvel. In turn, our characters, the stories we tell, and the Marvel Universe as a whole have grown.

We have been asked countless times about how "Women of Marvel" as a "platform" started, but as many of us know, it was never something any of us planned. In 2009, when the first Women of Marvel (WOM) panel premiered at San Diego Comic-Con (SDCC), we didn't have a plan or strategy, just the innate feeling that we wanted — *needed* — a place for both the women who worked at and with Marvel but also the women fans who craved a space in this vast fandom. That idea, of having a collective voice, a space for women and nonbinary folks, was key to the success of those first panels. As the years went by and we continued to host these panels, they proved to be the catalyst for some of the most magical moments of every year. With lines out the door, standing room only, it was clear that these spaces held the next generations of Marvel fandom. Not just a home, a place of community, but a space where we all could belong.

A few years later, we came together, along with our colleagues Jeanine Schaefer and Adri Cowan, to create the WOM podcast. To say we were scrappy in the beginning would be putting it lightly. We were a low-tech podcast, fitting in any way we could. Driven by our goal to embrace our community with open arms, with the content that we knew we wanted to see. Over time, we learned how to create a more structured and curated podcast with better sound and editing, but, along the way, regardless of the quality, we were embraced back. Almost ten years later, we are still here.

As the podcast evolved, so did we. In our search to create quality, engaging content, we too learned not just the true story of women at Marvel but the true Marvel secret, that women have always been a part of telling our stories. From Fabulous Flo Steinberg and the endless letters to fans that she wrote in Stan's voice, to Marie Severin and her army of colorists, to Paty Cockrum, a true firecracker who started the first archive of character art in the '70s. We also learned that there were so many others, past and present, shaping the Marvel Universe. Writers like Linda Fite, Jean Thomas, and Carole Seuling and artists like Janice Chiang, one of the first Chinese-American letterers. We learned about the era of Jo Duffy, Louise "Weezie" Simonson, and Ann Nocenti, with the iconic stories of *Luke Cage and Iron Fist*, *X-Men*, and *Daredevil*. But, somewhat unintentionally, we were also making room for the names to come.

We have not only been able to shine a light on this incredible work through the WOM podcast, pieces on Marvel.com like *Asked & Answered,* and the upcoming book *Super Visible*, but we have continued to help pave the way for incredible women and nonbinary talent through the Women of Marvel comics. Each of these pieces was a part of the celebration of a simple truth — we were here — and because of that, an awareness was built, both for comics leadership and for fans. We all realized what was possible.

When we began the panel all those years ago, there were no women or nonbinary characters with solo titles, and maybe a small handful of women were writing for Marvel. Now those lists have grown tremendously, with new characters joining the Marvel Universe, written and drawn by an increasing list of diverse creators from across the world. The best part is that behind the scenes, how we tell stories and what stories we tell continues to evolve.

We didn't know then what this would become or where the conversations would lead us. We only hoped to spark the conversation and to welcome more fans into our community. Today, fans who once sat in the audience or listened to the podcast now join us on stage as creators, producers, actors, and Marvel employees, each helping to continue the story of the Marvel Universe. That includes the first-of-its-kind, one-of-a-kind trade you have in your hands today.

Because in the end, we know now as we have always known in our hearts that this is Marvel…OUR universe.

JUDITH STEPHENS is a producer, cosplayer, and world traveler with ever-changing rainbow-colored hair. Born in Detroit, she moved to New York City in 2003 to attend college and fell in love with the city. While at Parsons studying photography, she discovered anime and cosplay while attending conventions. Since then, she has attended over 100 conventions across the United States and internationally as staff, photographer, and cosplayer, and has cosplayed over 25 characters, including Captain Marvel. As a Producer, Judith worked at Marvel for fifteen years, where she created series like *Marvel Becoming*, *Marvel Quickdraw*, *THWIP! The Big Marvel Show*, *Women of Marvel*, and more. A proud Queens resident, where she lives with her two cats, she spends her free time dining and traveling with friends. Judith is currently a host and producer of the *Women of Marvel* podcast and is co-author of *Super Visible: The Story of the Women of Marvel*.

SANA AMANAT is currently an Executive of Production & Development at Marvel Studios. Over her twelve years at the company, Sana has worked as an editor, content creator, and producer. She's worked on story and character development for much of her career, beginning with comic books then moving to animation, games, and live action. Her credits include comic book titles like *Captain Marvel*, *Miles Morales*, and *Hawkeye* and series *Marvel Rising* and *Marvel's Hero Project*. Sana is most known for co-creating a Muslim-American female super hero named Kamala Khan — the new *Ms. Marvel* — which gained worldwide media attention and sparked excitement and dialogue about identity and the Muslim-American narrative. She's championed representation in storytelling, striving to cultivate new voices within the entertainment industry by creating platforms like the *Women of Marvel*. She is currently producing the live-action *Ms. Marvel* series for Disney Plus.

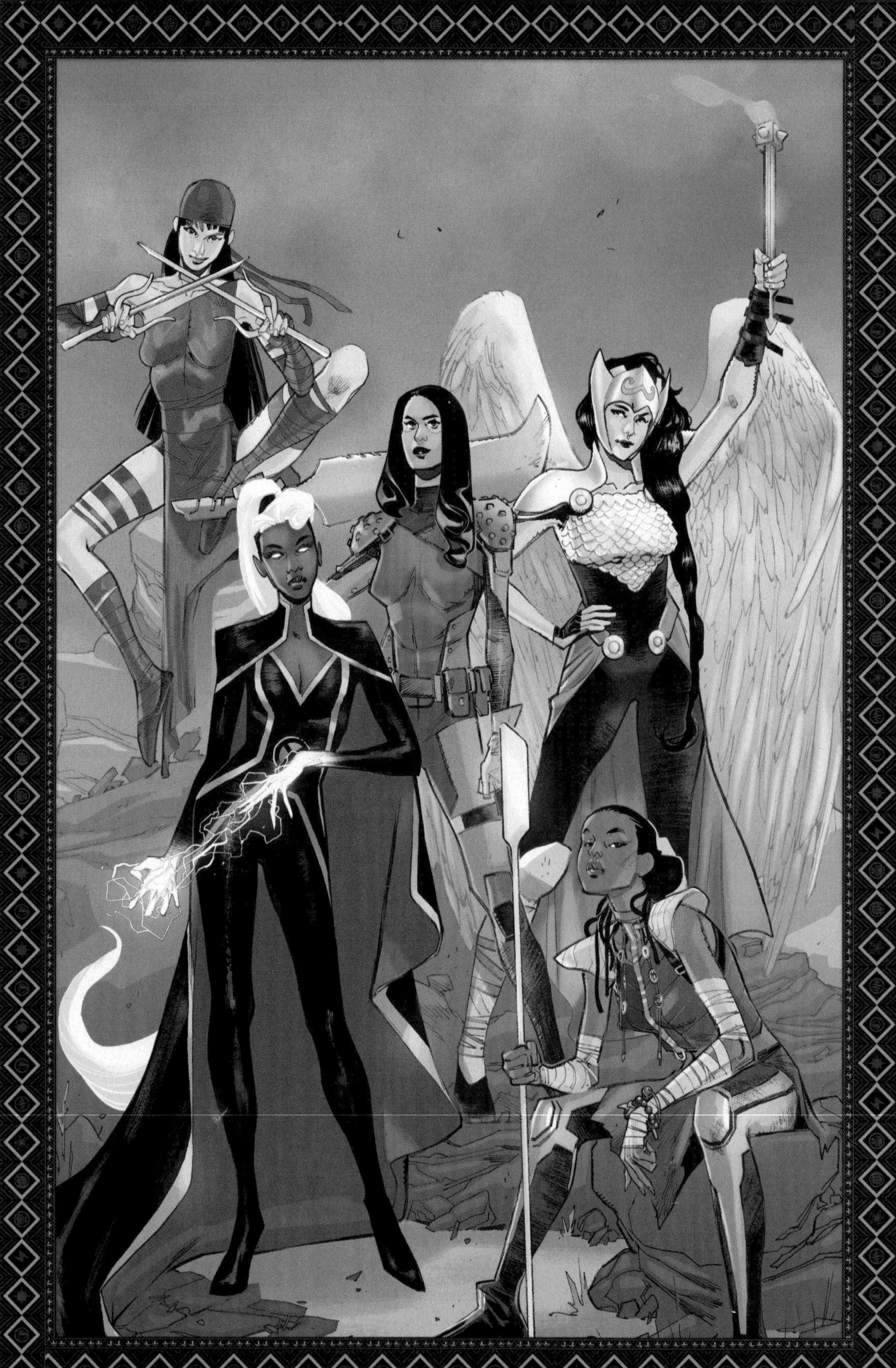

WOMEN OF MARVEL #1

INTRODUCTION BY LOUISE SIMONSON

Humanity exists on a spectrum. And each human's voice is different, speaking from their personal experience in the complex Venn diagram of their own life, expressing their individual point of view.

In the Olden Days of Marvel, the voices were mostly male. Marvel Comics was dominated by the people who founded it — Stan Lee, Jack Kirby, Steve Ditko. Like any creators, they were telling stories that interested them — mostly about guys who were smart, courageous, quirky and, in their own ways, heroes. Sure, they had problems, but without a problem, there's no story. The occasional female character appeared, usually to supply a dash of romance or intrigue, but the focus was mainly on the super-guys.

Of course, these stories drew a mostly male audience who identified with these heroes. Comics companies — Marvel and elsewhere — have never been strong on demographic surveys, so figures about actual readership were iffy. Back in the 1980s, when I started working at Marvel as an editor, I was told that the readership was 90-95% male. So it figures that the guys who loved Marvel Comics were mostly the ones who fought to work there as editors, writers and artists. Marie Severin, who had worked in comics from the 1950s as a colorist, penciler and inker, was the glaring exception.

But by the '80s, things were changing. *X-Men*, written by Chris Claremont, featured strong female characters, and its more diverse cast drew a larger-than-normal female audience. Jo Duffy and Ann Nocenti both edited and wrote brilliantly and successfully for 1980s Marvel.

I began editing for Marvel in 1980 and wrote their comics a few years later. I loved writing female characters, but, at first, I deliberately avoided books with female leads. I simply didn't want to be put on books that "everyone knew" would be canceled within six months. I got around that by writing *team* books with strong female leads…including a strange kid-team book, POWER PACK, with gorgeous art by June Brigman.

Then, in the 1990s, the *X-Men* animated series introduced these powerful, interesting women to a whole new audience of…women! Movies, cartoons and TV shows all helped introduce Marvel comics to a wider audience. Manga had millions of comics-loving female fans. And gradually, more women were reading Marvel comics. Comics sales reflected their interests, and, not surprisingly, as women's interest

in Marvel grew, more female editors, writers and artists began to lend their voices to Marvel stories.

Marvel stories told by women's voices have the heart-stopping heroic action Marvel readers have come to expect, of course. But the featured characters are more diverse, and the voices that tell their stories can be a bit more nuanced.

By 2021, Marvel readership seems to be more balanced. 60% men. 40% women. That's what I hear. Give or take 10 percentage points. Could even be 50-50.

This burgeoning group of female comics editors, writers, artists and readers is wonderful — smart, wise, honest and incredibly talented. The women of Marvel always were those things. But now, there are more of them!

"Weezie"
3/4/21

In addition to her pioneering work as an editor at Marvel in the '80s and the co-creator of POWER PACK, Louise Simonson also wrote fan-favorite runs on X-FACTOR, NEW MUTANTS and SUPERMAN: THE MAN OF STEEL.

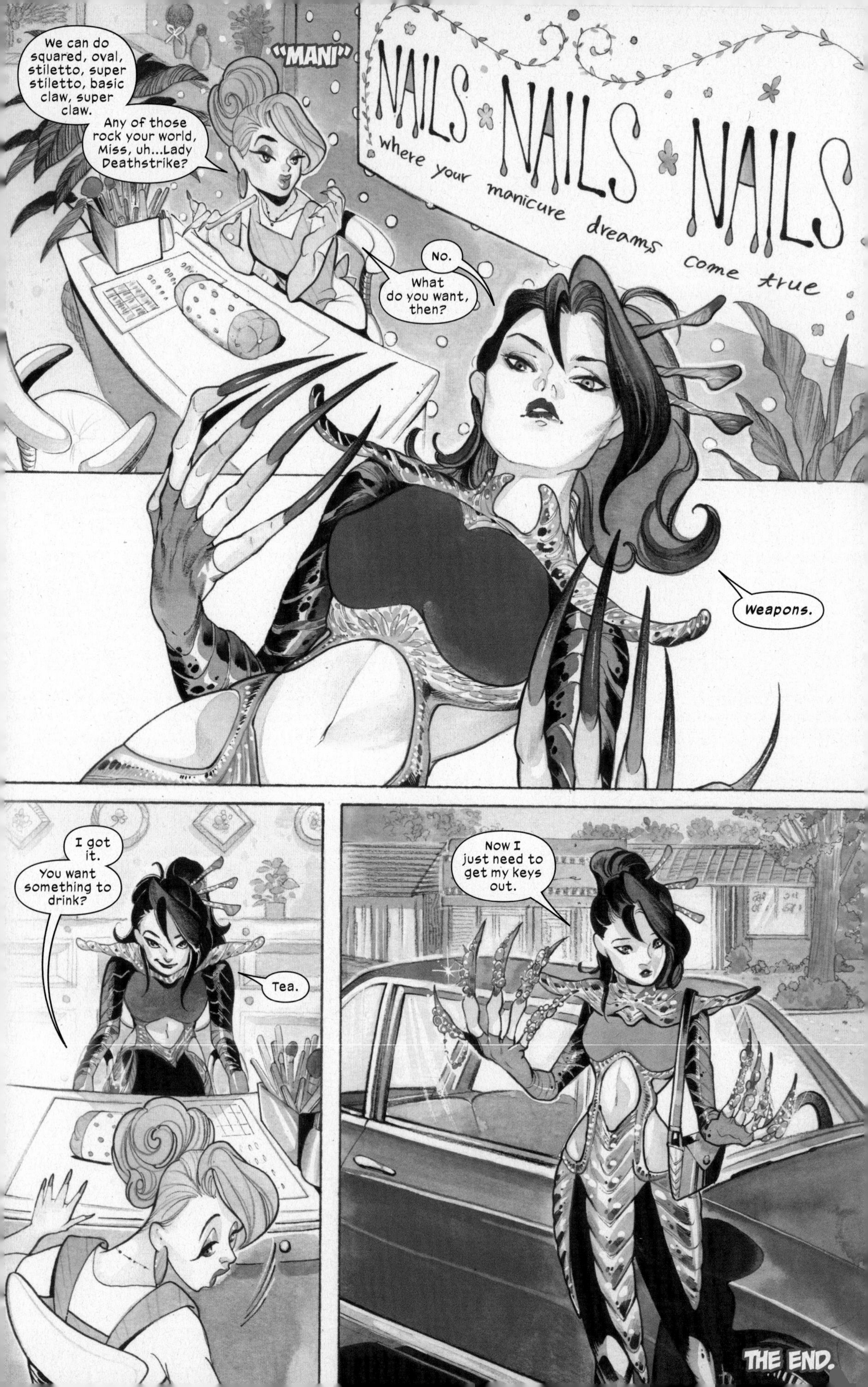
We can do squared, oval, stiletto, super stiletto, basic claw, super claw.
Any of those rock your world, Miss, uh...Lady Deathstrike?
"MANI"
NAILS NAILS NAILS
where your manicure dreams come true
No.
What do you want, then?
Weapons.
I got it.
You want something to drink?
Tea.
Now I just need to get my keys out.
THE END.

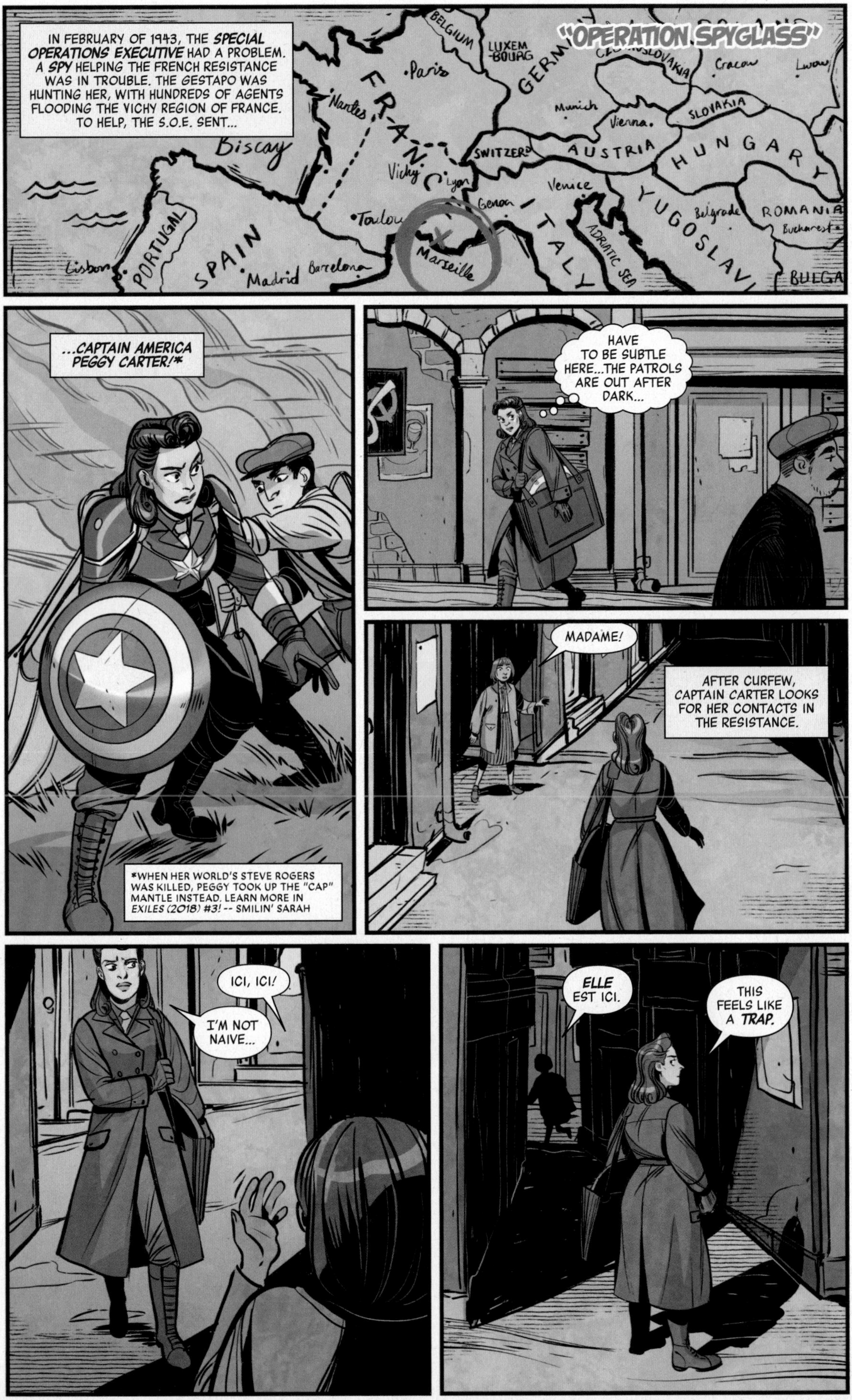
"OPERATION SPYGLASS"
IN FEBRUARY OF 1943, THE SPECIAL OPERATIONS EXECUTIVE HAD A PROBLEM. A SPY HELPING THE FRENCH RESISTANCE WAS IN TROUBLE. THE GESTAPO WAS HUNTING HER, WITH HUNDREDS OF AGENTS FLOODING THE VICHY REGION OF FRANCE. TO HELP, THE S.O.E. SENT...
BELGIUM
LUXEM BOURG
Paris
Nantes
FRANCE
Biscay
SWITZERd
AUSTRIA
HUNGARY
Munich
Vienna
SLOVAKIA
Cracow
Lwow
Vichy
Lyon
Genoa
Venice
YUGOSLAVI
Belgrade
ROMANIA
Bucharest
ITALY
ADRIATIC SEA
PORTUGAL
SPAIN
Lisbon
Madrid
Barcelona
Marseille
BULGA
...CAPTAIN AMERICA PEGGY CARTER!*
*WHEN HER WORLD'S STEVE ROGERS WAS KILLED, PEGGY TOOK UP THE "CAP" MANTLE INSTEAD. LEARN MORE IN EXILES (2018) #3! -- SMILIN' SARAH
HAVE TO BE SUBTLE HERE...THE PATROLS ARE OUT AFTER DARK...
MADAME!
AFTER CURFEW, CAPTAIN CARTER LOOKS FOR HER CONTACTS IN THE RESISTANCE.
ICI, ICI!
I'M NOT NAIVE...
ELLE EST ICI.
THIS FEELS LIKE A TRAP.

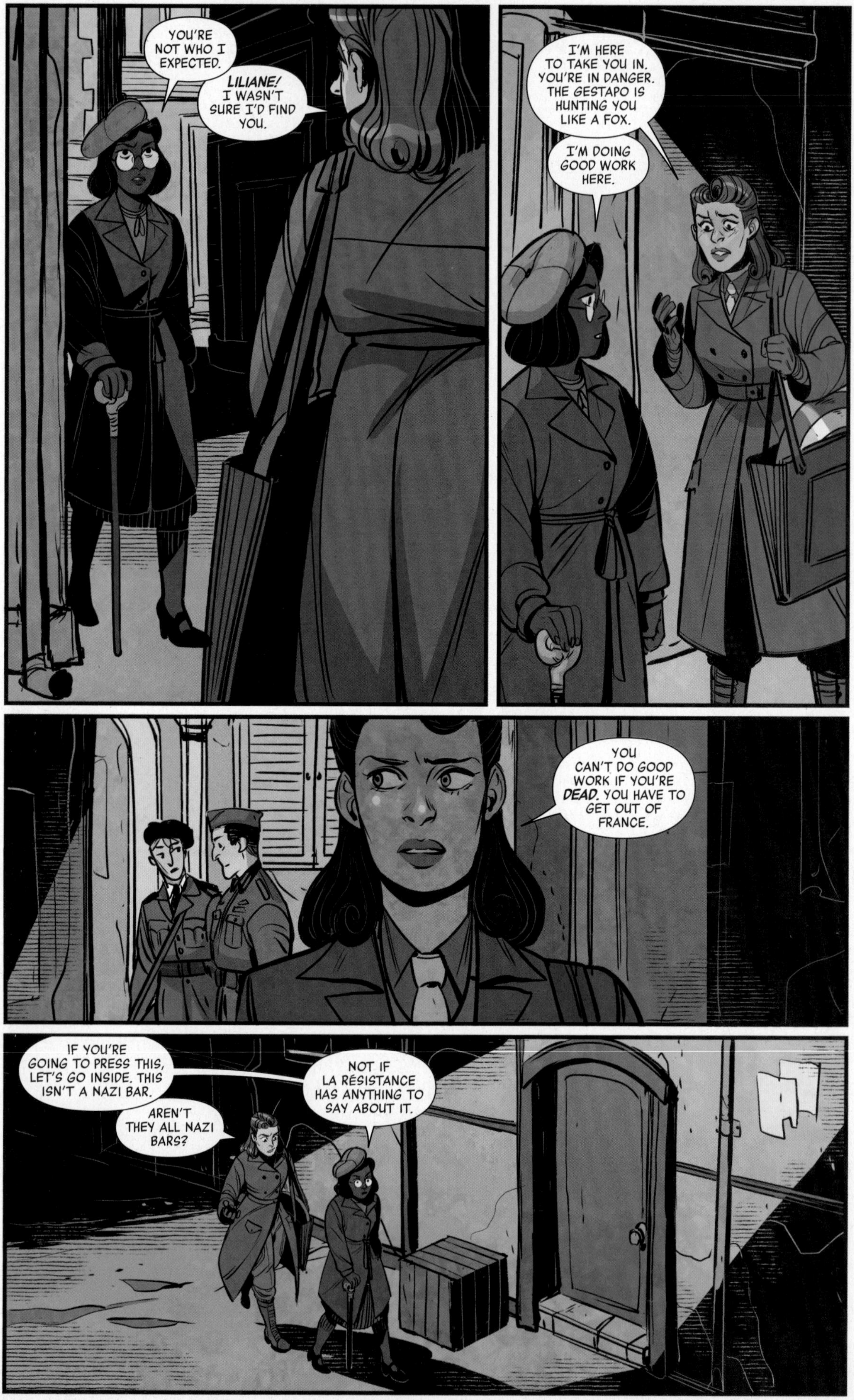
YOU'RE NOT WHO I EXPECTED.
LILIANE! I WASN'T SURE I'D FIND YOU.
I'M HERE TO TAKE YOU IN. YOU'RE IN DANGER. THE GESTAPO IS HUNTING YOU LIKE A FOX.
I'M DOING GOOD WORK HERE.
YOU CAN'T DO GOOD WORK IF YOU'RE DEAD. YOU HAVE TO GET OUT OF FRANCE.
IF YOU'RE GOING TO PRESS THIS, LET'S GO INSIDE. THIS ISN'T A NAZI BAR.
AREN'T THEY ALL NAZI BARS?
NOT IF LA RÉSISTANCE HAS ANYTHING TO SAY ABOUT IT.

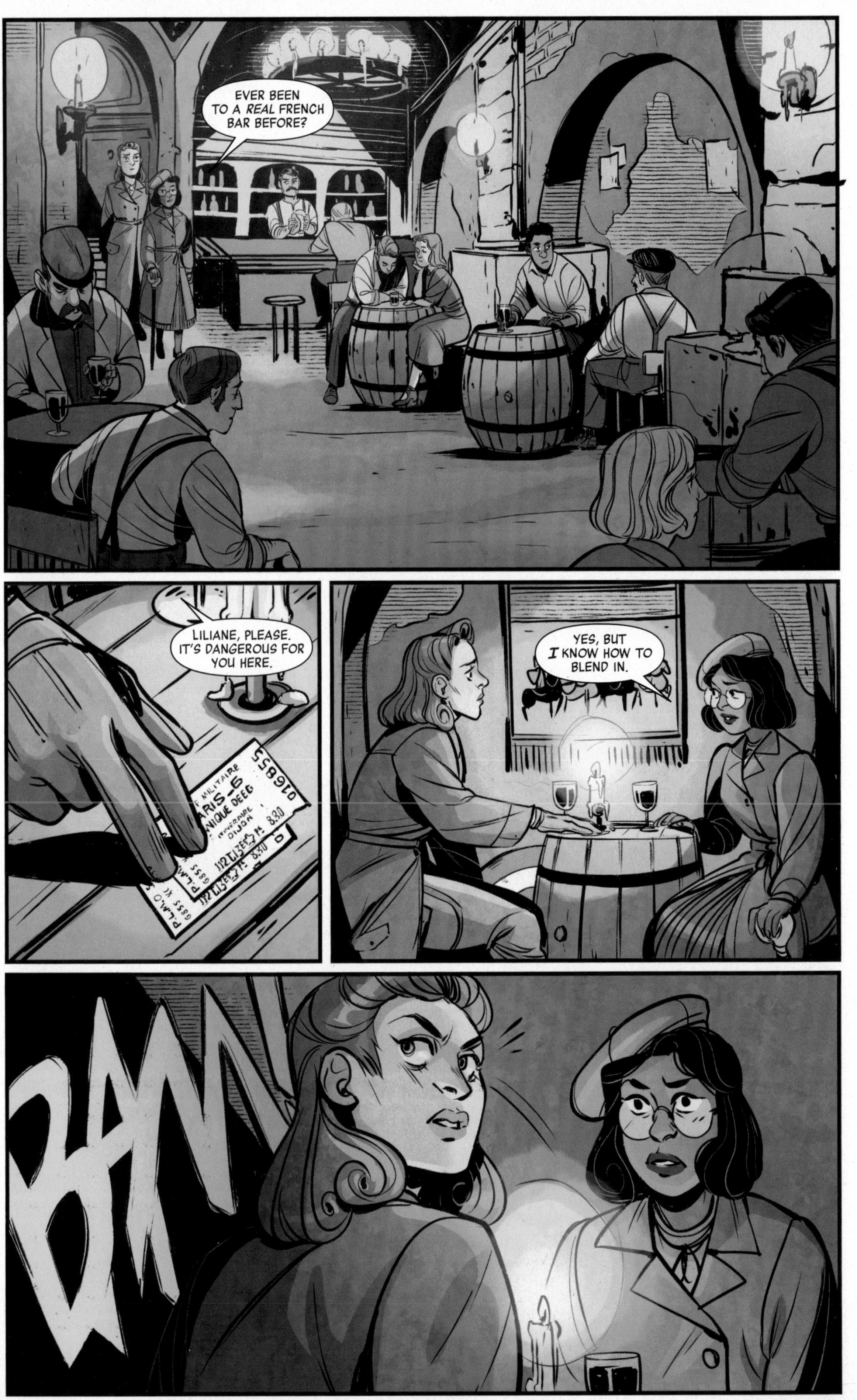
EVER BEEN TO A *REAL* FRENCH BAR BEFORE?
LILIANE, PLEASE. IT'S DANGEROUS FOR YOU HERE.
YES, BUT *I* KNOW HOW TO BLEND IN.
BAM

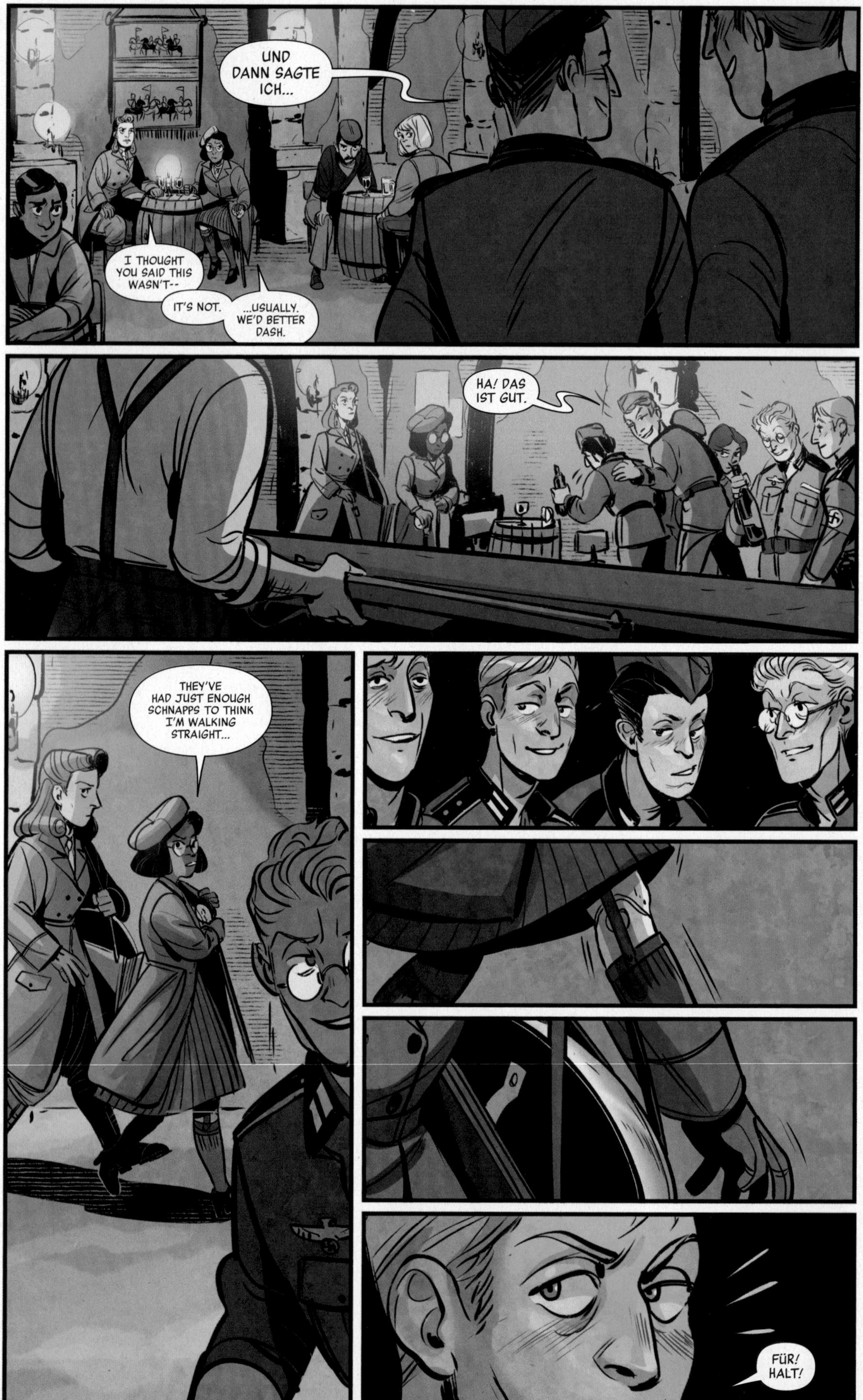
UND DANN SAGTE ICH...
I THOUGHT YOU SAID THIS WASN'T--
IT'S NOT.
...USUALLY. WE'D BETTER DASH.
HA! DAS IST GUT.
THEY'VE HAD JUST ENOUGH SCHNAPPS TO THINK I'M WALKING STRAIGHT...
FÜR! HALT!

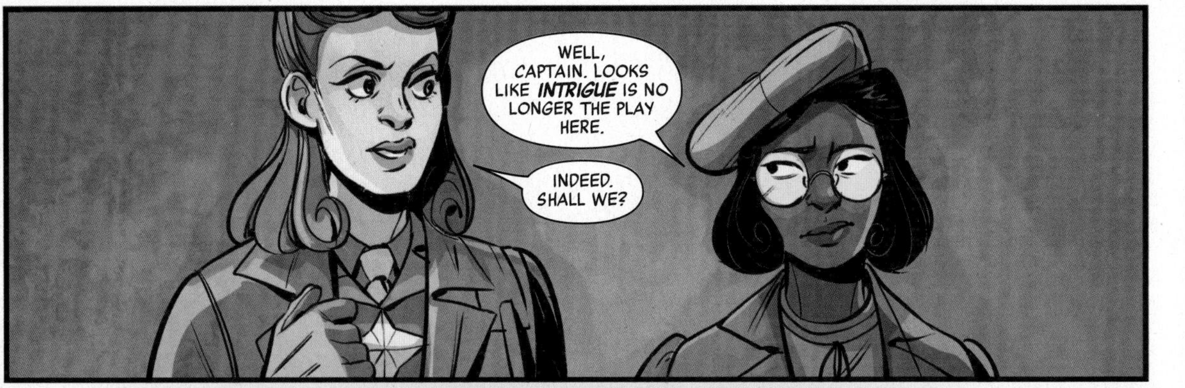
WELL, CAPTAIN. LOOKS LIKE INTRIGUE IS NO LONGER THE PLAY HERE.
INDEED. SHALL WE?

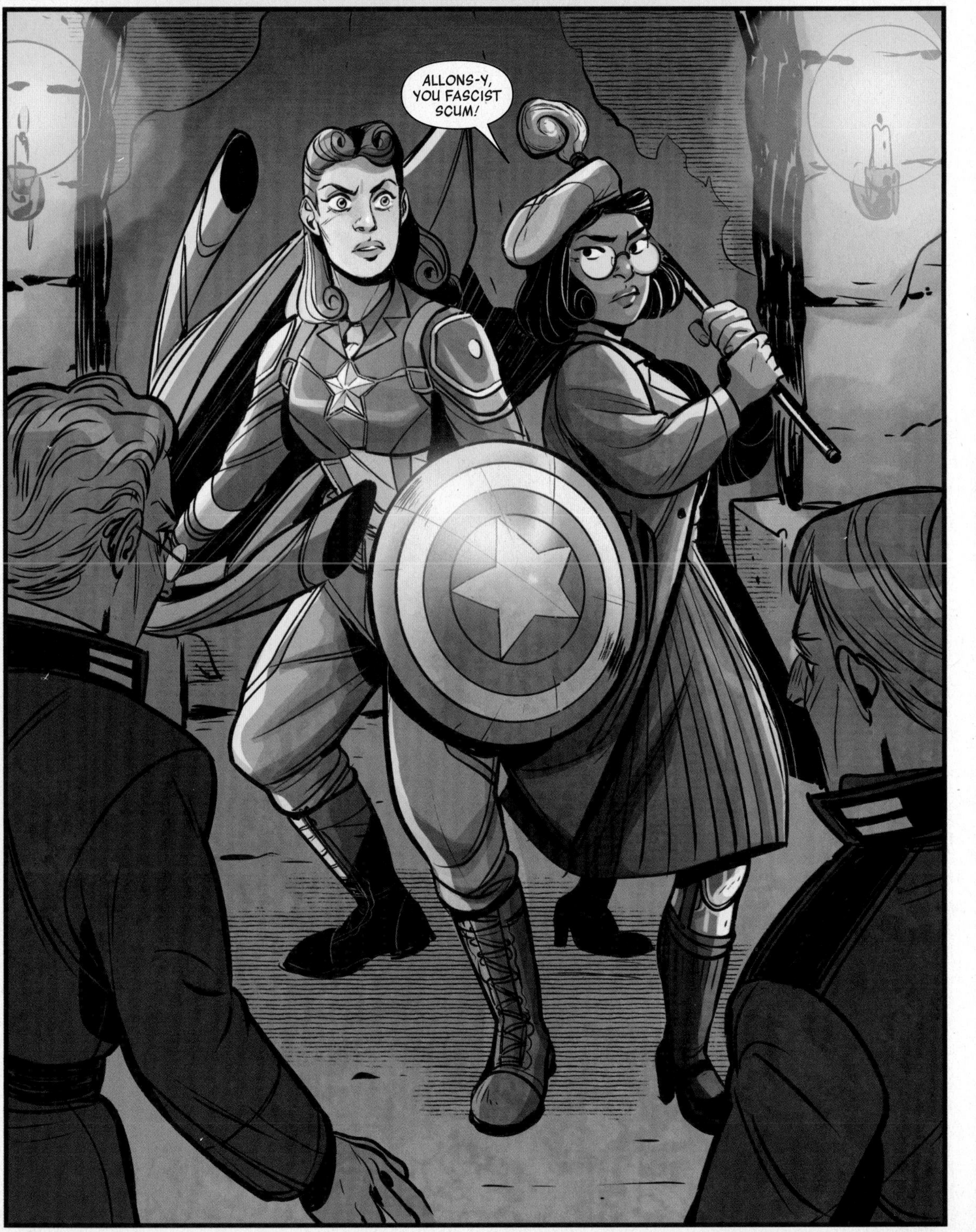
ALLONS-Y, YOU FASCIST SCUM!

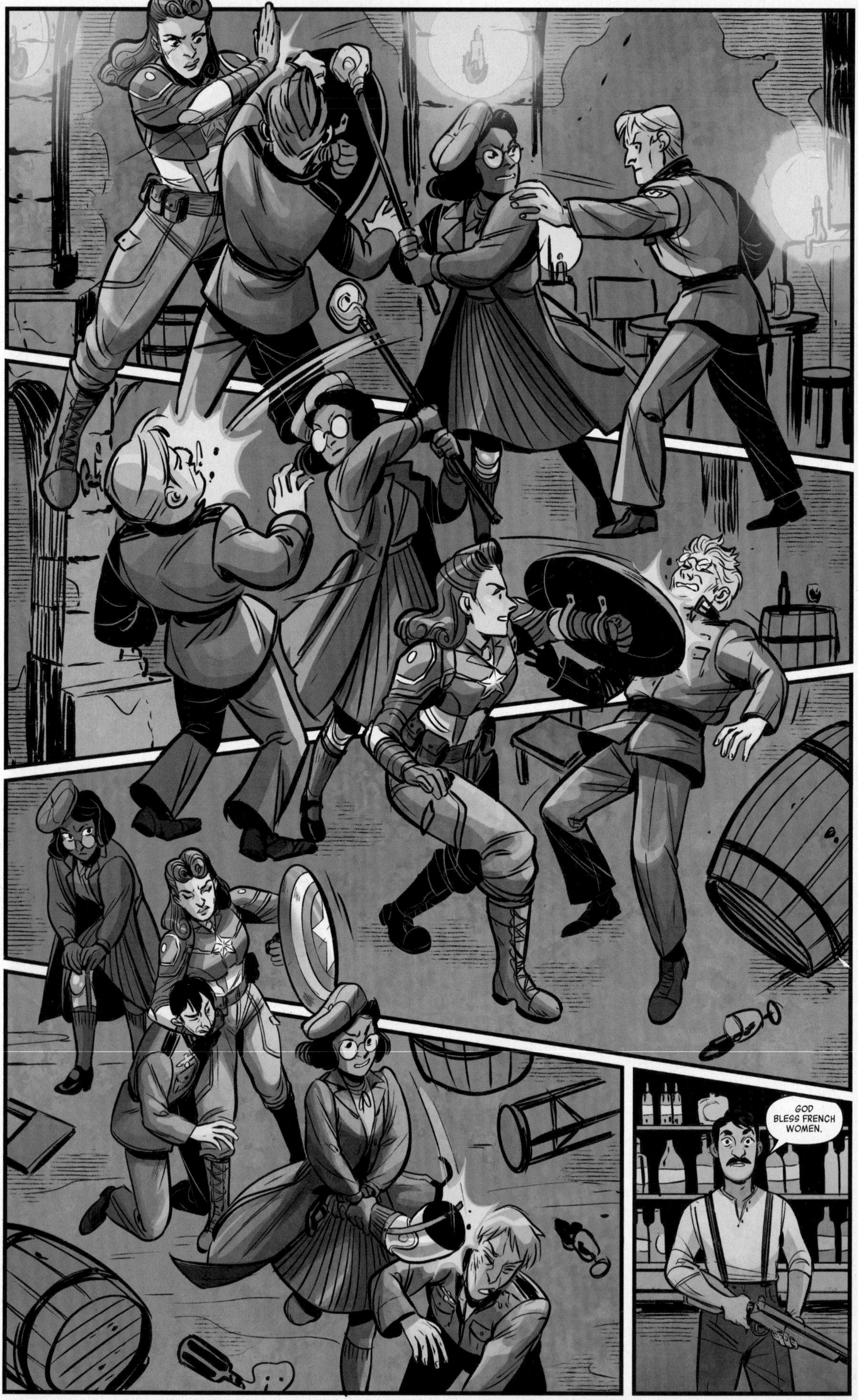
GOD BLESS FRENCH WOMEN.

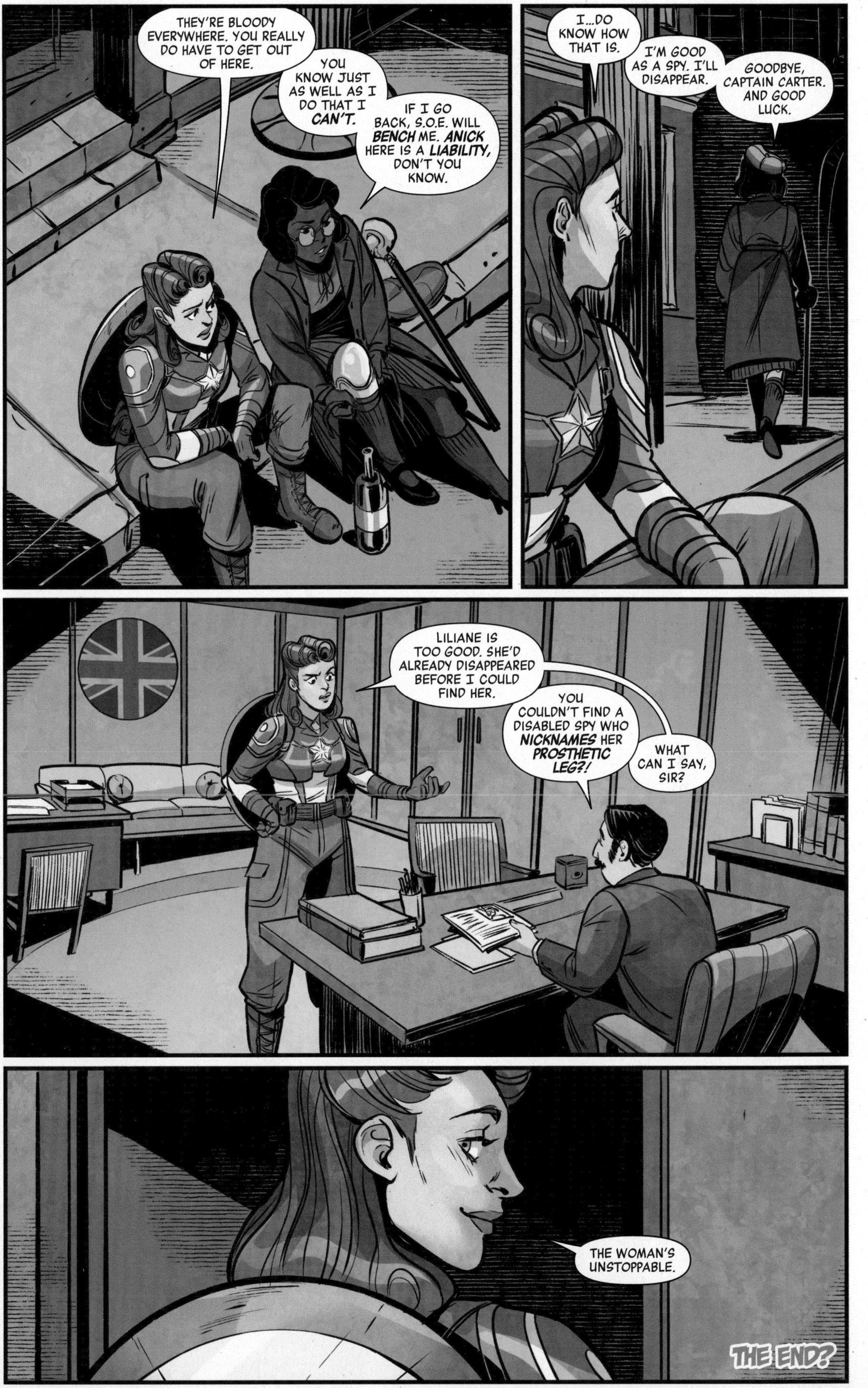
THEY'RE BLOODY EVERYWHERE. YOU REALLY DO HAVE TO GET OUT OF HERE.
YOU KNOW JUST AS WELL AS I DO THAT I CAN'T.
IF I GO BACK, S.O.E. WILL BENCH ME. ANICK HERE IS A LIABILITY, DON'T YOU KNOW.
I...DO KNOW HOW THAT IS.
I'M GOOD AS A SPY. I'LL DISAPPEAR.
GOODBYE, CAPTAIN CARTER. AND GOOD LUCK.
LILIANE IS TOO GOOD. SHE'D ALREADY DISAPPEARED BEFORE I COULD FIND HER.
YOU COULDN'T FIND A DISABLED SPY WHO NICKNAMES HER PROSTHETIC LEG?!
WHAT CAN I SAY, SIR?
THE WOMAN'S UNSTOPPABLE.
THE END?

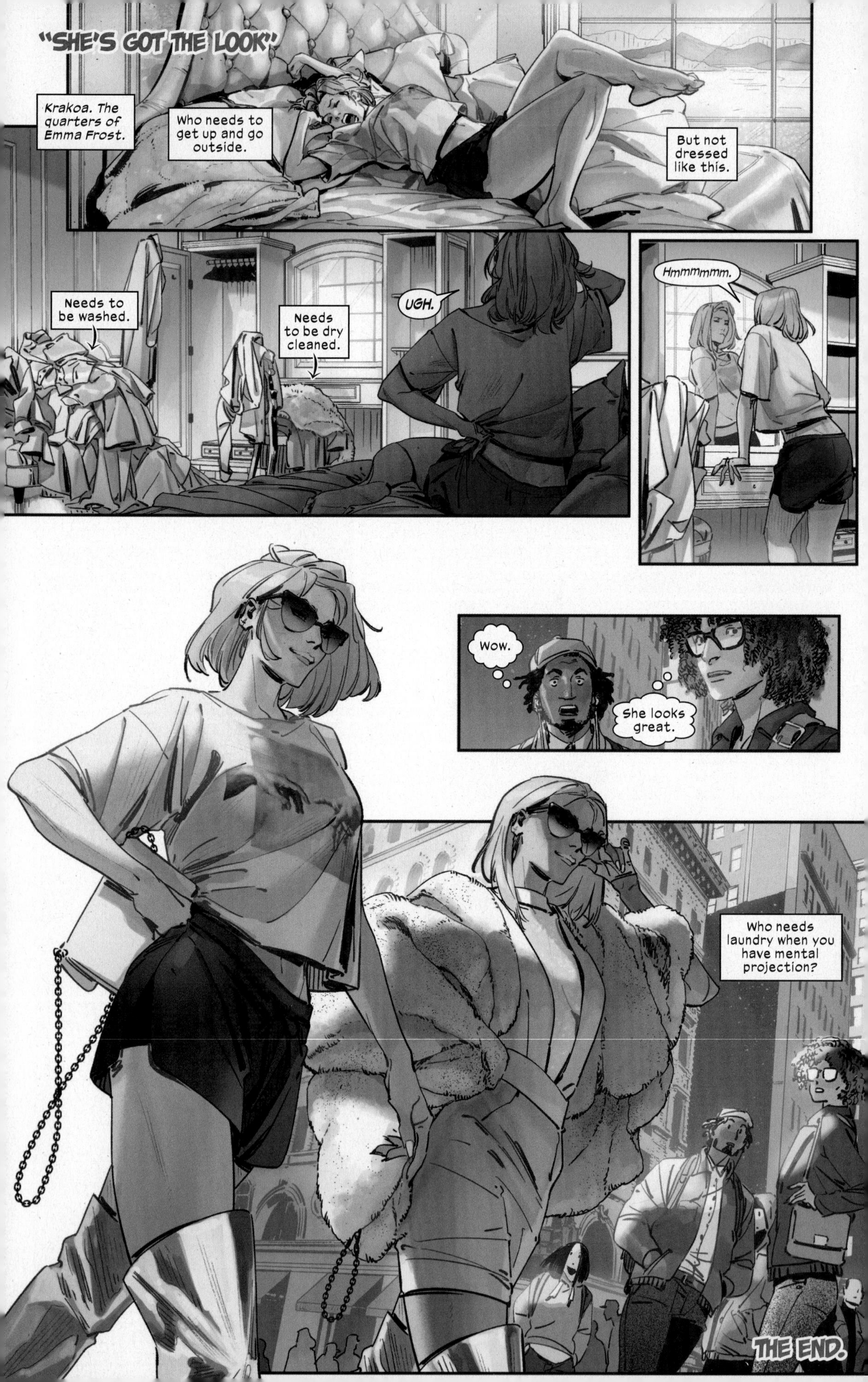
"SHE'S GOT THE LOOK"
Krakoa. The quarters of Emma Frost.
Who needs to get up and go outside.
But not dressed like this.
Needs to be washed.
Needs to be dry cleaned.
UGH.
Hmmmmmm.
Wow.
She looks great.
Who needs laundry when you have mental projection?
THE END.

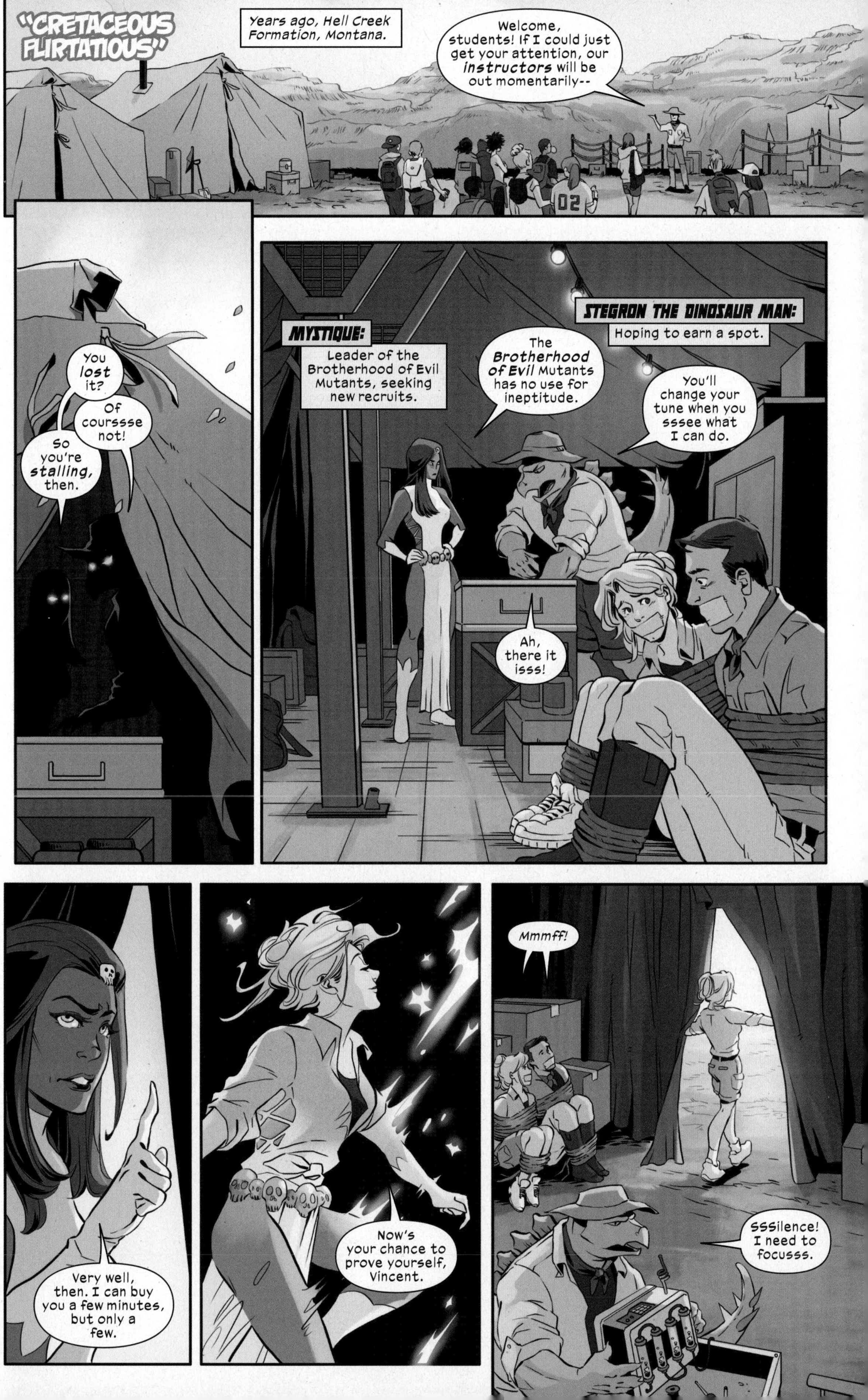
"CRETACEOUS FLIRTATIOUS"
Years ago, Hell Creek Formation, Montana.
Welcome, students! If I could just get your attention, our instructors will be out momentarily--
02
You lost it?
Of coursse not!
So you're stalling, then.
MYSTIQUE:
Leader of the Brotherhood of Evil Mutants, seeking new recruits.
The Brotherhood of Evil Mutants has no use for ineptitude.
STEGRON THE DINOSAUR MAN:
Hoping to earn a spot.
You'll change your tune when you sssee what I can do.
Ah, there it isss!
Very well, then. I can buy you a few minutes, but only a few.
Now's your chance to prove yourself, Vincent.
Mmmff!
SSSilence! I need to focusss.

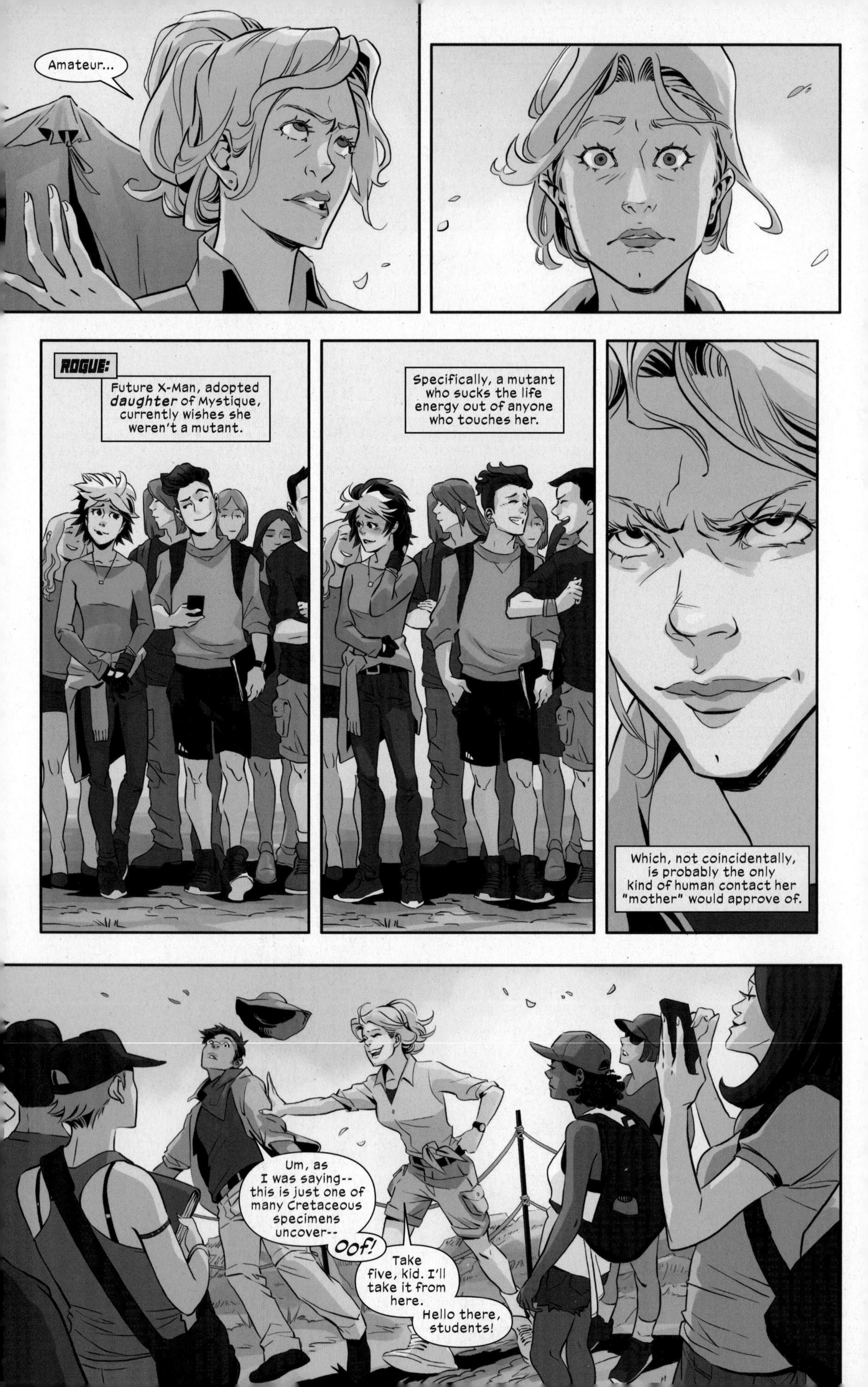
Amateur...
ROGUE:
Future X-Man, adopted daughter of Mystique, currently wishes she weren't a mutant.
Specifically, a mutant who sucks the life energy out of anyone who touches her.
Which, not coincidentally, is probably the only kind of human contact her "mother" would approve of.
Um, as I was saying-- this is just one of many Cretaceous specimens uncover--
OOF!
Take five, kid. I'll take it from here.
Hello there, students!

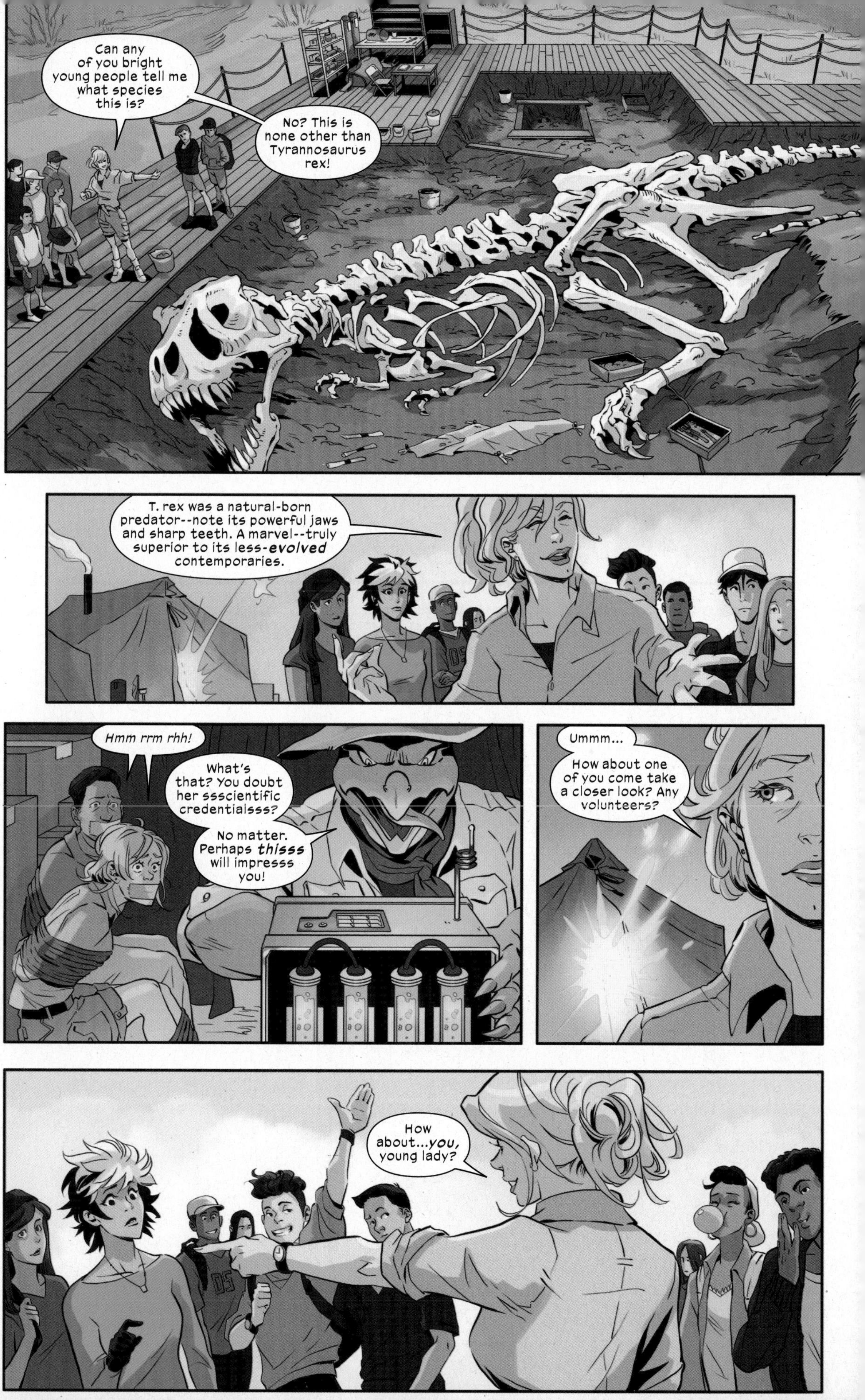
Can any of you bright young people tell me what species this is?
No? This is none other than Tyrannosaurus rex!
T. rex was a natural-born predator--note its powerful jaws and sharp teeth. A marvel--truly superior to its less-*evolved* contemporaries.
Hmm rrm rhh!
What's that? You doubt her ssscientific credentialsss?
No matter. Perhaps *thisss* will impresss you!
Ummm...
How about one of you come take a closer look? Any volunteers?
How about...*you*, young lady?

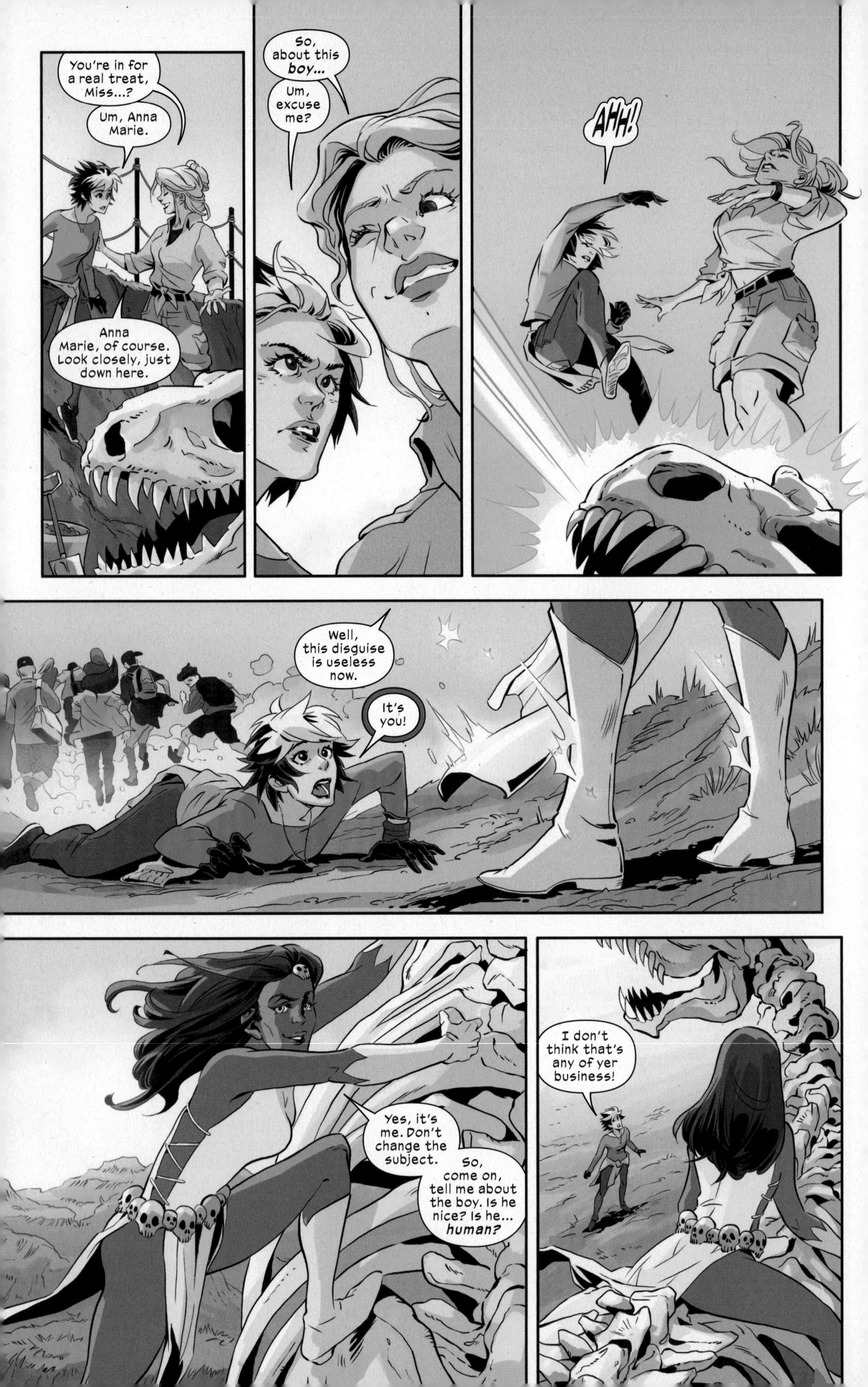
You're in for a real treat, Miss...?
Um, Anna Marie.
Anna Marie, of course. Look closely, just down here.
So, about this *boy*...
Um, excuse me?
AHH!
Well, this disguise is useless now.
It's you!
Yes, it's me. Don't change the subject.
So, come on, tell me about the boy. Is he nice? Is he... *human?*
I don't think that's any of yer business!

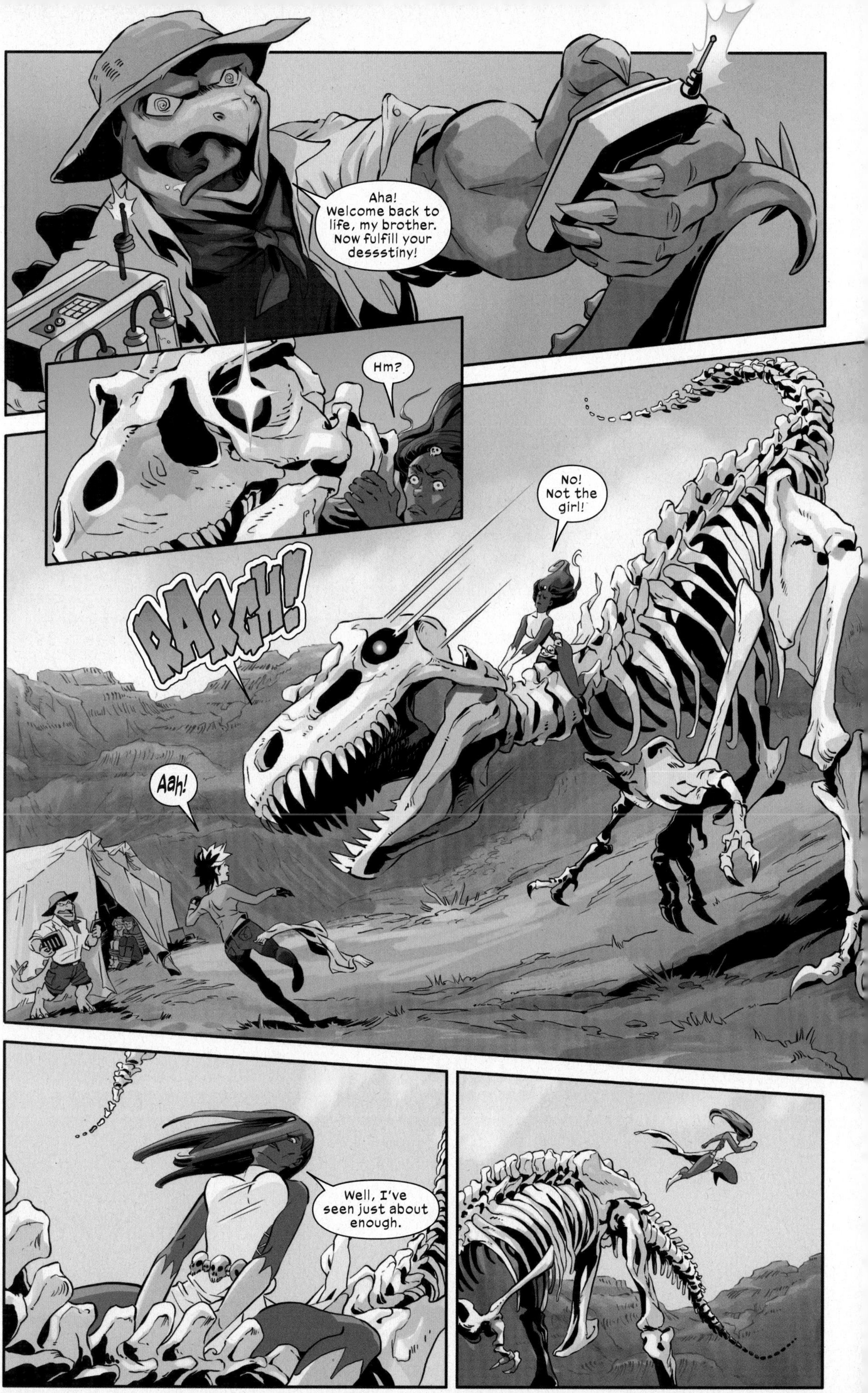
Aha! Welcome back to life, my brother. Now fulfill your dessstiny!
Hm?
No! Not the girl!
RARGH!
Aah!
Well, I've seen just about enough.

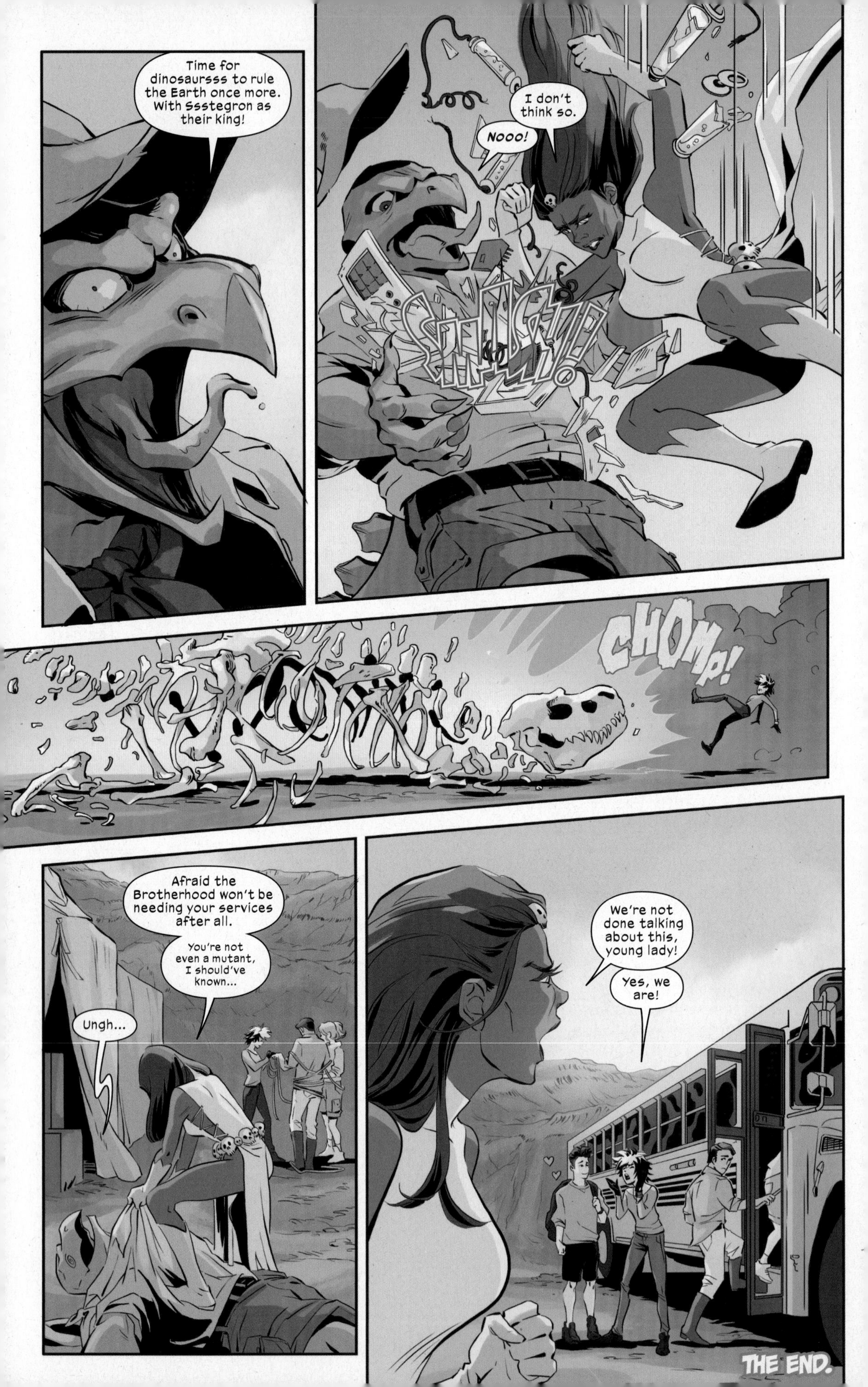
Time for dinosaursss to rule the Earth once more. With Ssstegron as their king!
I don't think so.
NOOO!
CHOMP!
Afraid the Brotherhood won't be needing your services after all.
You're not even a mutant, I should've known...
Ungh...
We're not done talking about this, young lady!
Yes, we are!
THE END.

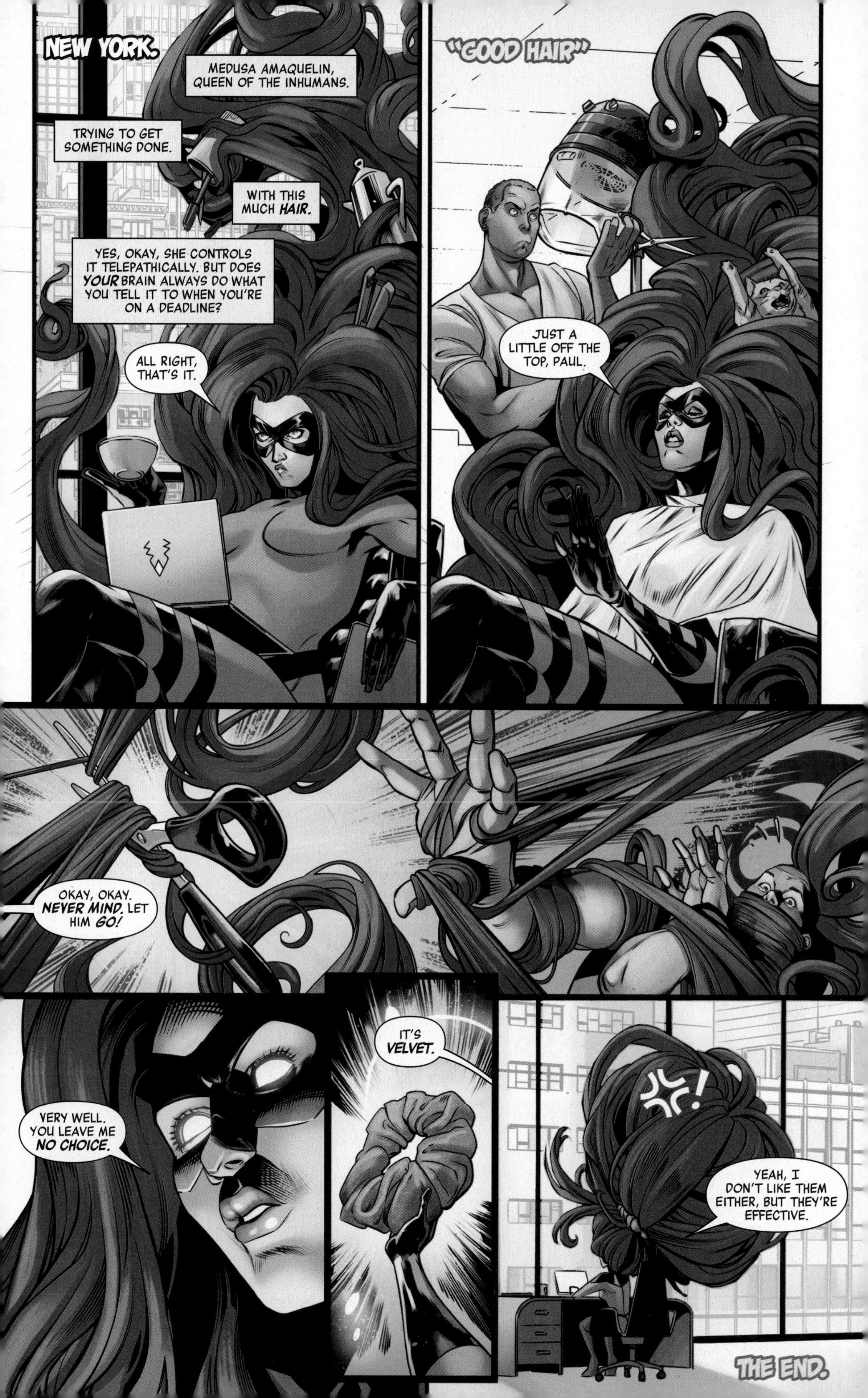
NEW YORK.
MEDUSA AMAQUELIN, QUEEN OF THE INHUMANS.
TRYING TO GET SOMETHING DONE.
WITH THIS MUCH HAIR.
YES, OKAY, SHE CONTROLS IT TELEPATHICALLY. BUT DOES YOUR BRAIN ALWAYS DO WHAT YOU TELL IT TO WHEN YOU'RE ON A DEADLINE?
ALL RIGHT, THAT'S IT.
"GOOD HAIR"
JUST A LITTLE OFF THE TOP, PAUL.
OKAY, OKAY. NEVER MIND. LET HIM GO!
VERY WELL. YOU LEAVE ME NO CHOICE.
IT'S VELVET.
YEAH, I DON'T LIKE THEM EITHER, BUT THEY'RE EFFECTIVE.
THE END.

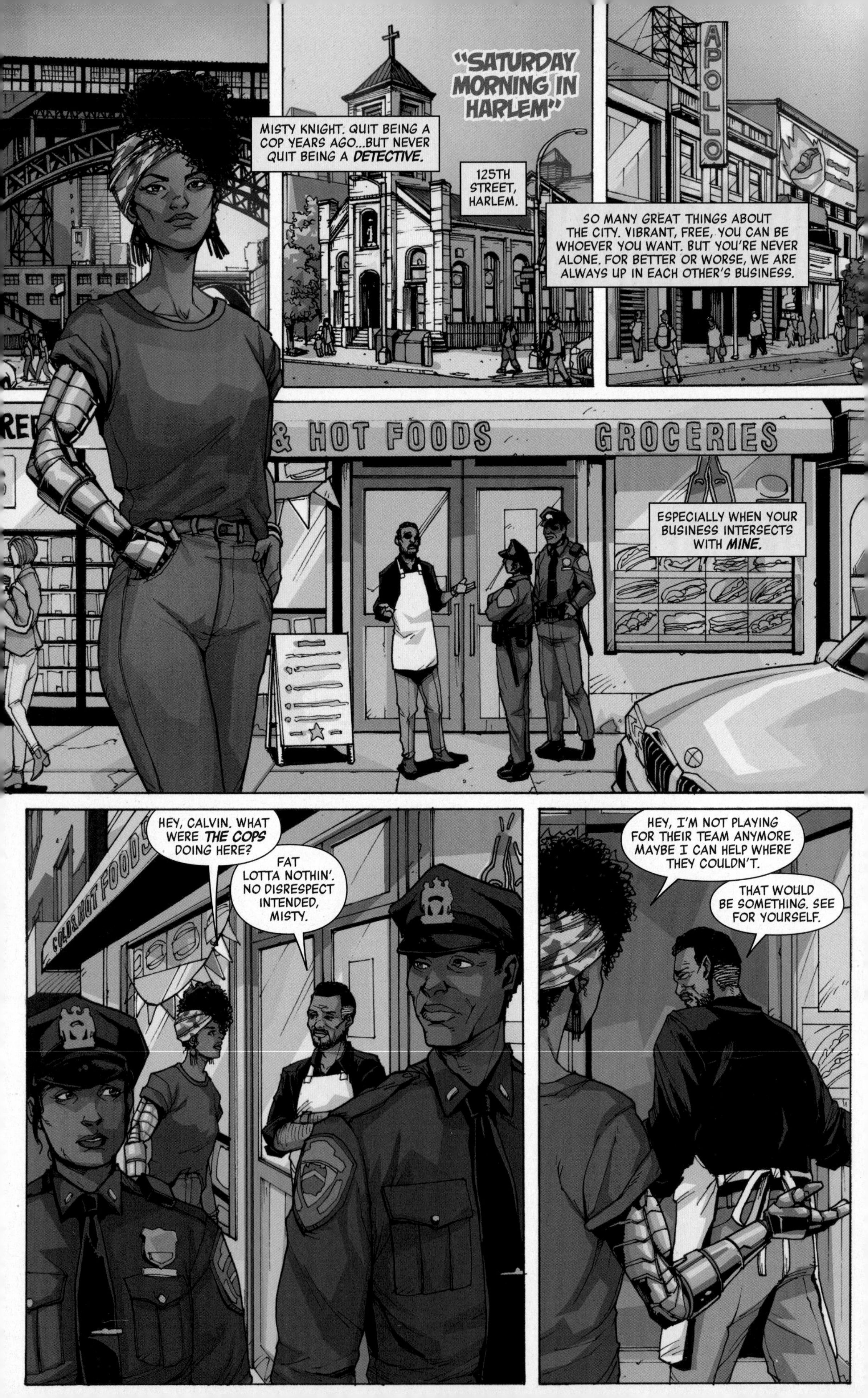
MISTY KNIGHT. QUIT BEING A COP YEARS AGO...BUT NEVER QUIT BEING A DETECTIVE.
"SATURDAY MORNING IN HARLEM"
125TH STREET, HARLEM.
APOLLO
SO MANY GREAT THINGS ABOUT THE CITY. VIBRANT, FREE, YOU CAN BE WHOEVER YOU WANT. BUT YOU'RE NEVER ALONE. FOR BETTER OR WORSE, WE ARE ALWAYS UP IN EACH OTHER'S BUSINESS.
& HOT FOODS
GROCERIES
ESPECIALLY WHEN YOUR BUSINESS INTERSECTS WITH MINE.
HEY, CALVIN. WHAT WERE THE COPS DOING HERE?
FAT LOTTA NOTHIN'. NO DISRESPECT INTENDED, MISTY.
HEY, I'M NOT PLAYING FOR THEIR TEAM ANYMORE. MAYBE I CAN HELP WHERE THEY COULDN'T.
THAT WOULD BE SOMETHING. SEE FOR YOURSELF.

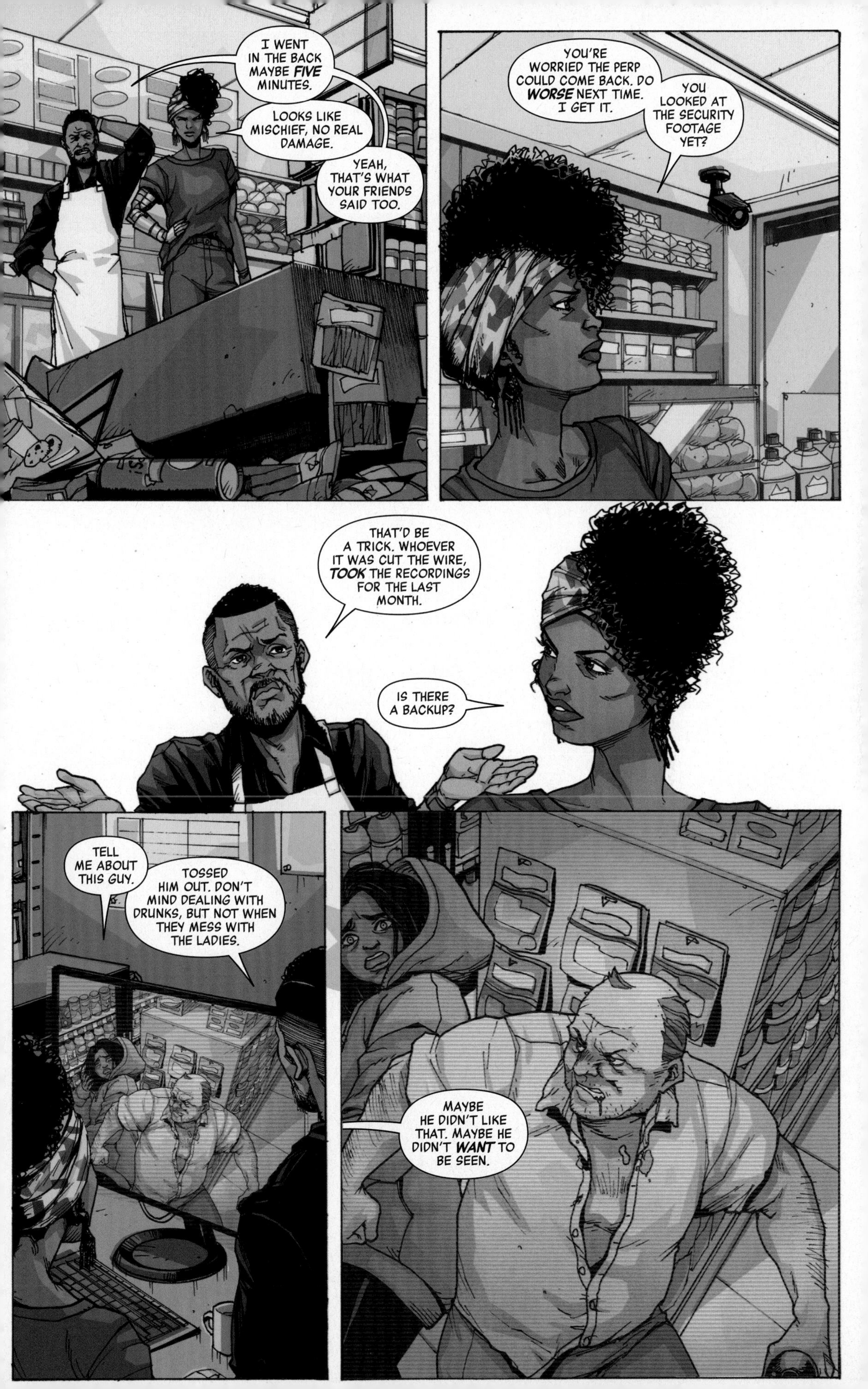
I WENT IN THE BACK MAYBE FIVE MINUTES.
LOOKS LIKE MISCHIEF, NO REAL DAMAGE.
YEAH, THAT'S WHAT YOUR FRIENDS SAID TOO.
YOU'RE WORRIED THE PERP COULD COME BACK. DO WORSE NEXT TIME. I GET IT.
YOU LOOKED AT THE SECURITY FOOTAGE YET?
THAT'D BE A TRICK. WHOEVER IT WAS CUT THE WIRE, TOOK THE RECORDINGS FOR THE LAST MONTH.
IS THERE A BACKUP?
TELL ME ABOUT THIS GUY.
TOSSED HIM OUT. DON'T MIND DEALING WITH DRUNKS, BUT NOT WHEN THEY MESS WITH THE LADIES.
MAYBE HE DIDN'T LIKE THAT. MAYBE HE DIDN'T WANT TO BE SEEN.

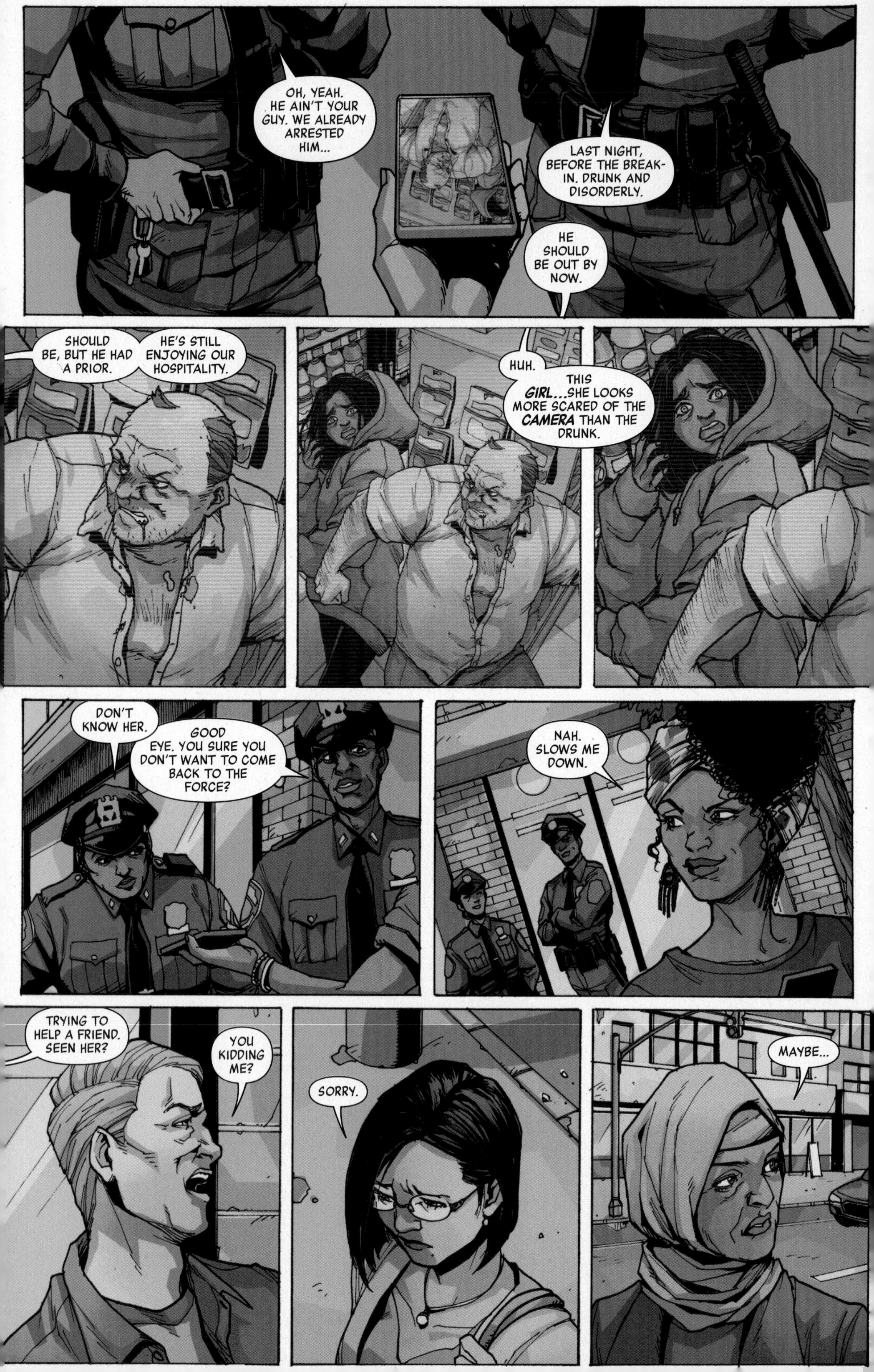
OH, YEAH. HE AIN'T YOUR GUY. WE ALREADY ARRESTED HIM...
LAST NIGHT, BEFORE THE BREAK-IN. DRUNK AND DISORDERLY.
HE SHOULD BE OUT BY NOW.
SHOULD BE, BUT HE HAD A PRIOR.
HE'S STILL ENJOYING OUR HOSPITALITY.
HUH.
THIS GIRL...SHE LOOKS MORE SCARED OF THE CAMERA THAN THE DRUNK.
DON'T KNOW HER.
GOOD EYE. YOU SURE YOU DON'T WANT TO COME BACK TO THE FORCE?
NAH. SLOWS ME DOWN.
TRYING TO HELP A FRIEND. SEEN HER?
YOU KIDDING ME?
SORRY.
MAYBE...

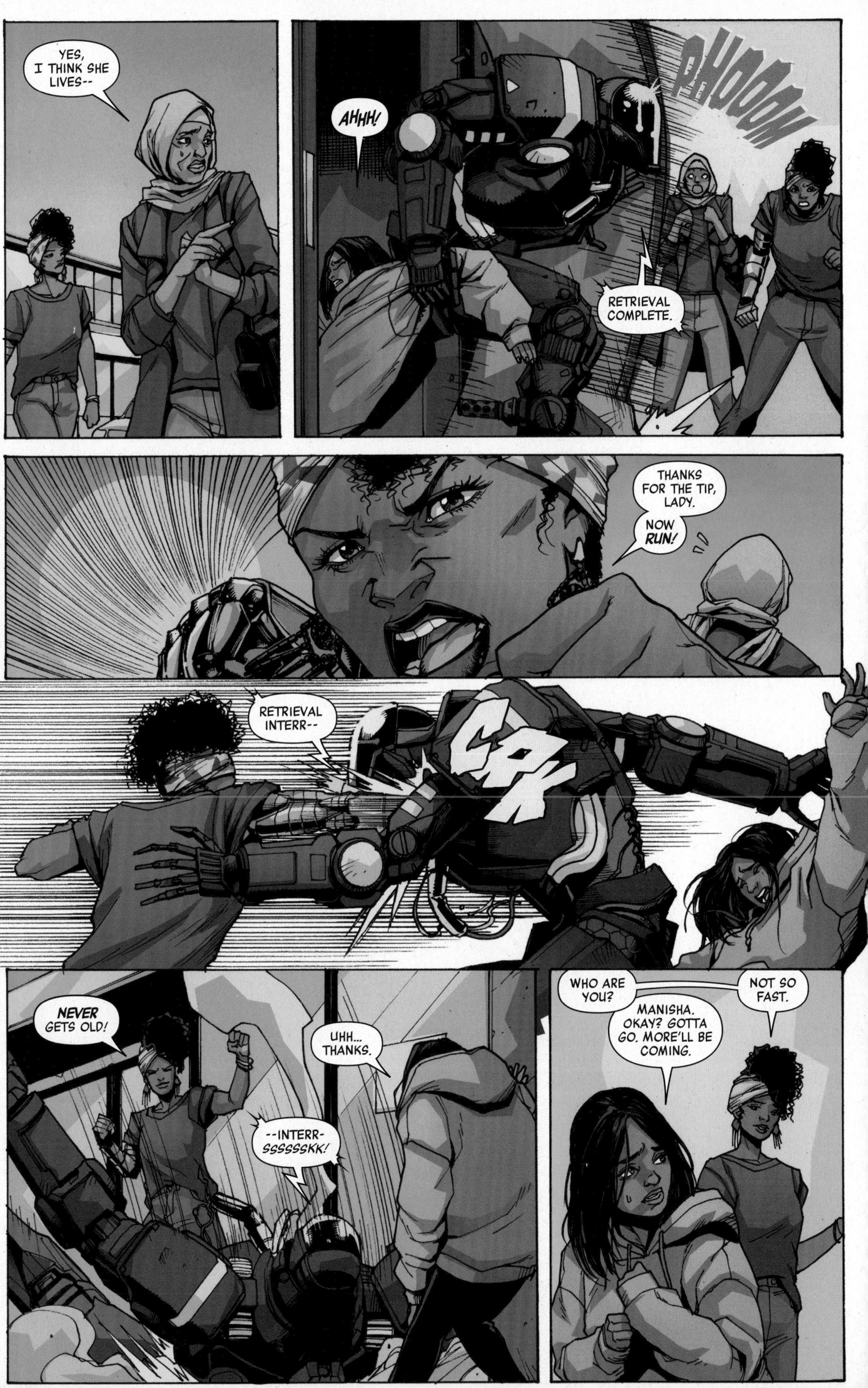
YES, I THINK SHE LIVES--
AHHH!
PHOOOM
RETRIEVAL COMPLETE.
THANKS FOR THE TIP, LADY.
NOW RUN!
RETRIEVAL INTERR--
CRK
NEVER GETS OLD!
UHH... THANKS.
--INTERR-SSSSSSKK!
WHO ARE YOU?
MANISHA. OKAY? GOTTA GO. MORE'LL BE COMING.
NOT SO FAST.

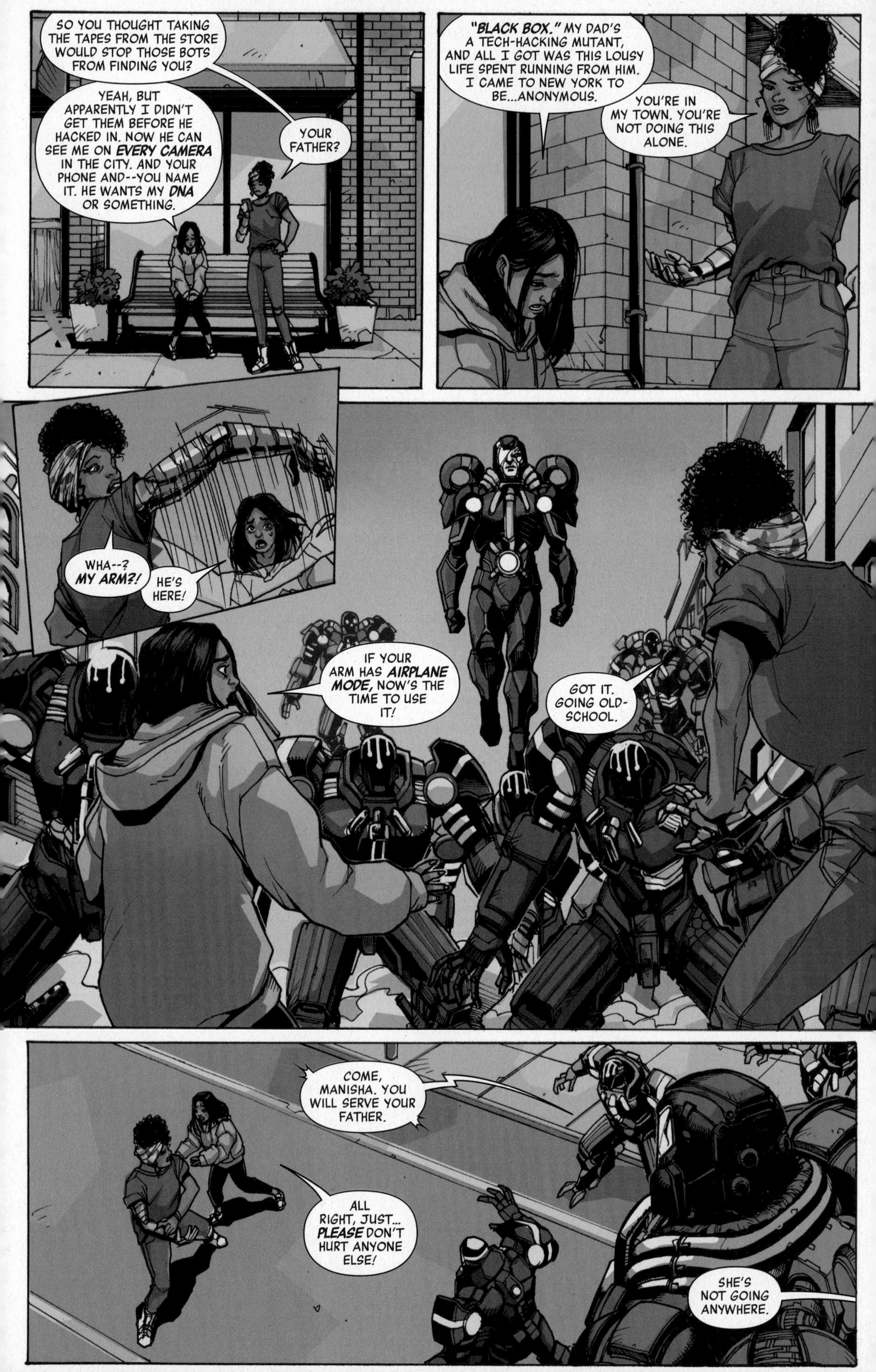
SO YOU THOUGHT TAKING THE TAPES FROM THE STORE WOULD STOP THOSE BOTS FROM FINDING YOU?
YEAH, BUT APPARENTLY I DIDN'T GET THEM BEFORE HE HACKED IN. NOW HE CAN SEE ME ON EVERY CAMERA IN THE CITY. AND YOUR PHONE AND--YOU NAME IT. HE WANTS MY DNA OR SOMETHING.
YOUR FATHER?
"BLACK BOX." MY DAD'S A TECH-HACKING MUTANT, AND ALL I GOT WAS THIS LOUSY LIFE SPENT RUNNING FROM HIM. I CAME TO NEW YORK TO BE...ANONYMOUS.
YOU'RE IN MY TOWN. YOU'RE NOT DOING THIS ALONE.
WHA--? MY ARM?!
HE'S HERE!
IF YOUR ARM HAS AIRPLANE MODE, NOW'S THE TIME TO USE IT!
GOT IT. GOING OLD-SCHOOL.
COME, MANISHA. YOU WILL SERVE YOUR FATHER.
ALL RIGHT, JUST... PLEASE DON'T HURT ANYONE ELSE!
SHE'S NOT GOING ANYWHERE.

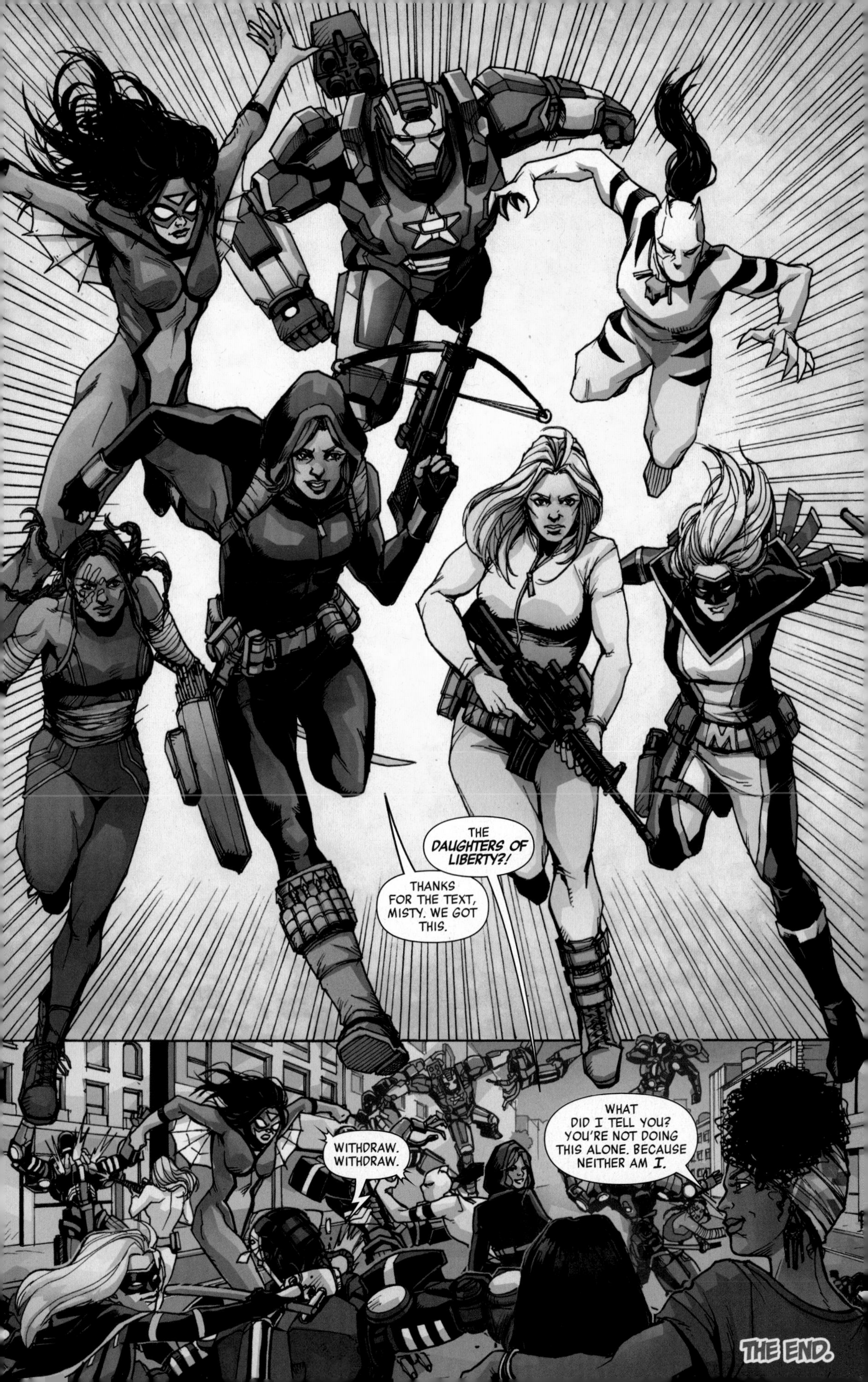
THE DAUGHTERS OF LIBERTY?!
THANKS FOR THE TEXT, MISTY. WE GOT THIS.
WITHDRAW. WITHDRAW.
WHAT DID I TELL YOU? YOU'RE NOT DOING THIS ALONE. BECAUSE NEITHER AM I.
THE END.

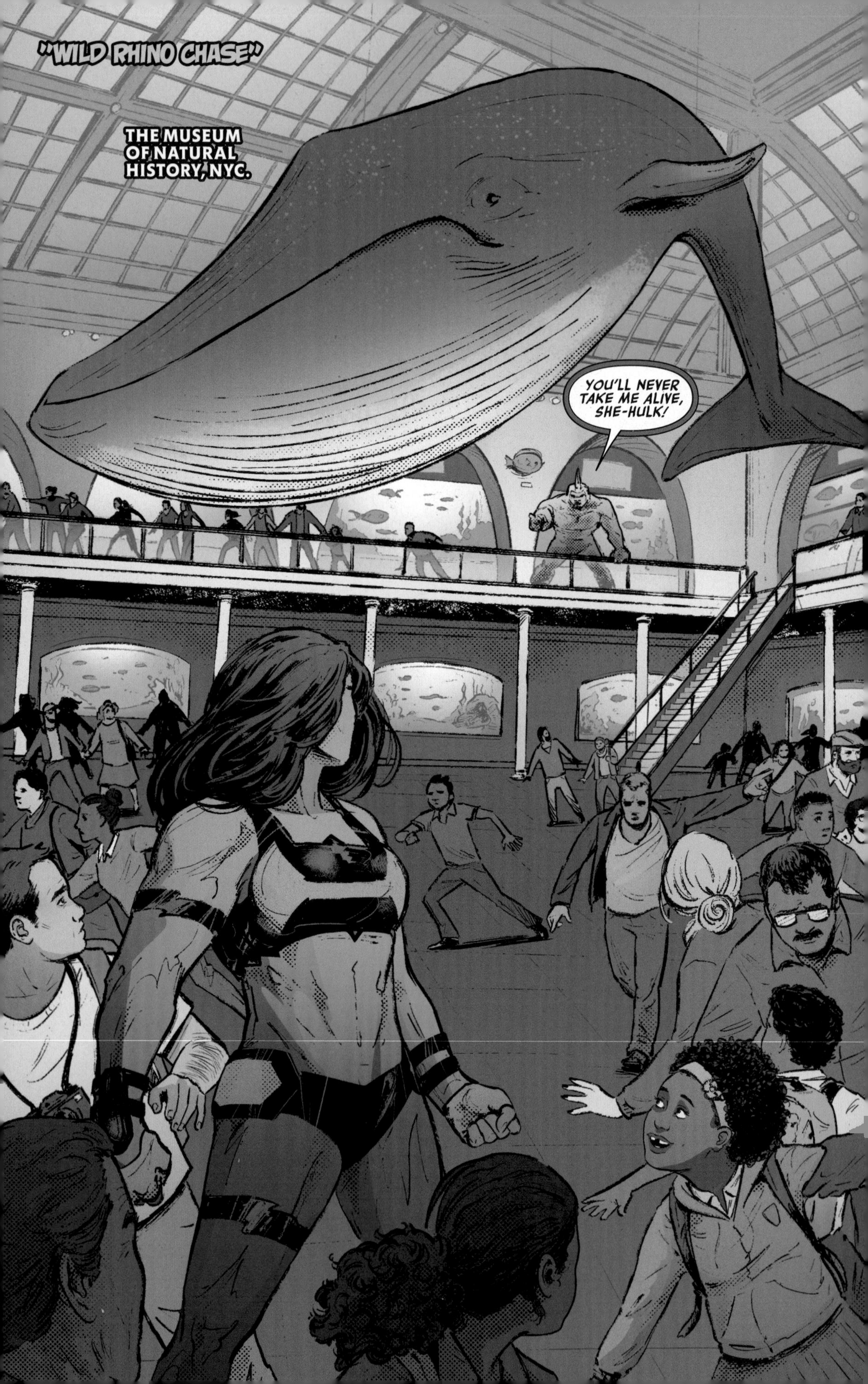
"WILD RHINO CHASE"
THE MUSEUM OF NATURAL HISTORY, NYC.
YOU'LL NEVER TAKE ME ALIVE, SHE-HULK!

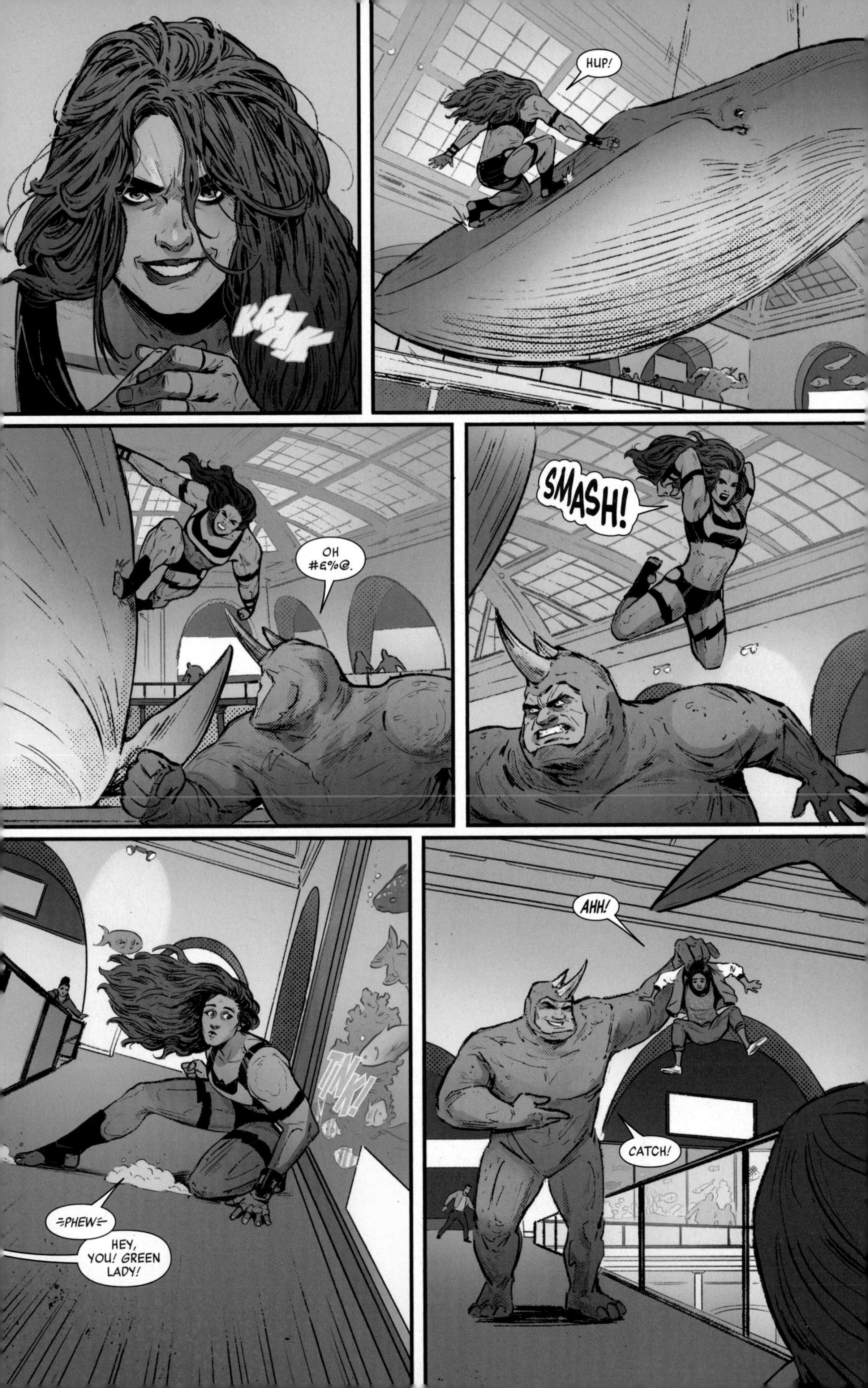
KRAK
HUP!
OH #&%@.
SMASH!
TINK!
AHH!
CATCH!
=PHEW=
HEY, YOU! GREEN LADY!

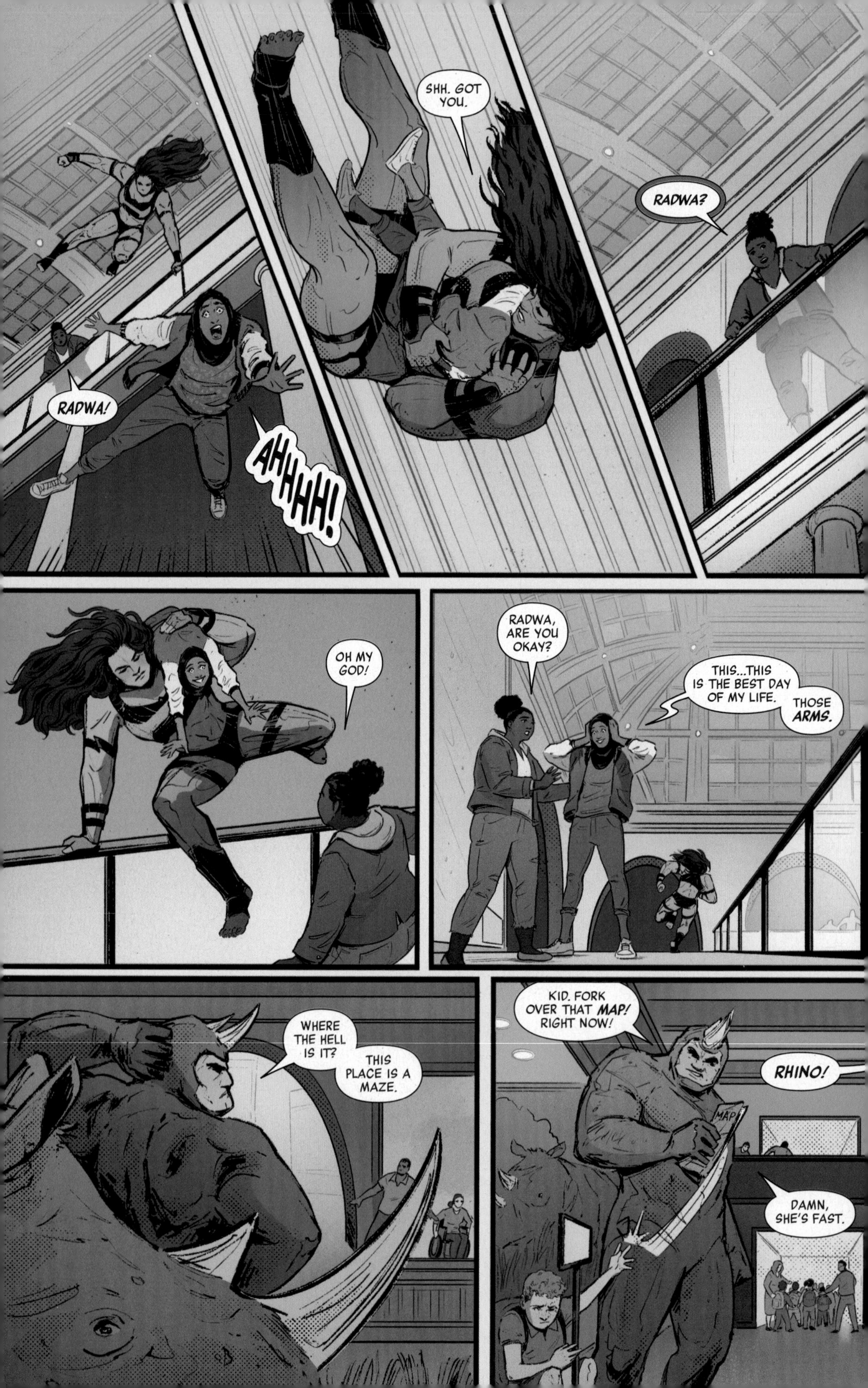
RADWA!
AHHHH!
SHH. GOT YOU.
RADWA?
OH MY GOD!
RADWA, ARE YOU OKAY?
THIS...THIS IS THE BEST DAY OF MY LIFE.
THOSE ARMS.
WHERE THE HELL IS IT?
THIS PLACE IS A MAZE.
KID. FORK OVER THAT MAP! RIGHT NOW!
MAP
RHINO!
DAMN, SHE'S FAST.

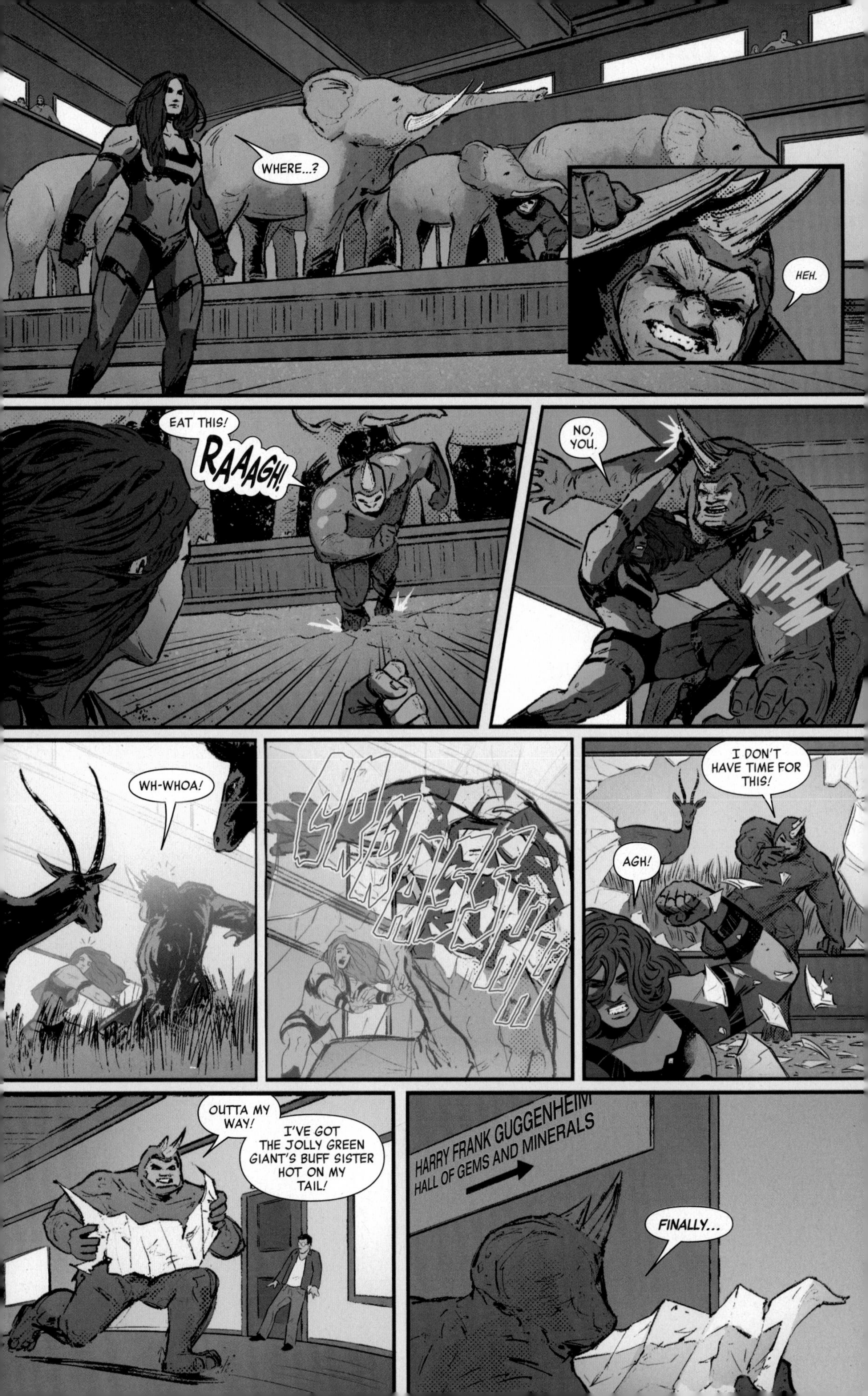
WHERE...?
HEH.
EAT THIS!
RAAAGH!
NO, YOU.
WHAM
WH-WHOA!
I DON'T HAVE TIME FOR THIS!
AGH!
OUTTA MY WAY!
I'VE GOT THE JOLLY GREEN GIANT'S BUFF SISTER HOT ON MY TAIL!
HARRY FRANK GUGGENHEIM HALL OF GEMS AND MINERALS
FINALLY...

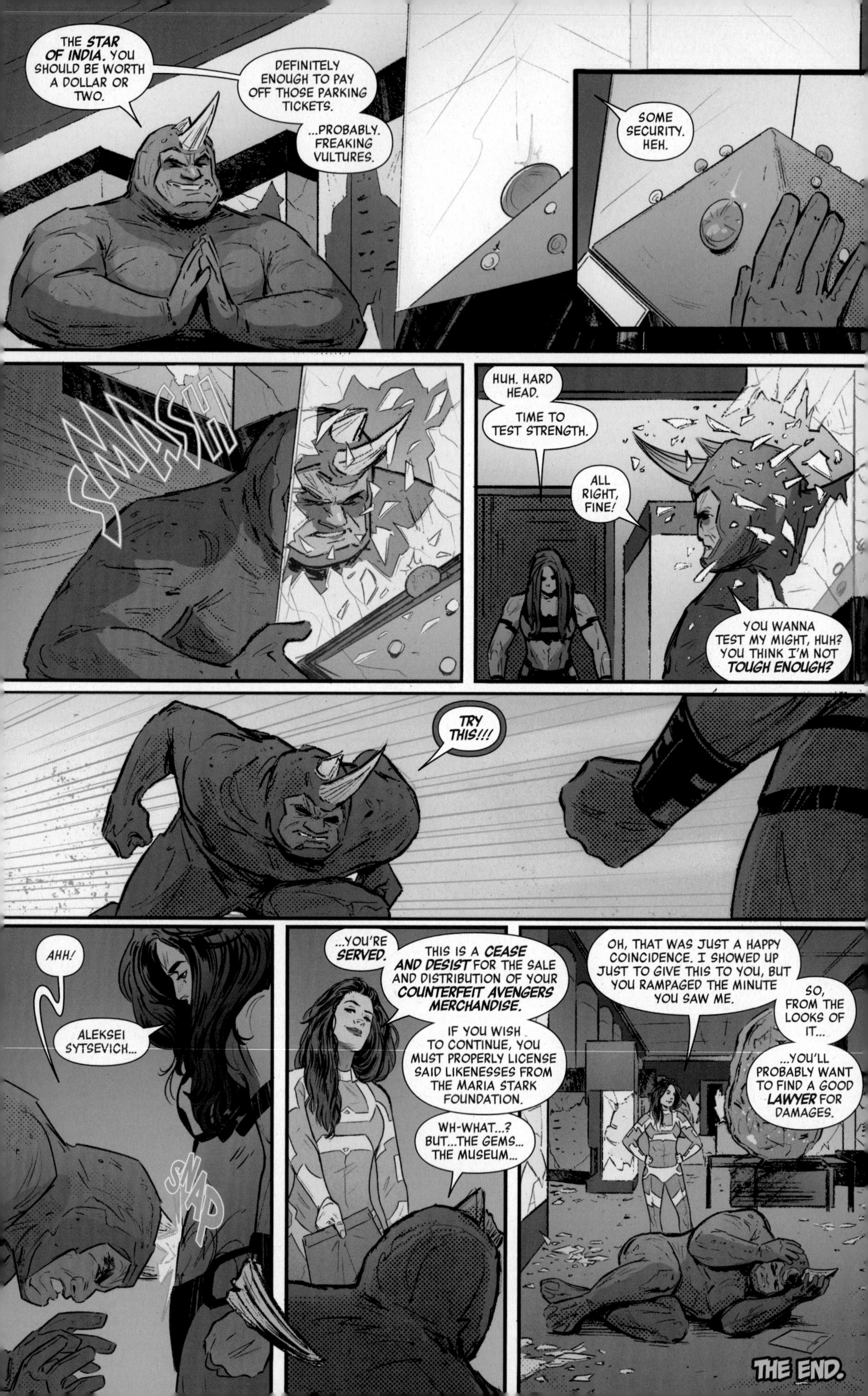
THE STAR OF INDIA. YOU SHOULD BE WORTH A DOLLAR OR TWO.
DEFINITELY ENOUGH TO PAY OFF THOSE PARKING TICKETS.
...PROBABLY. FREAKING VULTURES.
SOME SECURITY. HEH.
SMASH!!
HUH. HARD HEAD.
TIME TO TEST STRENGTH.
ALL RIGHT, FINE!
YOU WANNA TEST MY MIGHT, HUH? YOU THINK I'M NOT TOUGH ENOUGH?
TRY THIS!!!
AHH!
ALEKSEI SYTSEVICH...
SNAP
...YOU'RE SERVED.
THIS IS A CEASE AND DESIST FOR THE SALE AND DISTRIBUTION OF YOUR COUNTERFEIT AVENGERS MERCHANDISE.
IF YOU WISH TO CONTINUE, YOU MUST PROPERLY LICENSE SAID LIKENESSES FROM THE MARIA STARK FOUNDATION.
WH-WHAT...? BUT...THE GEMS... THE MUSEUM...
OH, THAT WAS JUST A HAPPY COINCIDENCE. I SHOWED UP JUST TO GIVE THIS TO YOU, BUT YOU RAMPAGED THE MINUTE YOU SAW ME.
SO, FROM THE LOOKS OF IT...
...YOU'LL PROBABLY WANT TO FIND A GOOD LAWYER FOR DAMAGES.
THE END.

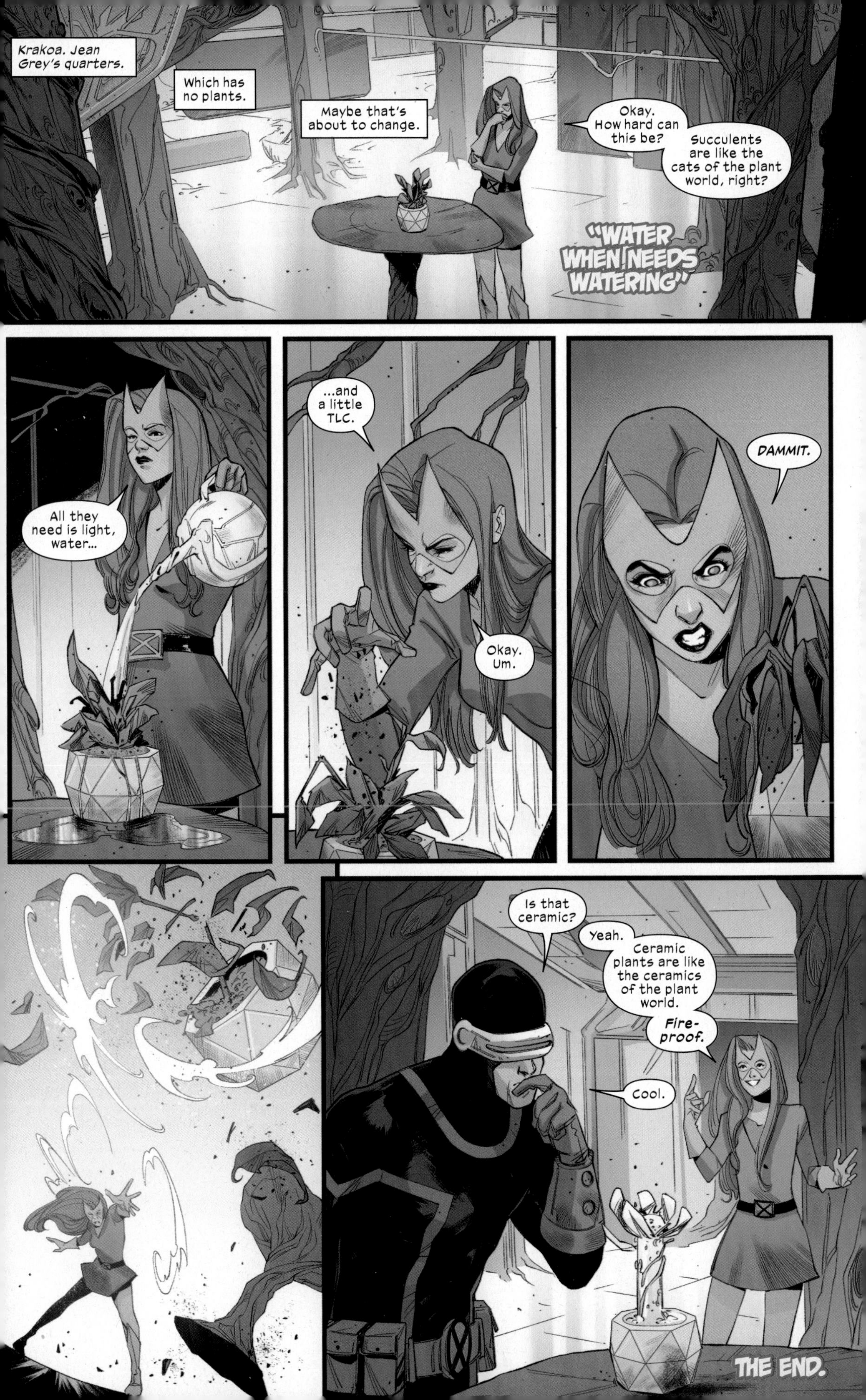
Krakoa. Jean Grey's quarters.
Which has no plants.
Maybe that's about to change.
Okay. How hard can this be?
Succulents are like the cats of the plant world, right?
"WATER WHEN NEEDS WATERING"
All they need is light, water...
...and a little TLC.
Okay. Um.
DAMMIT.
Is that ceramic?
Yeah.
Ceramic plants are like the ceramics of the plant world.
Fire-proof.
Cool.
THE END.

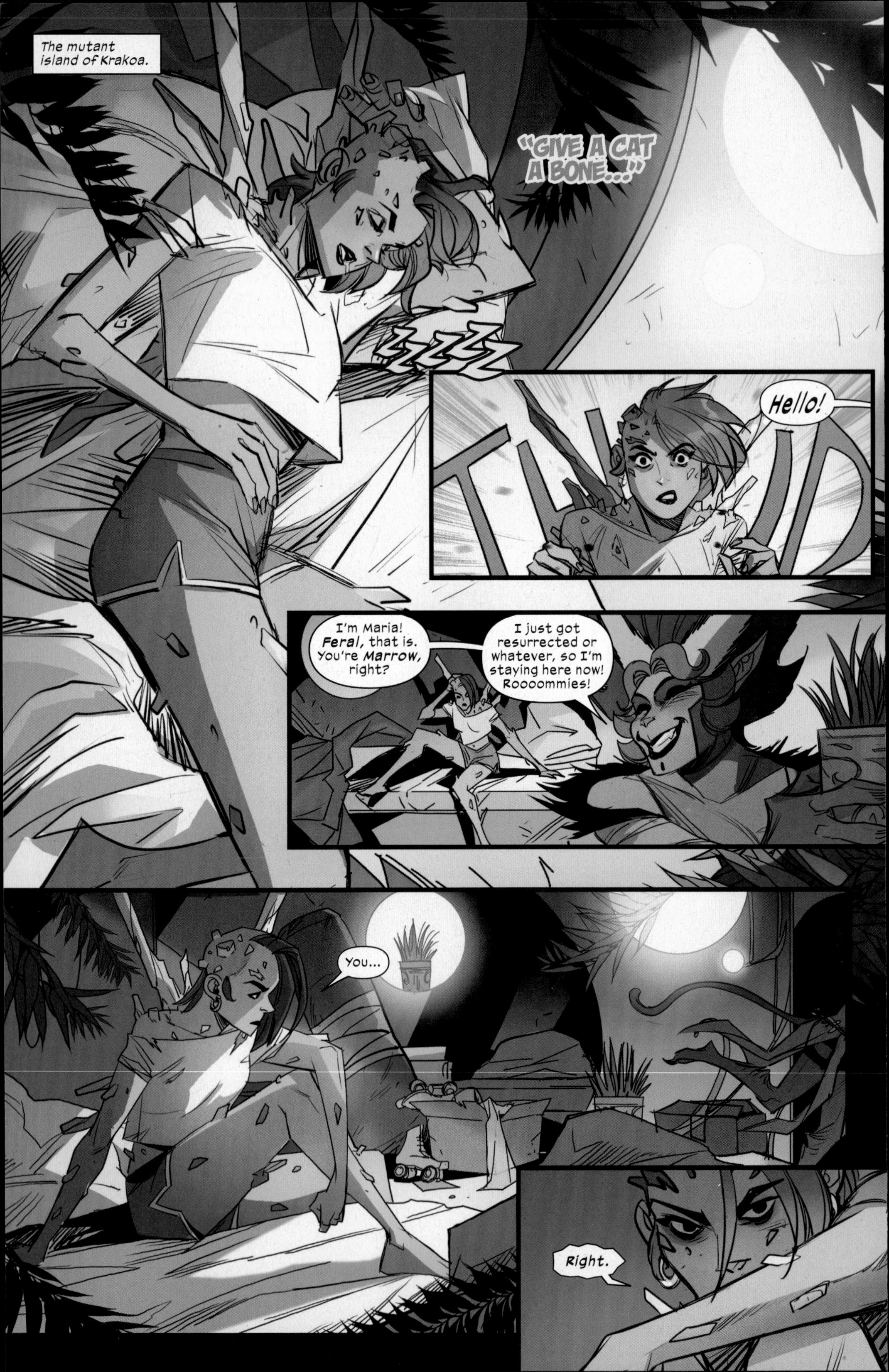
The mutant island of Krakoa.
"GIVE A CAT A BONE..."
ZZZZ
THUD
Hello!
I'm Maria! Feral, that is. You're Marrow, right?
I just got resurrected or whatever, so I'm staying here now! Rooommies!
You...
Right.

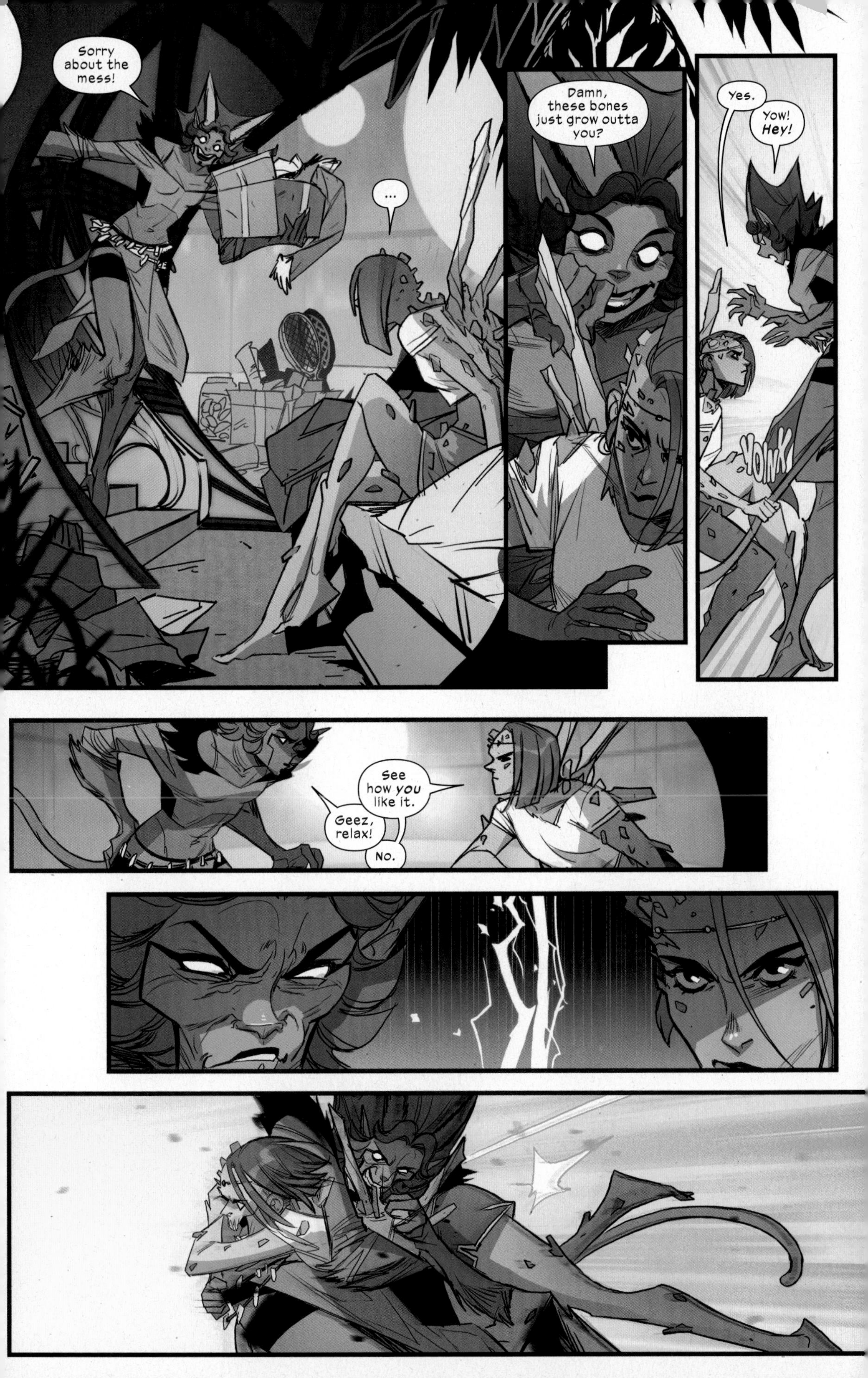
Sorry about the mess!
...
Damn, these bones just grow outta you?
Yes.
Yow! Hey!
YOINK
See how you like it.
Geez, relax!
No.

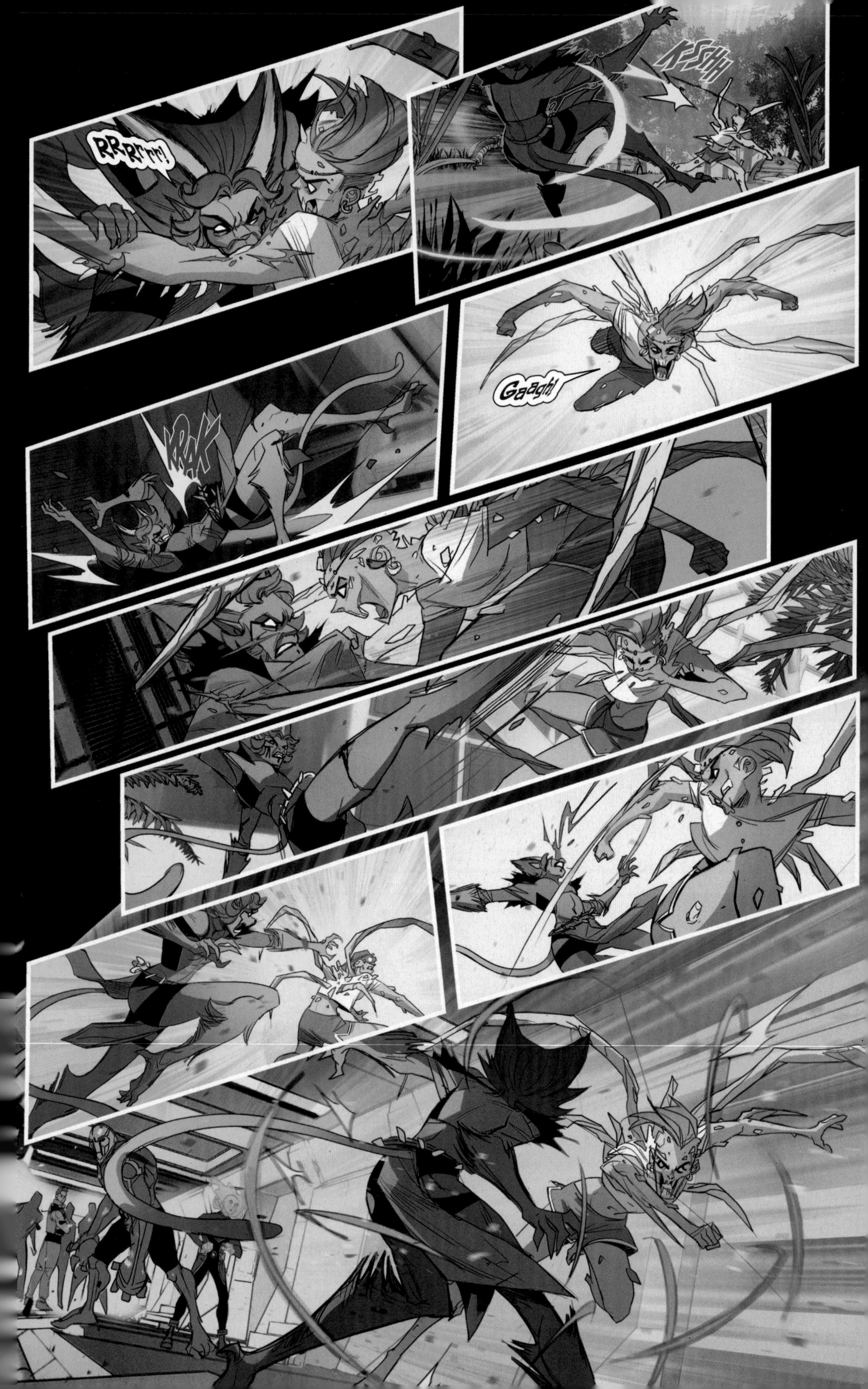
RRRR'T'T!
KSHH
Gaagh!
KRAK

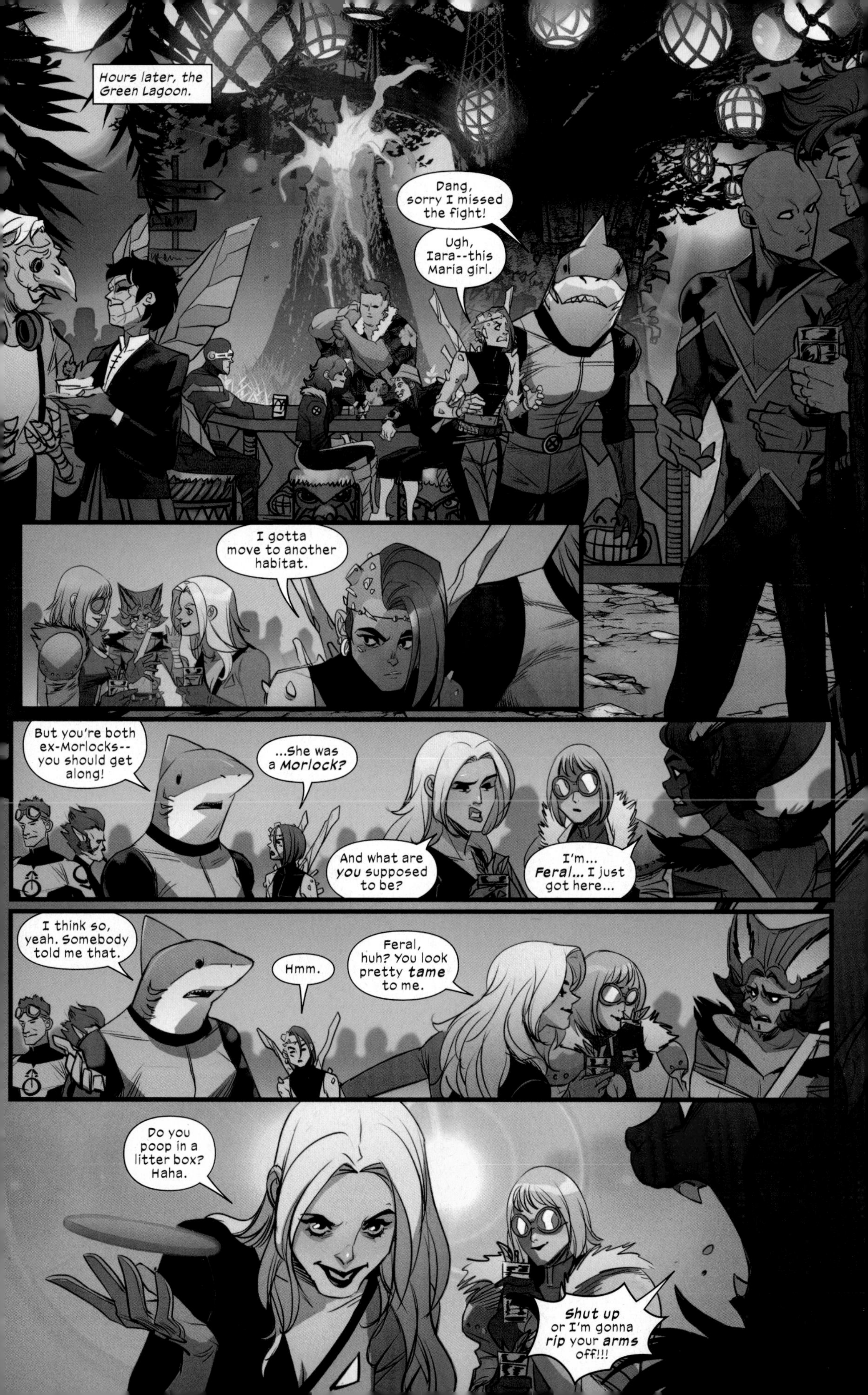
Hours later, the Green Lagoon.
Dang, sorry I missed the fight!
Ugh, Iara--this Maria girl.
I gotta move to another habitat.
But you're both ex-Morlocks--you should get along!
...She was a Morlock?
And what are you supposed to be?
I'm... Feral... I just got here...
I think so, yeah. Somebody told me that.
Hmm.
Feral, huh? You look pretty tame to me.
Do you poop in a litter box? Haha.
Shut up or I'm gonna rip your arms off!!!

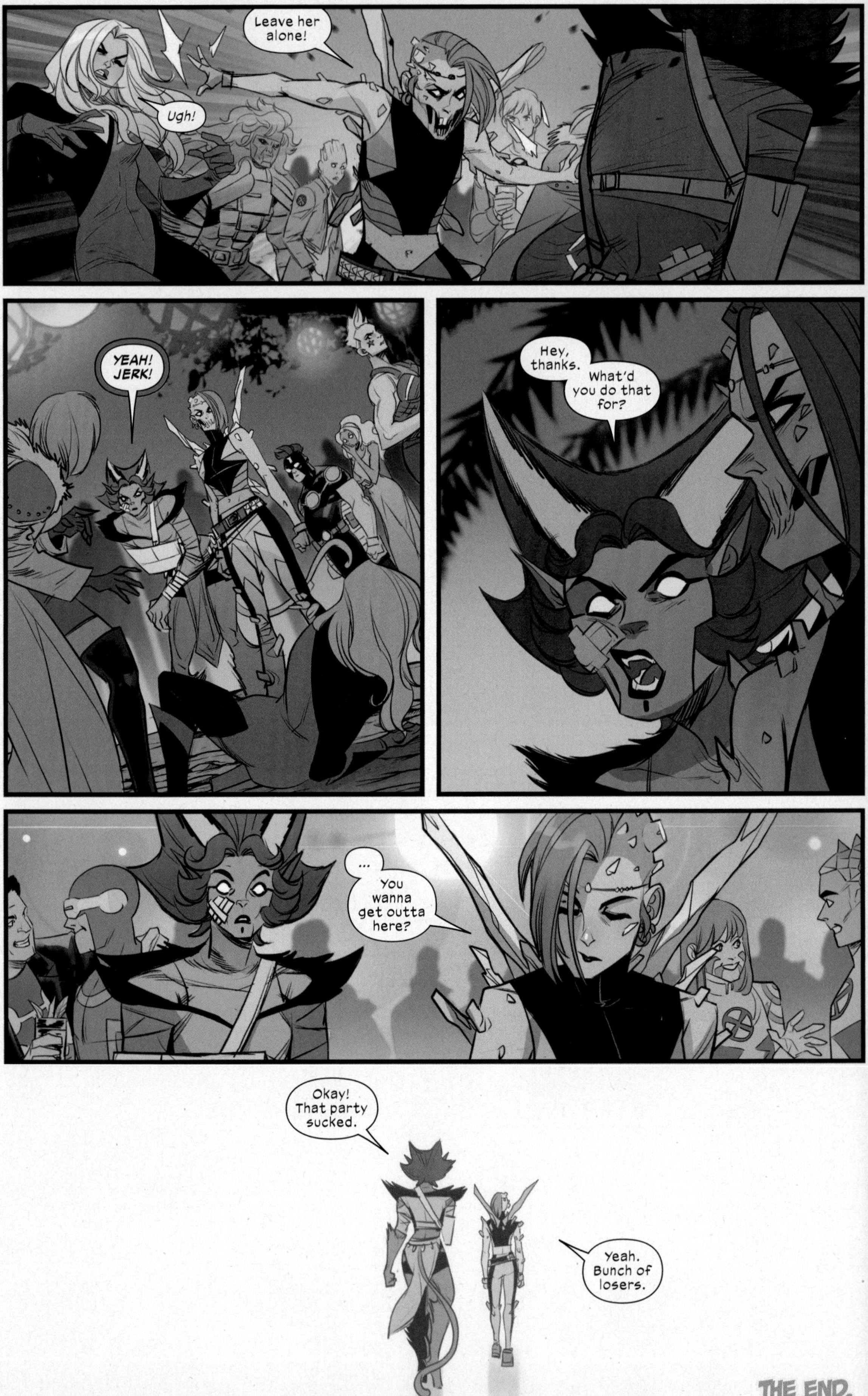
Leave her alone!
Ugh!
YEAH! JERK!
Hey, thanks.
What'd you do that for?
... You wanna get outta here?
Okay! That party sucked.
Yeah. Bunch of losers.
THE END.

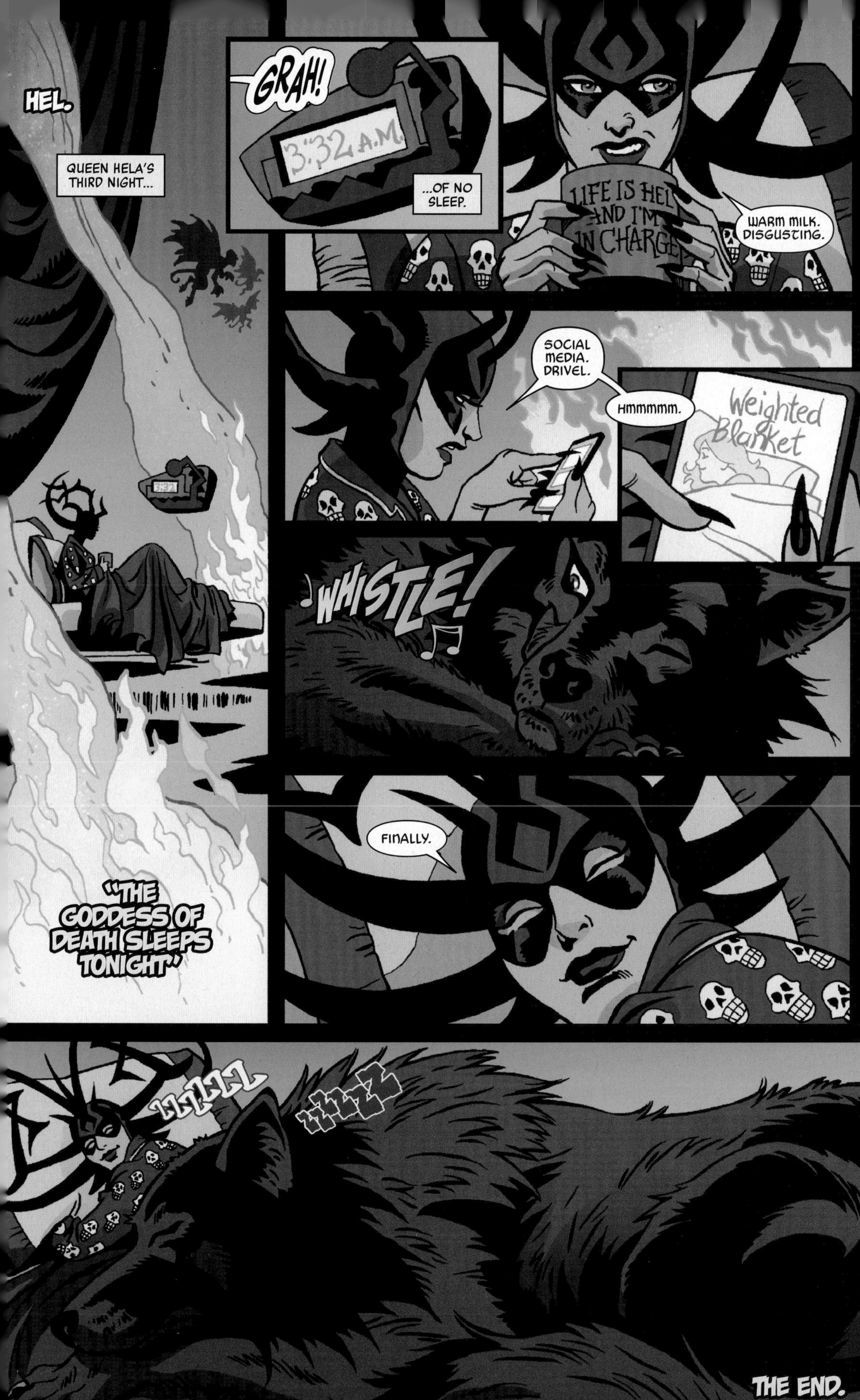
HEL.
QUEEN HELA'S THIRD NIGHT...
GRAH!
3:32 A.M.
...OF NO SLEEP.
LIFE IS HEL AND I'M IN CHARGE
WARM MILK. DISGUSTING.
SOCIAL MEDIA. DRIVEL.
HMMMMM.
Weighted Blanket
WHISTLE!
FINALLY.
"THE GODDESS OF DEATH SLEEPS TONIGHT"
ZZZZZ
ZZZZZ
THE END.

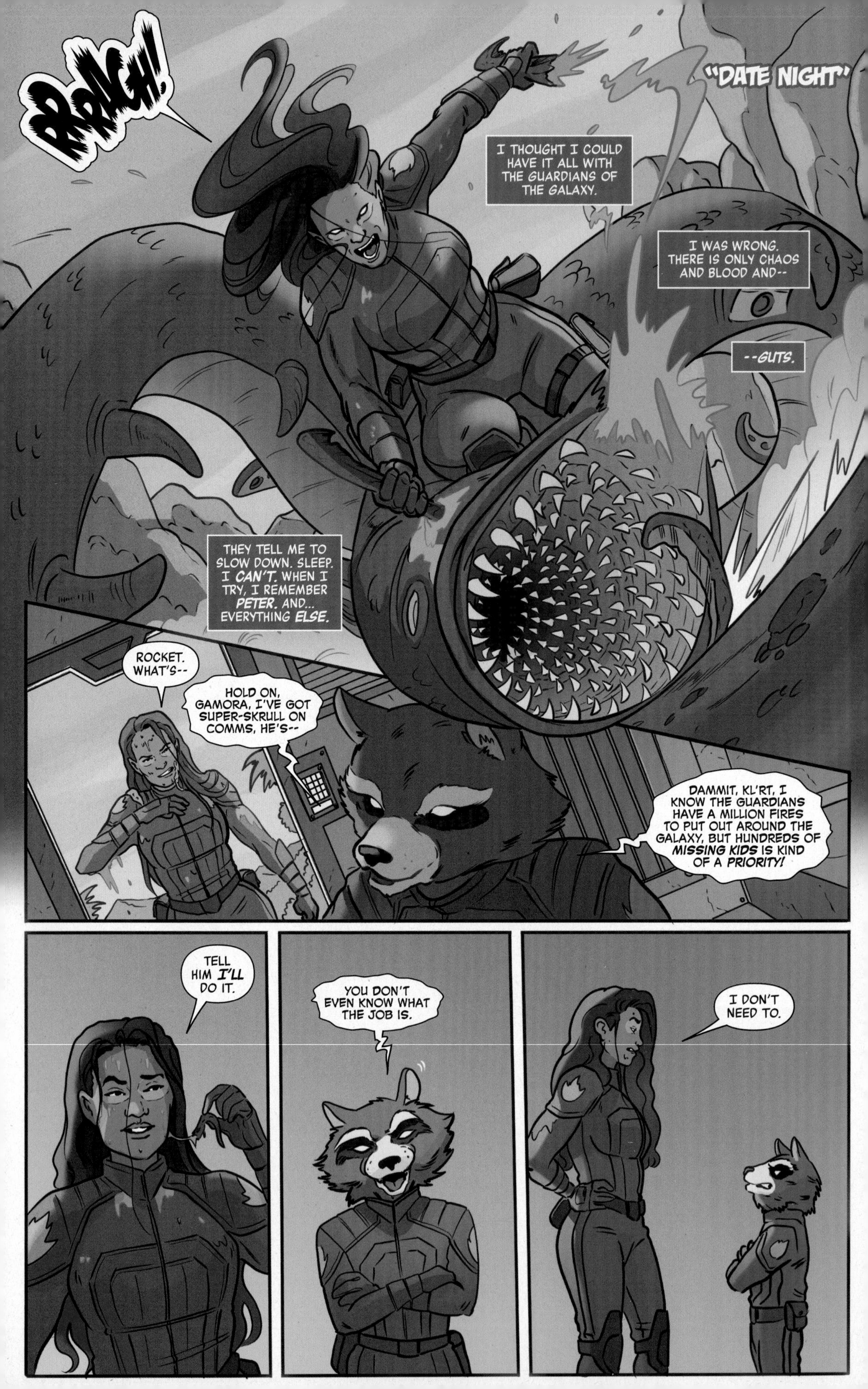

BRAGH!
"DATE NIGHT"
I THOUGHT I COULD HAVE IT ALL WITH THE GUARDIANS OF THE GALAXY.
I WAS WRONG. THERE IS ONLY CHAOS AND BLOOD AND--
--GUTS.
THEY TELL ME TO SLOW DOWN. SLEEP. I CAN'T. WHEN I TRY, I REMEMBER PETER. AND... EVERYTHING ELSE.
ROCKET. WHAT'S--
HOLD ON, GAMORA, I'VE GOT SUPER-SKRULL ON COMMS, HE'S--
DAMMIT, KL'RT, I KNOW THE GUARDIANS HAVE A MILLION FIRES TO PUT OUT AROUND THE GALAXY, BUT HUNDREDS OF MISSING KIDS IS KIND OF A PRIORITY!
TELL HIM I'LL DO IT.
YOU DON'T EVEN KNOW WHAT THE JOB IS.
I DON'T NEED TO.

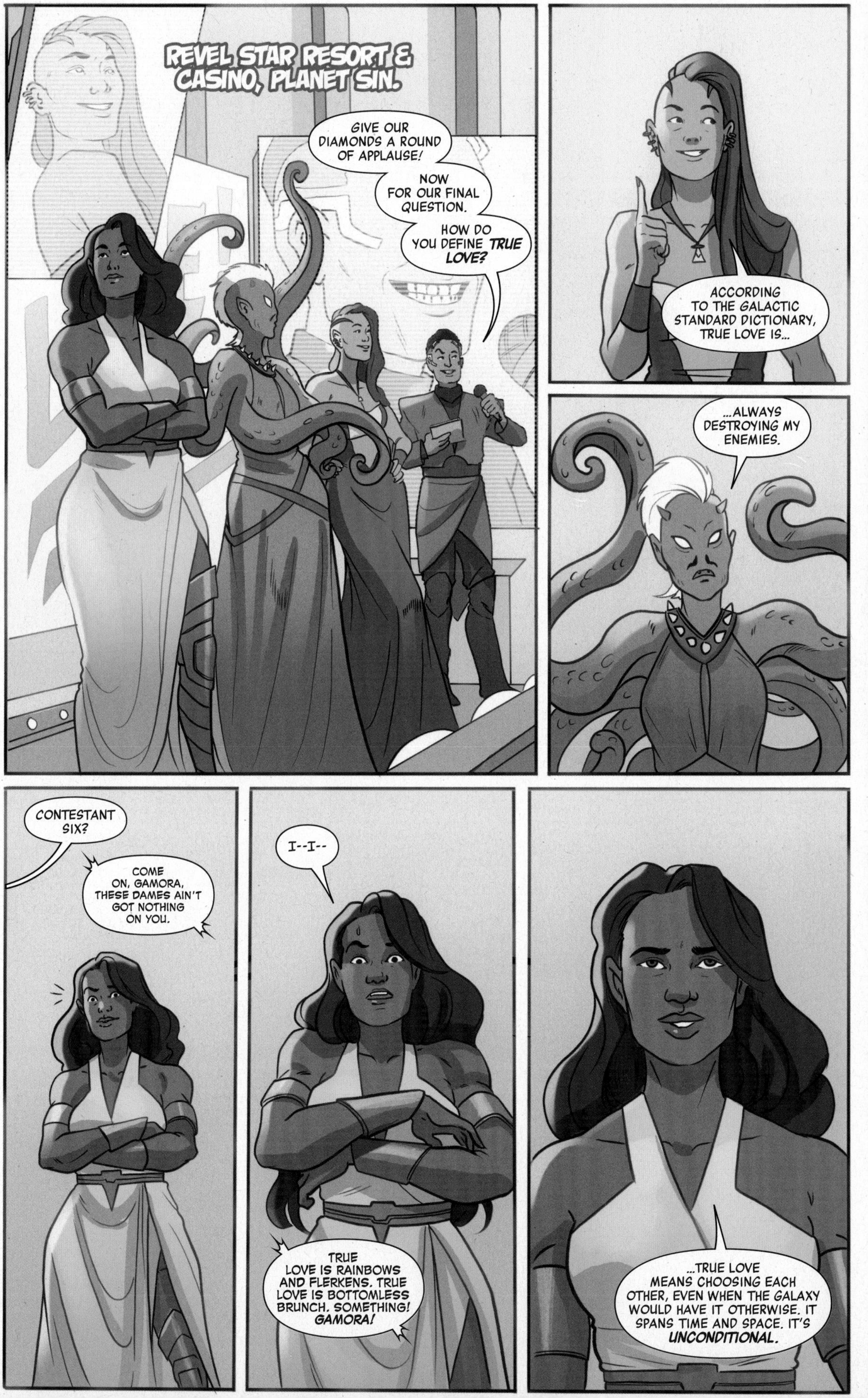
REVEL STAR RESORT & CASINO, PLANET SIN.
GIVE OUR DIAMONDS A ROUND OF APPLAUSE!
NOW FOR OUR FINAL QUESTION.
HOW DO YOU DEFINE TRUE LOVE?
ACCORDING TO THE GALACTIC STANDARD DICTIONARY, TRUE LOVE IS...
...ALWAYS DESTROYING MY ENEMIES.
CONTESTANT SIX?
COME ON, GAMORA, THESE DAMES AIN'T GOT NOTHING ON YOU.
I--I--
TRUE LOVE IS RAINBOWS AND FLERKENS. TRUE LOVE IS BOTTOMLESS BRUNCH. SOMETHING! GAMORA!
...TRUE LOVE MEANS CHOOSING EACH OTHER, EVEN WHEN THE GALAXY WOULD HAVE IT OTHERWISE. IT SPANS TIME AND SPACE. IT'S UNCONDITIONAL.

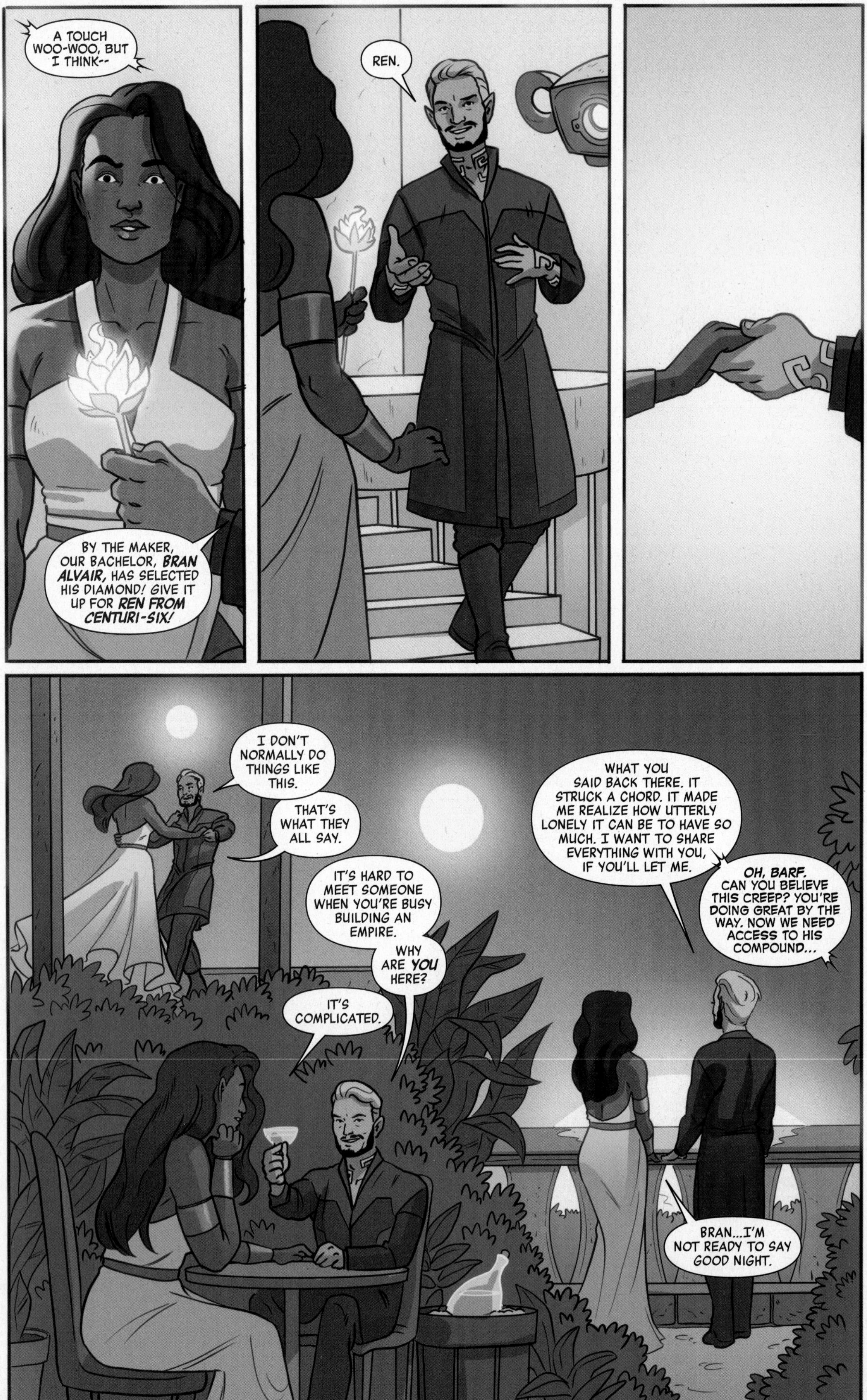
A TOUCH WOO-WOO, BUT I THINK--
BY THE MAKER, OUR BACHELOR, BRAN ALVAIR, HAS SELECTED HIS DIAMOND! GIVE IT UP FOR REN FROM CENTURI-SIX!
REN.
I DON'T NORMALLY DO THINGS LIKE THIS.
THAT'S WHAT THEY ALL SAY.
IT'S HARD TO MEET SOMEONE WHEN YOU'RE BUSY BUILDING AN EMPIRE.
WHY ARE YOU HERE?
IT'S COMPLICATED.
WHAT YOU SAID BACK THERE. IT STRUCK A CHORD. IT MADE ME REALIZE HOW UTTERLY LONELY IT CAN BE TO HAVE SO MUCH. I WANT TO SHARE EVERYTHING WITH YOU, IF YOU'LL LET ME.
OH, BARF. CAN YOU BELIEVE THIS CREEP? YOU'RE DOING GREAT BY THE WAY. NOW WE NEED ACCESS TO HIS COMPOUND...
BRAN...I'M NOT READY TO SAY GOOD NIGHT.

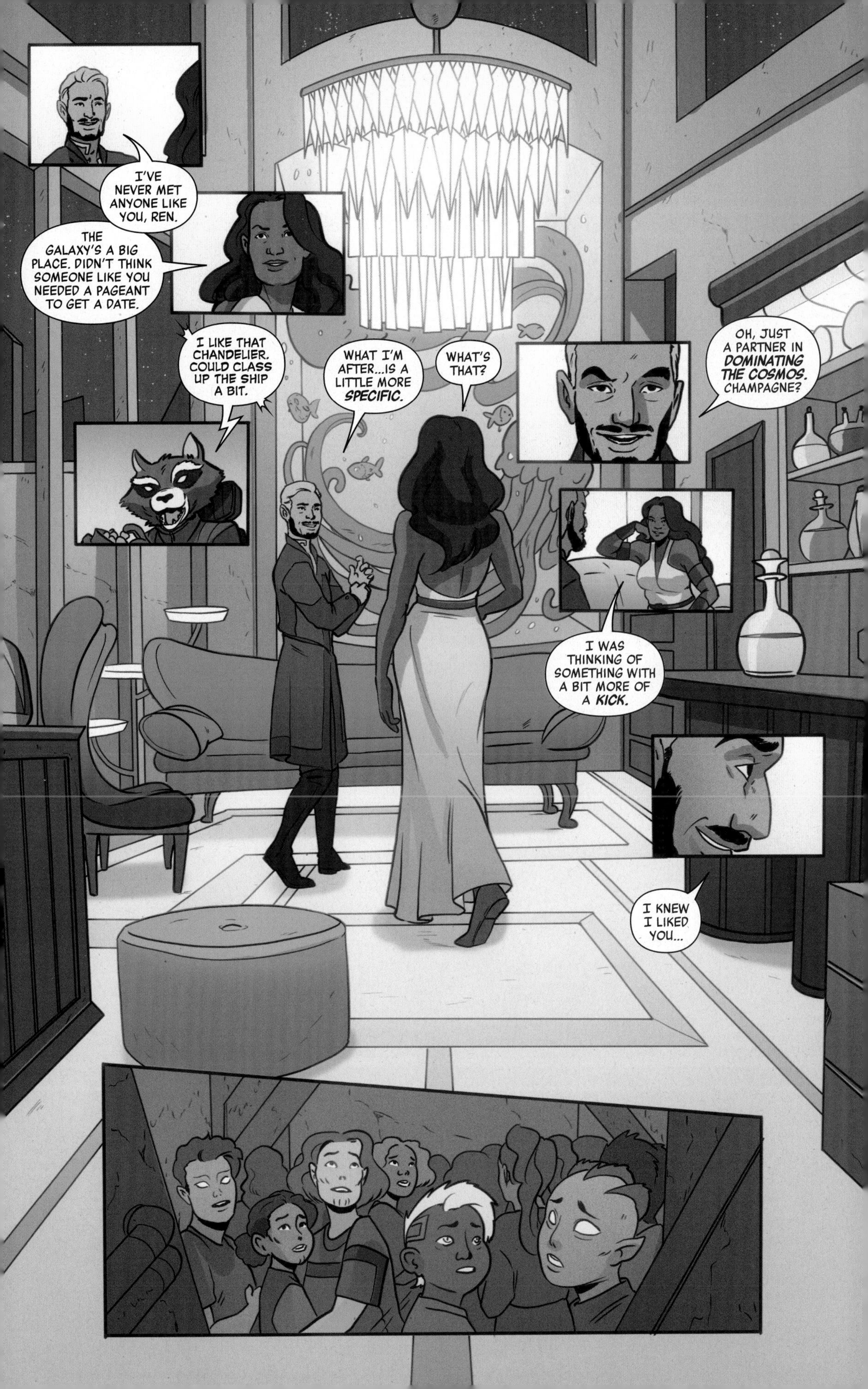
I'VE NEVER MET ANYONE LIKE YOU, REN.
THE GALAXY'S A BIG PLACE. DIDN'T THINK SOMEONE LIKE YOU NEEDED A PAGEANT TO GET A DATE.
I LIKE THAT CHANDELIER. COULD CLASS UP THE SHIP A BIT.
WHAT I'M AFTER...IS A LITTLE MORE SPECIFIC.
WHAT'S THAT?
OH, JUST A PARTNER IN DOMINATING THE COSMOS. CHAMPAGNE?
I WAS THINKING OF SOMETHING WITH A BIT MORE OF A KICK.
I KNEW I LIKED YOU...

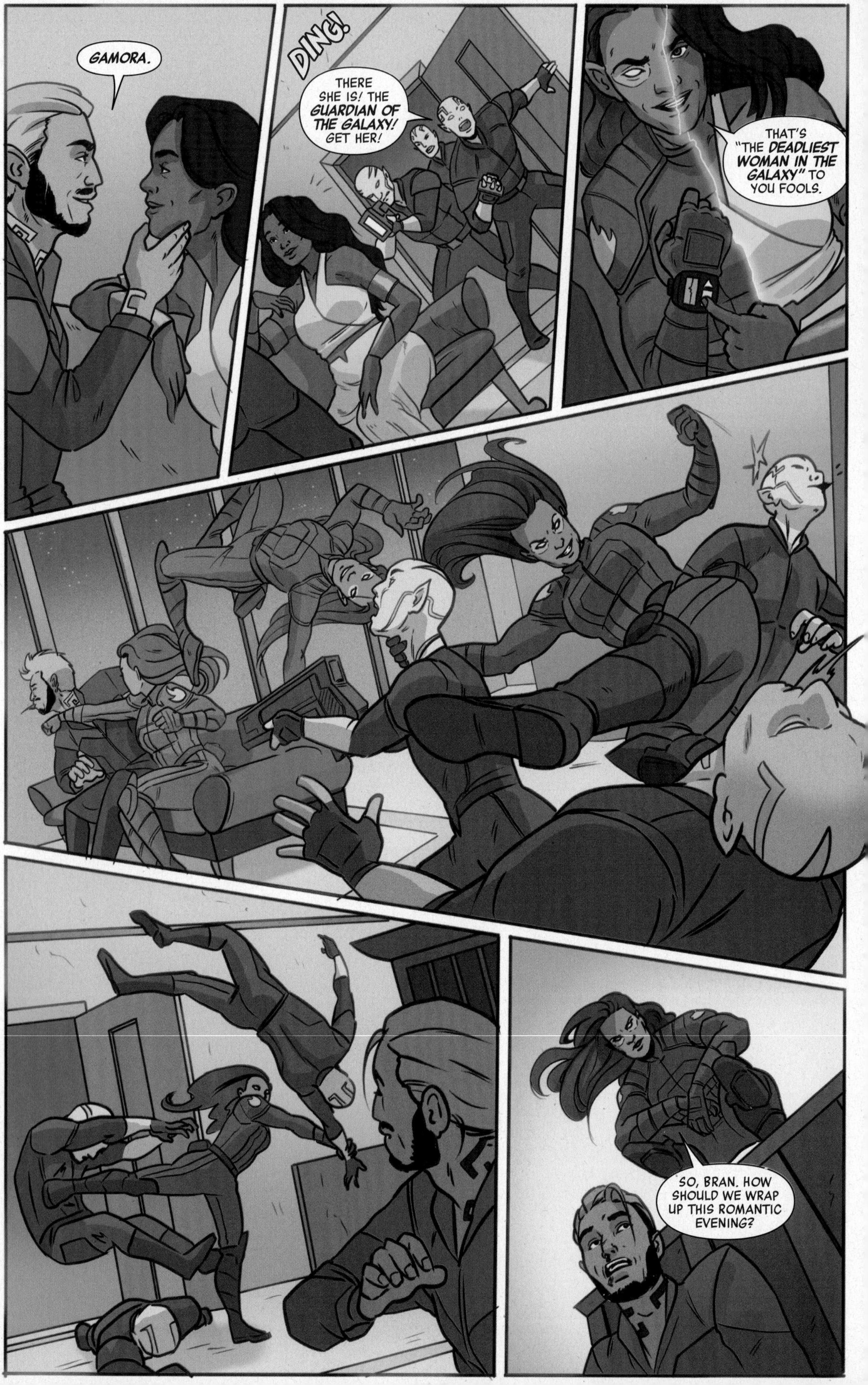
GAMORA.
DING!
THERE SHE IS! THE GUARDIAN OF THE GALAXY! GET HER!
THAT'S "THE DEADLIEST WOMAN IN THE GALAXY" TO YOU FOOLS.
SO, BRAN. HOW SHOULD WE WRAP UP THIS ROMANTIC EVENING?

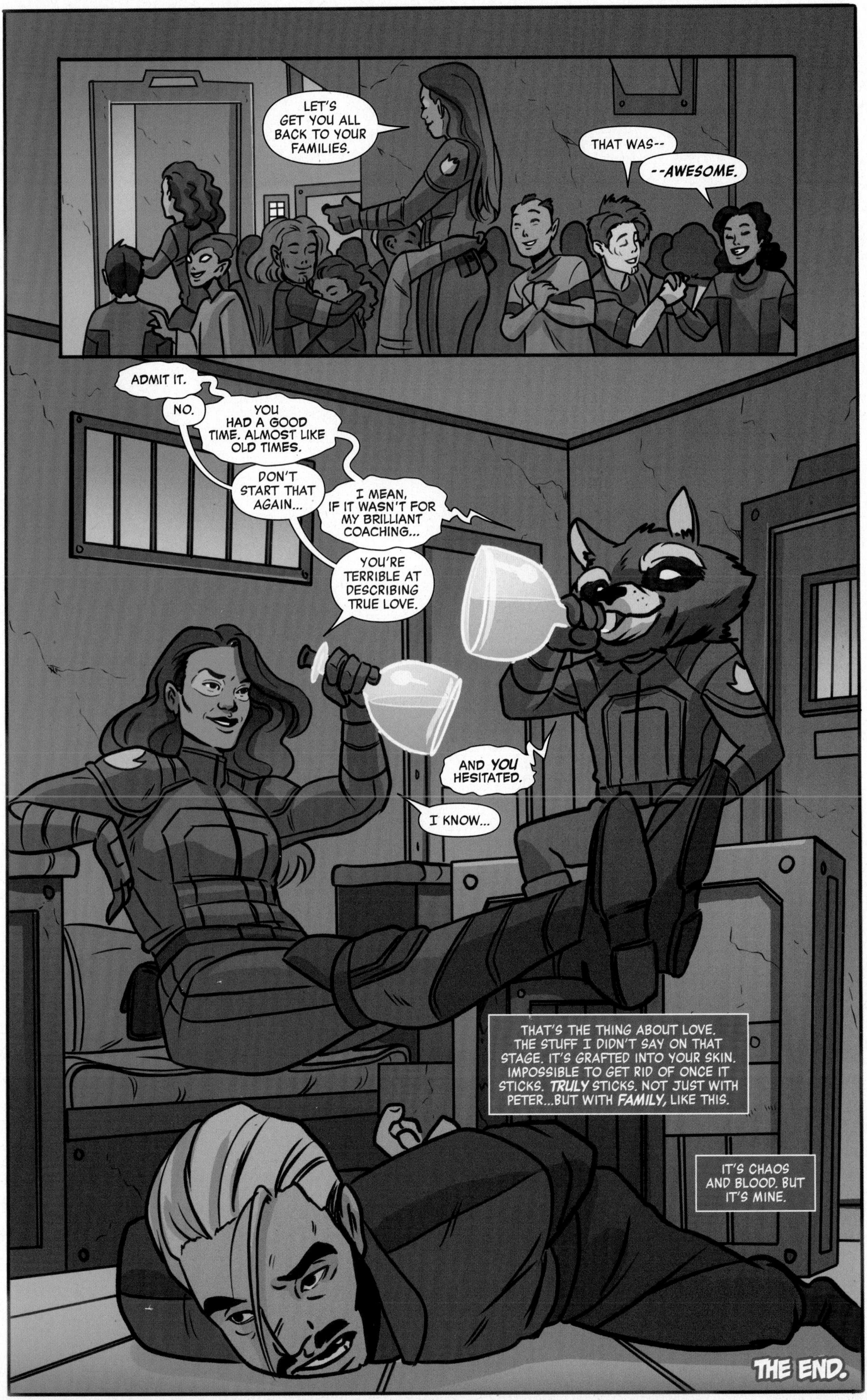

LET'S GET YOU ALL BACK TO YOUR FAMILIES.
THAT WAS--
--AWESOME.
ADMIT IT.
NO.
YOU HAD A GOOD TIME. ALMOST LIKE OLD TIMES.
DON'T START THAT AGAIN...
I MEAN, IF IT WASN'T FOR MY BRILLIANT COACHING...
YOU'RE TERRIBLE AT DESCRIBING TRUE LOVE.
AND YOU HESITATED.
I KNOW...
THAT'S THE THING ABOUT LOVE. THE STUFF I DIDN'T SAY ON THAT STAGE. IT'S GRAFTED INTO YOUR SKIN. IMPOSSIBLE TO GET RID OF ONCE IT STICKS. TRULY STICKS. NOT JUST WITH PETER...BUT WITH FAMILY, LIKE THIS.
IT'S CHAOS AND BLOOD. BUT IT'S MINE.
THE END.

Through the Women of Marvel program, we celebrate not only the creators and characters we love, but also the incredible staff who bring our comics to life behind the scenes. The truth is, women have always made comics — and now, like Weezie said in the intro, there are more of us than ever. Here is just a snapshot of the many hardworking heroines at Marvel Comics and *their* favorite Women of Marvel:

LINDSEY COHICK
Assistant Editor, 3 years at Marvel

"Lately I've become really attached to Felicia Hardy — the Black Cat — thanks to her solo series, where she's more than just a love interest. On the contrary, she doesn't have time for romance! She's too busy pulling off heists, getting in over her head and problem-solving her way out, usually with a little help from her crew, Bruno and Dr. Korpse. Felicia embodies one of my favorite character archetypes: the 'morally gray with a heart of gold' type. She shows (on a textual and meta-textual level) that your past doesn't define you."

ANNALISE BISSA
Associate Editor, 4.5 years at Marvel

"Storm is the very definition of the phrase 'contains multitudes' — power, grace, grief, joy — and she is one of the greatest mutants, X-Men and comics characters of all time!"

JACQUE PORTE
Director, S&P & Proofreading, 7 years at Marvel

"Fabulous Flo Steinberg left me with three things I hold dear: a newspaper clipping of three happy llamas ('The Girls,' as she called them), her directive to 'always have something sweet in the afternoon' and an anatomically correct Bullpen trophy/creature made from an old ink can and pen. I take these as reminders to appreciate my team, practice self-care and always be a bit silly."

SARAH SATHER
Publishing Talent and Scheduling Coordinator, 2.5 years at Marvel

"I've learned a lot from my favorite women of Marvel, on and off the page. Jane Foster as Thor taught me that I am braver and far more resilient than I may realize. That great power is inside of us always. And that love and hammers can conquer cancer and even death. I love you, Jane. Thanks for everything."

ALANNA SMITH
Editor, 6 years at Marvel

"One of my favorite Marvel women is the dearly departed Fabulous Flo Steinberg. She was such a warm and welcoming but also bitingly funny presence, and if I can bring even a fraction of the joy to this office that she did, I'll consider my time at Marvel a success!"

CAITLIN O'CONNELL
Associate Editor of Special Projects/Juvenile Publishing, 6 years at Marvel

"My favorite female character is Nadia Van Dyne, a science cinnamon roll, but my favorite Lady of Marvel has to be Jacque Porte — my first boss at Marvel, a career consultant extraordinaire and my friend."

STACIE ZUCKER
Designer, Special Projects, 6 years at Marvel

"On a spiritual level, Gamora is my gal! At her core, she's someone who trusts her instincts and stays true to her heart to do what's right, and I also try to live my life that way."

DANIELLE DAKE
Print Production Coordinator, 5 years at Marvel

"My favorite lady of Marvel is Brunnhilde, who shows that female Asgardians are just as powerful!"

KATERI WOODY
Associate Managing Editor, 6 years at Marvel

"My favorite lady of Marvel is the inimitable Sharon Carter! She's a top-notch spy and an overall delightful character."

SHANNON ANDREWS BALLESTEROS

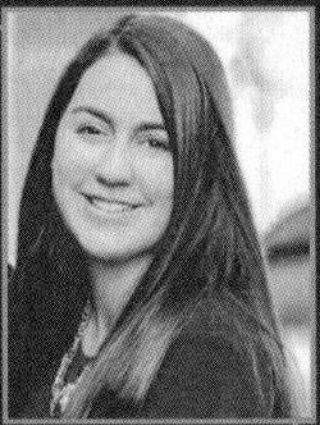

Assistant Managing Editor, 5 years at Marvel

"There are so many fearless Marvel ladies to choose as my favorite character, but Squirrel Girl is always at the top of my list. I admire her determination to help people, her drive to always better herself and, most of all, her ability to make people laugh. Whenever I go to conventions, I'm always blown away by how many young girls and women cosplay as Squirrel Girl. She's a hero who everyone can look up to, and she kicks butt just as hard as she'll make you laugh. We all need a positive role model like that!"

JENNIFER GRÜNWALD

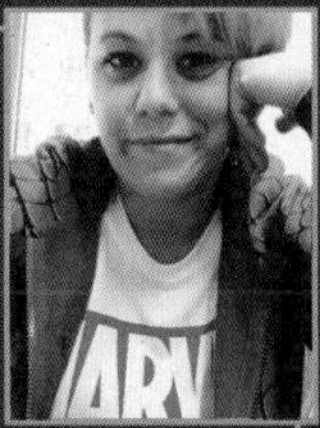

ARV

Director, Production & Special Projects, 19 years at Marvel

"My career here can be traced back to falling in love with Rogue from the '90s *X-Men* cartoon. Loved her strength, her hair and her accent. She remains my favorite."

KAT GREGOROWICZ

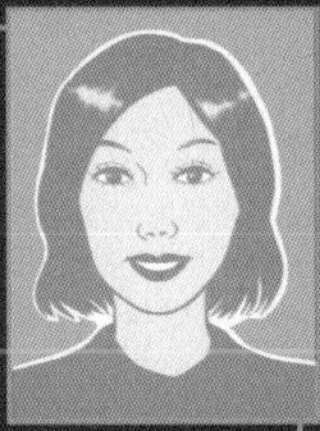

Assistant Editor, 2 years at Marvel

"My favorite female character has to be Emma Frost. I feel like she encompasses it all — she's sexy, outspoken and has awesome powers. I like that she has confidence and goes after what she wants. She knows how to be a star and doesn't lessen herself for anyone. And when female creators can be part of her story, that's even better."

MARA PANTANO

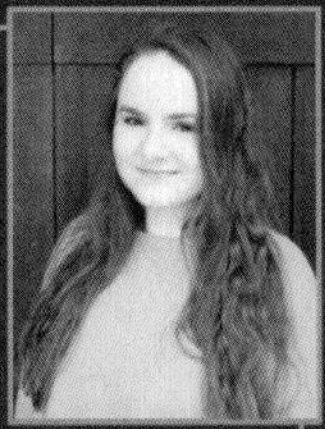

Associate Manager, Print Production, 7 years at Marvel

"My favorite lady of Marvel is Medusa. Who wouldn't want super-powerful hair?!"

EMILY NEWCOMEN

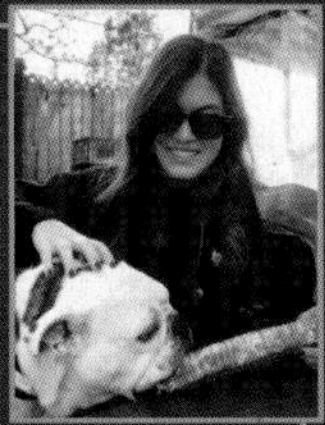

Associate Manager, Talent Relations, 5 years, 2 months at Marvel

"I love She-Hulk. I love the idea that she is in control of her emotions and can harness that power for the well-being of others — not to mention she's absolutely fabulous, like a giant '90s supermodel."

LISA MONTALBANO

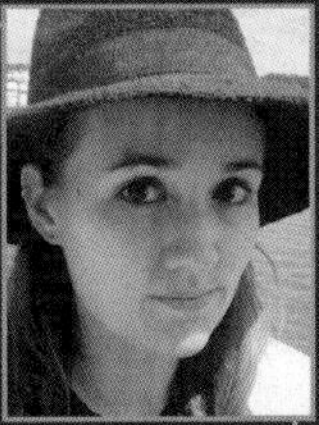

Associate Manager, Talent Relations, 4 years at Marvel

"Kate Bishop has been a favorite of mine since her first appearance in YOUNG AVENGERS, where she shows no fear stepping into new and potentially dangerous situations to help others."

LAUREN BISOM

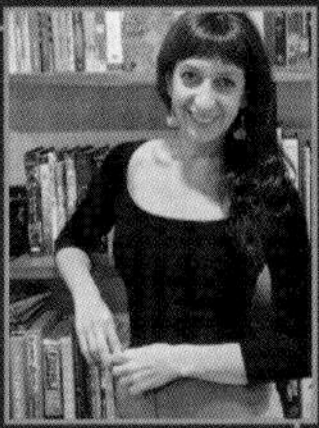

Senior Editor, 2 years at Marvel

"My favorite fictional lady of Marvel would have to be Moon Girl. Not only does Lunella Lafayette have one of the best sidekicks around in Devil Dinosaur, but I love that she never doubts her own abilities and won't stand for those around her doubting them either. One of my real-life super hero creators is Louise Simonson, one of the first writers I worked with when I entered comics. Her initial support and gentle guidance helped give me the confidence to trust my own abilities — just like Moon Girl!"

SARAH BRUNSTAD

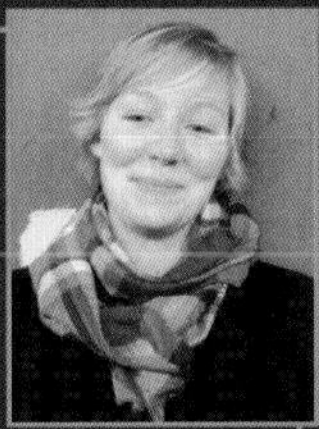

Editor, 8.5 years at Marvel

"You're seeing many of my favorite women of Marvel represented in this book already, but I'd like to shout out the indomitable Marie Severin, an amazing artist whose legacy goes so much further than I think she even knew."

ANGÉLIQUE ROCHÉ

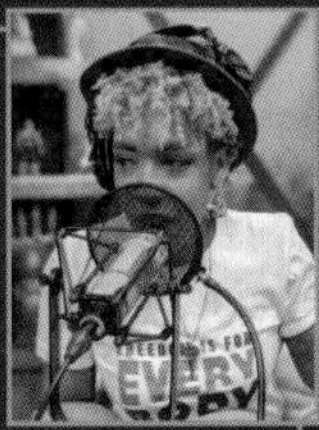

Host/Producer/Consultant, 4 years at Marvel

"Honestly, what I love about Monica Rambeau can be summed up in a quote from the woman herself: "Well, Auntie Monica is not $+^@*!& laughing."

To learn more about "Fabulous Flo," who guided many generations of creators and staff through Marvel, please see our tribute to her at **www.marvel.com/articles/comics/marvel-remembers-flo-steinberg** Born in 1939, Flo joined Marvel in the 1960s and was a presence in the offices nearly up until her death in 2017. We love you, Flo.

POWER POSE

SPOTLIGHTING WOMEN OF COLOR IN THE MARVEL UNIVERSE

BY ANGÉLIQUE ROCHÉ

They say you shouldn't judge a book by its cover — but there IS something to be said about the power of a good comic book cover. Who among us has not wandered through a comic book store, scanned the solicits or been browsing through Marvel Unlimited when a cover of our favorite character or even a new character, storyline or arc unexpectedly — sometimes suddenly — grabbed our attention. From main covers to variants, omnibuses to trade paperbacks, the exposition and tone-setting of a cover speaks volumes — sometimes literally.

So when the editorial team asked if I could choose ten covers spotlighting Marvel's women of color, I knew exactly what to do. I started by asking the most amazing fans in the Multiverse — you — what your favorite covers through the years have been. The response was overwhelming. Out of the several hundred comments on Twitter, I managed to narrow it down to ten covers that embodied the spirit of empowerment, vulnerability, diversity, and badassery that so many of us love about our favorite Marvel super heroes.

#1 THE MIGHTY AVENGERS (1985) #255

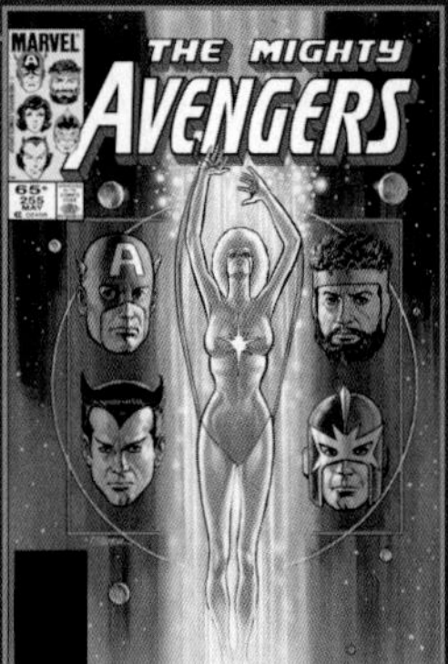
MARVEL
THE MIGHTY
AVENGERS

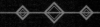

Cover art by Tom Palmer and issue written by Roger Stern. One of my personal favorites, this color-rich cover spotlights Monica Rambeau, then known as Captain Marvel, traveling at the speed of light through space to check on Sanctuary II, Thanos' former starship — where trouble awaits.

#2 THE RUNAWAYS (2017) #12

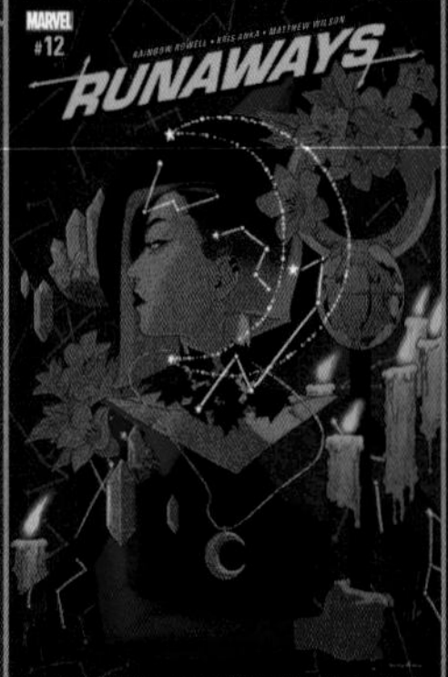
MARVEL
#12
RUNAWAYS

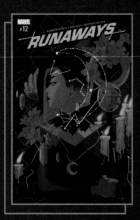

Cover art by Kris Anka and issue written by Rainbow Rowell. This beautiful cover and its distinct coloring spotlights Nico Minoru with her magical staff and sets the tone for the internal conflict regarding both her staff and her relationship with fellow Runaway Karolina Dean.

#3 AMAZING FANTASY (2004) #1

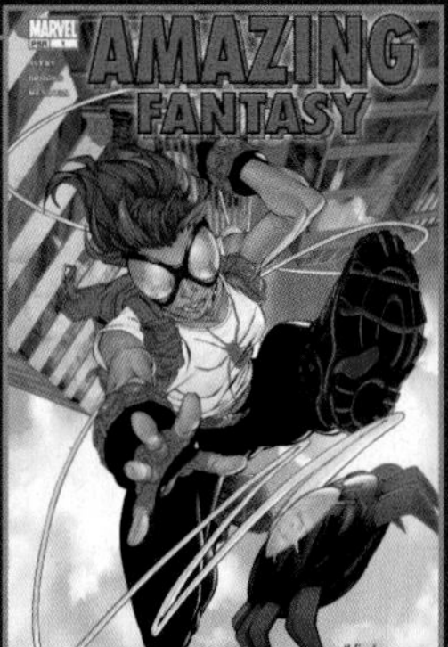
MARVEL
AMAZING
FANTASY

Cover art by Mark Brooks (with Jaime Mendoza and Danimation) and issue written by Fiona Avery. This cover marks the first appearance of Anya Corazon, A.K.A. Spider-Girl. Billed as the teen-friendly adventures of an all-new, all-different heroine, this cover was the perfect introduction of Araña as she THWIPS into the Marvel Universe!

#4 EXILES (2018) #1

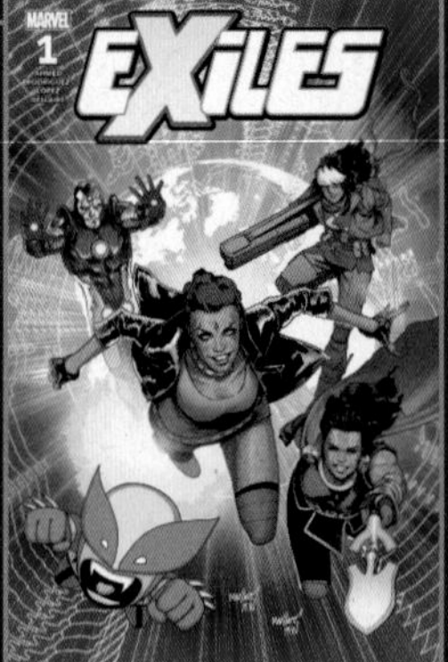
MARVEL
1
EXILES

Cover art by David Marquez (with Matthew Wilson) and issue written by Saladin Ahmed. This cover spotlights a new team of Exiles — heroes from many different realities — led by X-Man and native Bahamian Blink with Old Woman Kamala Khan and Valkyrie as they join forces with Iron Lad and Wolvie to save the Multiverse from a mysterious force threatening all of existence.

#5 INFINITY GAUNTLET (2015) #5

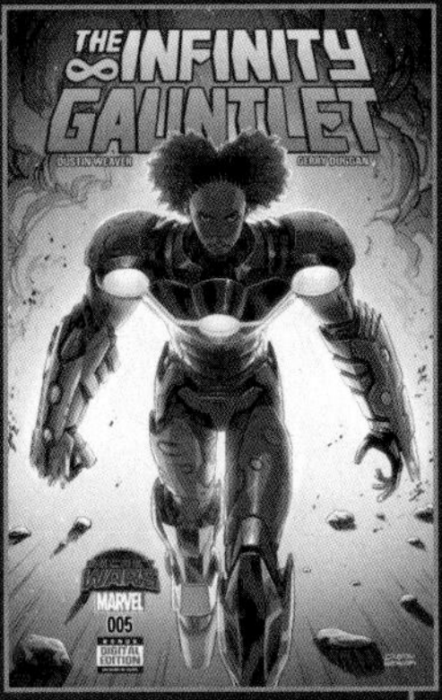
THE INFINITY GAUNTLET
DUSTIN WEAVER
GERRY DUGGAN
MARVEL
005
DIGITAL EDITION

Cover art by Dustin Weaver and issue written by Gerry Duggan and Dustin Weaver. This badass cover signaled the emergence of Anwen Bakian, A.K.A. Nova (Earth-94241) of the Bakian clan. The series gives the backstory of Anwen and her family and sets the stage for her becoming Nova and eventually fighting against the Multiverse's mightiest foe, Thanos.

#8 ATLANTIS ATTACKS (2020) #4

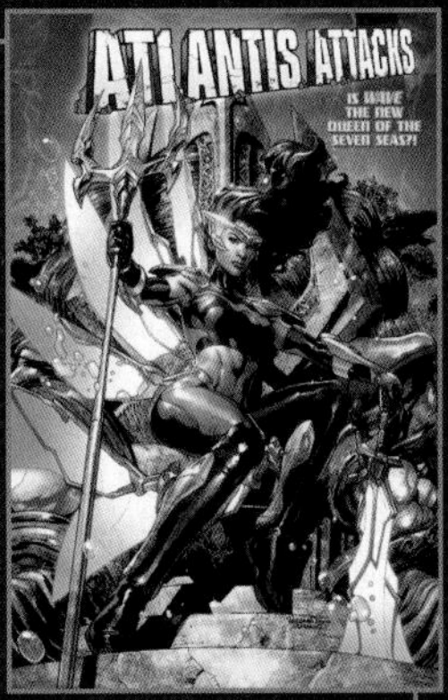
ATLANTIS ATTACKS
IS WAVE THE NEW QUEEN OF THE SEVEN SEAS?!

Cover art by Carlo Pagulayan (with Jason Paz and Rain Beredo) and issue written by Greg Pak. Filipina super hero Wave was empowered by evil scientists, only to change sides and join the heroes known as Triumph Division. Later joining the Agents of Atlas, Wave found herself in conflict with Atlantis, which led to the mysteries teased in this recent issue!

#6 SILK (2021) #1

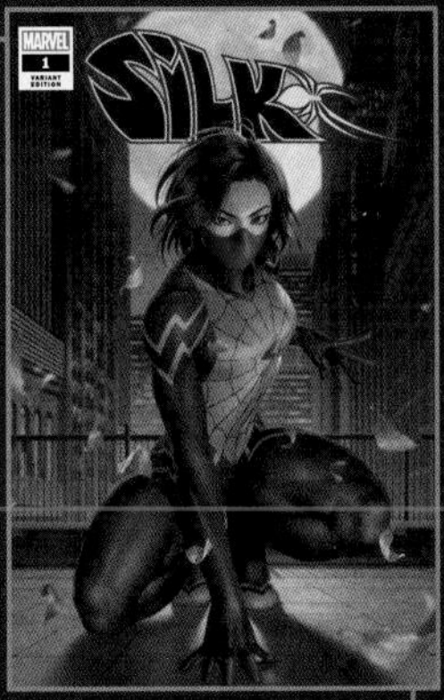
MARVEL
1
VARIANT EDITION
SILK

Variant cover art by Junggeun Yoon and issue written by Maurene Goo. The newest cover on the list, this variant is from Silk's recently launched solo series, written by acclaimed novelist Maurene Goo and drawn by superstar artist Takeshi Miyazawa. SILK follows Cindy Moon's adventures as a journalist at *Threats and Menaces* by day and a super hero by night.

#9 IRONHEART (2018) #12

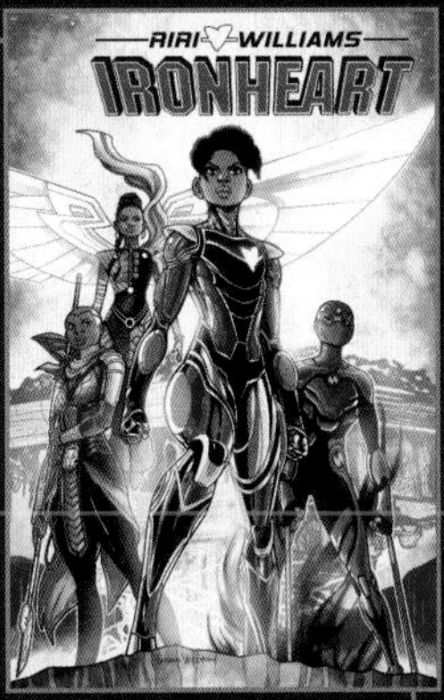
RIRI WILLIAMS
IRONHEART

Cover art by Luciano Vecchio and issue written by Eve L. Ewing. This cover spotlights not just one, but FOUR iconic female super heroes of color as Ironheart concludes her Wakandan adventure with the aid of Shuri, Silhouette and Okoye.

#7 AMERICA (2017) #2

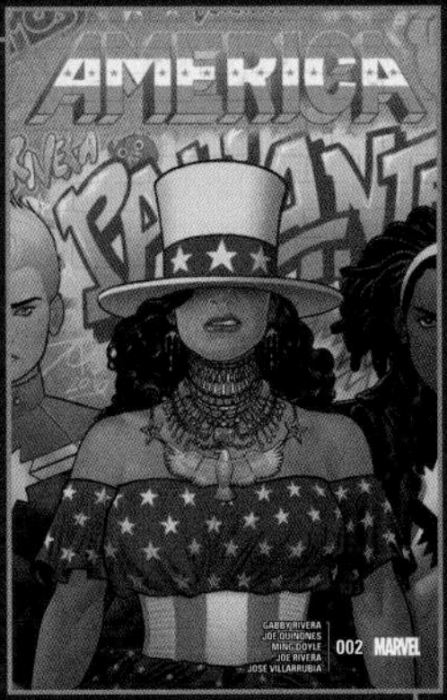
AMERICA
002
MARVEL

Cover art by Joe Quinones and issue written by Gabby Rivera. A true crossover of pop culture and comics, this iconic cover pays homage to none other than Queen Bey herself, Beyoncé, and features both Carol Danvers, A.K.A. Captain Marvel, and Monica Rambeau, A.K.A. Spectrum, "in formation" with Multiversal hero America Chavez.

#10 MARVEL'S VOICES: INDIGENOUS VOICES (2020) #1

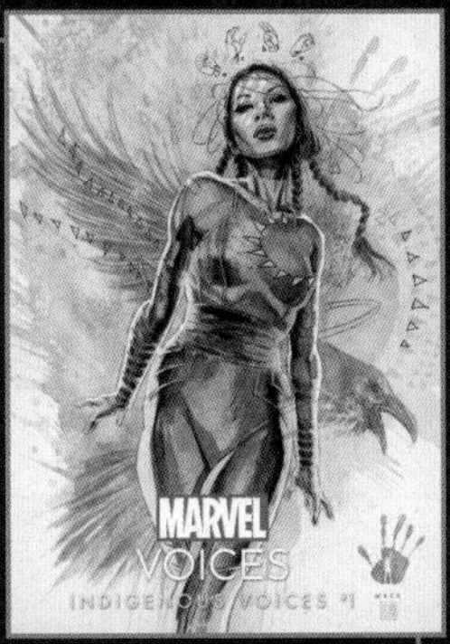
MARVEL
VOICES
INDIGENOUS VOICES #1

Variant cover art by David Mack and issue written by multiple contributors. Last year, Native American and Indigenous artists and writers came together to create a collection of Marvel stories for National Native American Heritage Month, including this cover featuring Maya Lopez, A.K.A. Echo.

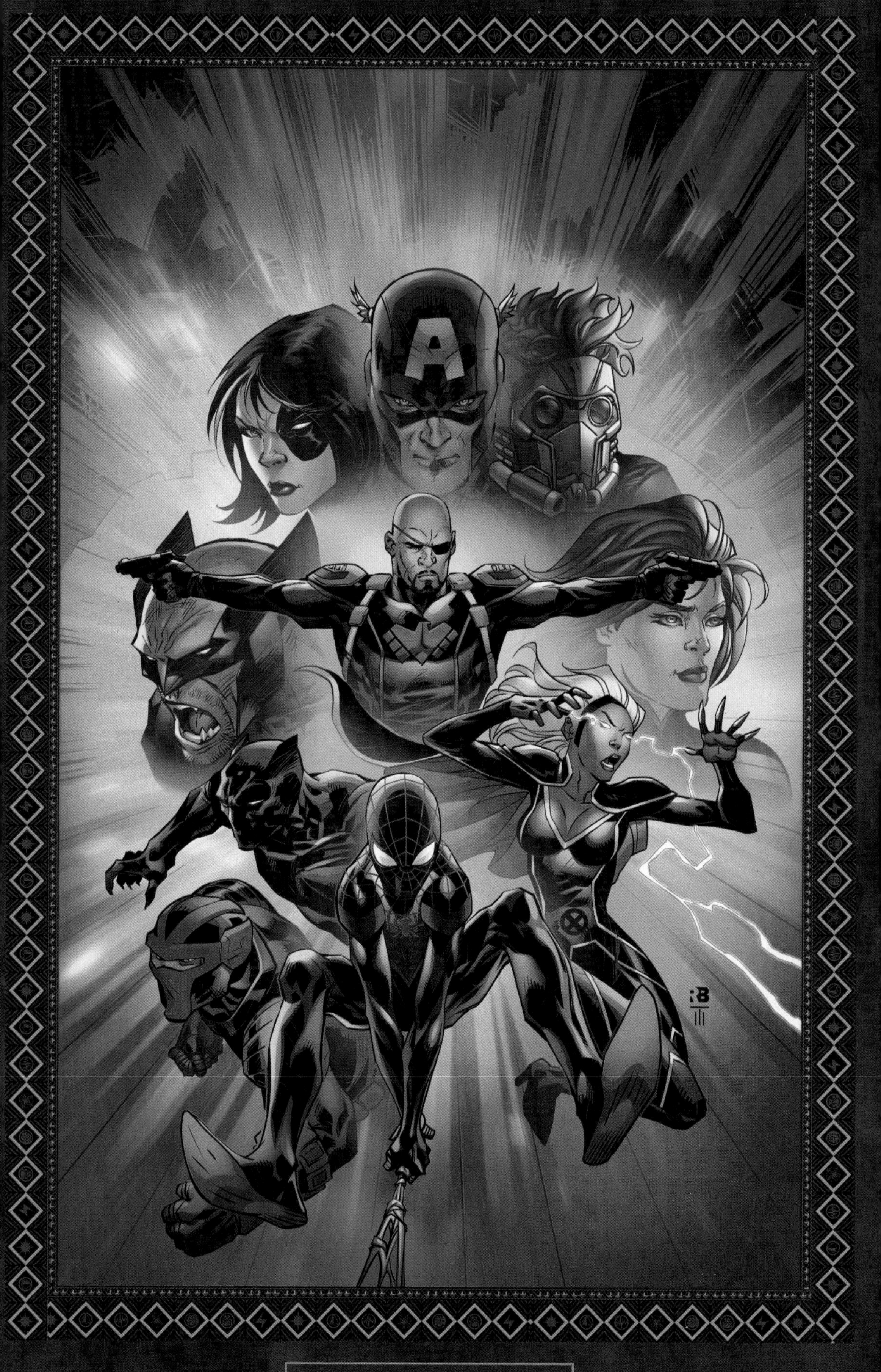

MARVEL'S VOICES #1

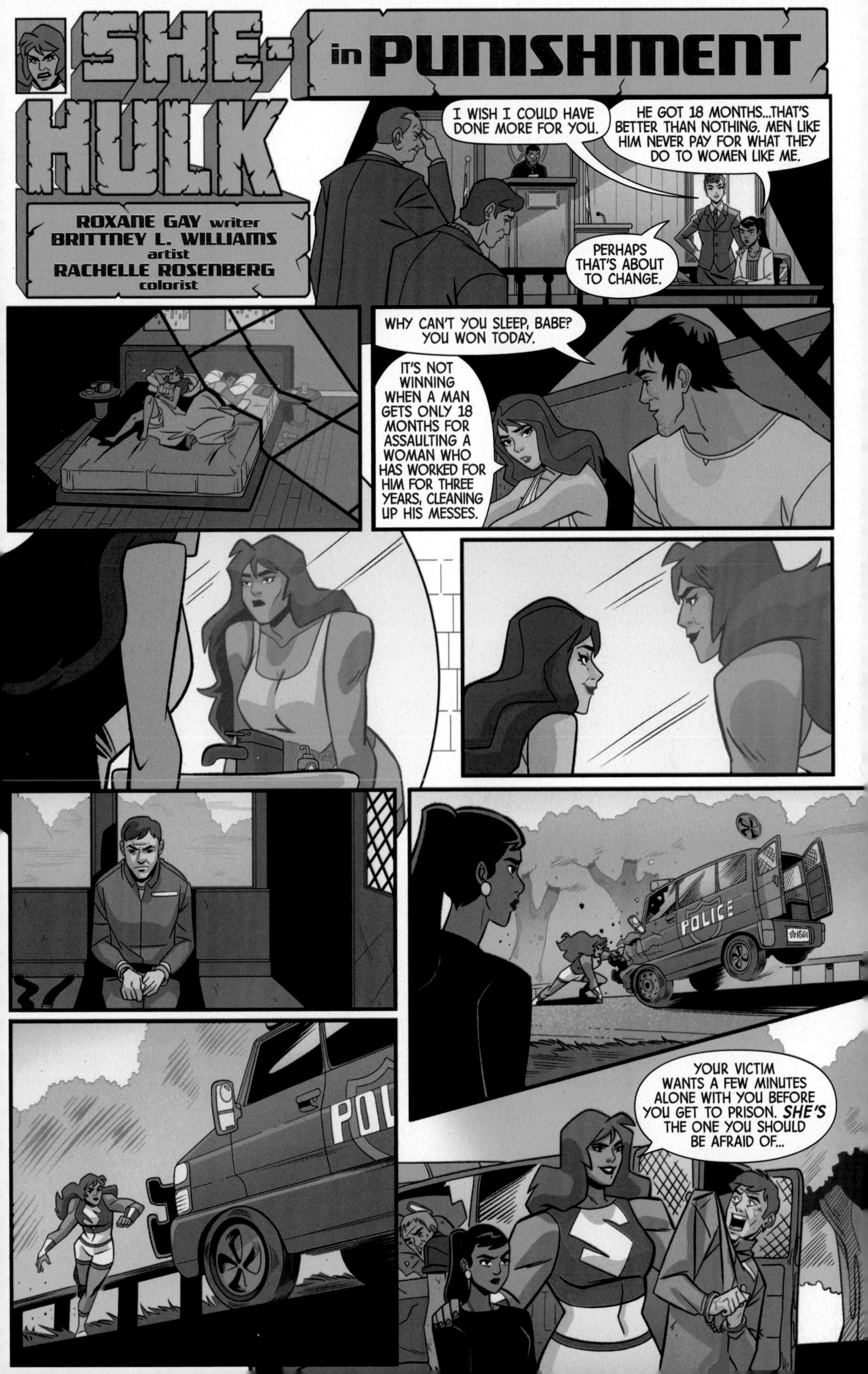
SHE-HULK in PUNISHMENT
ROXANE GAY writer
BRITTNEY L. WILLIAMS artist
RACHELLE ROSENBERG colorist
I WISH I COULD HAVE DONE MORE FOR YOU.
HE GOT 18 MONTHS...THAT'S BETTER THAN NOTHING. MEN LIKE HIM NEVER PAY FOR WHAT THEY DO TO WOMEN LIKE ME.
PERHAPS THAT'S ABOUT TO CHANGE.
WHY CAN'T YOU SLEEP, BABE? YOU WON TODAY.
IT'S NOT WINNING WHEN A MAN GETS ONLY 18 MONTHS FOR ASSAULTING A WOMAN WHO HAS WORKED FOR HIM FOR THREE YEARS, CLEANING UP HIS MESSES.
POLICE
POL
YOUR VICTIM WANTS A FEW MINUTES ALONE WITH YOU BEFORE YOU GET TO PRISON. SHE'S THE ONE YOU SHOULD BE AFRAID OF...

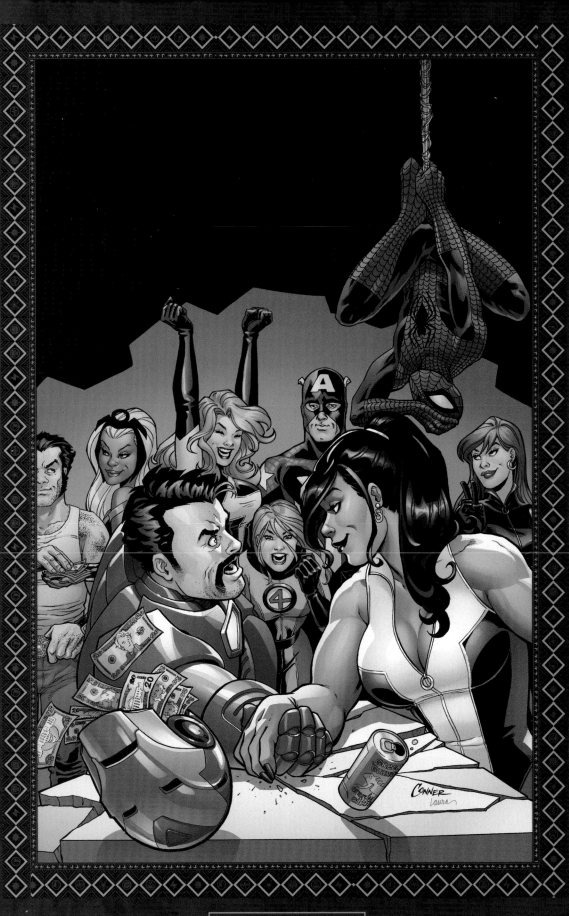

GIRL COMICS #1

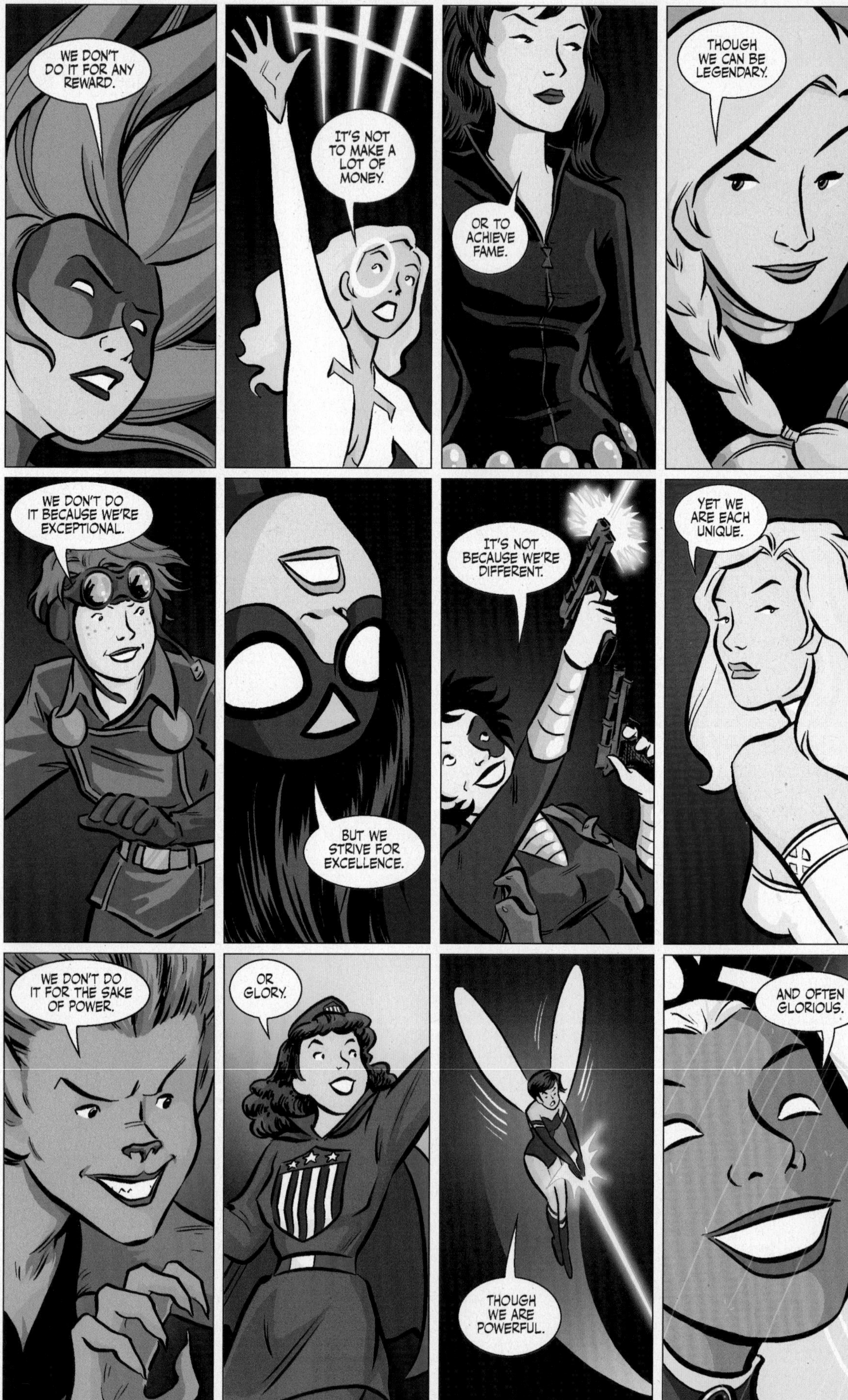
WE DON'T DO IT FOR ANY REWARD.
IT'S NOT TO MAKE A LOT OF MONEY.
OR TO ACHIEVE FAME.
THOUGH WE CAN BE LEGENDARY.
WE DON'T DO IT BECAUSE WE'RE EXCEPTIONAL.
BUT WE STRIVE FOR EXCELLENCE.
IT'S NOT BECAUSE WE'RE DIFFERENT.
YET WE ARE EACH UNIQUE.
WE DON'T DO IT FOR THE SAKE OF POWER.
OR GLORY.
THOUGH WE ARE POWERFUL.
AND OFTEN GLORIOUS.

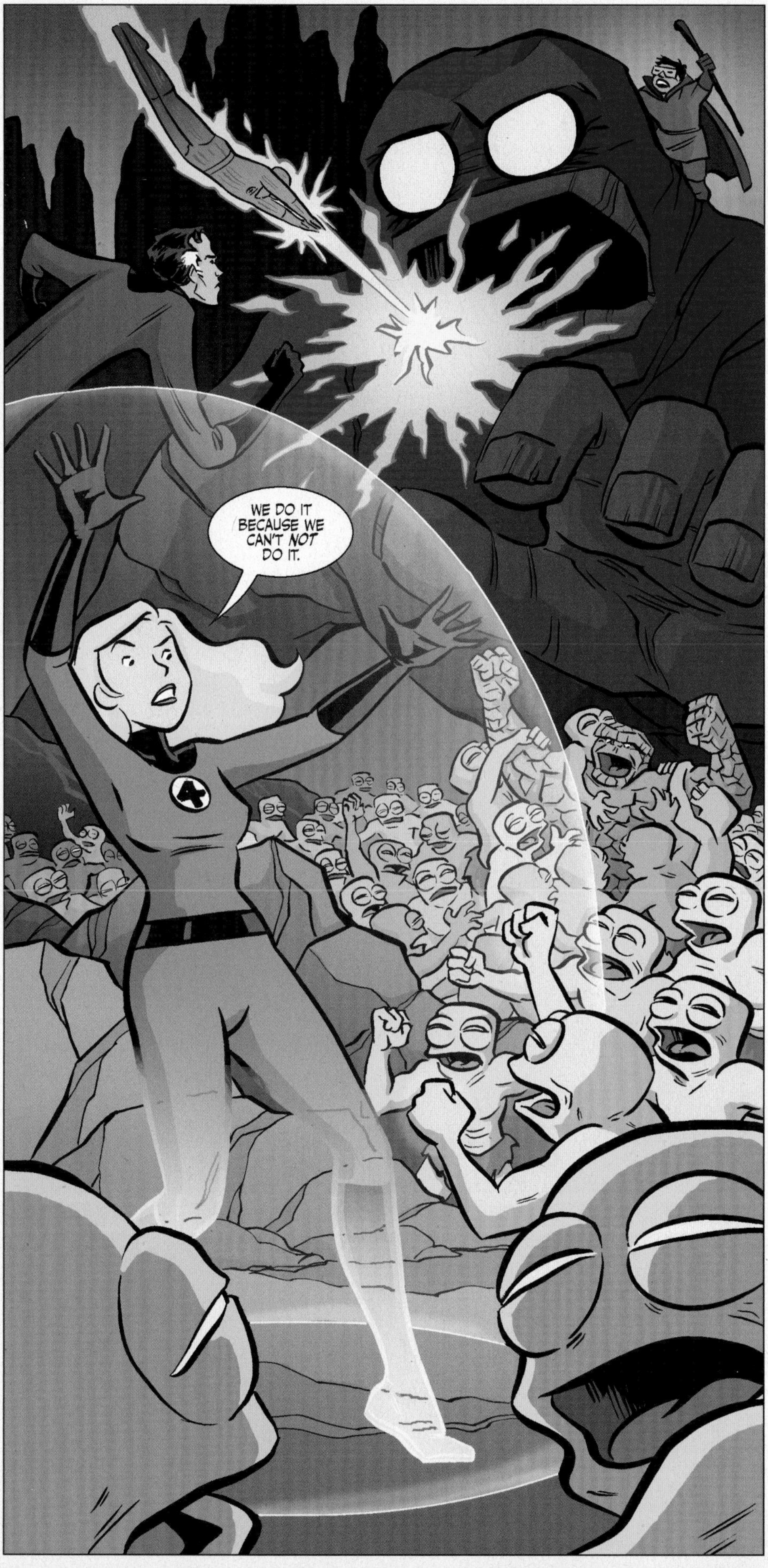
WE DO IT BECAUSE WE CAN'T *NOT* DO IT.

GIRL COMICS

Part One of Three

INTRODUCTION:
COLLEEN COOVER

COVER ART:
AMANDA CONNER & LAURA MARTIN

PRODUCTION:
IRENE LEE

ASSISTANT EDITORS:
SANA AMANAT & RACHEL PINNELAS

ASSOCIATE EDITOR:
LAUREN SANKOVITCH

EDITOR:
JEANINE SCHAEFER

EDITOR IN CHIEF:
JOE QUESADA

PUBLISHER:
DAN BUCKLEY

EXEC. PRODUCER:
ALAN FINE

SPECIAL THANKS:
SPRING HOTELING

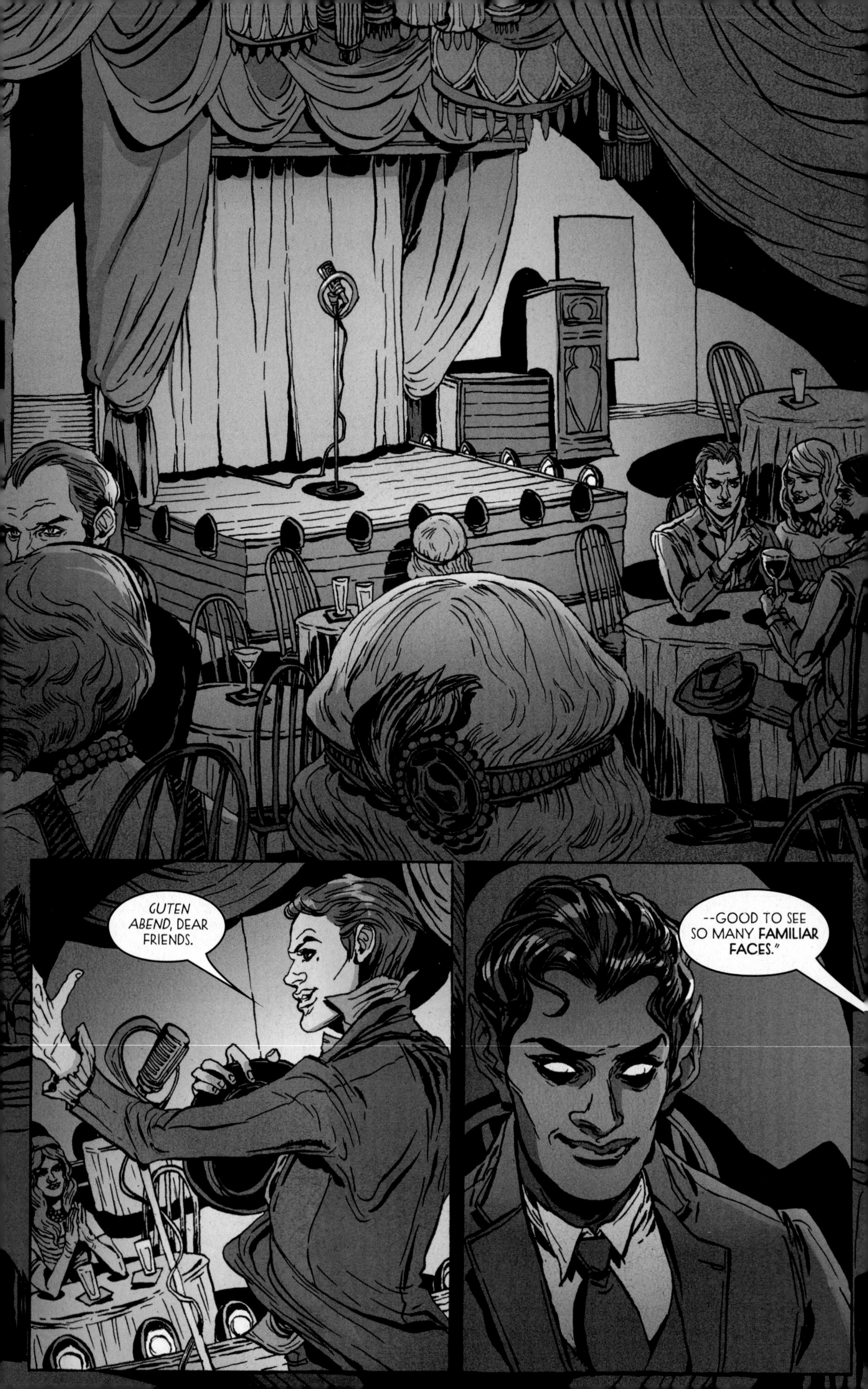
GUTEN ABEND, DEAR FRIENDS.
--GOOD TO SEE SO MANY FAMILIAR FACES."

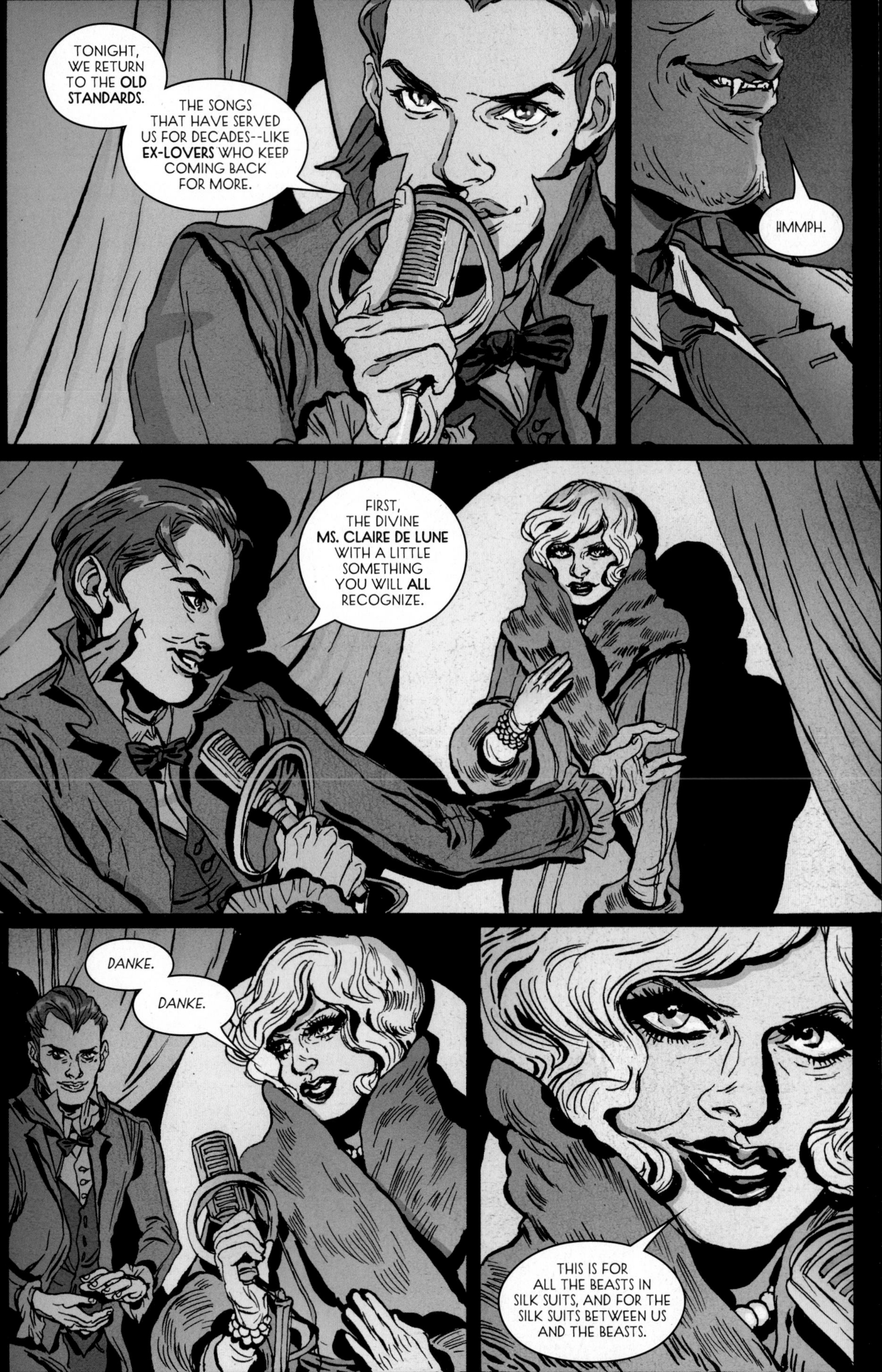
TONIGHT, WE RETURN TO THE **OLD STANDARDS.**
THE SONGS THAT HAVE SERVED US FOR DECADES--LIKE **EX-LOVERS** WHO KEEP COMING BACK FOR MORE.
HMMPH.
FIRST, THE DIVINE **MS. CLAIRE DE LUNE** WITH A LITTLE SOMETHING YOU WILL **ALL** RECOGNIZE.
DANKE.
DANKE.
THIS IS FOR ALL THE BEASTS IN SILK SUITS, AND FOR THE SILK SUITS BETWEEN US AND THE BEASTS.

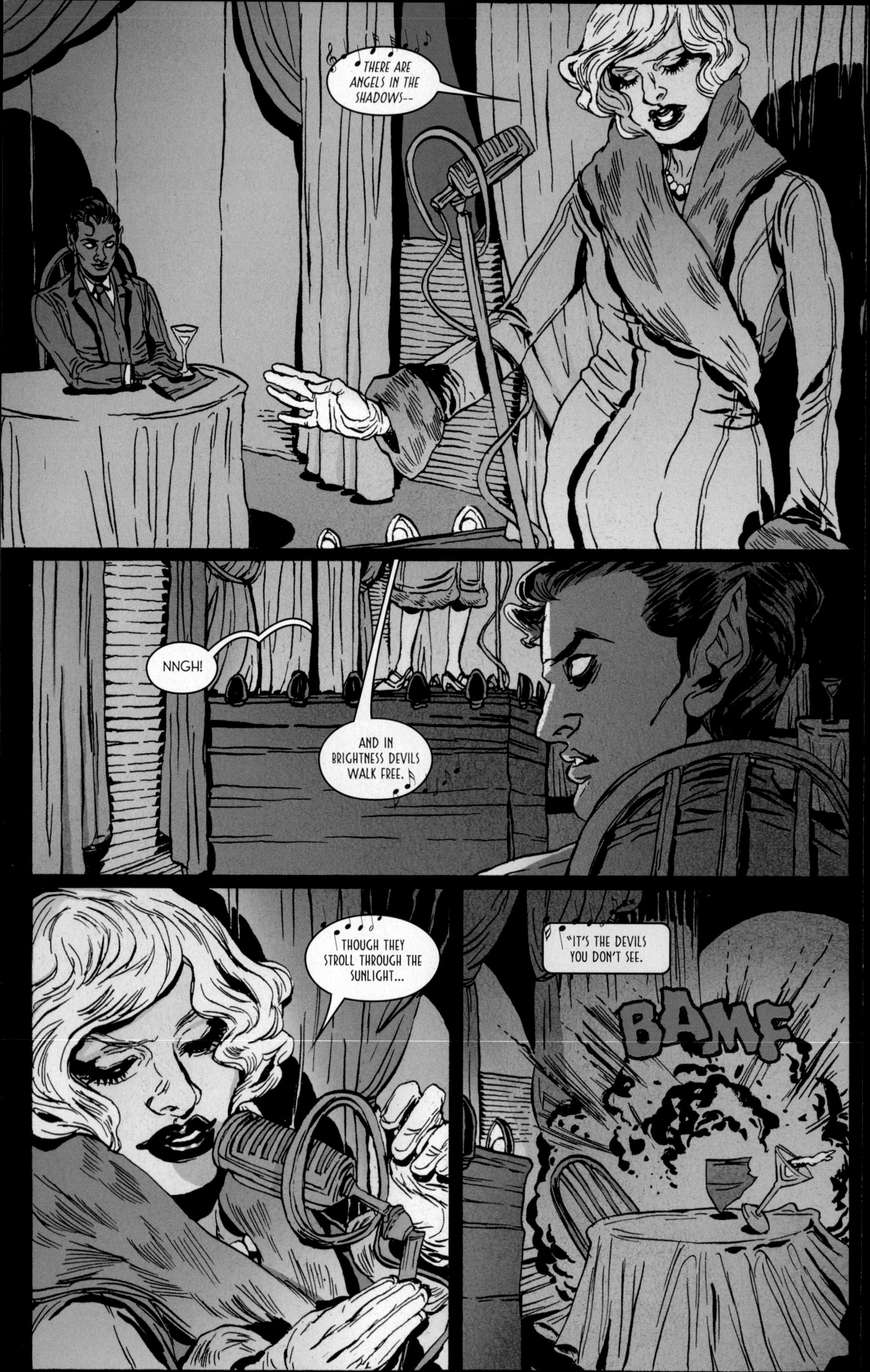
THERE ARE ANGELS IN THE SHADOWS--
NNGH!
AND IN BRIGHTNESS DEVILS WALK FREE.
THOUGH THEY STROLL THROUGH THE SUNLIGHT...
"IT'S THE DEVILS YOU DON'T SEE.
BAMF

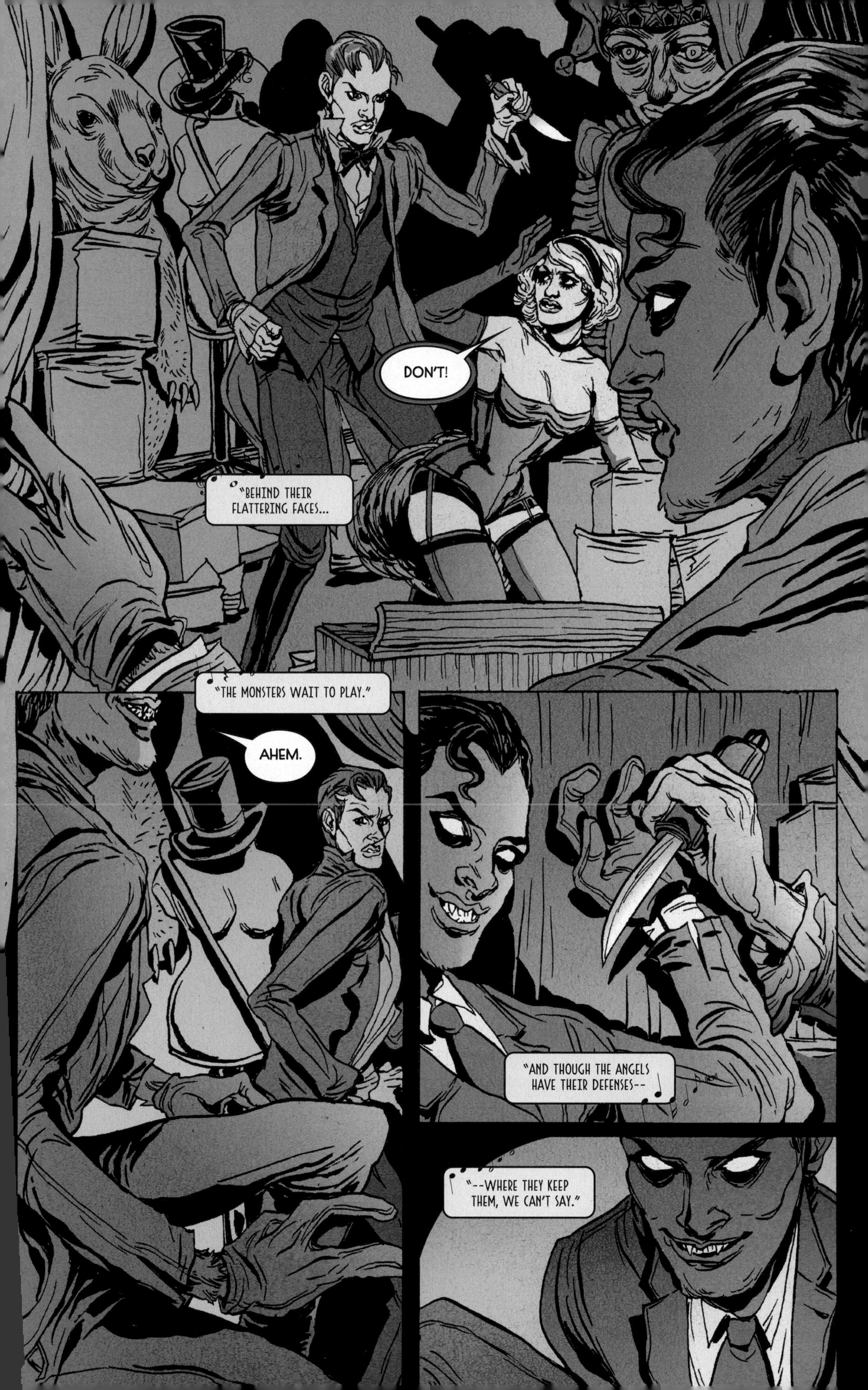
DON'T!
"BEHIND THEIR FLATTERING FACES...
"THE MONSTERS WAIT TO PLAY."
AHEM.
"AND THOUGH THE ANGELS HAVE THEIR DEFENSES--
"--WHERE THEY KEEP THEM, WE CAN'T SAY."

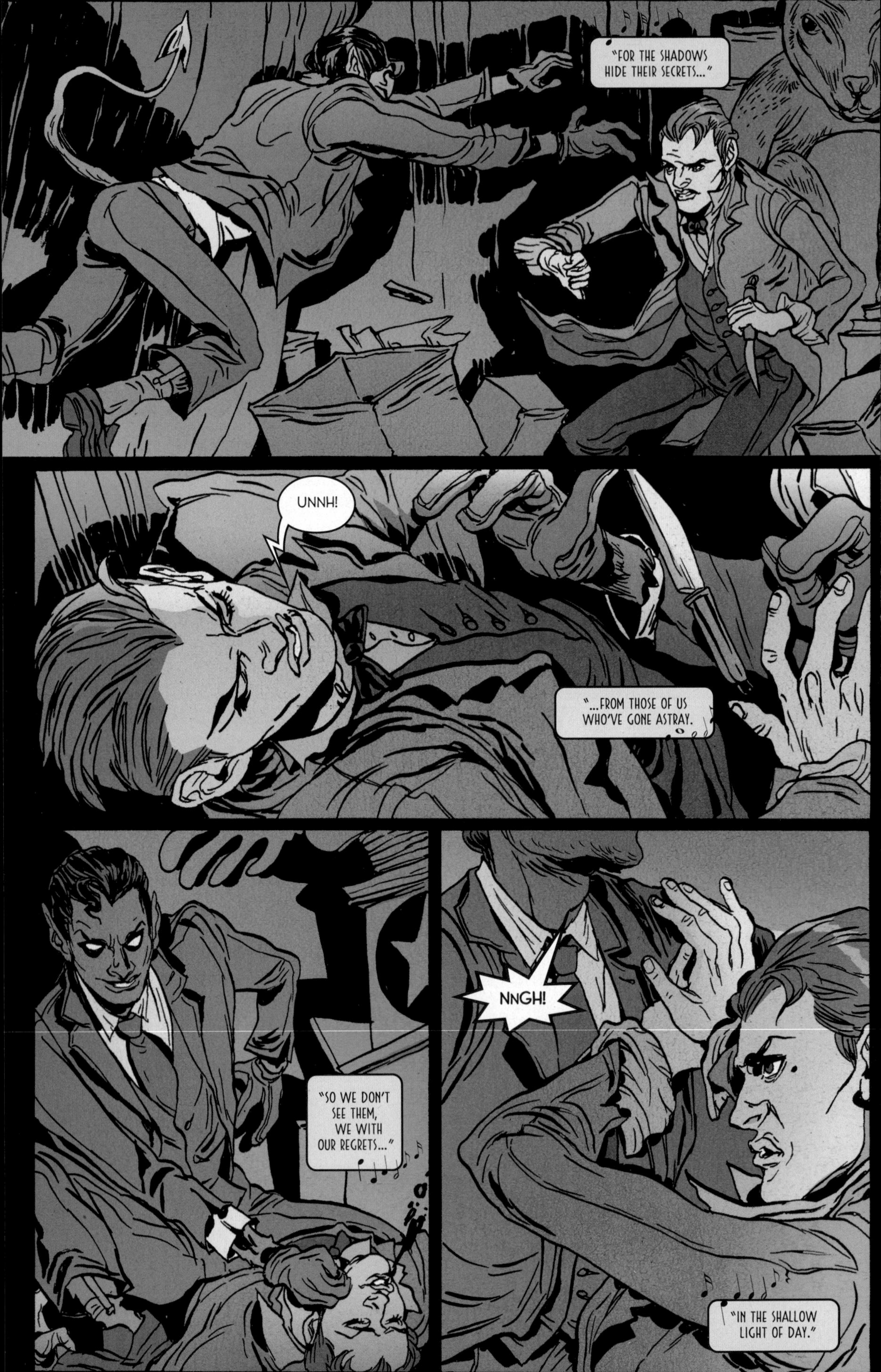
"FOR THE SHADOWS HIDE THEIR SECRETS..."
UNNH!
"...FROM THOSE OF US WHO'VE GONE ASTRAY.
"SO WE DON'T SEE THEM, WE WITH OUR REGRETS..."
NNGH!
"IN THE SHALLOW LIGHT OF DAY."

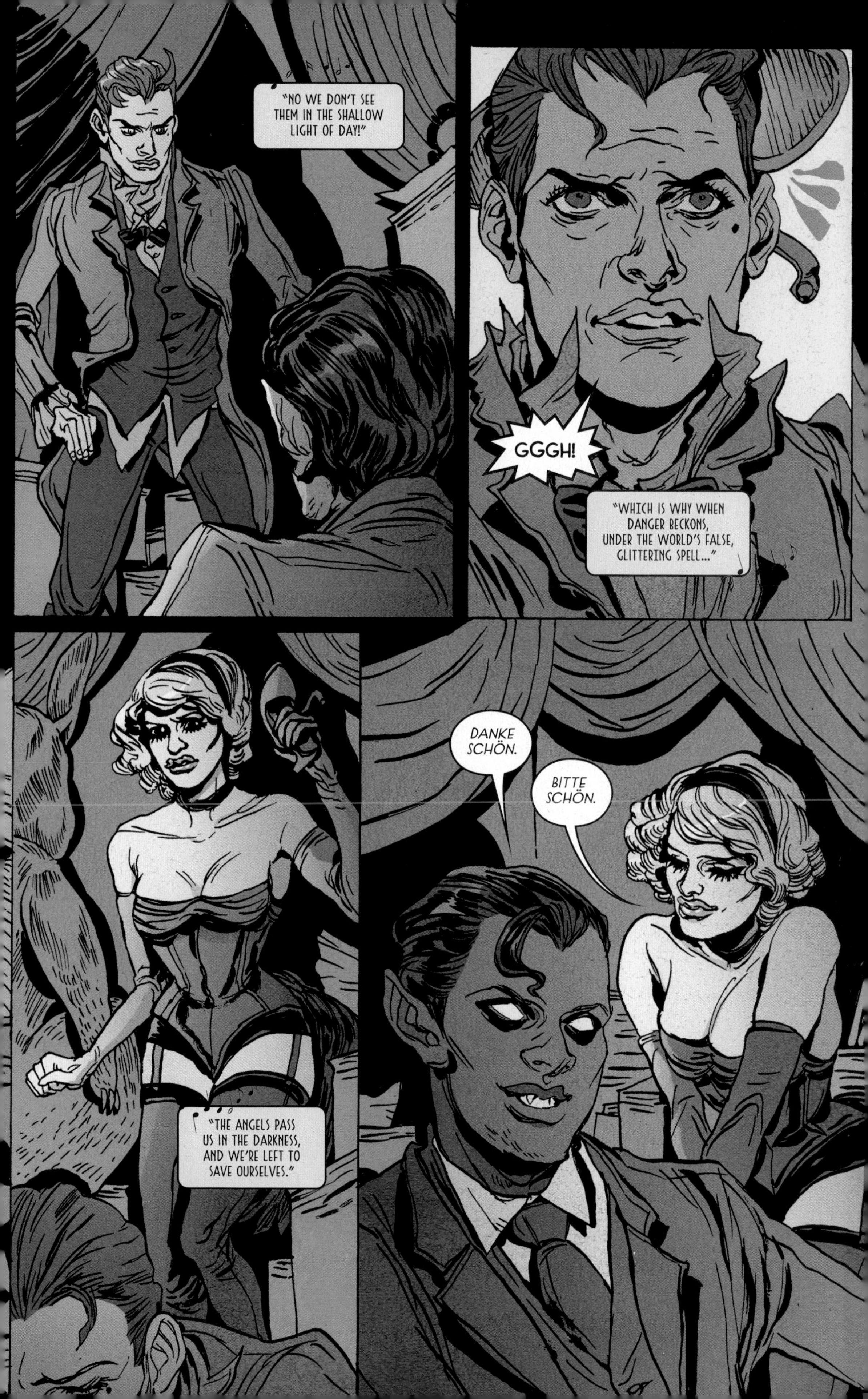
"NO WE DON'T SEE THEM IN THE SHALLOW LIGHT OF DAY!"
GGGH!
"WHICH IS WHY WHEN DANGER BECKONS, UNDER THE WORLD'S FALSE, GLITTERING SPELL..."
"THE ANGELS PASS US IN THE DARKNESS, AND WE'RE LEFT TO SAVE OURSELVES."
DANKE SCHÖN.
BITTE SCHÖN.

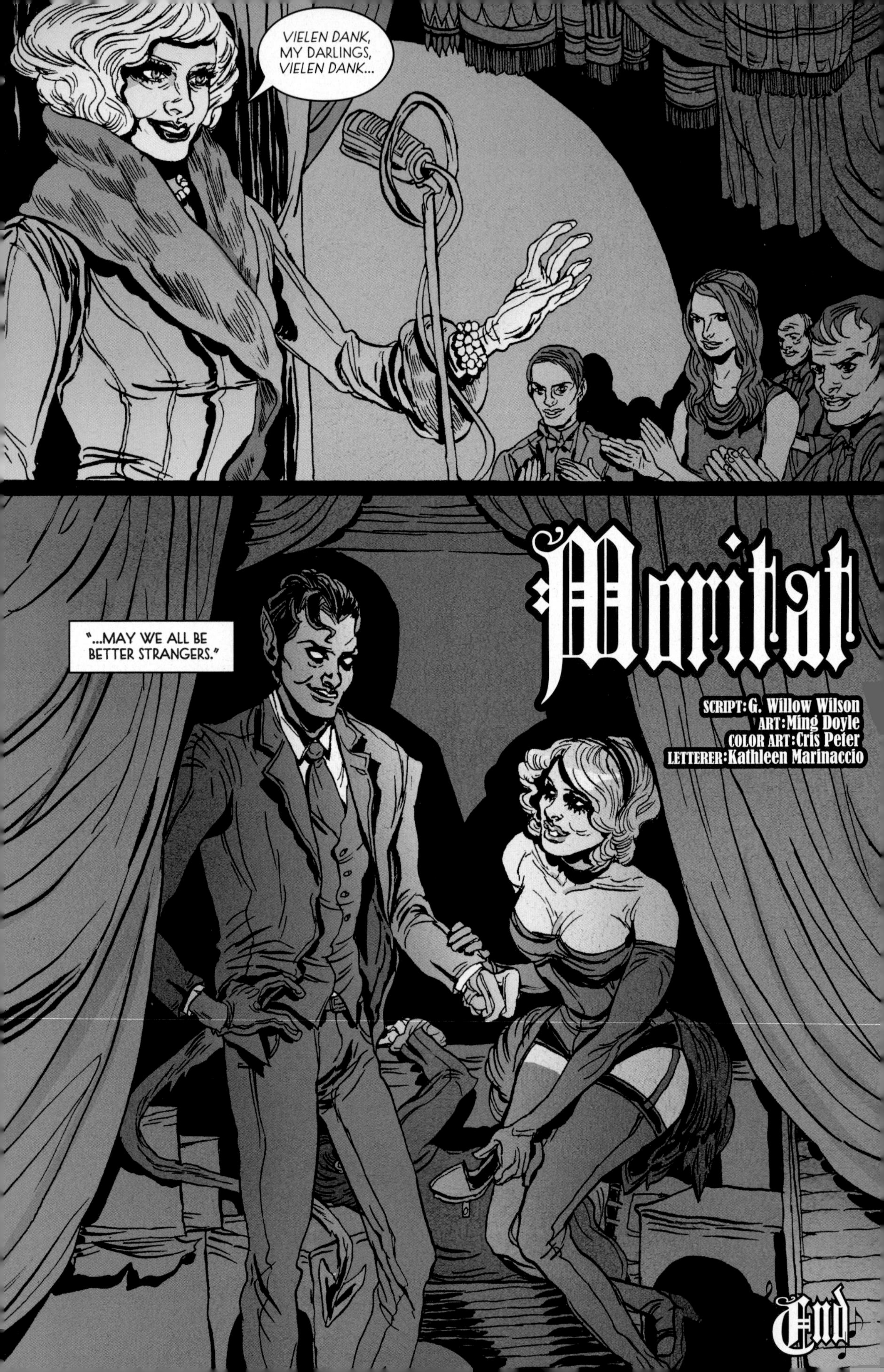
VIELEN DANK, MY DARLINGS, VIELEN DANK...
"...MAY WE ALL BE BETTER STRANGERS."
Moritat
SCRIPT: G. Willow Wilson
ART: Ming Doyle
COLOR ART: Cris Peter
LETTERER: Kathleen Marinaccio
End

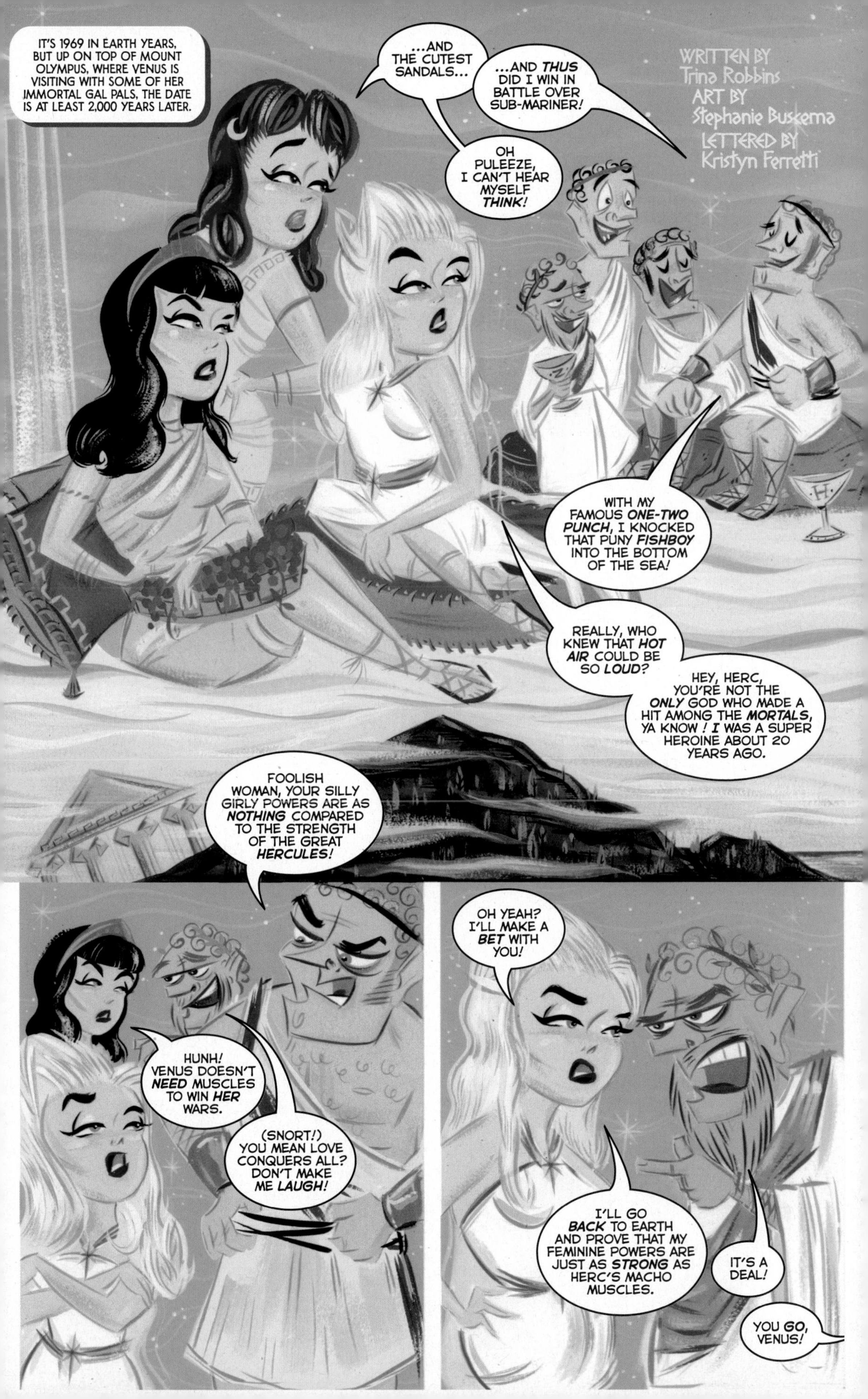
IT'S 1969 IN EARTH YEARS, BUT UP ON TOP OF MOUNT OLYMPUS, WHERE VENUS IS VISITING WITH SOME OF HER IMMORTAL GAL PALS, THE DATE IS AT LEAST 2,000 YEARS LATER.
...AND THE CUTEST SANDALS...
...AND THUS DID I WIN IN BATTLE OVER SUB-MARINER!
OH PULEEZE, I CAN'T HEAR MYSELF THINK!
WRITTEN BY Trina Robbins
ART BY Stephanie Buscema
LETTERED BY Kristyn Ferretti
WITH MY FAMOUS ONE-TWO PUNCH, I KNOCKED THAT PUNY FISHBOY INTO THE BOTTOM OF THE SEA!
REALLY, WHO KNEW THAT HOT AIR COULD BE SO LOUD?
HEY, HERC, YOU'RE NOT THE ONLY GOD WHO MADE A HIT AMONG THE MORTALS, YA KNOW ! I WAS A SUPER HEROINE ABOUT 20 YEARS AGO.
FOOLISH WOMAN, YOUR SILLY GIRLY POWERS ARE AS NOTHING COMPARED TO THE STRENGTH OF THE GREAT HERCULES!
HUNH! VENUS DOESN'T NEED MUSCLES TO WIN HER WARS.
(SNORT!) YOU MEAN LOVE CONQUERS ALL? DON'T MAKE ME LAUGH!
OH YEAH? I'LL MAKE A BET WITH YOU!
I'LL GO BACK TO EARTH AND PROVE THAT MY FEMININE POWERS ARE JUST AS STRONG AS HERC'S MACHO MUSCLES.
IT'S A DEAL!
YOU GO, VENUS!

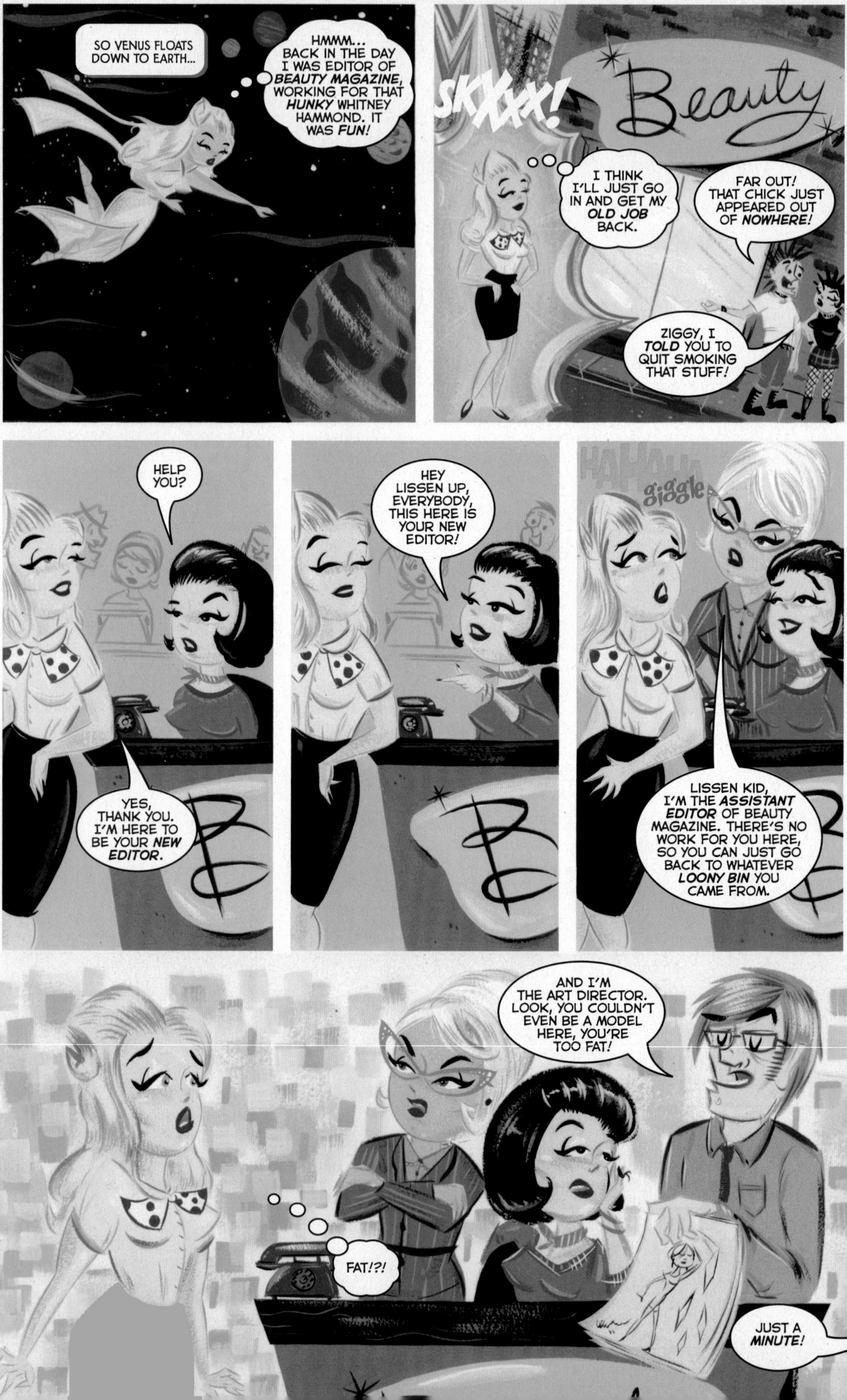
SO VENUS FLOATS DOWN TO EARTH...
HMMM... BACK IN THE DAY I WAS EDITOR OF BEAUTY MAGAZINE, WORKING FOR THAT HUNKY WHITNEY HAMMOND. IT WAS FUN!
SKXXX!
Beauty
I THINK I'LL JUST GO IN AND GET MY OLD JOB BACK.
FAR OUT! THAT CHICK JUST APPEARED OUT OF NOWHERE!
ZIGGY, I TOLD YOU TO QUIT SMOKING THAT STUFF!
HELP YOU?
YES, THANK YOU. I'M HERE TO BE YOUR NEW EDITOR.
HEY LISSEN UP, EVERYBODY, THIS HERE IS YOUR NEW EDITOR!
HAHAHA
giggle
LISSEN KID, I'M THE ASSISTANT EDITOR OF BEAUTY MAGAZINE. THERE'S NO WORK FOR YOU HERE, SO YOU CAN JUST GO BACK TO WHATEVER LOONY BIN YOU CAME FROM.
AND I'M THE ART DIRECTOR. LOOK, YOU COULDN'T EVEN BE A MODEL HERE, YOU'RE TOO FAT!
FAT!?!
JUST A MINUTE!

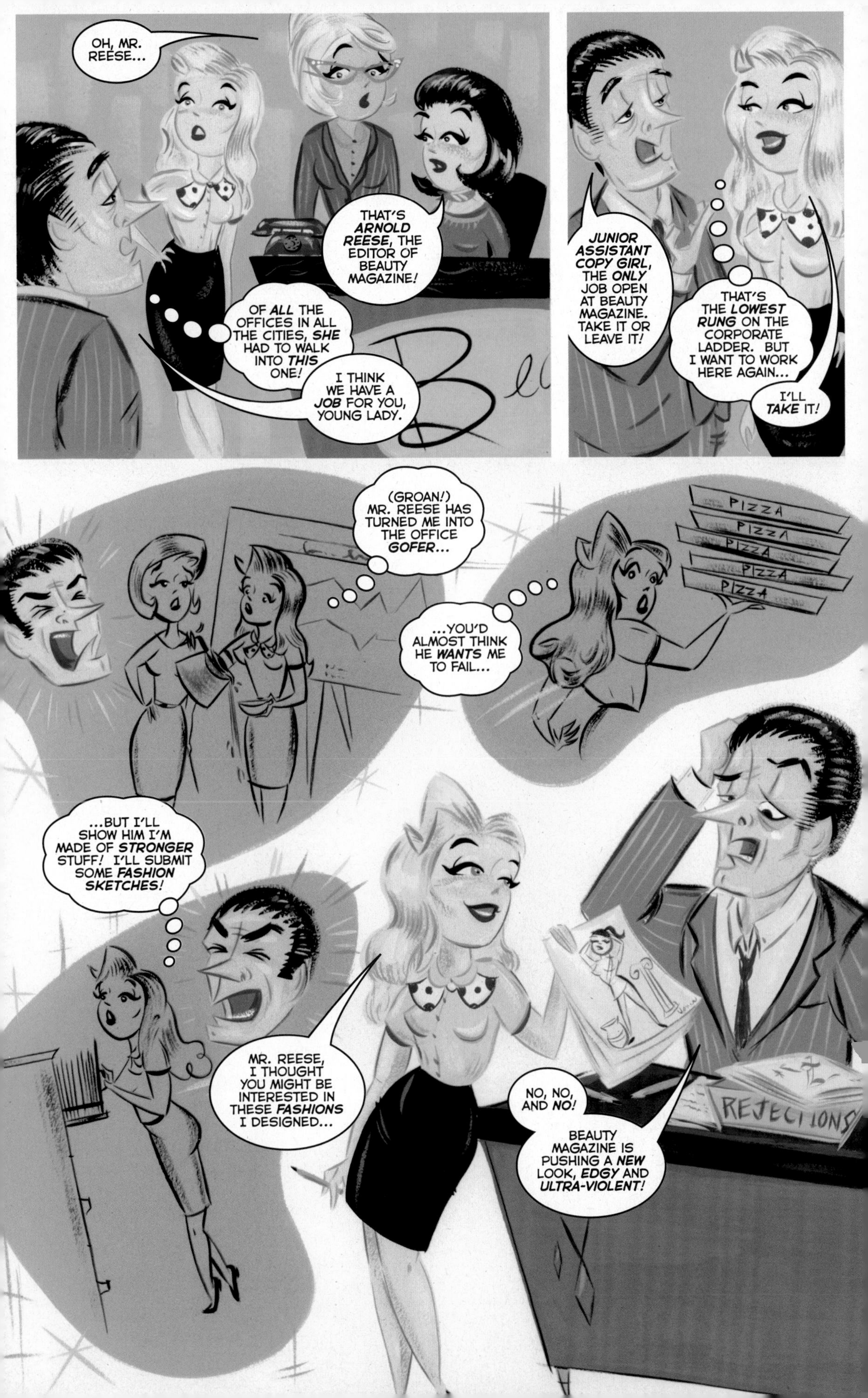

OH, MR. REESE...
THAT'S ARNOLD REESE, THE EDITOR OF BEAUTY MAGAZINE!
OF ALL THE OFFICES IN ALL THE CITIES, SHE HAD TO WALK INTO THIS ONE!
I THINK WE HAVE A JOB FOR YOU, YOUNG LADY.
JUNIOR ASSISTANT COPY GIRL, THE ONLY JOB OPEN AT BEAUTY MAGAZINE. TAKE IT OR LEAVE IT!
THAT'S THE LOWEST RUNG ON THE CORPORATE LADDER. BUT I WANT TO WORK HERE AGAIN...
I'LL TAKE IT!
(GROAN!) MR. REESE HAS TURNED ME INTO THE OFFICE GOFER...
...YOU'D ALMOST THINK HE WANTS ME TO FAIL...
PIZZA
PIZZA
PIZZA
PIZZA
PIZZA
...BUT I'LL SHOW HIM I'M MADE OF STRONGER STUFF! I'LL SUBMIT SOME FASHION SKETCHES!
MR. REESE, I THOUGHT YOU MIGHT BE INTERESTED IN THESE FASHIONS I DESIGNED...
NO, NO, AND NO!
BEAUTY MAGAZINE IS PUSHING A NEW LOOK, EDGY AND ULTRA-VIOLENT!
REJECTIONS

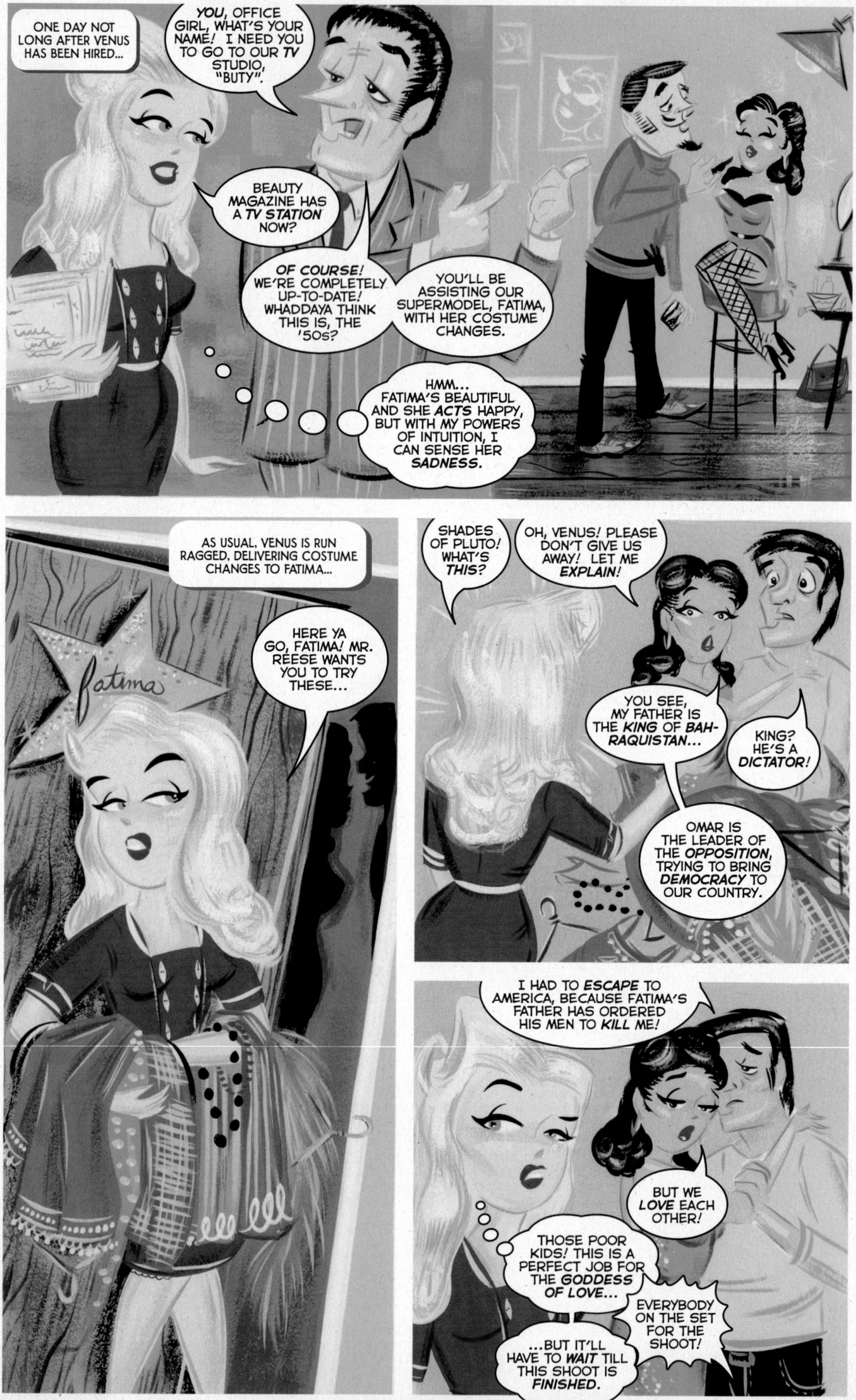
ONE DAY NOT LONG AFTER VENUS HAS BEEN HIRED...
YOU, OFFICE GIRL, WHAT'S YOUR NAME! I NEED YOU TO GO TO OUR TV STUDIO, "BUTY".
BEAUTY MAGAZINE HAS A TV STATION NOW?
OF COURSE! WE'RE COMPLETELY UP-TO-DATE! WHADDAYA THINK THIS IS, THE '50S?
YOU'LL BE ASSISTING OUR SUPERMODEL, FATIMA, WITH HER COSTUME CHANGES.
HMM... FATIMA'S BEAUTIFUL AND SHE ACTS HAPPY, BUT WITH MY POWERS OF INTUITION, I CAN SENSE HER SADNESS.
AS USUAL, VENUS IS RUN RAGGED, DELIVERING COSTUME CHANGES TO FATIMA...
fatima
HERE YA GO, FATIMA! MR. REESE WANTS YOU TO TRY THESE...
SHADES OF PLUTO! WHAT'S THIS?
OH, VENUS! PLEASE DON'T GIVE US AWAY! LET ME EXPLAIN!
YOU SEE, MY FATHER IS THE KING OF BAH-RAQUISTAN...
KING? HE'S A DICTATOR!
OMAR IS THE LEADER OF THE OPPOSITION, TRYING TO BRING DEMOCRACY TO OUR COUNTRY.
I HAD TO ESCAPE TO AMERICA, BECAUSE FATIMA'S FATHER HAS ORDERED HIS MEN TO KILL ME!
BUT WE LOVE EACH OTHER!
THOSE POOR KIDS! THIS IS A PERFECT JOB FOR THE GODDESS OF LOVE...
...BUT IT'LL HAVE TO WAIT TILL THIS SHOOT IS FINISHED.
EVERYBODY ON THE SET FOR THE SHOOT!

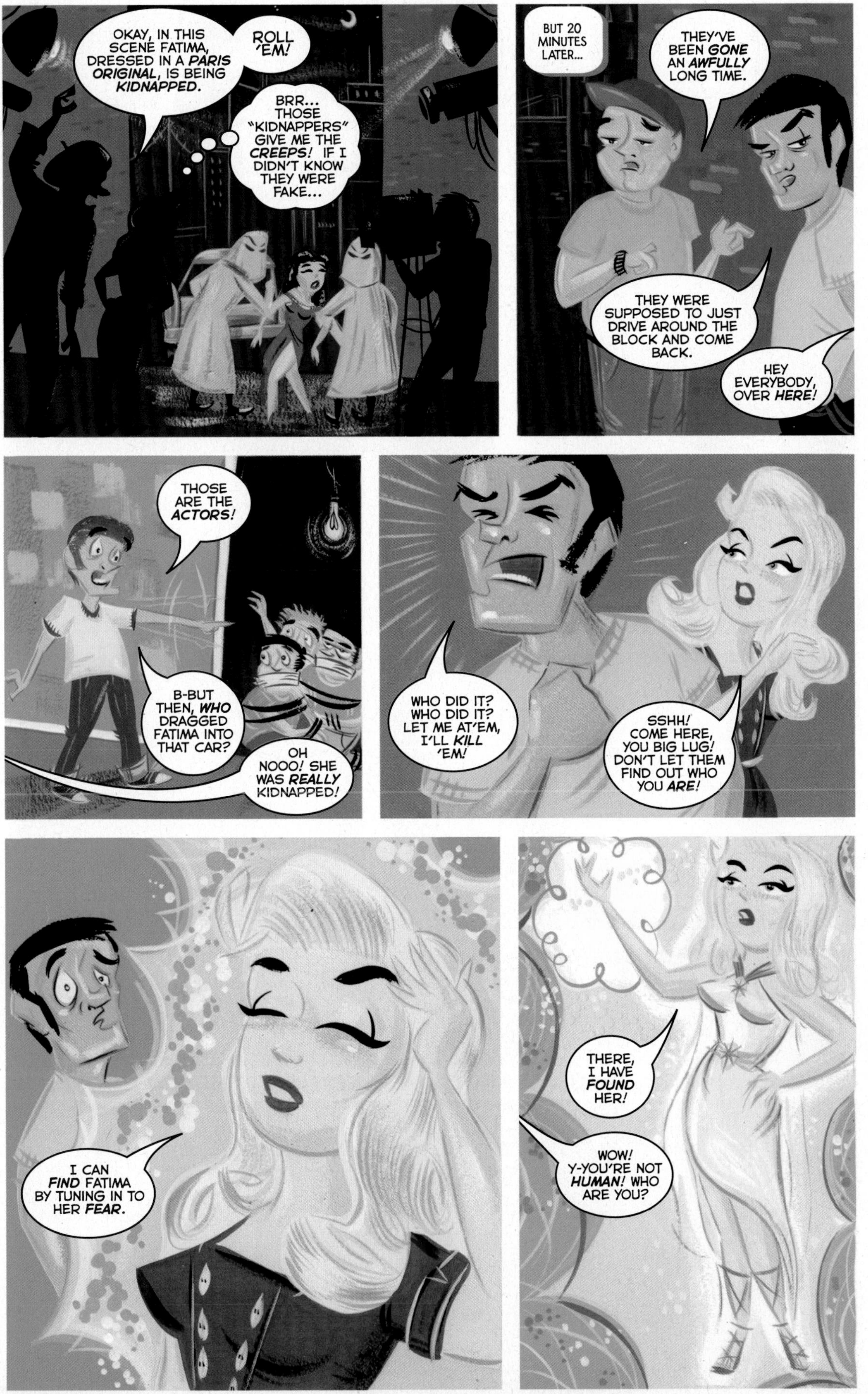
OKAY, IN THIS SCENE FATIMA, DRESSED IN A PARIS ORIGINAL, IS BEING KIDNAPPED.
ROLL 'EM!
BRR... THOSE "KIDNAPPERS" GIVE ME THE CREEPS! IF I DIDN'T KNOW THEY WERE FAKE...
BUT 20 MINUTES LATER...
THEY'VE BEEN GONE AN AWFULLY LONG TIME.
THEY WERE SUPPOSED TO JUST DRIVE AROUND THE BLOCK AND COME BACK.
HEY EVERYBODY, OVER HERE!
THOSE ARE THE ACTORS!
B-BUT THEN, WHO DRAGGED FATIMA INTO THAT CAR?
OH NOOO! SHE WAS REALLY KIDNAPPED!
WHO DID IT? WHO DID IT? LET ME AT'EM, I'LL KILL 'EM!
SSHH! COME HERE, YOU BIG LUG! DON'T LET THEM FIND OUT WHO YOU ARE!
I CAN FIND FATIMA BY TUNING IN TO HER FEAR.
THERE, I HAVE FOUND HER!
WOW! Y-YOU'RE NOT HUMAN! WHO ARE YOU?

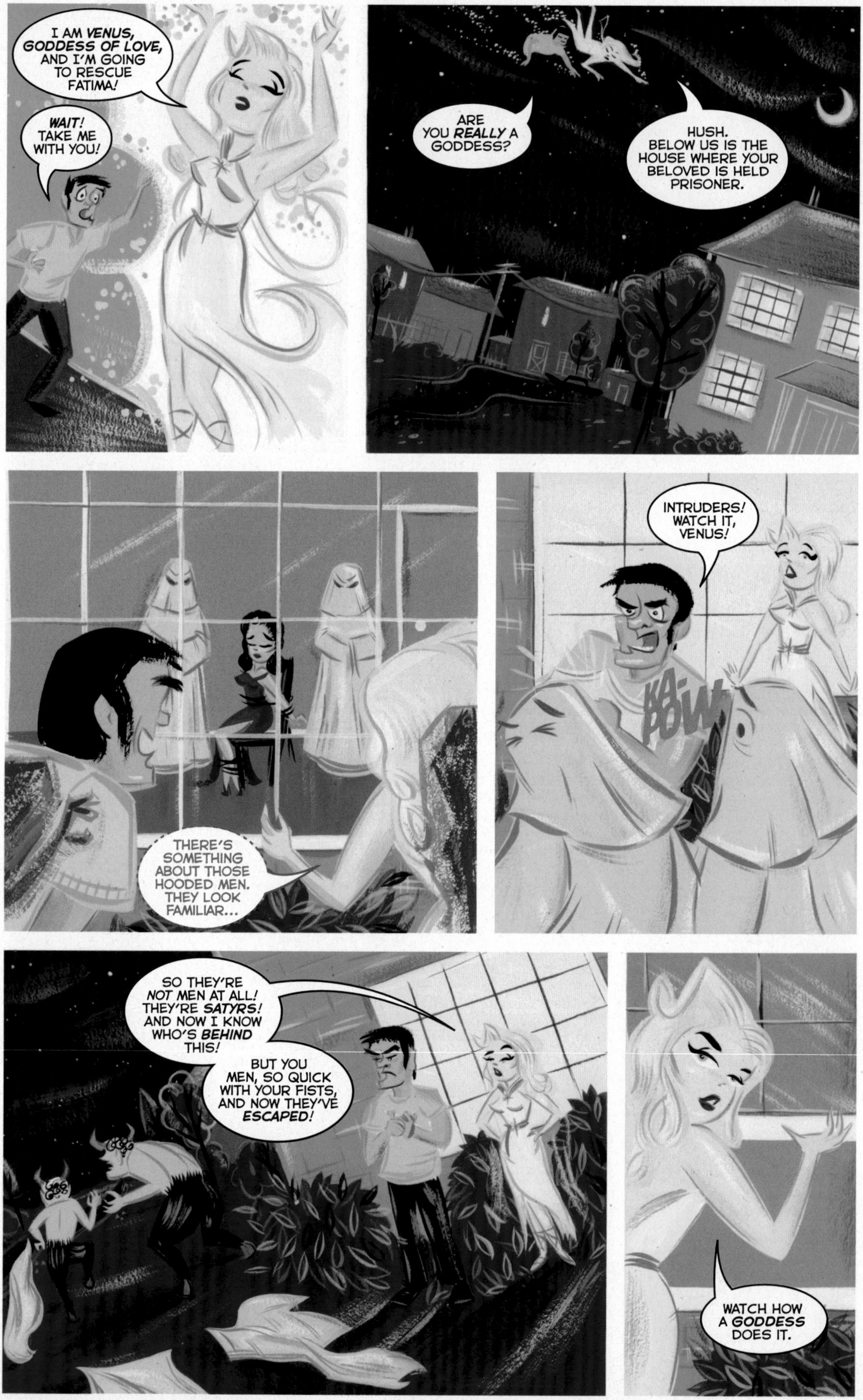

I AM VENUS, GODDESS OF LOVE, AND I'M GOING TO RESCUE FATIMA!
WAIT! TAKE ME WITH YOU!
ARE YOU REALLY A GODDESS?
HUSH. BELOW US IS THE HOUSE WHERE YOUR BELOVED IS HELD PRISONER.
THERE'S SOMETHING ABOUT THOSE HOODED MEN. THEY LOOK FAMILIAR...
INTRUDERS! WATCH IT, VENUS!
KA-POW
SO THEY'RE NOT MEN AT ALL! THEY'RE SATYRS! AND NOW I KNOW WHO'S BEHIND THIS!
BUT YOU MEN, SO QUICK WITH YOUR FISTS, AND NOW THEY'VE ESCAPED!
WATCH HOW A GODDESS DOES IT.

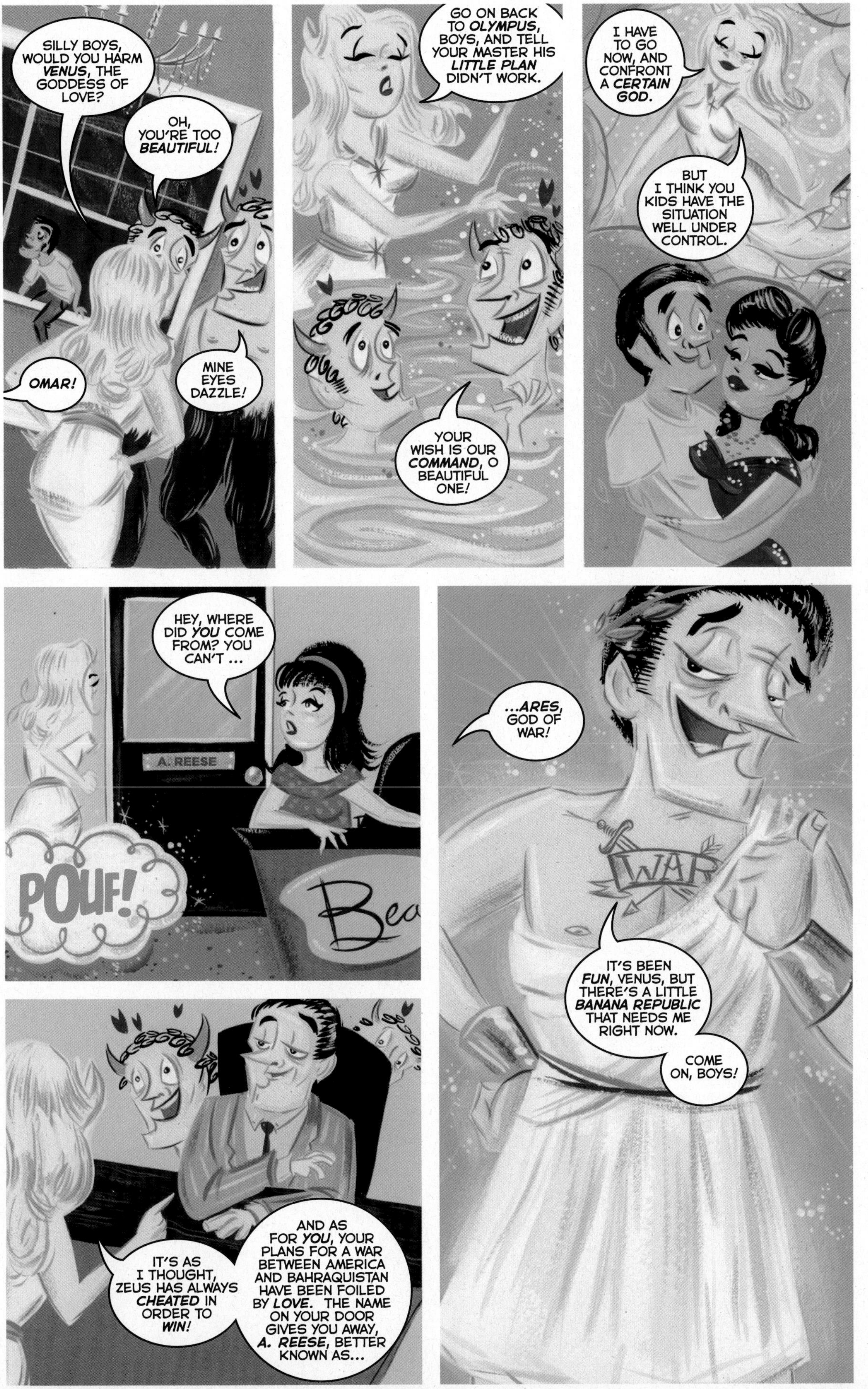
SILLY BOYS, WOULD YOU HARM VENUS, THE GODDESS OF LOVE?
OH, YOU'RE TOO BEAUTIFUL!
OMAR!
MINE EYES DAZZLE!
GO ON BACK TO OLYMPUS, BOYS, AND TELL YOUR MASTER HIS LITTLE PLAN DIDN'T WORK.
YOUR WISH IS OUR COMMAND, O BEAUTIFUL ONE!
I HAVE TO GO NOW, AND CONFRONT A CERTAIN GOD.
BUT I THINK YOU KIDS HAVE THE SITUATION WELL UNDER CONTROL.
HEY, WHERE DID YOU COME FROM? YOU CAN'T ...
A. REESE
POUF!
Bea
IT'S AS I THOUGHT, ZEUS HAS ALWAYS CHEATED IN ORDER TO WIN!
AND AS FOR YOU, YOUR PLANS FOR A WAR BETWEEN AMERICA AND BAHRAQUISTAN HAVE BEEN FOILED BY LOVE. THE NAME ON YOUR DOOR GIVES YOU AWAY, A. REESE, BETTER KNOWN AS...
...ARES, GOD OF WAR!
WAR
IT'S BEEN FUN, VENUS, BUT THERE'S A LITTLE BANANA REPUBLIC THAT NEEDS ME RIGHT NOW.
COME ON, BOYS!

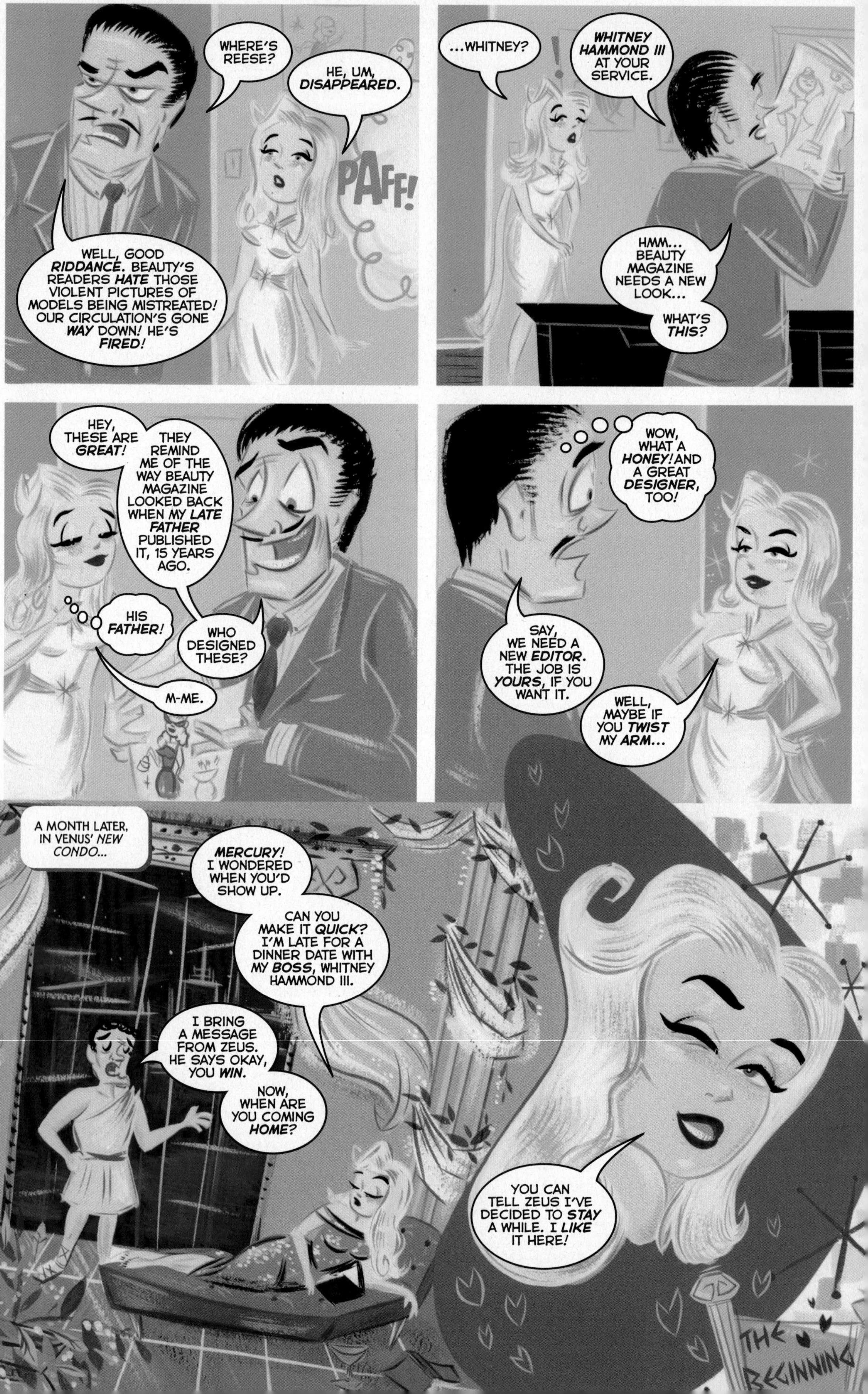
WHERE'S REESE?
HE, UM, DISAPPEARED.
PAFF!
WELL, GOOD RIDDANCE. BEAUTY'S READERS HATE THOSE VIOLENT PICTURES OF MODELS BEING MISTREATED! OUR CIRCULATION'S GONE WAY DOWN! HE'S FIRED!
...WHITNEY?
WHITNEY HAMMOND III AT YOUR SERVICE.
HMM... BEAUTY MAGAZINE NEEDS A NEW LOOK...
WHAT'S THIS?
HEY, THESE ARE GREAT!
THEY REMIND ME OF THE WAY BEAUTY MAGAZINE LOOKED BACK WHEN MY LATE FATHER PUBLISHED IT, 15 YEARS AGO.
HIS FATHER!
WHO DESIGNED THESE?
M-ME.
WOW, WHAT A HONEY! AND A GREAT DESIGNER, TOO!
SAY, WE NEED A NEW EDITOR. THE JOB IS YOURS, IF YOU WANT IT.
WELL, MAYBE IF YOU TWIST MY ARM...
A MONTH LATER, IN VENUS' NEW CONDO...
MERCURY! I WONDERED WHEN YOU'D SHOW UP.
CAN YOU MAKE IT QUICK? I'M LATE FOR A DINNER DATE WITH MY BOSS, WHITNEY HAMMOND III.
I BRING A MESSAGE FROM ZEUS. HE SAYS OKAY, YOU WIN.
NOW, WHEN ARE YOU COMING HOME?
YOU CAN TELL ZEUS I'VE DECIDED TO STAY A WHILE. I LIKE IT HERE!
THE BEGINNING

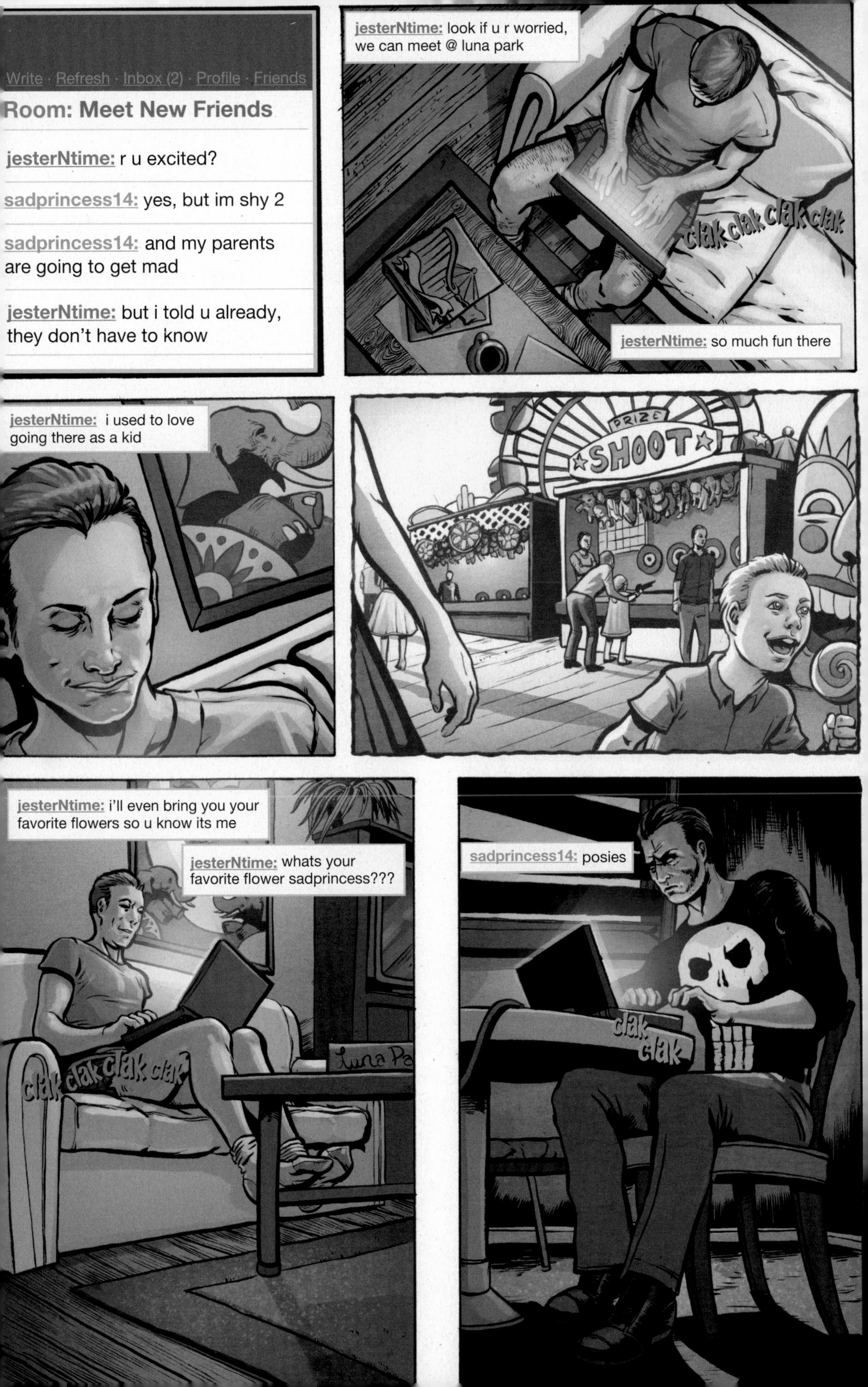
Write · Refresh · Inbox (2) · Profile · Friends
Room: Meet New Friends
jesterNtime: r u excited?
sadprincess14: yes, but im shy 2
sadprincess14: and my parents are going to get mad
jesterNtime: but i told u already, they don't have to know
jesterNtime: look if u r worried, we can meet @ luna park
clak clak clak clak
jesterNtime: so much fun there
jesterNtime: i used to love going there as a kid
PRIZE
SHOOT
jesterNtime: i'll even bring you your favorite flowers so u know its me
jesterNtime: whats your favorite flower sadprincess???
clak clak clak clak
Luna Pa
sadprincess14: posies
clak clak

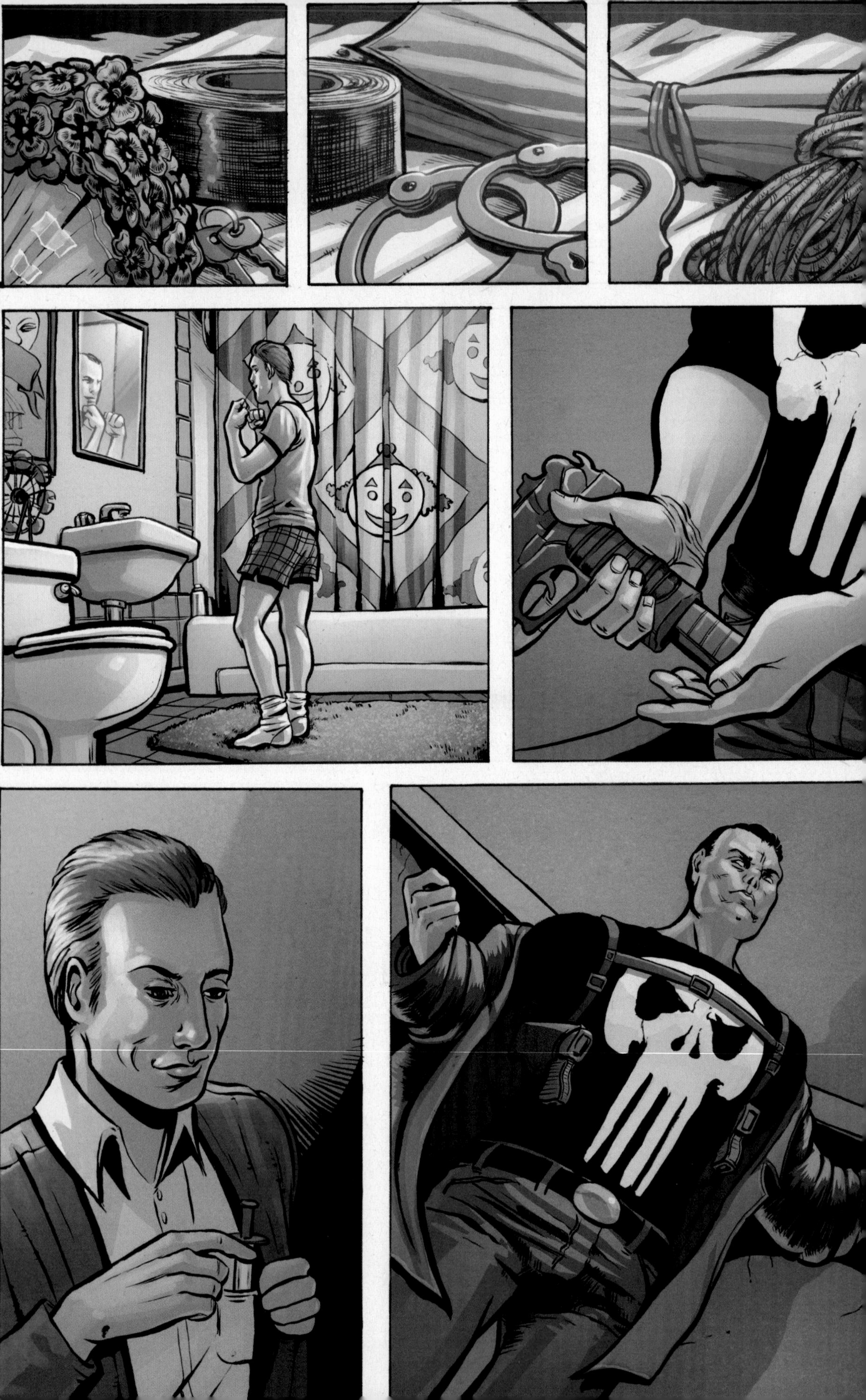

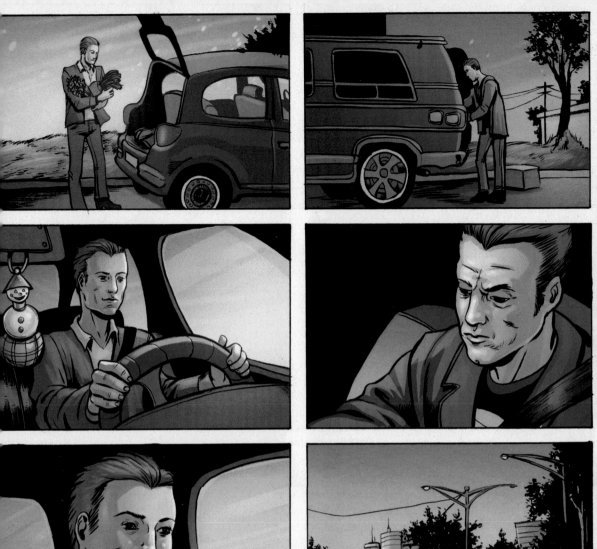

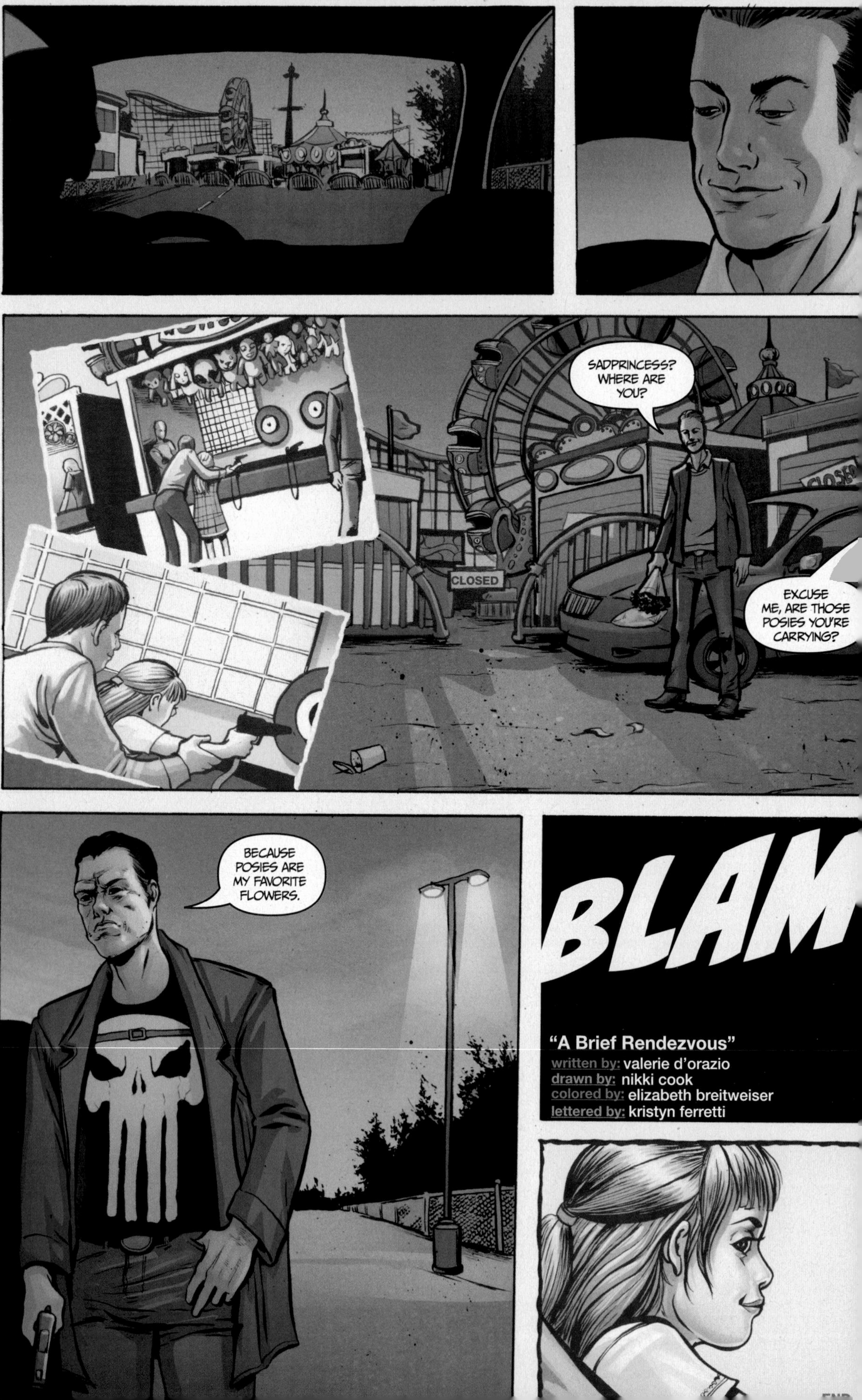

SADPRINCESS? WHERE ARE YOU?
CLOSED
CLOSED
EXCUSE ME, ARE THOSE POSIES YOU'RE CARRYING?
BECAUSE POSIES ARE MY FAVORITE FLOWERS.
BLAM
"A Brief Rendezvous"
written by: valerie d'orazio
drawn by: nikki cook
colored by: elizabeth breitweiser
lettered by: kristyn ferretti

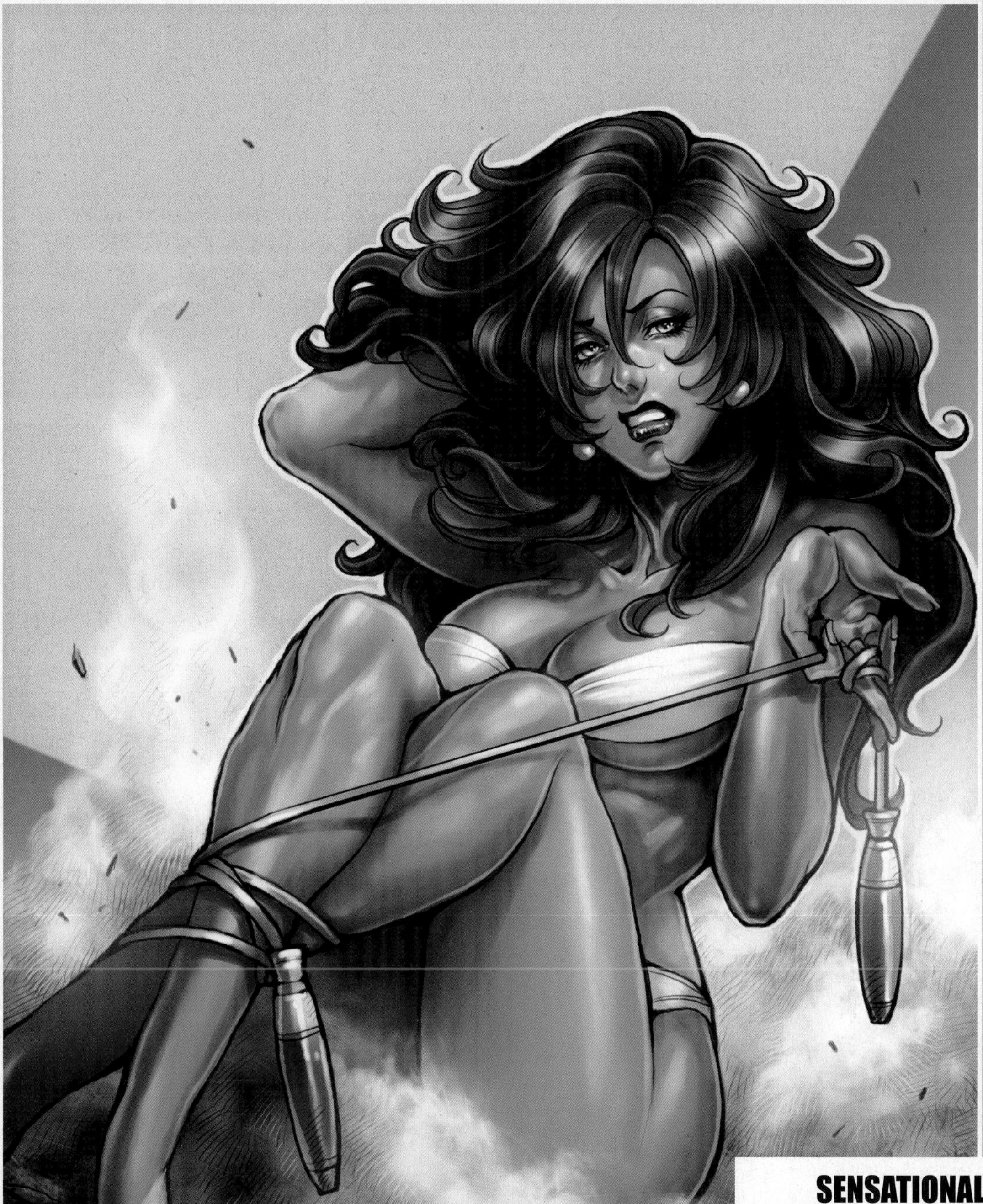

SENSATIONAL SHE-HULK#40 1992

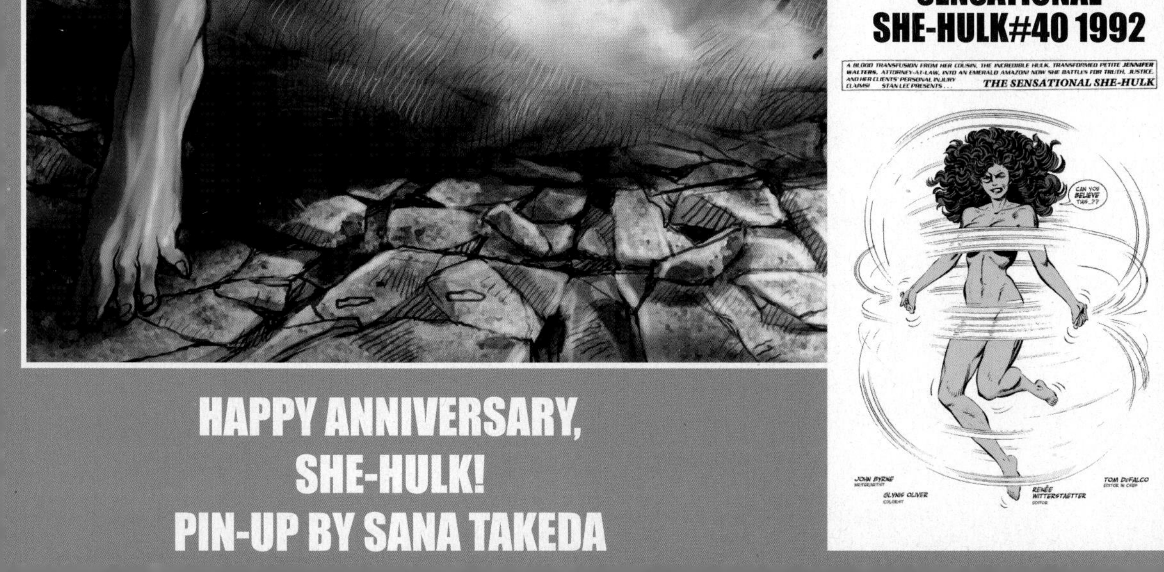
A BLOOD TRANSFUSION FROM HER COUSIN, THE INCREDIBLE HULK, TRANSFORMED PETITE JENNIFER WALTERS, ATTORNEY-AT-LAW, INTO AN EMERALD AMAZON! NOW SHE BATTLES FOR TRUTH, JUSTICE, AND HER CLIENTS' PERSONAL INJURY CLAIMS! STAN LEE PRESENTS . . .
THE SENSATIONAL SHE-HULK
CAN YOU BELIEVE THIS..??
JOHN BYRNE
GLYNIS OLIVER
RENÉE WITTERSTAETTER
TOM DeFALCO
EDITOR IN CHIEF

HAPPY ANNIVERSARY, SHE-HULK!

PIN-UP BY SANA TAKEDA

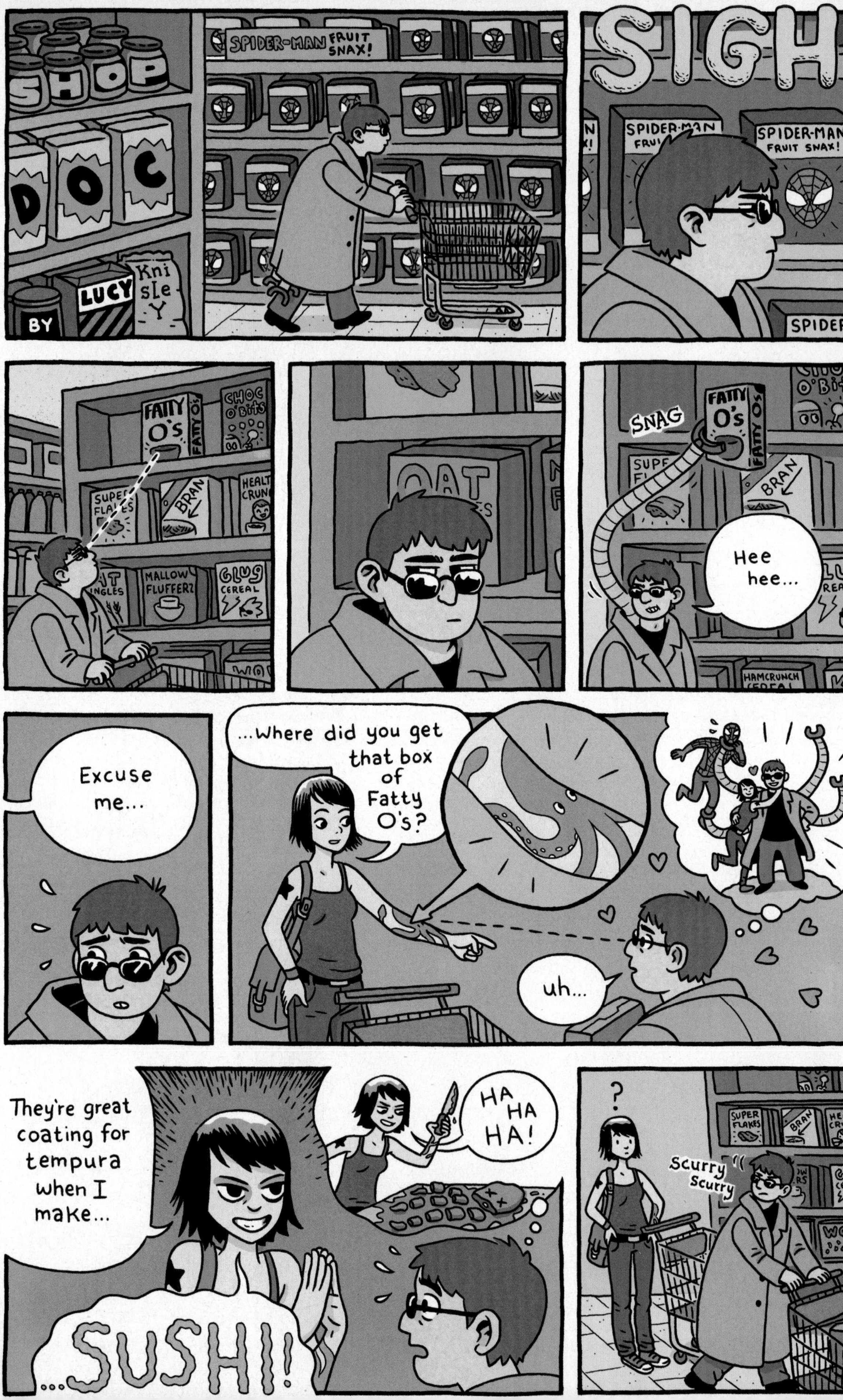
SHOP
DOC
BY
LUCY
Knisley
SPIDER-MAN FRUIT SNAX!
SIGH
SPIDER-MAN FRUIT SNAX!
SPIDER
FATTY O's
CHOC O'BITS
SUPER FLAKES
BRAN
MALLOW FLUFFERZ
GLUG CEREAL
OAT
SNAG
Hee hee...
HAMCRUNCH CEREAL
Excuse me...
...Where did you get that box of Fatty O's?
uh...
They're great coating for tempura when I make...
...SUSHI!
HA HA HA!
?
Scurry Scurry

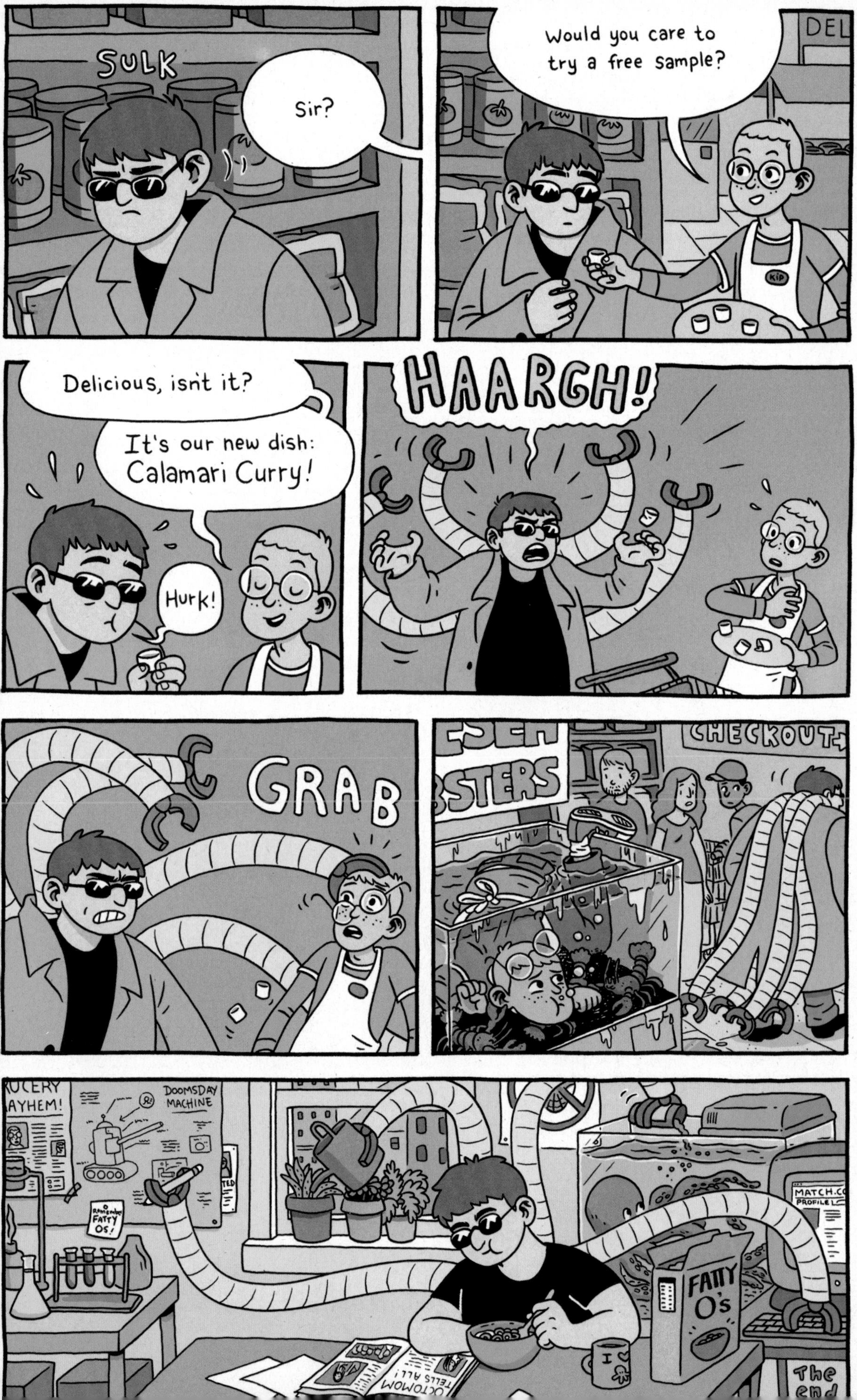

SULK
Sir?
Would you care to try a free sample?
KIP
Delicious, isn't it?
It's our new dish: Calamari Curry!
Hurk!
HAARGH!
GRAB
CHECKOUT
DOOMSDAY MACHINE
Remember FATTY Os!
FATTY O's
I ♡
The end

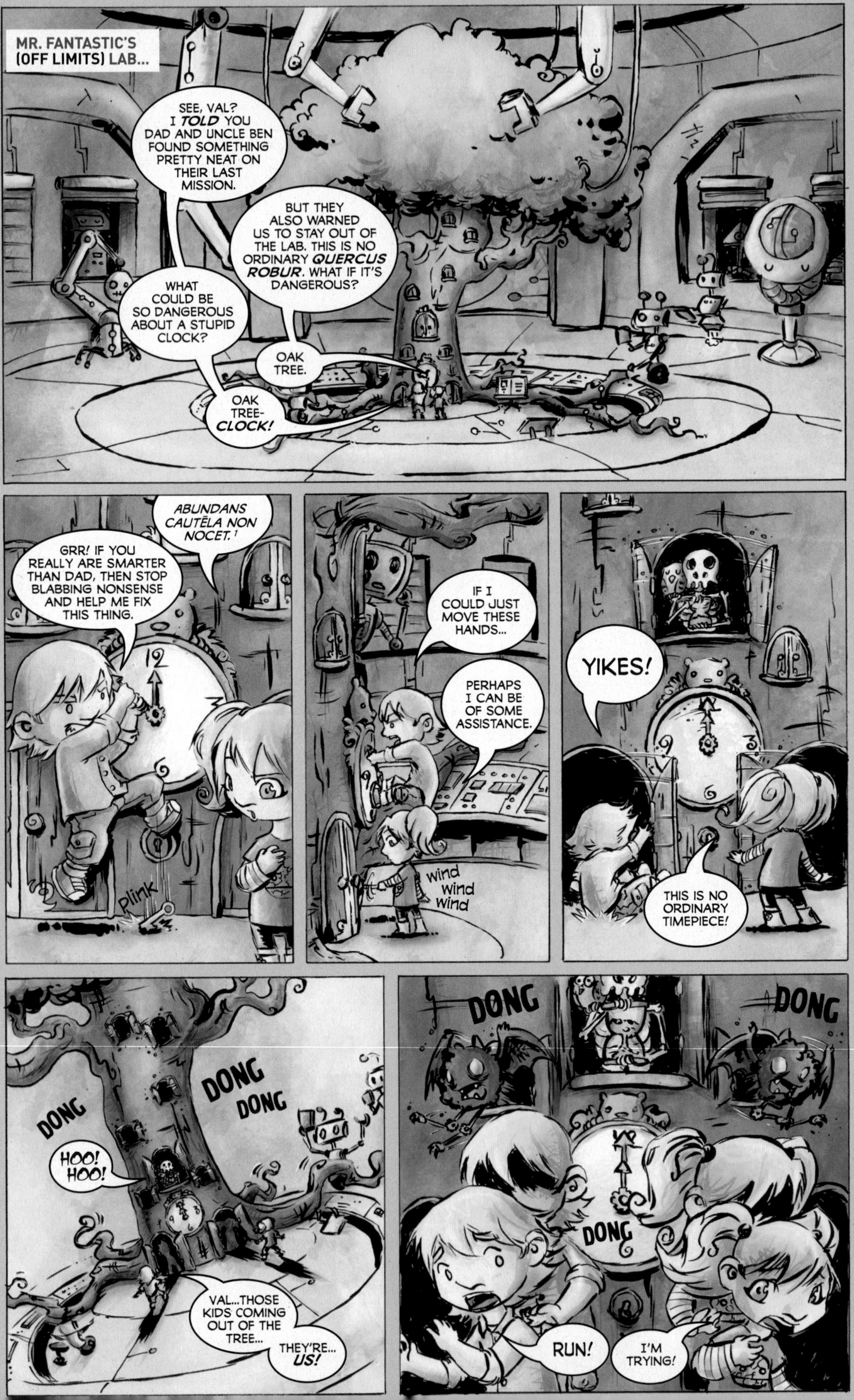
MR. FANTASTIC'S (OFF LIMITS) LAB...
SEE, VAL? I *TOLD* YOU DAD AND UNCLE BEN FOUND SOMETHING PRETTY NEAT ON THEIR LAST MISSION.
BUT THEY ALSO WARNED US TO STAY OUT OF THE LAB. THIS IS NO ORDINARY *QUERCUS ROBUR*. WHAT IF IT'S DANGEROUS?
WHAT COULD BE SO DANGEROUS ABOUT A STUPID CLOCK?
OAK TREE.
OAK TREE-*CLOCK!*
ABUNDANS CAUTĒLA NON NOCET.[1]
GRR! IF YOU REALLY ARE SMARTER THAN DAD, THEN STOP BLABBING NONSENSE AND HELP ME FIX THIS THING.
plink
IF I COULD JUST MOVE THESE HANDS...
PERHAPS I CAN BE OF SOME ASSISTANCE.
wind wind wind
YIKES!
THIS IS NO ORDINARY TIMEPIECE!
DONG
DONG
DONG
HOO! HOO!
VAL...THOSE KIDS COMING OUT OF THE TREE...
THEY'RE... *US!*
DONG
DONG
DONG
RUN!
I'M TRYING!

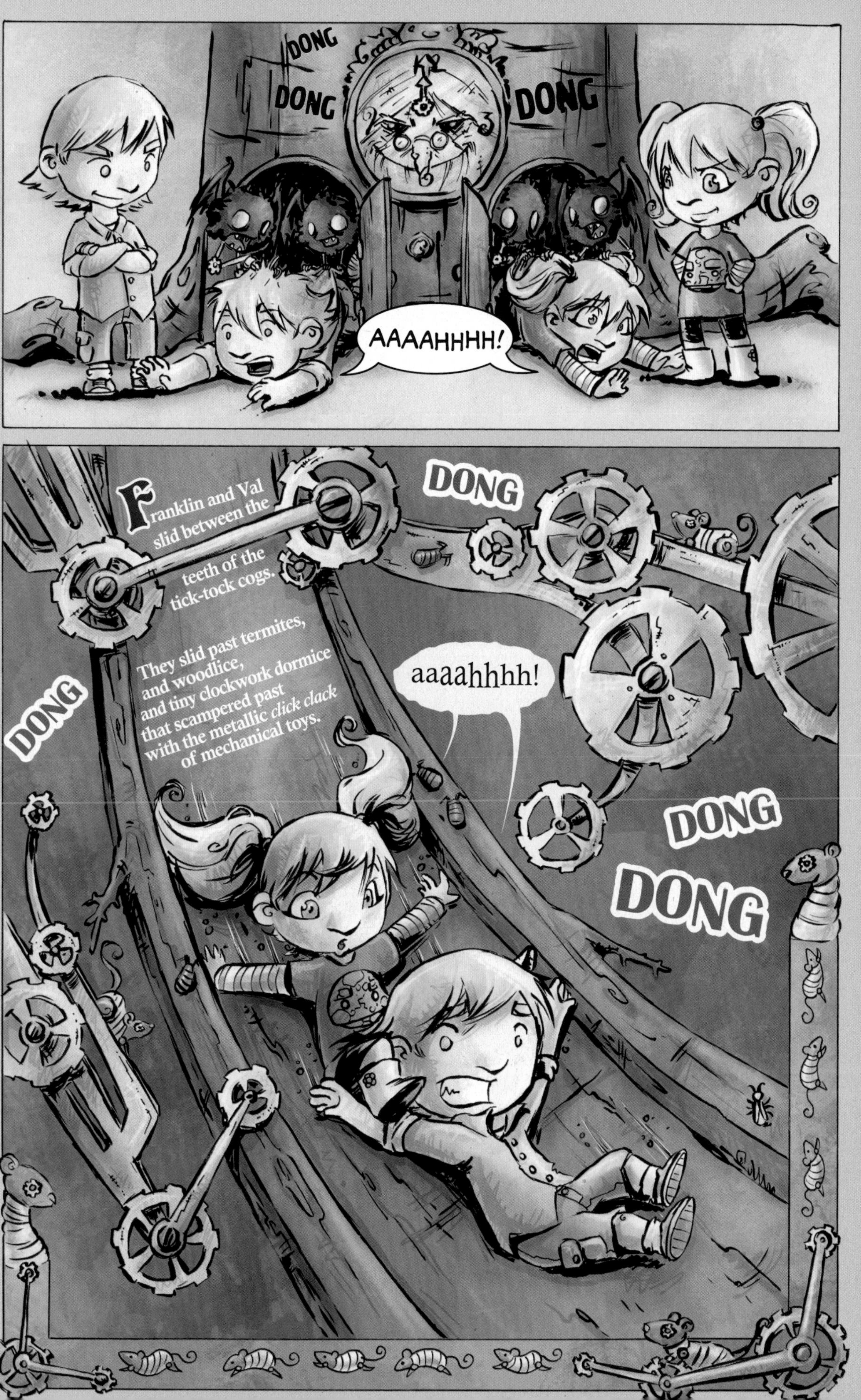
DONG
DONG
DONG
AAAAHHHH!
Franklin and Val slid between the teeth of the tick-tock cogs.
They slid past termites, and woodlice, and tiny clockwork dormice that scampered past with the metallic *click clack* of mechanical toys.
DONG
DONG
aaaahhhh!
DONG
DONG

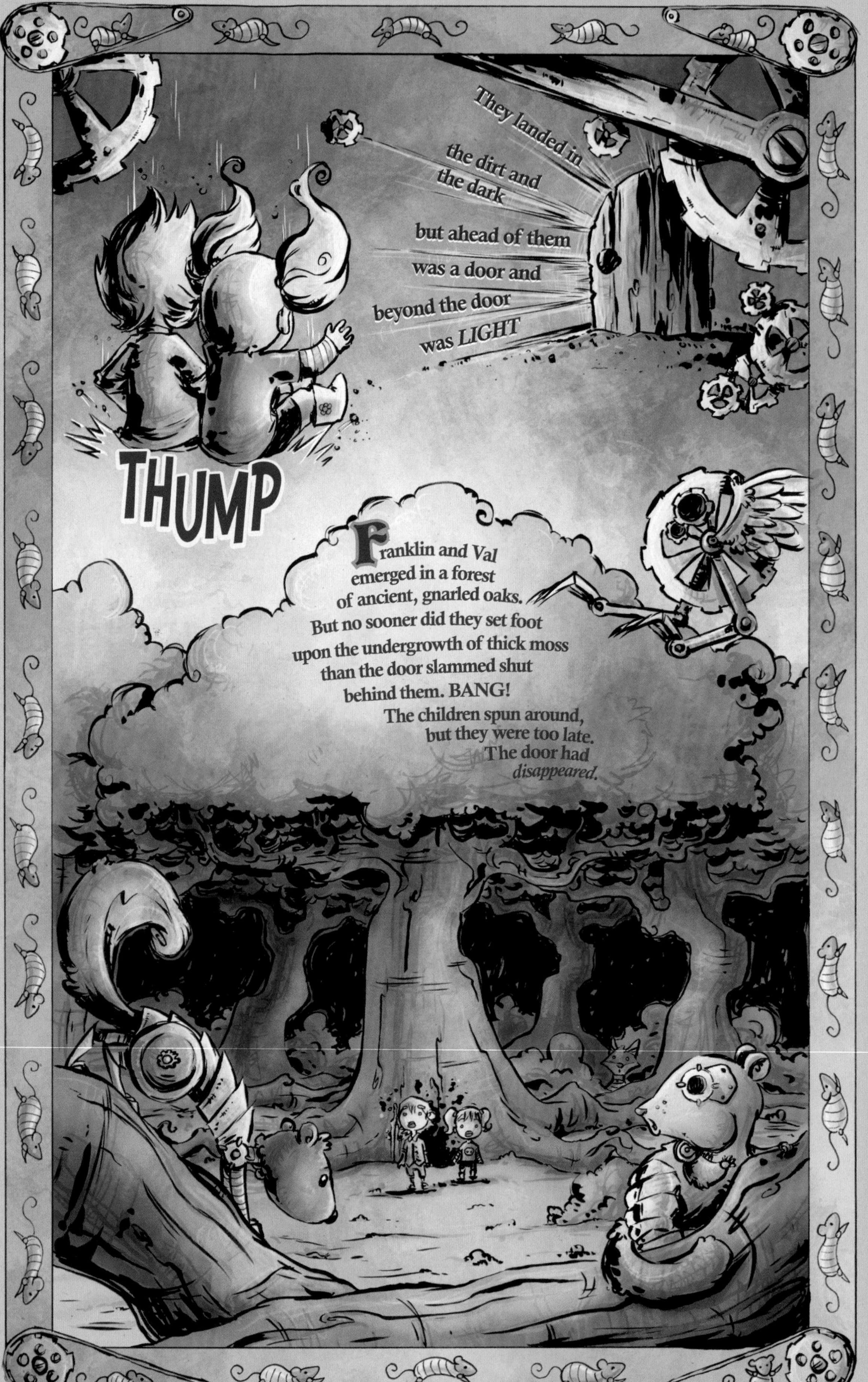

They landed in
the dirt and
the dark
but ahead of them
was a door and
beyond the door
was *LIGHT*
THUMP
Franklin and Val emerged in a forest of ancient, gnarled oaks. But no sooner did they set foot upon the undergrowth of thick moss than the door slammed shut behind them. BANG! The children spun around, but they were too late. The door had *disappeared.*

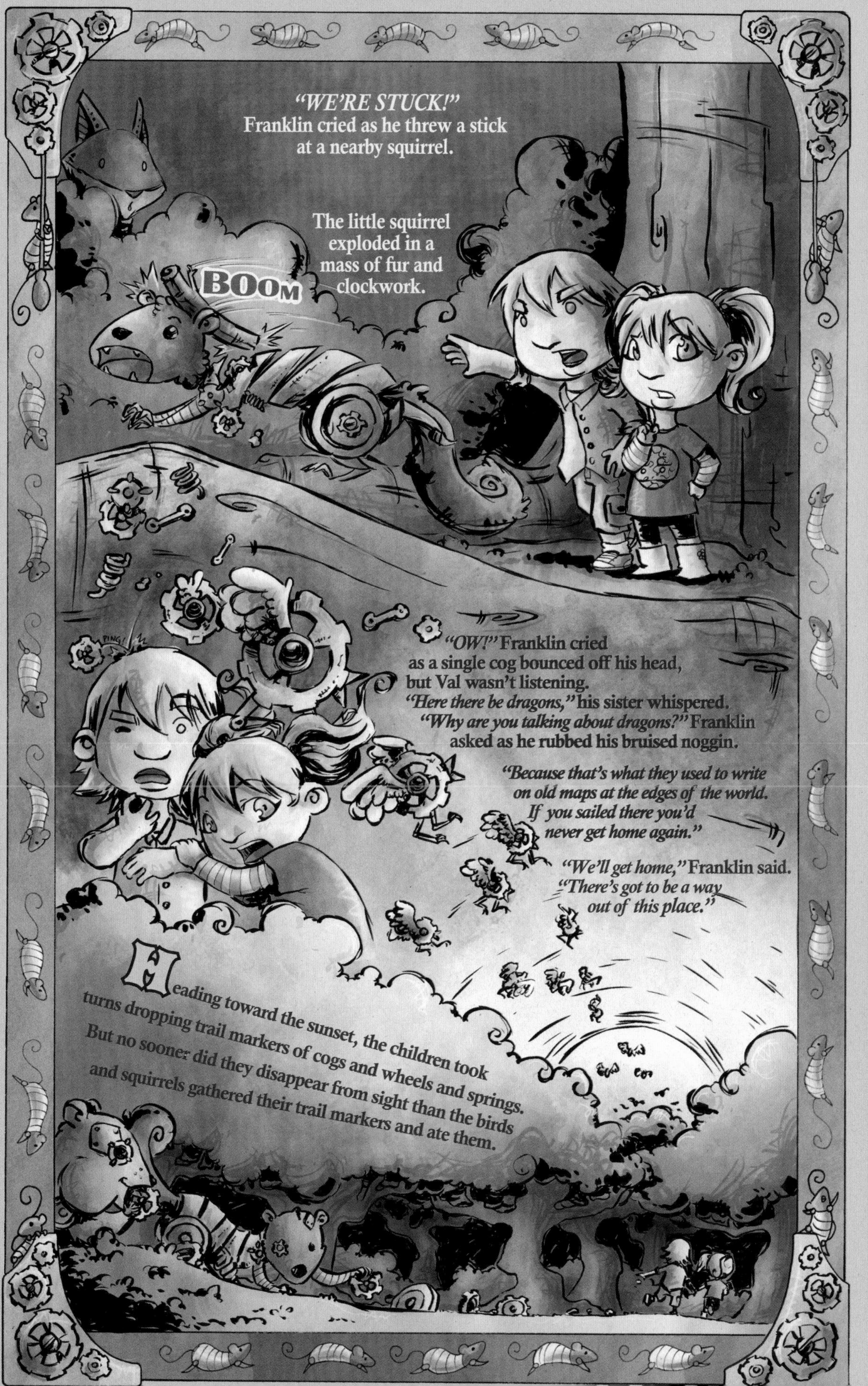
"WE'RE STUCK!"
Franklin cried as he threw a stick at a nearby squirrel.
BOOM
The little squirrel exploded in a mass of fur and clockwork.
"OW!" Franklin cried as a single cog bounced off his head, but Val wasn't listening.
"Here there be dragons," his sister whispered.
"Why are you talking about dragons?" Franklin asked as he rubbed his bruised noggin.
"Because that's what they used to write on old maps at the edges of the world. If you sailed there you'd never get home again."
"We'll get home," Franklin said. "There's got to be a way out of this place."
Heading toward the sunset, the children took turns dropping trail markers of cogs and wheels and springs. But no sooner did they disappear from sight than the birds and squirrels gathered their trail markers and ate them.

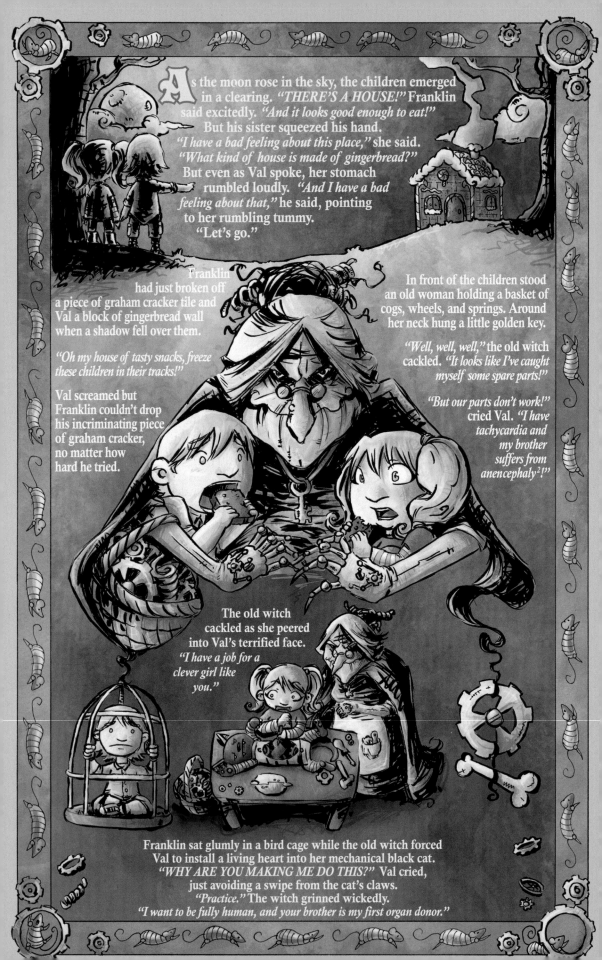

As the moon rose in the sky, the children emerged in a clearing. *"THERE'S A HOUSE!"* Franklin said excitedly. *"And it looks good enough to eat!"* But his sister squeezed his hand. *"I have a bad feeling about this place,"* she said. *"What kind of house is made of gingerbread?"* But even as Val spoke, her stomach rumbled loudly. *"And I have a bad feeling about that,"* he said, pointing to her rumbling tummy. *"Let's go."*

Franklin had just broken off a piece of graham cracker tile and Val a block of gingerbread wall when a shadow fell over them.

"Oh my house of tasty snacks, freeze these children in their tracks!"

Val screamed but Franklin couldn't drop his incriminating piece of graham cracker, no matter how hard he tried.

In front of the children stood an old woman holding a basket of cogs, wheels, and springs. Around her neck hung a little golden key.

"Well, well, well," the old witch cackled. *"It looks like I've caught myself some spare parts!"*

"But our parts don't work!" cried Val. *"I have tachycardia and my brother suffers from anencephaly[2]!"*

The old witch cackled as she peered into Val's terrified face. *"I have a job for a clever girl like you."*

Franklin sat glumly in a bird cage while the old witch forced Val to install a living heart into her mechanical black cat. *"WHY ARE YOU MAKING ME DO THIS?"* Val cried, just avoiding a swipe from the cat's claws. *"Practice."* The witch grinned wickedly. *"I want to be fully human, and your brother is my first organ donor."*

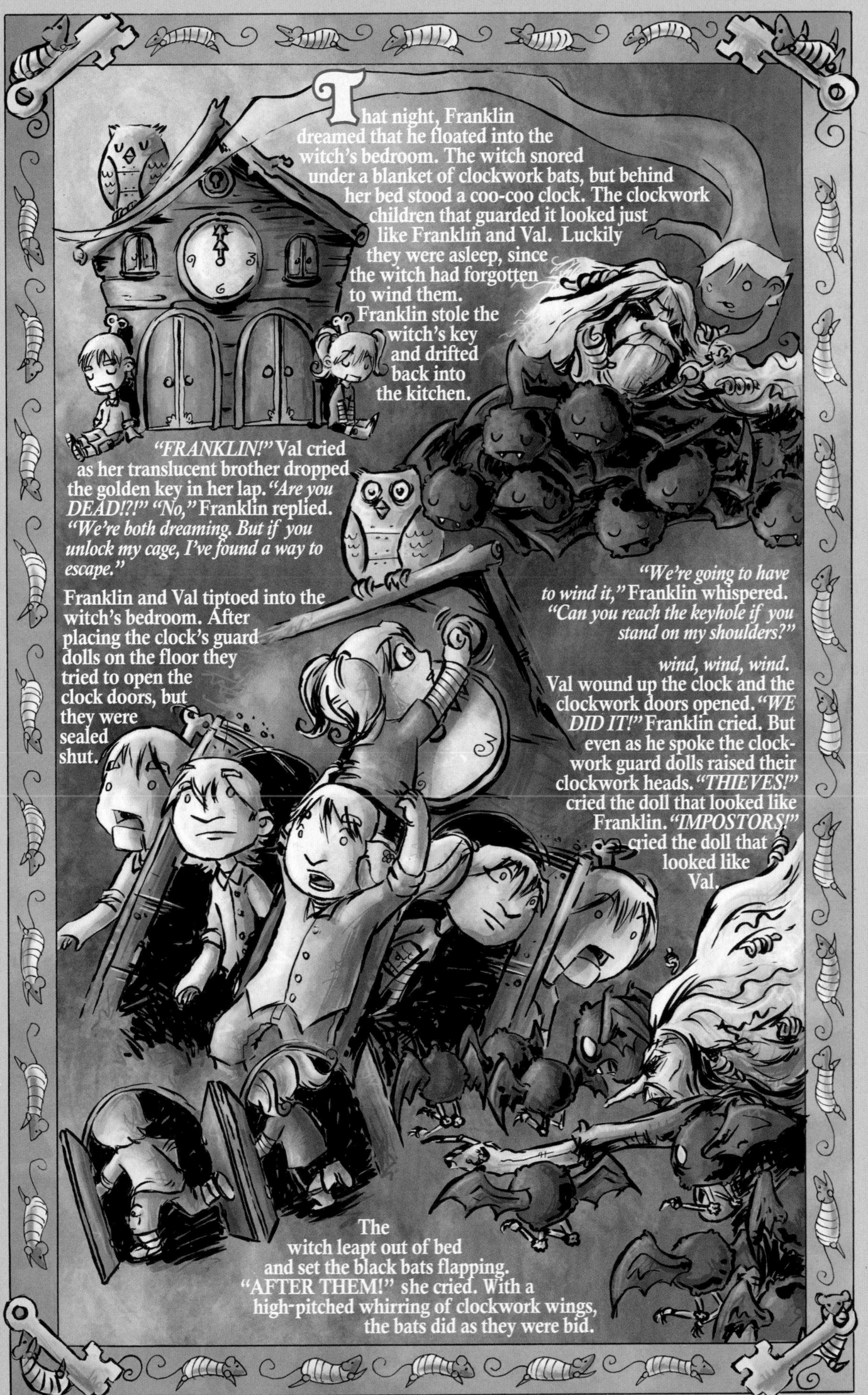
That night, Franklin dreamed that he floated into the witch's bedroom. The witch snored under a blanket of clockwork bats, but behind her bed stood a coo-coo clock. The clockwork children that guarded it looked just like Franklin and Val. Luckily they were asleep, since the witch had forgotten to wind them. Franklin stole the witch's key and drifted back into the kitchen.
"FRANKLIN!" Val cried as her translucent brother dropped the golden key in her lap. *"Are you DEAD!?!"* *"No,"* Franklin replied. *"We're both dreaming. But if you unlock my cage, I've found a way to escape."*
Franklin and Val tiptoed into the witch's bedroom. After placing the clock's guard dolls on the floor they tried to open the clock doors, but they were sealed shut.
"We're going to have to wind it," Franklin whispered. *"Can you reach the keyhole if you stand on my shoulders?"*
wind, wind, wind.
Val wound up the clock and the clockwork doors opened. *"WE DID IT!"* Franklin cried. But even as he spoke the clockwork guard dolls raised their clockwork heads. *"THIEVES!"* cried the doll that looked like Franklin. *"IMPOSTORS!"* cried the doll that looked like Val.
The witch leapt out of bed and set the black bats flapping. "AFTER THEM!" she cried. With a high-pitched whirring of clockwork wings, the bats did as they were bid.

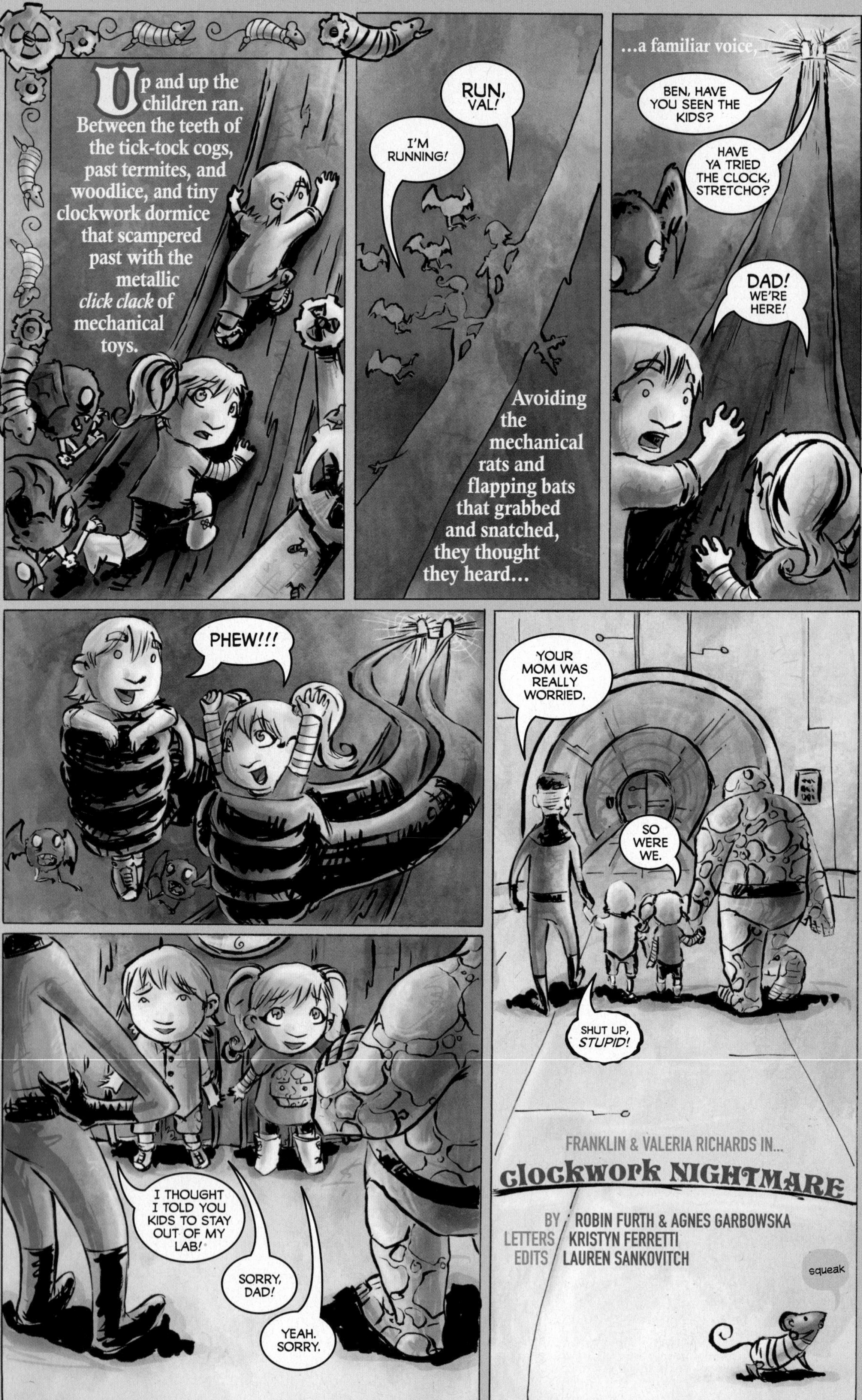
Up and up the children ran. Between the teeth of the tick-tock cogs, past termites, and woodlice, and tiny clockwork dormice that scampered past with the metallic *click clack* of mechanical toys.
RUN, VAL!
I'M RUNNING!
Avoiding the mechanical rats and flapping bats that grabbed and snatched, they thought they heard…
…a familiar voice,
BEN, HAVE YOU SEEN THE KIDS?
HAVE YA TRIED THE CLOCK, STRETCHO?
DAD! WE'RE HERE!
PHEW!!!
YOUR MOM WAS REALLY WORRIED.
SO WERE WE.
SHUT UP, *STUPID!*
I THOUGHT I TOLD YOU KIDS TO STAY OUT OF MY LAB!
SORRY, DAD!
YEAH. SORRY.
FRANKLIN & VALERIA RICHARDS IN…
CLOCKWORK NIGHTMARE
BY / ROBIN FURTH & AGNES GARBOWSKA
LETTERS / KRISTYN FERRETTI
EDITS / LAUREN SANKOVITCH
squeak

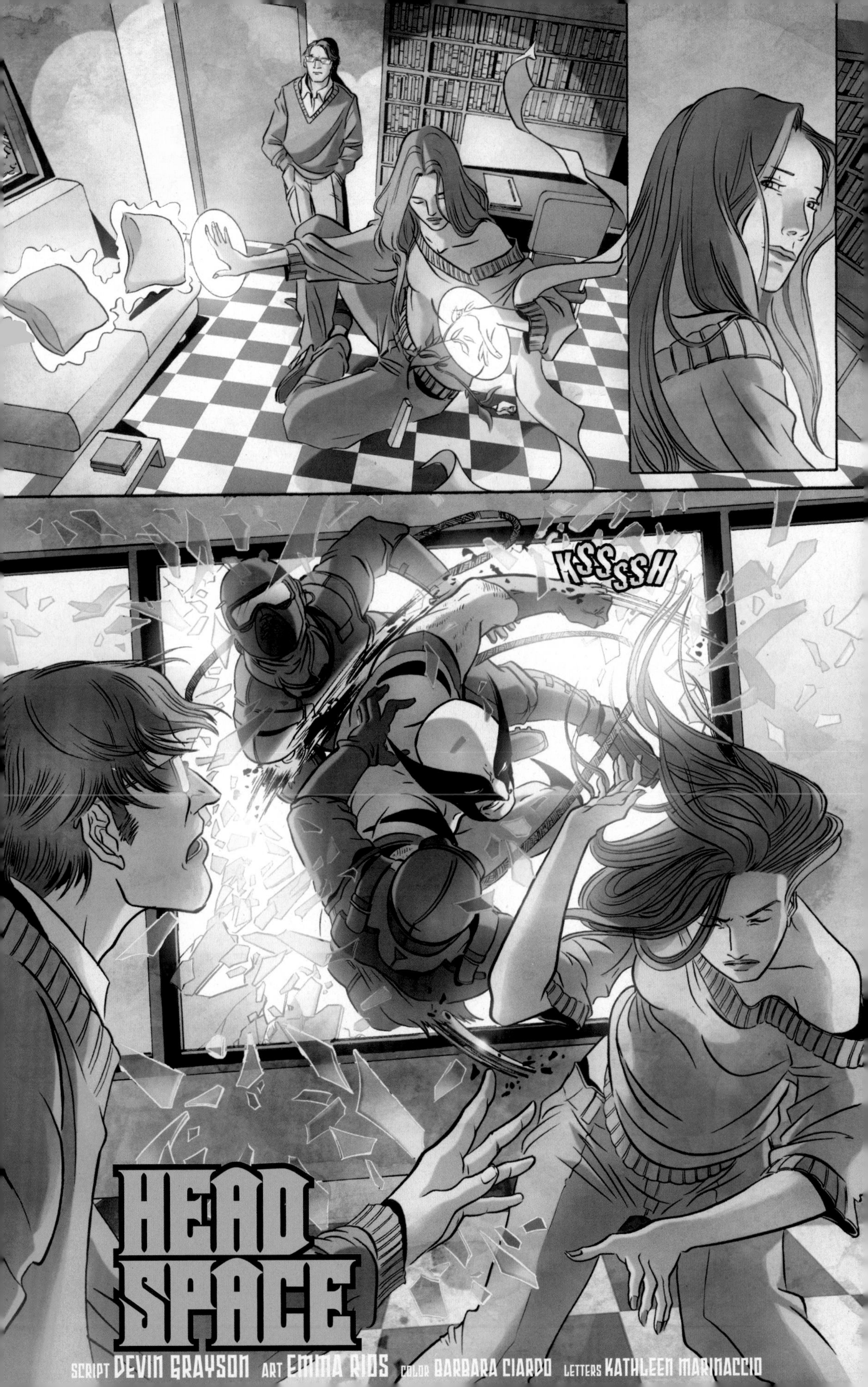
KSSSSH
HEAD SPACE
SCRIPT DEVIN GRAYSON ART EMMA RIOS COLOR BARBARA CIARDO LETTERS KATHLEEN MARINACCIO

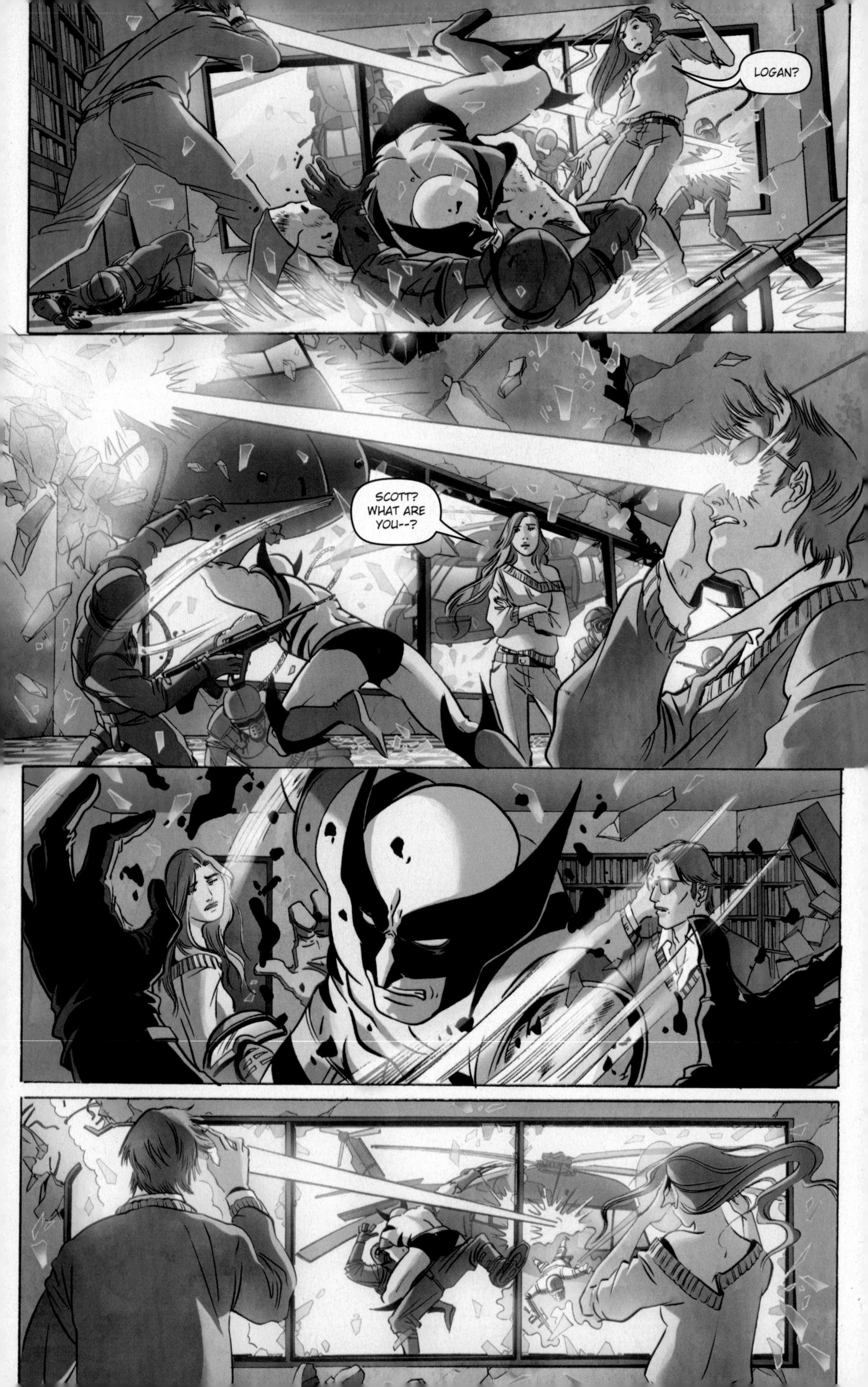
LOGAN?
SCOTT? WHAT ARE YOU--?

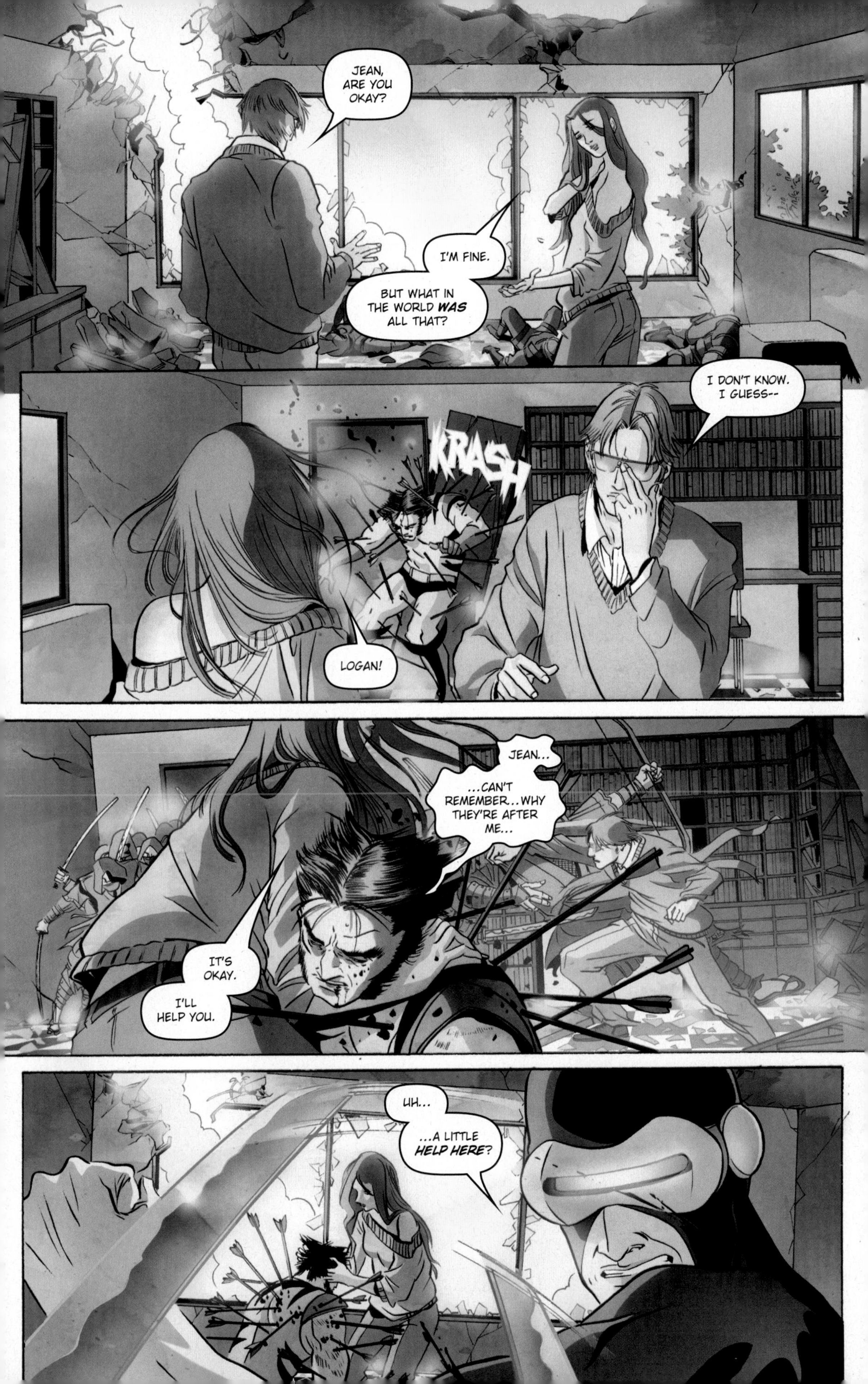
JEAN, ARE YOU OKAY?
I'M FINE.
BUT WHAT IN THE WORLD *WAS* ALL THAT?
I DON'T KNOW. I GUESS--
KRASH
LOGAN!
JEAN...
...CAN'T REMEMBER...WHY THEY'RE AFTER ME...
IT'S OKAY.
I'LL HELP YOU.
UH...
...A LITTLE *HELP HERE*?

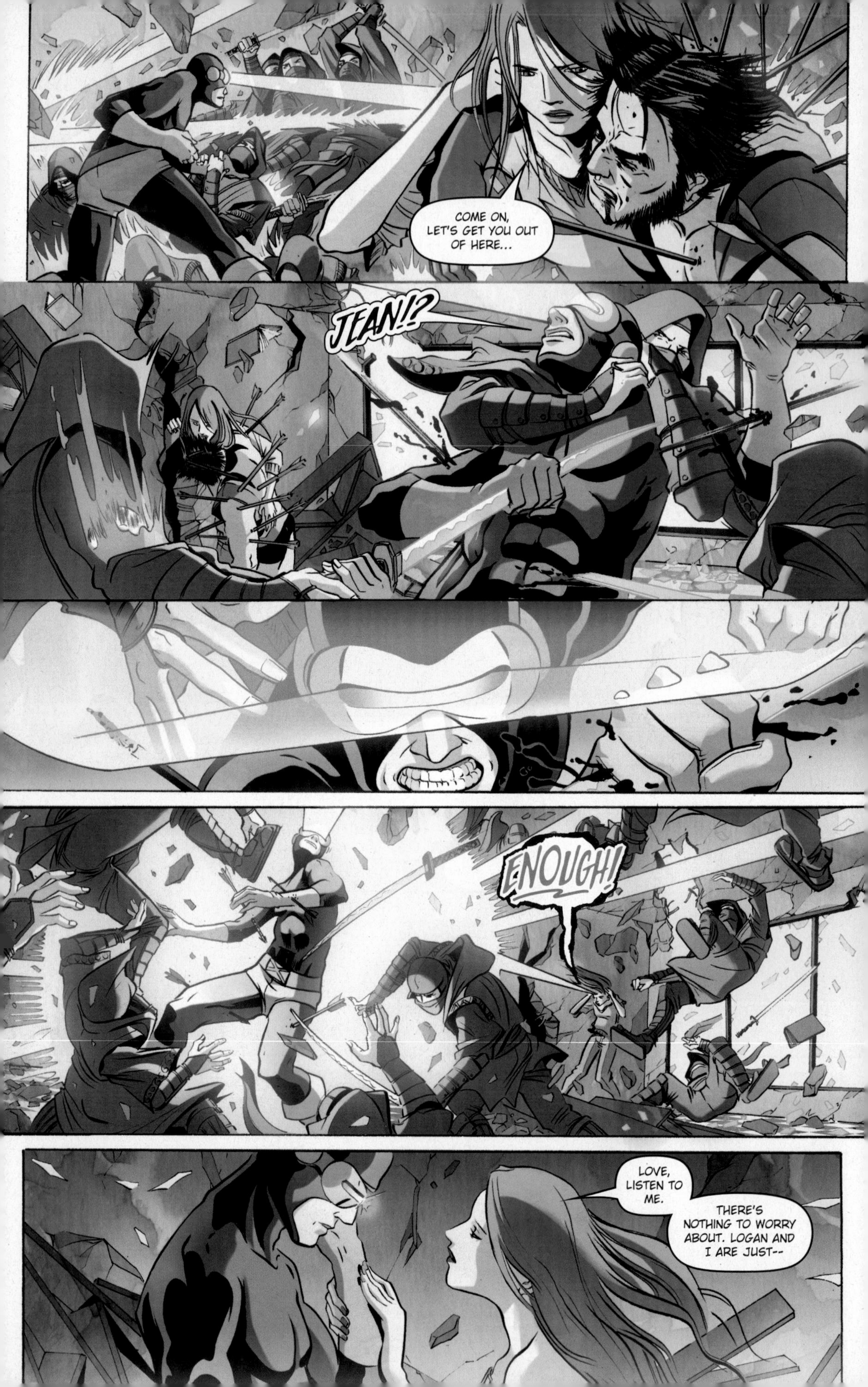
COME ON, LET'S GET YOU OUT OF HERE...
JEAN!?
ENOUGH!
LOVE, LISTEN TO ME.
THERE'S NOTHING TO WORRY ABOUT. LOGAN AND I ARE JUST--

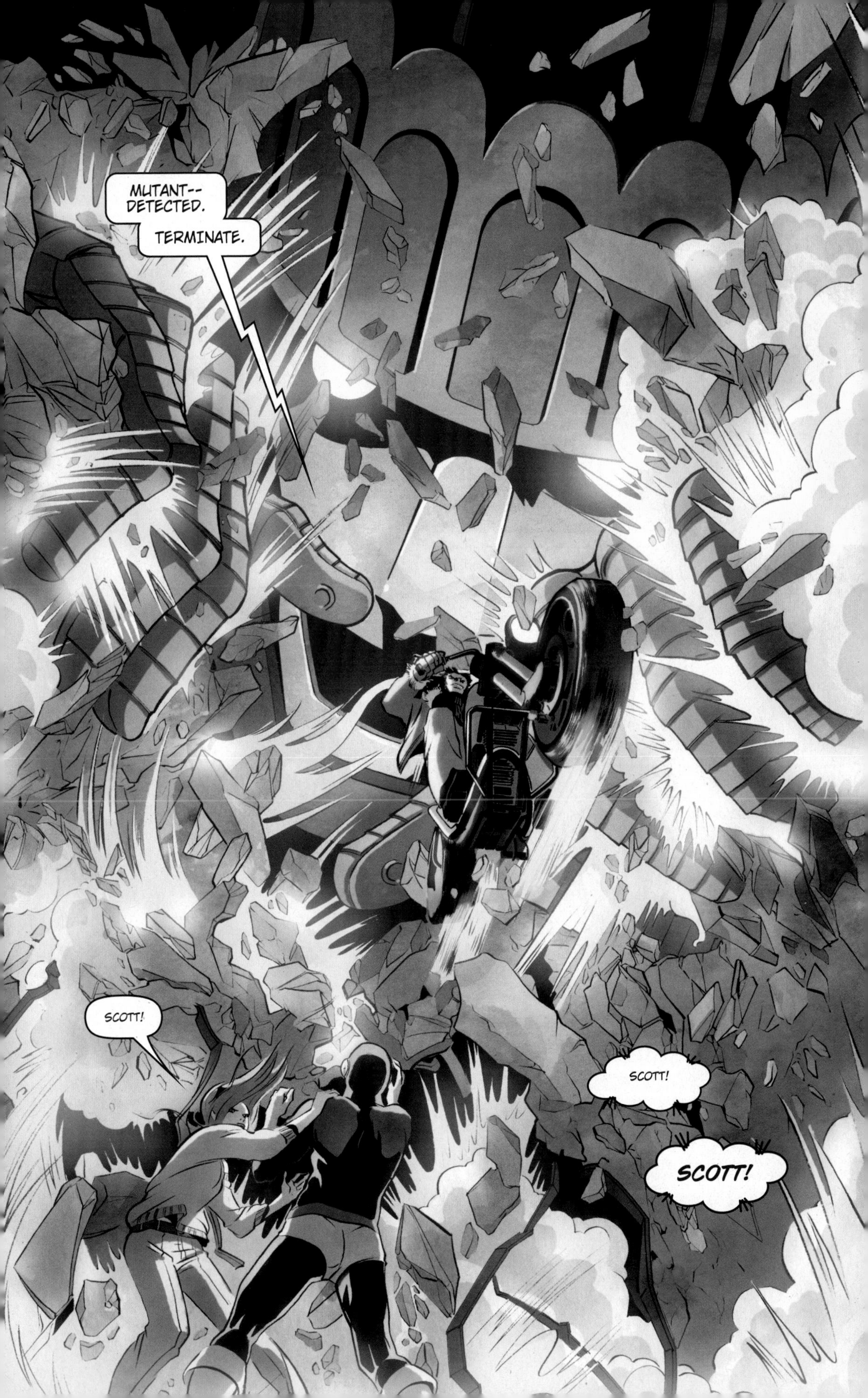
MUTANT--
DETECTED.
TERMINATE.
SCOTT!
SCOTT!
SCOTT!

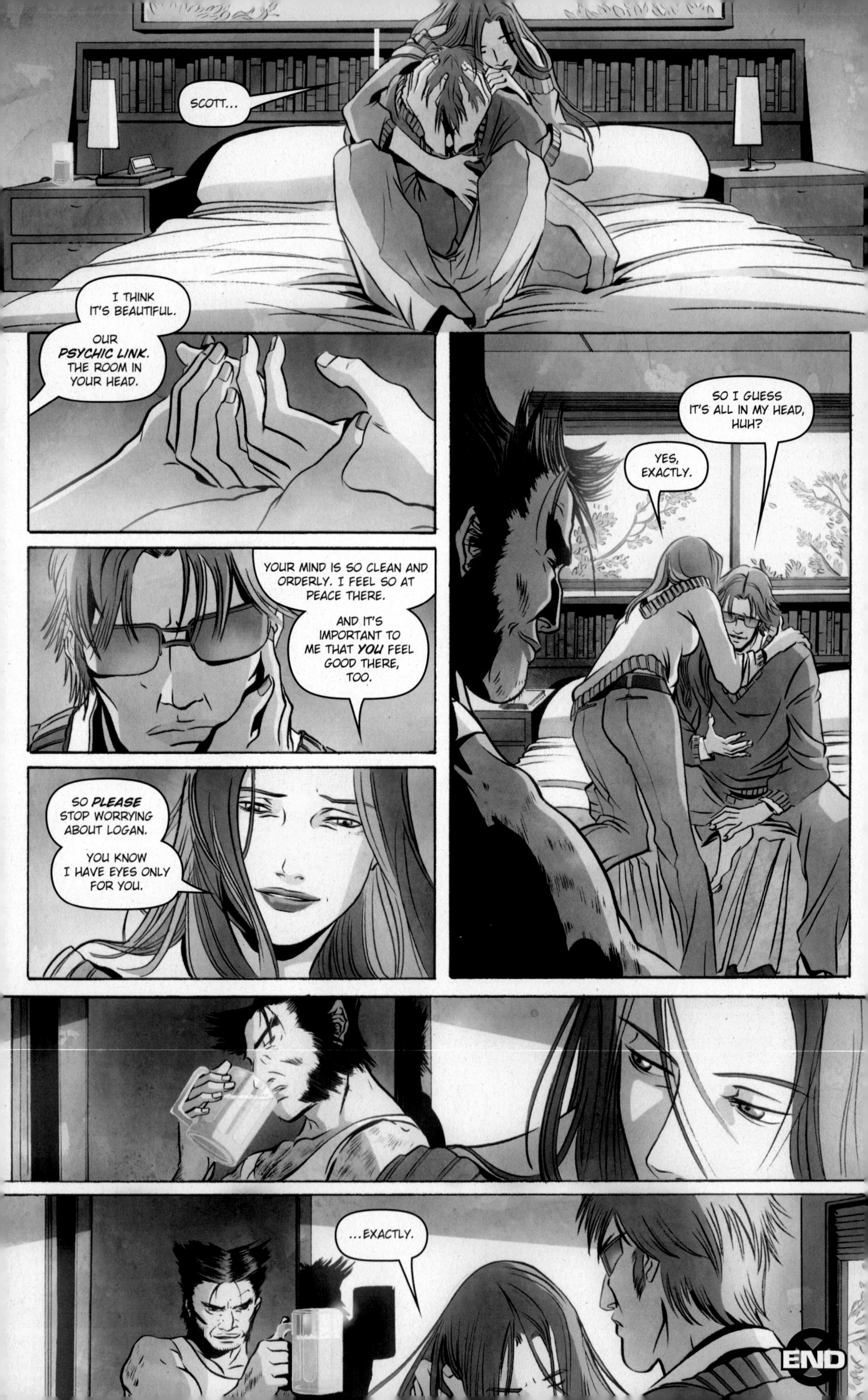
SCOTT...
I THINK IT'S BEAUTIFUL.
OUR PSYCHIC LINK. THE ROOM IN YOUR HEAD.
YOUR MIND IS SO CLEAN AND ORDERLY. I FEEL SO AT PEACE THERE.
AND IT'S IMPORTANT TO ME THAT YOU FEEL GOOD THERE, TOO.
SO PLEASE STOP WORRYING ABOUT LOGAN.
YOU KNOW I HAVE EYES ONLY FOR YOU.
SO I GUESS IT'S ALL IN MY HEAD, HUH?
YES, EXACTLY.
...EXACTLY.
END

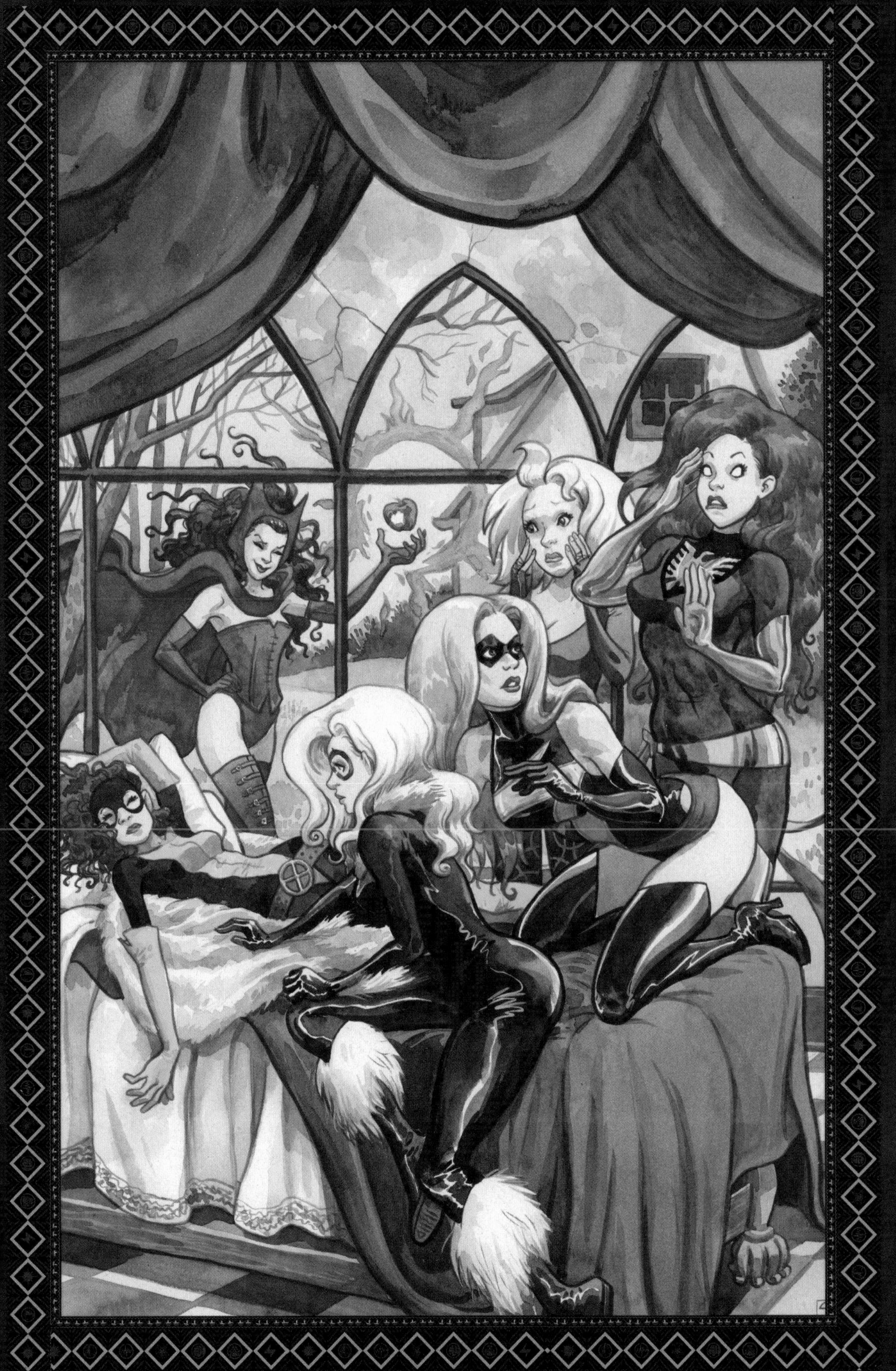

GIRL COMICS #2

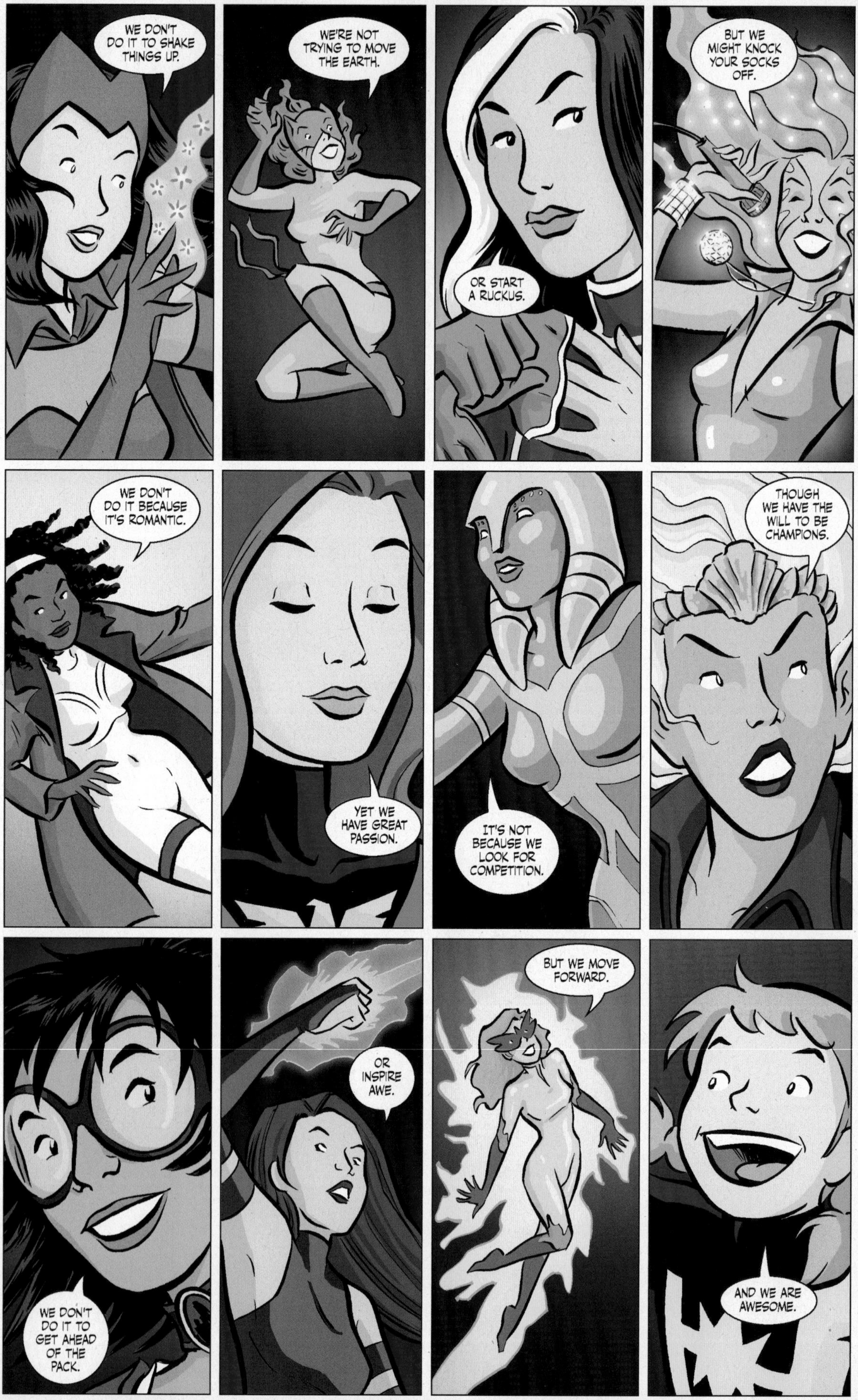
WE DON'T DO IT TO SHAKE THINGS UP.
WE'RE NOT TRYING TO MOVE THE EARTH.
OR START A RUCKUS.
BUT WE MIGHT KNOCK YOUR SOCKS OFF.
WE DON'T DO IT BECAUSE IT'S ROMANTIC.
YET WE HAVE GREAT PASSION.
IT'S NOT BECAUSE WE LOOK FOR COMPETITION.
THOUGH WE HAVE THE WILL TO BE CHAMPIONS.
WE DON'T DO IT TO GET AHEAD OF THE PACK.
OR INSPIRE AWE.
BUT WE MOVE FORWARD.
AND WE ARE AWESOME.

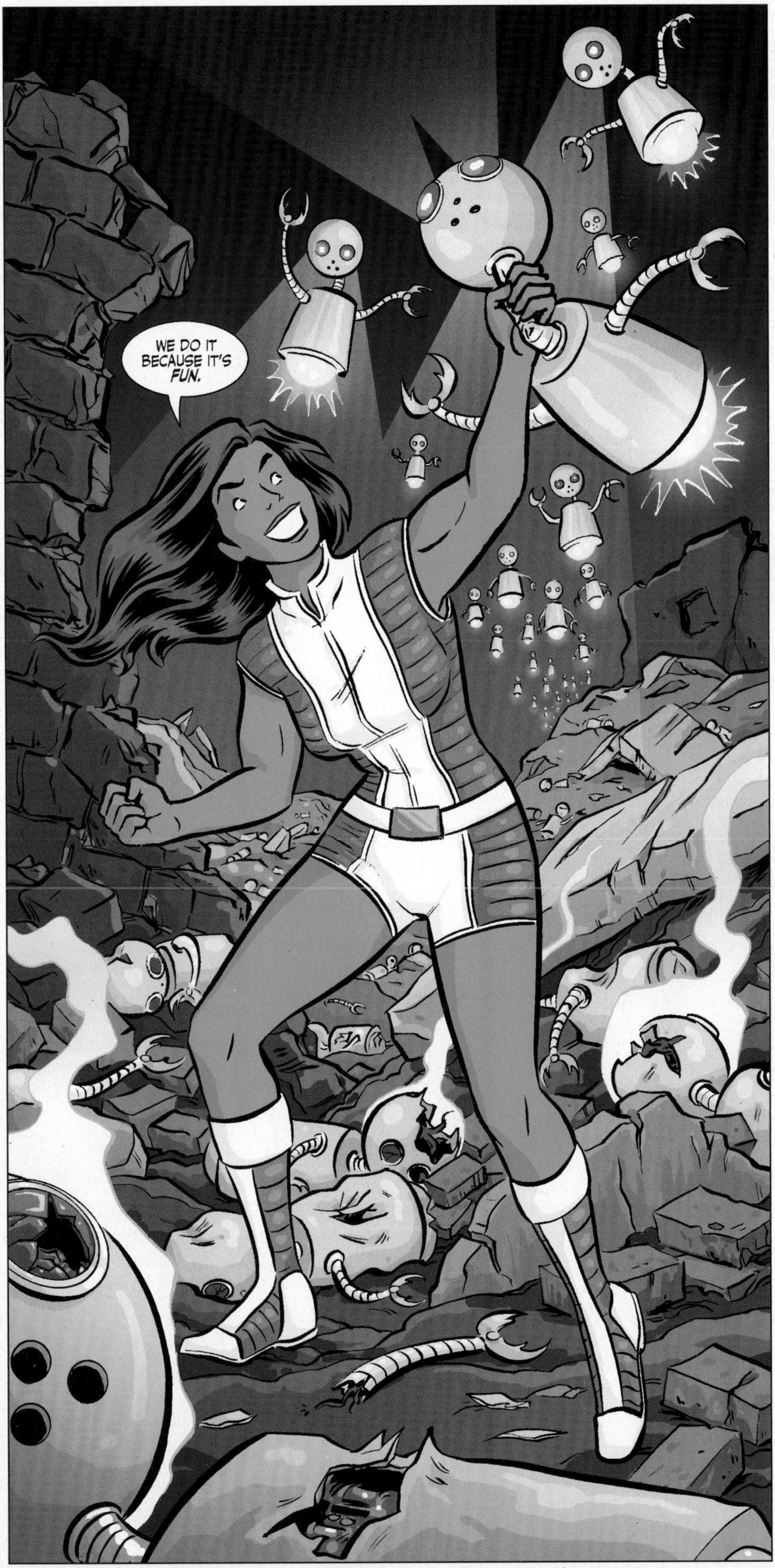
WE DO IT BECAUSE IT'S FUN.

GIRL COMICS

Part Two of Three

INTRODUCTION:
COLLEEN COOVER

COVER ART:
JILL THOMPSON

PRODUCTION:
IRENE LEE

ASSISTANT EDITORS:
SANA AMANAT & RACHEL PINNELAS

ASSOCIATE EDITOR:
LAUREN SANKOVITCH

EDITOR:
JEANINE SCHAEFER

EDITOR IN CHIEF:
JOE QUESADA

PUBLISHER:
DAN BUCKLEY

EXEC. PRODUCER:
ALAN FINE

SPECIAL THANKS:
SPRING HOTELING

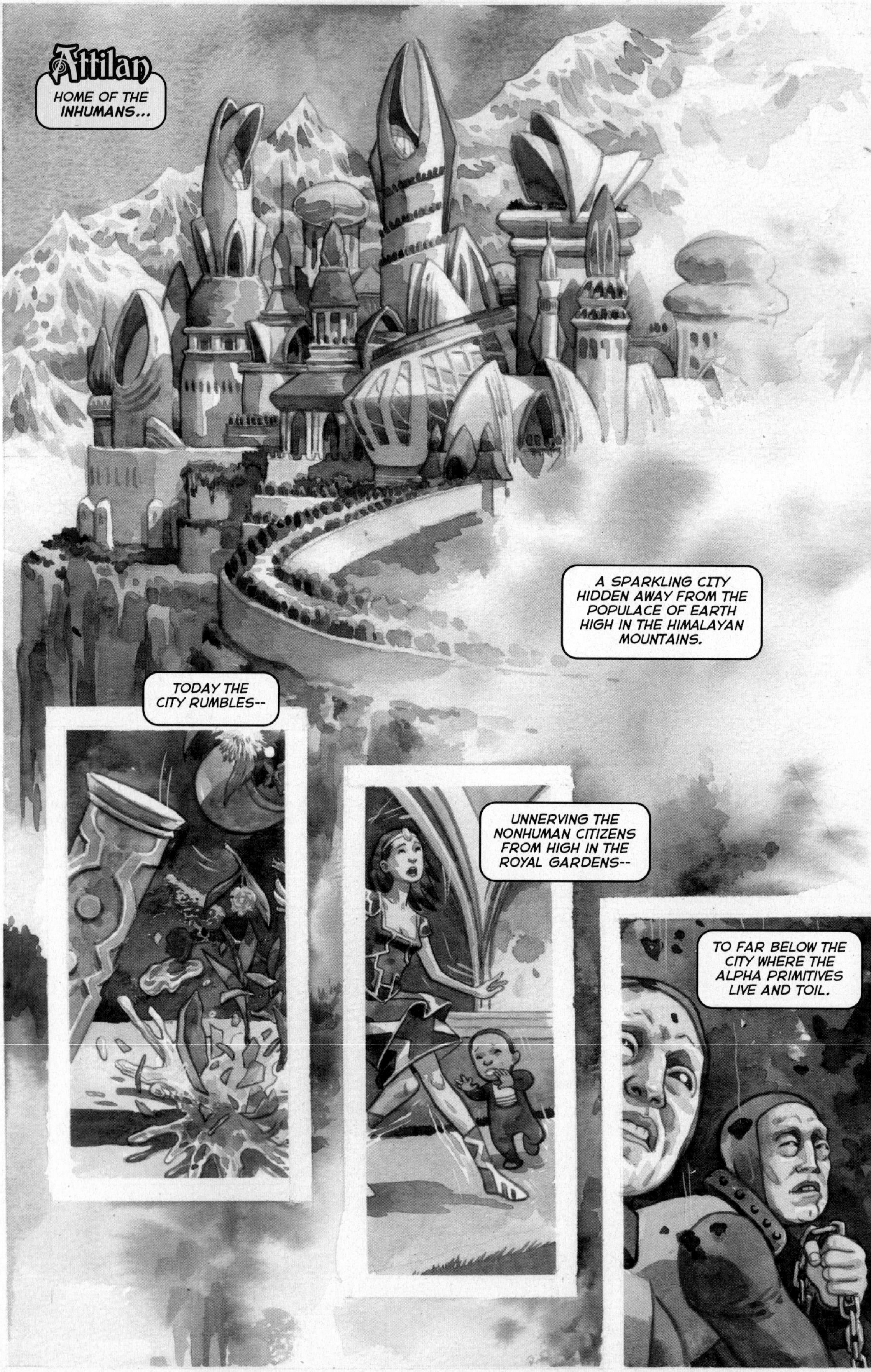
Attilan
HOME OF THE INHUMANS...
A SPARKLING CITY HIDDEN AWAY FROM THE POPULACE OF EARTH HIGH IN THE HIMALAYAN MOUNTAINS.
TODAY THE CITY RUMBLES--
UNNERVING THE NONHUMAN CITIZENS FROM HIGH IN THE ROYAL GARDENS--
TO FAR BELOW THE CITY WHERE THE ALPHA PRIMITIVES LIVE AND TOIL.

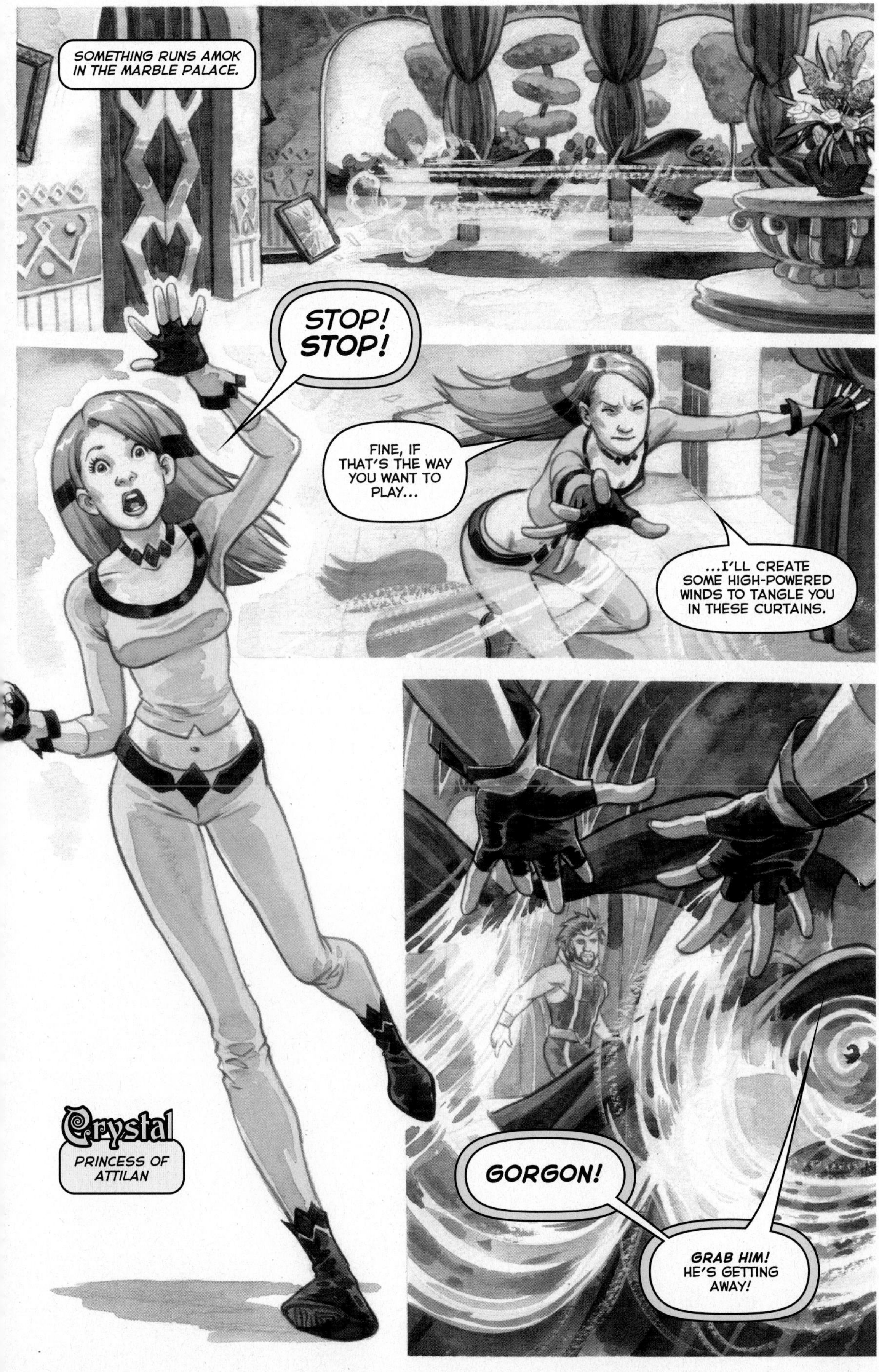
SOMETHING RUNS AMOK IN THE MARBLE PALACE.
STOP! STOP!
FINE, IF THAT'S THE WAY YOU WANT TO PLAY...
...I'LL CREATE SOME HIGH-POWERED WINDS TO TANGLE YOU IN THESE CURTAINS.
Crystal
PRINCESS OF ATTILAN
GORGON!
GRAB HIM! HE'S GETTING AWAY!

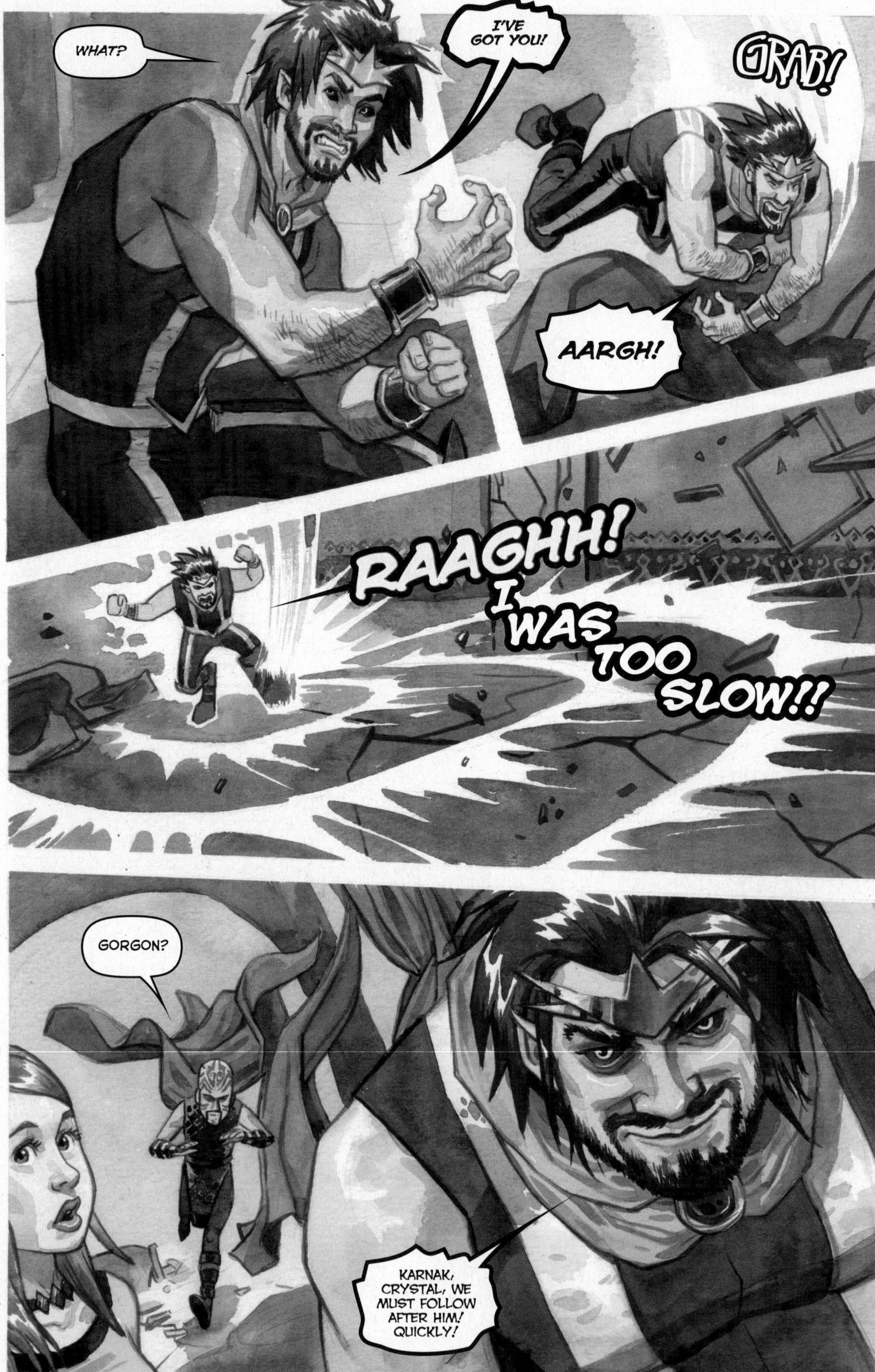
WHAT?
I'VE GOT YOU!
GRAB!
AARGH!
RAAGHH! I WAS TOO SLOW!!
GORGON?
KARNAK, CRYSTAL, WE MUST FOLLOW AFTER HIM! QUICKLY!

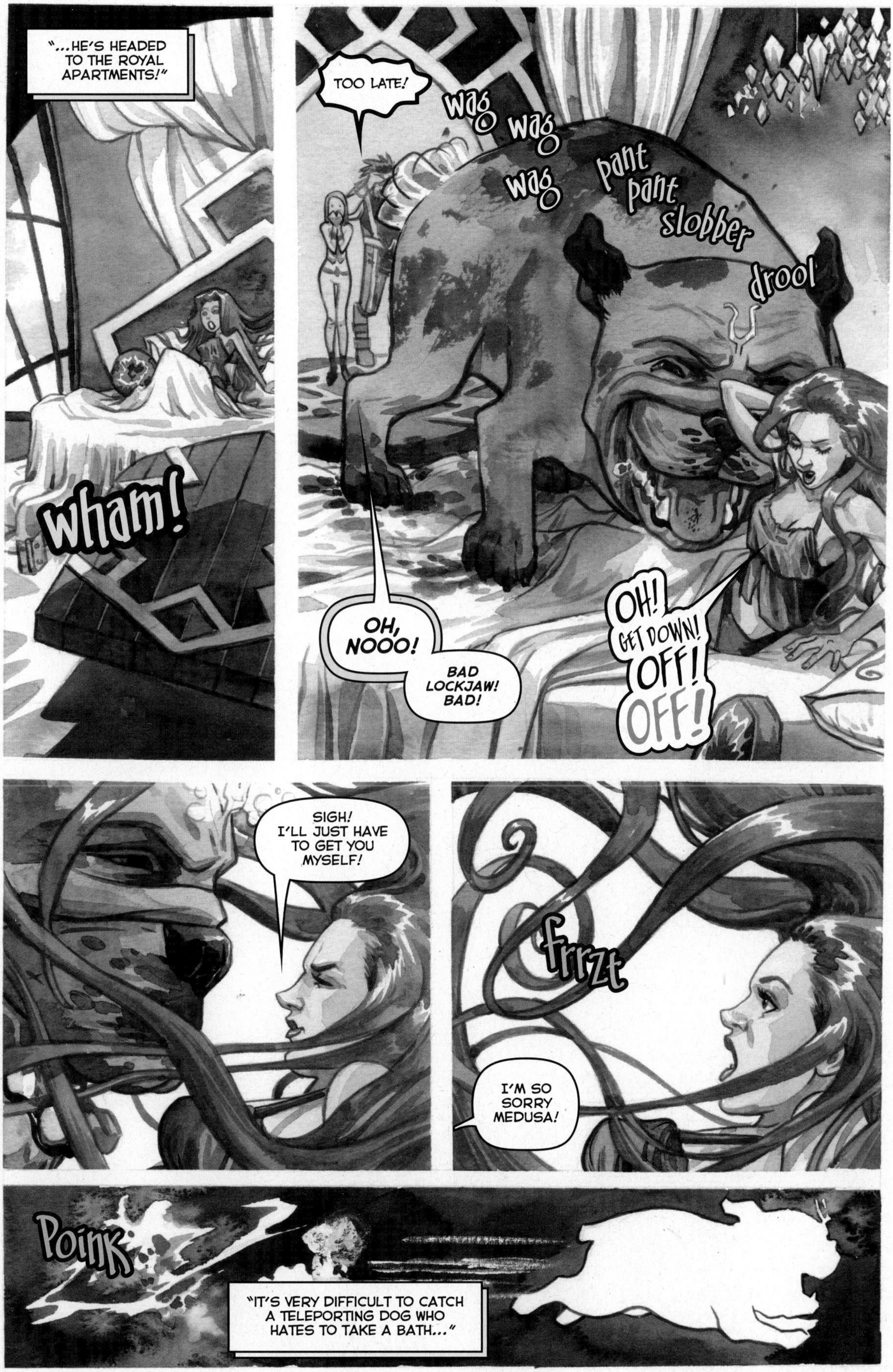
"...HE'S HEADED TO THE ROYAL APARTMENTS!"
wham!
TOO LATE!
wag wag wag
pant pant slobber
drool
OH, NOOO!
BAD LOCKJAW! BAD!
OH! GET DOWN! OFF! OFF!
SIGH! I'LL JUST HAVE TO GET YOU MYSELF!
frrzt
I'M SO SORRY MEDUSA!
Poink
"IT'S VERY DIFFICULT TO CATCH A TELEPORTING DOG WHO HATES TO TAKE A BATH..."

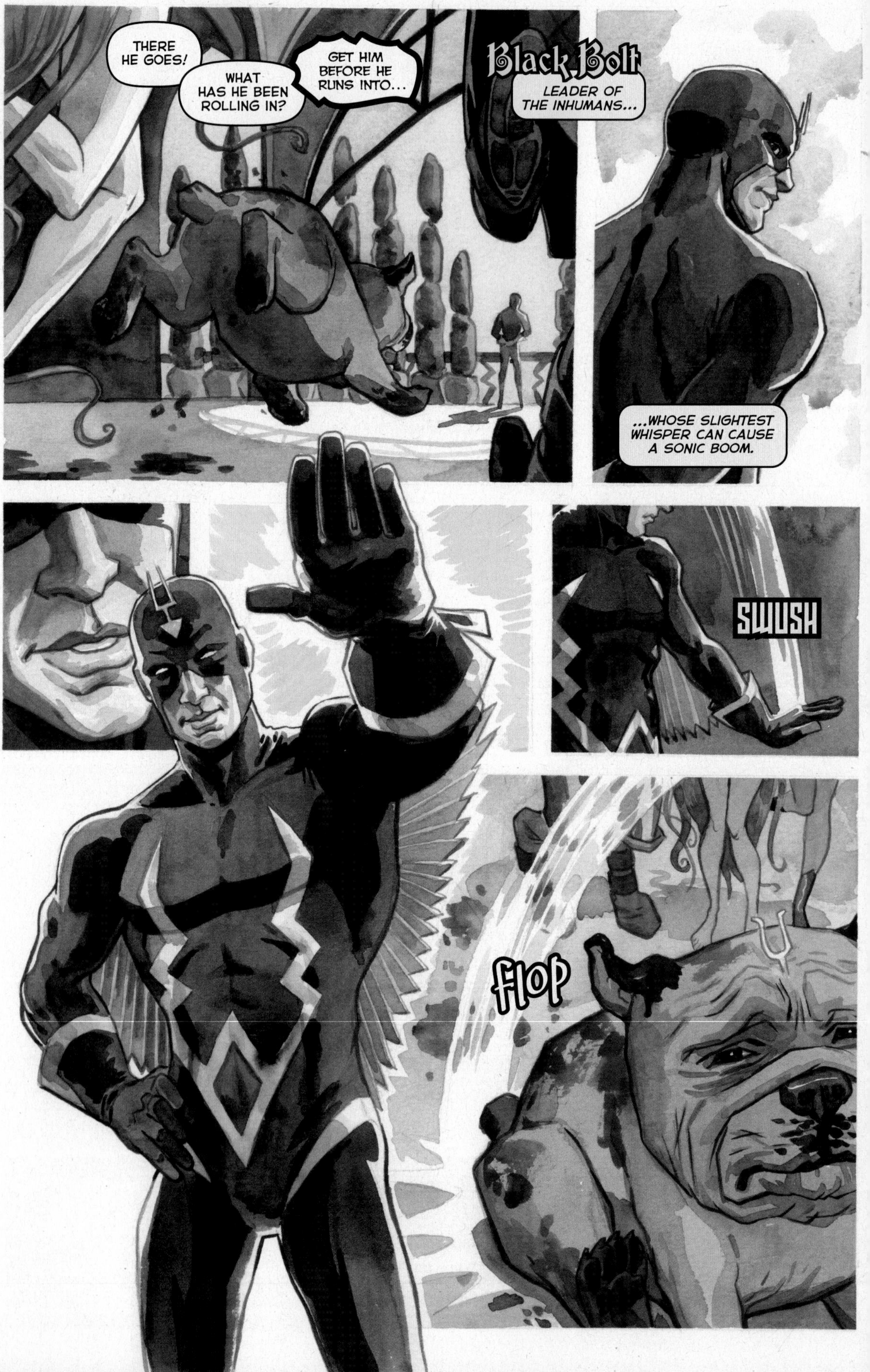
THERE HE GOES!
WHAT HAS HE BEEN ROLLING IN?
GET HIM BEFORE HE RUNS INTO...
Black Bolt
LEADER OF THE INHUMANS...
...WHOSE SLIGHTEST WHISPER CAN CAUSE A SONIC BOOM.
SWUSH
flop

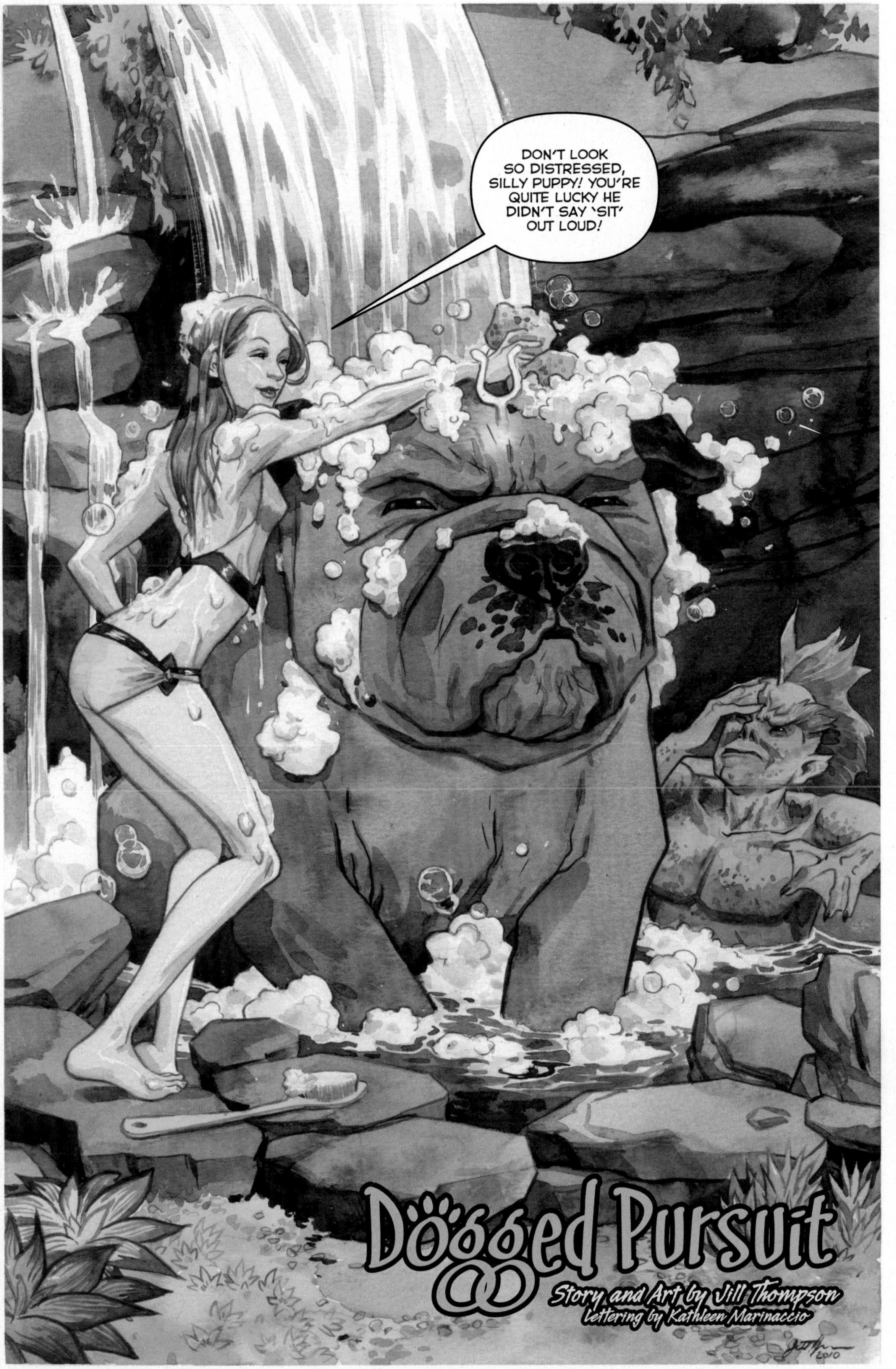
DON'T LOOK SO DISTRESSED, SILLY PUPPY! YOU'RE QUITE LUCKY HE DIDN'T SAY 'SIT' OUT LOUD!
Dogged Pursuit
Story and Art by Jill Thompson
lettering by Kathleen Marinaccio

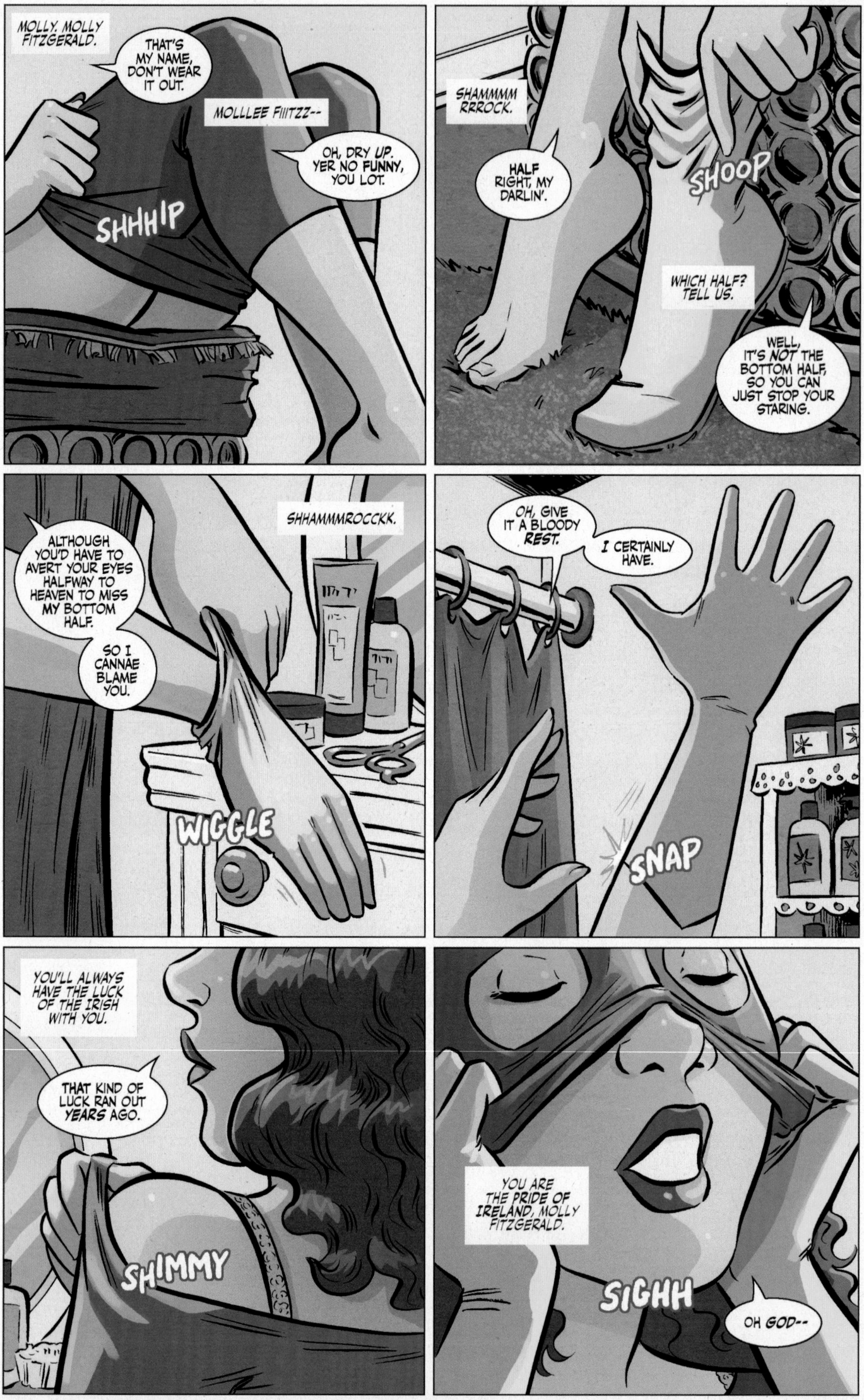
MOLLY. MOLLY FITZGERALD.
THAT'S MY NAME, DON'T WEAR IT OUT.
MOLLLEE FIIITZZ--
OH, DRY UP. YER NO FUNNY, YOU LOT.
SHHHIP
SHAMMMM RRROCK.
HALF RIGHT, MY DARLIN'.
SHOOP
WHICH HALF? TELL US.
WELL, IT'S NOT THE BOTTOM HALF, SO YOU CAN JUST STOP YOUR STARING.
ALTHOUGH YOU'D HAVE TO AVERT YOUR EYES HALFWAY TO HEAVEN TO MISS MY BOTTOM HALF.
SO I CANNAE BLAME YOU.
SHHAMMMROCCKK.
WIGGLE
OH, GIVE IT A BLOODY REST.
I CERTAINLY HAVE.
SNAP
YOU'LL ALWAYS HAVE THE LUCK OF THE IRISH WITH YOU.
THAT KIND OF LUCK RAN OUT YEARS AGO.
SHIMMY
YOU ARE THE PRIDE OF IRELAND, MOLLY FITZGERALD.
SIGHH
OH GOD--

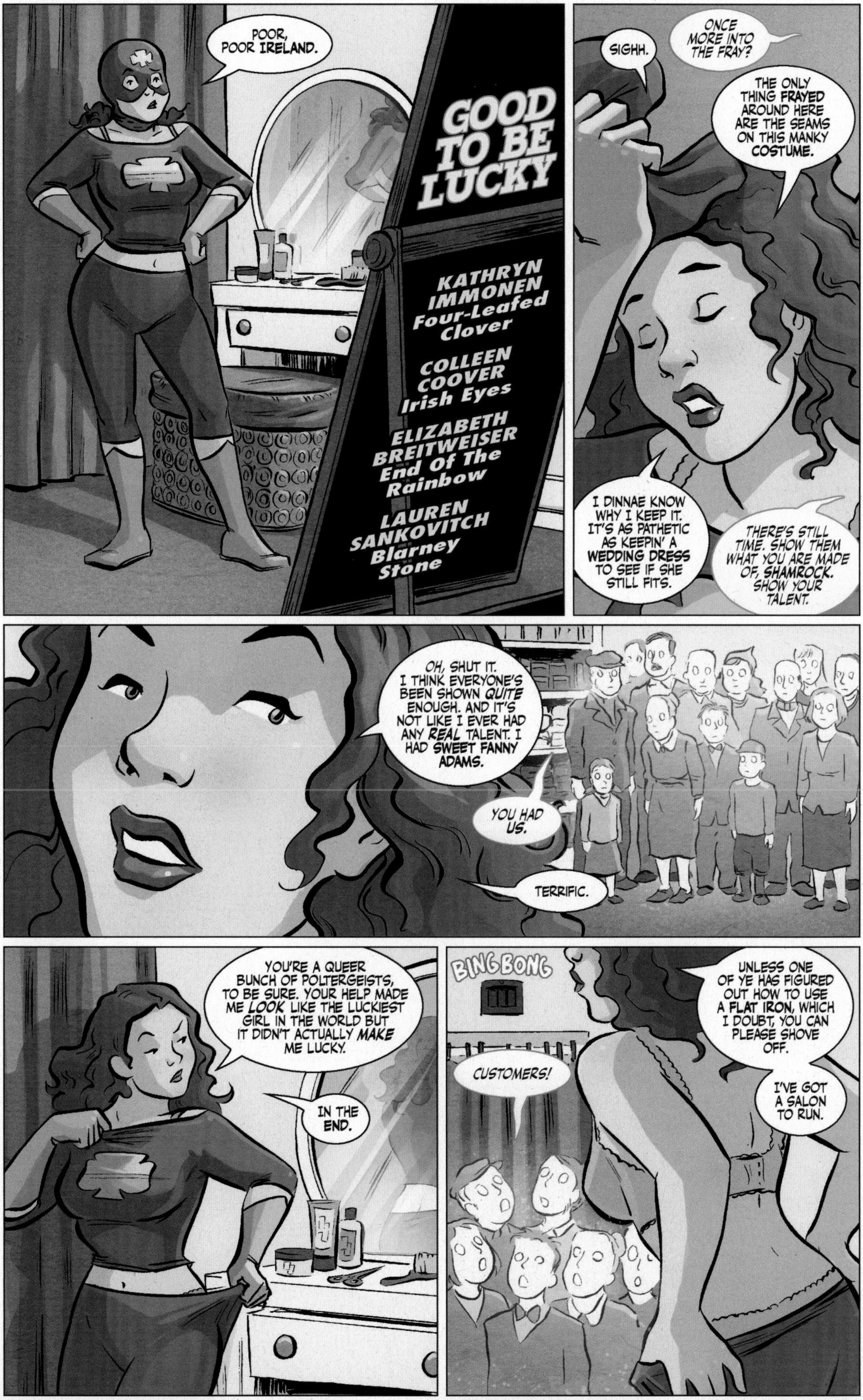
POOR, POOR IRELAND.
GOOD TO BE LUCKY
KATHRYN IMMONEN Four-Leafed Clover
COLLEEN COOVER Irish Eyes
ELIZABETH BREITWEISER End Of The Rainbow
LAUREN SANKOVITCH Blarney Stone
SIGHH.
ONCE MORE INTO THE FRAY?
THE ONLY THING FRAYED AROUND HERE ARE THE SEAMS ON THIS MANKY COSTUME.
I DINNAE KNOW WHY I KEEP IT. IT'S AS PATHETIC AS KEEPIN' A WEDDING DRESS TO SEE IF SHE STILL FITS.
THERE'S STILL TIME. SHOW THEM WHAT YOU ARE MADE OF, SHAMROCK. SHOW YOUR TALENT.
OH, SHUT IT. I THINK EVERYONE'S BEEN SHOWN QUITE ENOUGH. AND IT'S NOT LIKE I EVER HAD ANY REAL TALENT. I HAD SWEET FANNY ADAMS.
YOU HAD US.
TERRIFIC.
YOU'RE A QUEER BUNCH OF POLTERGEISTS, TO BE SURE. YOUR HELP MADE ME LOOK LIKE THE LUCKIEST GIRL IN THE WORLD BUT IT DIDN'T ACTUALLY MAKE ME LUCKY.
IN THE END.
BING BONG
CUSTOMERS!
UNLESS ONE OF YE HAS FIGURED OUT HOW TO USE A FLAT IRON, WHICH I DOUBT, YOU CAN PLEASE SHOVE OFF.
I'VE GOT A SALON TO RUN.

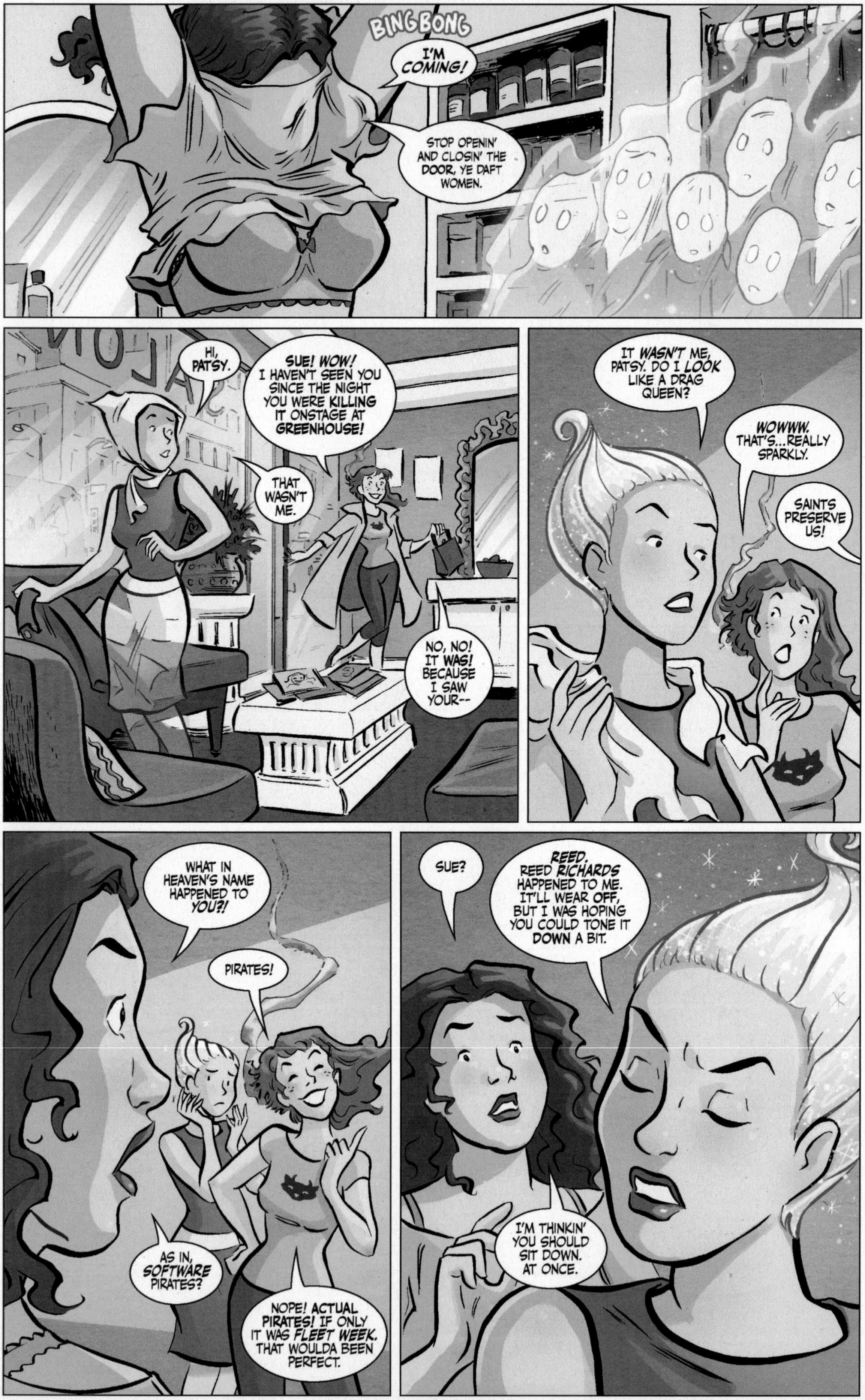
BING BONG
I'M COMING!
STOP OPENIN' AND CLOSIN' THE DOOR, YE DAFT WOMEN.
HI, PATSY.
SUE! WOW! I HAVEN'T SEEN YOU SINCE THE NIGHT YOU WERE KILLING IT ONSTAGE AT GREENHOUSE!
THAT WASN'T ME.
NO, NO! IT WAS! BECAUSE I SAW YOUR--
IT WASN'T ME, PATSY. DO I LOOK LIKE A DRAG QUEEN?
WOWWW. THAT'S...REALLY SPARKLY.
SAINTS PRESERVE US!
WHAT IN HEAVEN'S NAME HAPPENED TO YOU?!
PIRATES!
AS IN, SOFTWARE PIRATES?
NOPE! ACTUAL PIRATES! IF ONLY IT WAS FLEET WEEK. THAT WOULDA BEEN PERFECT.
SUE?
REED. REED RICHARDS HAPPENED TO ME. IT'LL WEAR OFF, BUT I WAS HOPING YOU COULD TONE IT DOWN A BIT.
I'M THINKIN' YOU SHOULD SIT DOWN. AT ONCE.

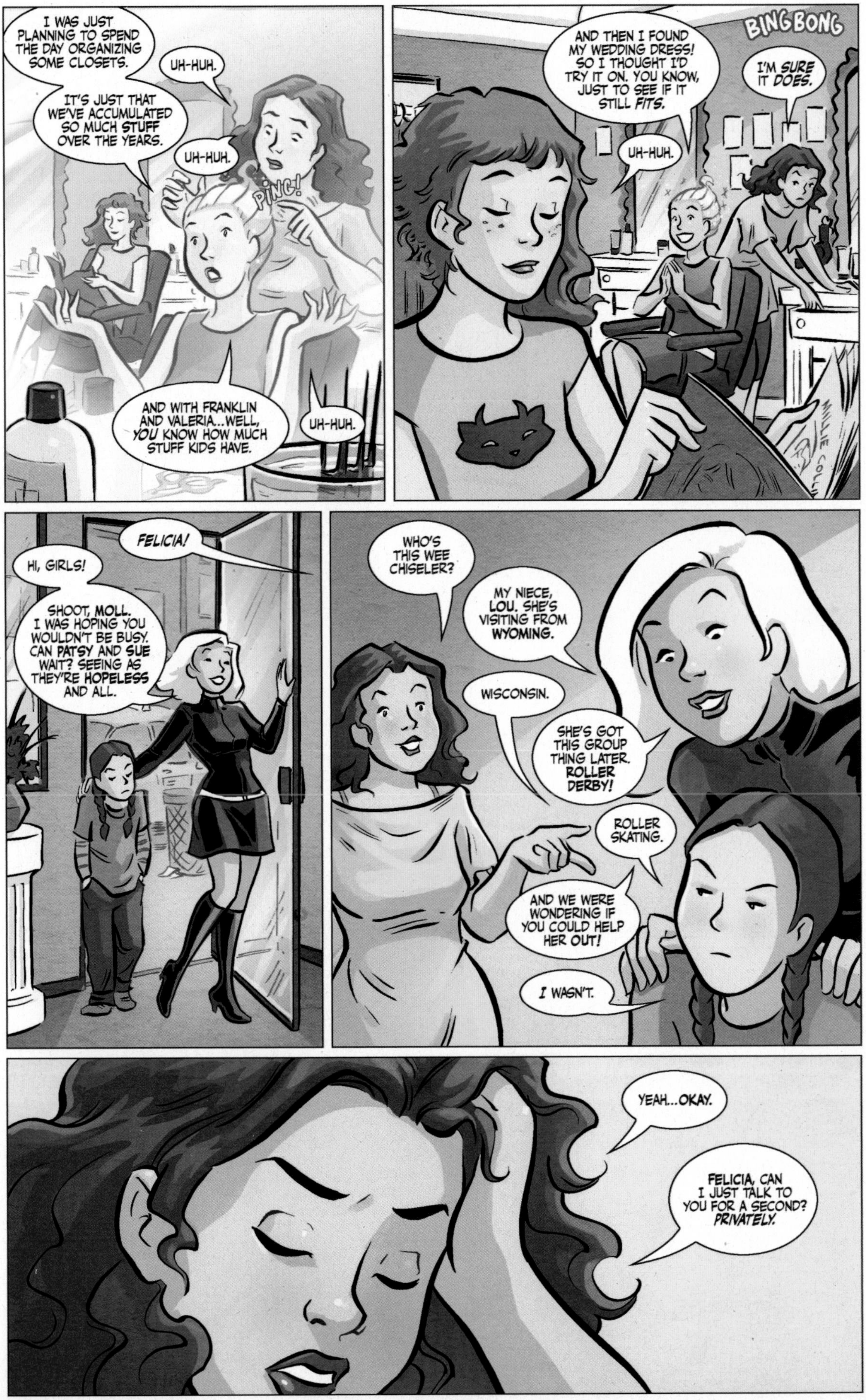
I WAS JUST PLANNING TO SPEND THE DAY ORGANIZING SOME CLOSETS.
UH-HUH.
IT'S JUST THAT WE'VE ACCUMULATED SO MUCH STUFF OVER THE YEARS.
UH-HUH.
PING!
AND WITH FRANKLIN AND VALERIA...WELL, YOU KNOW HOW MUCH STUFF KIDS HAVE.
UH-HUH.
AND THEN I FOUND MY WEDDING DRESS! SO I THOUGHT I'D TRY IT ON. YOU KNOW, JUST TO SEE IF IT STILL FITS.
UH-HUH.
BING BONG
I'M SURE IT DOES.
FELICIA!
HI, GIRLS!
SHOOT, MOLL. I WAS HOPING YOU WOULDN'T BE BUSY. CAN PATSY AND SUE WAIT? SEEING AS THEY'RE HOPELESS AND ALL.
WHO'S THIS WEE CHISELER?
MY NIECE, LOU. SHE'S VISITING FROM WYOMING.
WISCONSIN.
SHE'S GOT THIS GROUP THING LATER. ROLLER DERBY!
ROLLER SKATING.
AND WE WERE WONDERING IF YOU COULD HELP HER OUT!
I WASN'T.
YEAH...OKAY.
FELICIA, CAN I JUST TALK TO YOU FOR A SECOND? PRIVATELY.

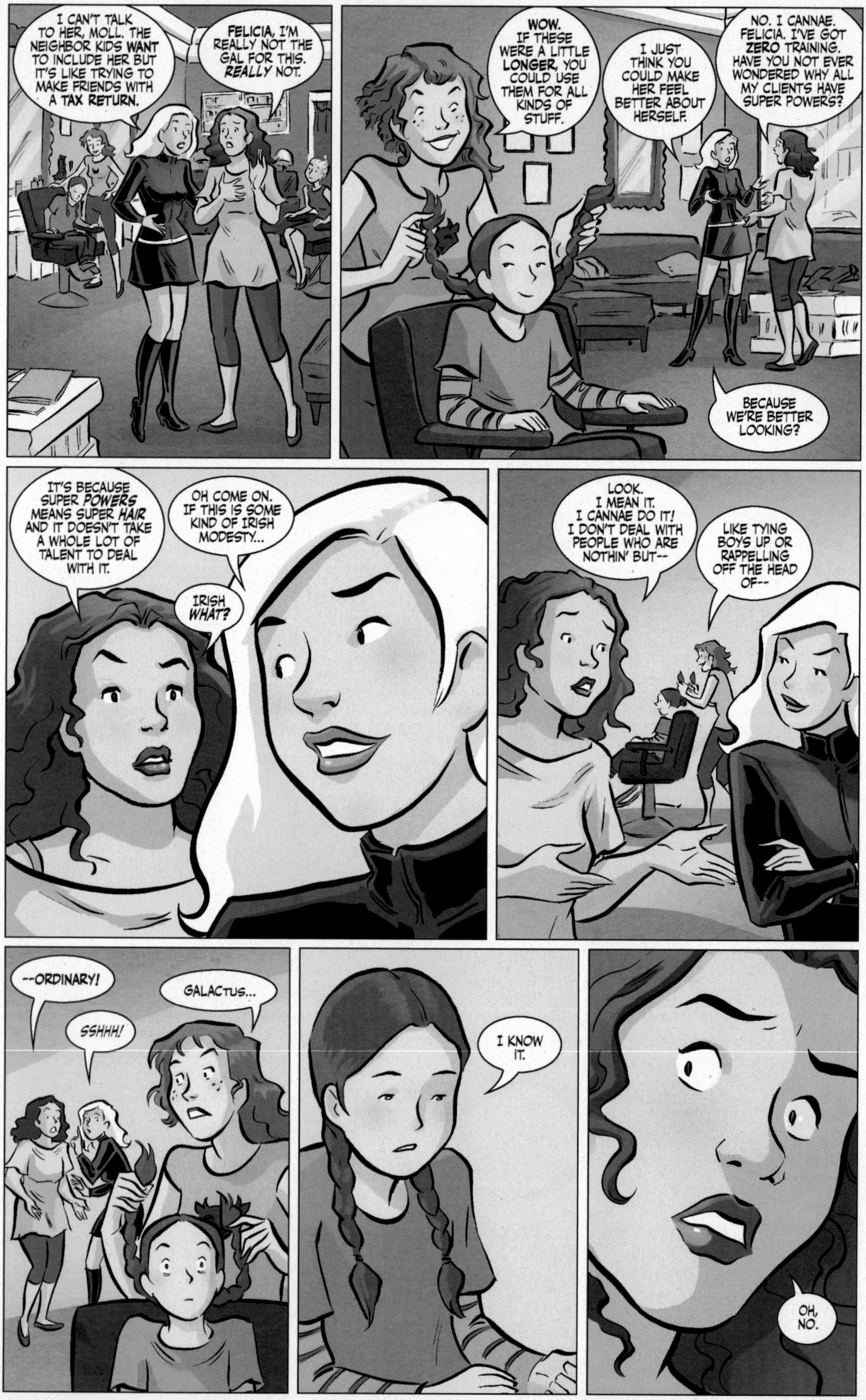
I CAN'T TALK TO HER, MOLL. THE NEIGHBOR KIDS WANT TO INCLUDE HER BUT IT'S LIKE TRYING TO MAKE FRIENDS WITH A TAX RETURN.
FELICIA, I'M REALLY NOT THE GAL FOR THIS. REALLY NOT.
WOW. IF THESE WERE A LITTLE LONGER, YOU COULD USE THEM FOR ALL KINDS OF STUFF.
I JUST THINK YOU COULD MAKE HER FEEL BETTER ABOUT HERSELF.
NO. I CANNAE. FELICIA. I'VE GOT ZERO TRAINING. HAVE YOU NOT EVER WONDERED WHY ALL MY CLIENTS HAVE SUPER POWERS?
BECAUSE WE'RE BETTER LOOKING?
IT'S BECAUSE SUPER POWERS MEANS SUPER HAIR AND IT DOESN'T TAKE A WHOLE LOT OF TALENT TO DEAL WITH IT.
OH COME ON. IF THIS IS SOME KIND OF IRISH MODESTY...
IRISH WHAT?
LOOK. I MEAN IT. I CANNAE DO IT! I DON'T DEAL WITH PEOPLE WHO ARE NOTHIN' BUT--
LIKE TYING BOYS UP OR RAPPELLING OFF THE HEAD OF--
--ORDINARY!
GALACTUS...
SSHHH!
I KNOW IT.
OH, NO.

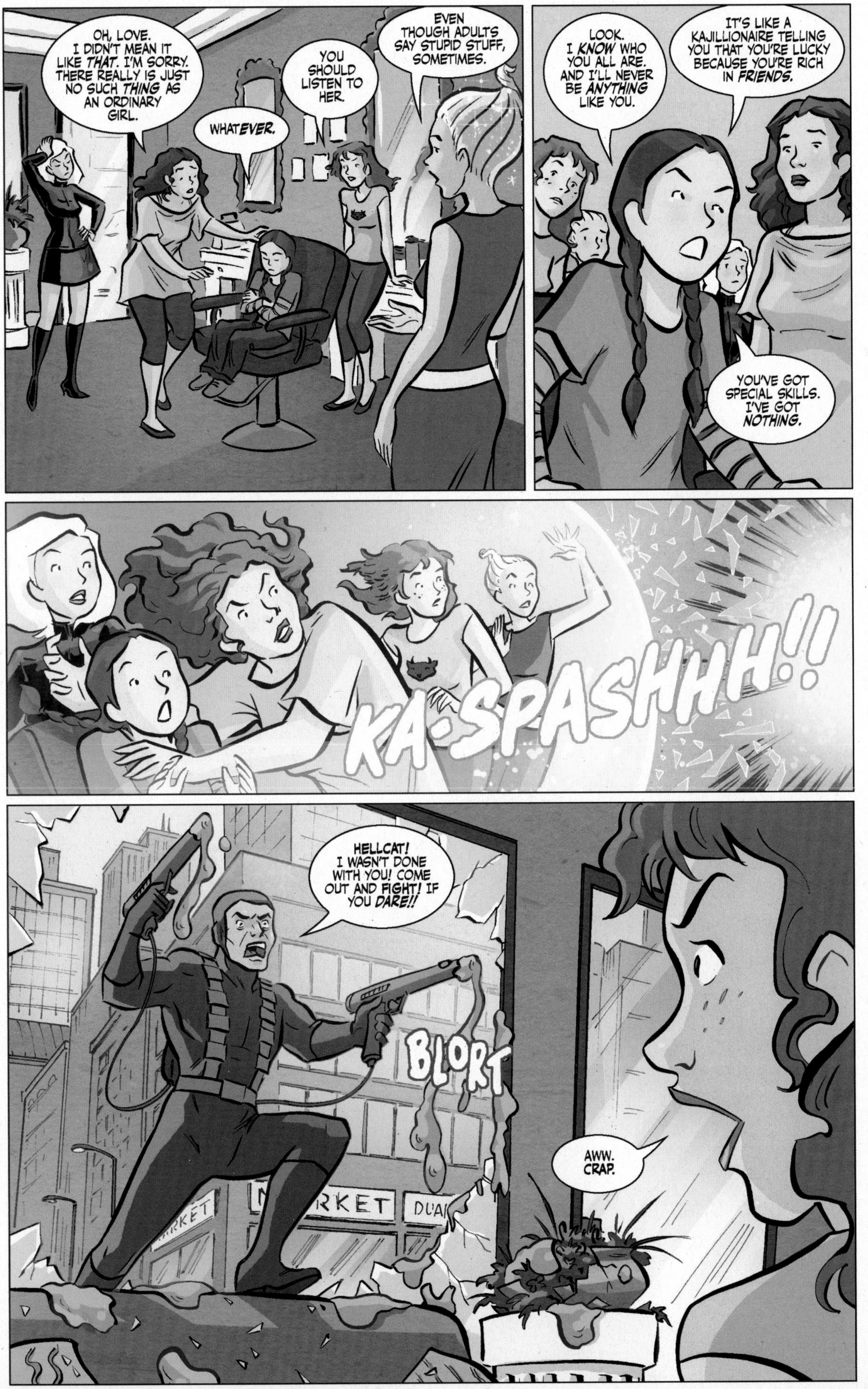
OH, LOVE. I DIDN'T MEAN IT LIKE THAT. I'M SORRY. THERE REALLY IS JUST NO SUCH THING AS AN ORDINARY GIRL.
WHATEVER.
YOU SHOULD LISTEN TO HER.
EVEN THOUGH ADULTS SAY STUPID STUFF, SOMETIMES.
LOOK. I KNOW WHO YOU ALL ARE. AND I'LL NEVER BE ANYTHING LIKE YOU.
IT'S LIKE A KAJILLIONAIRE TELLING YOU THAT YOU'RE LUCKY BECAUSE YOU'RE RICH IN FRIENDS.
YOU'VE GOT SPECIAL SKILLS. I'VE GOT NOTHING.
KA-SPASHHH!!
HELLCAT! I WASN'T DONE WITH YOU! COME OUT AND FIGHT! IF YOU DARE!!
BLORT
AWW. CRAP.

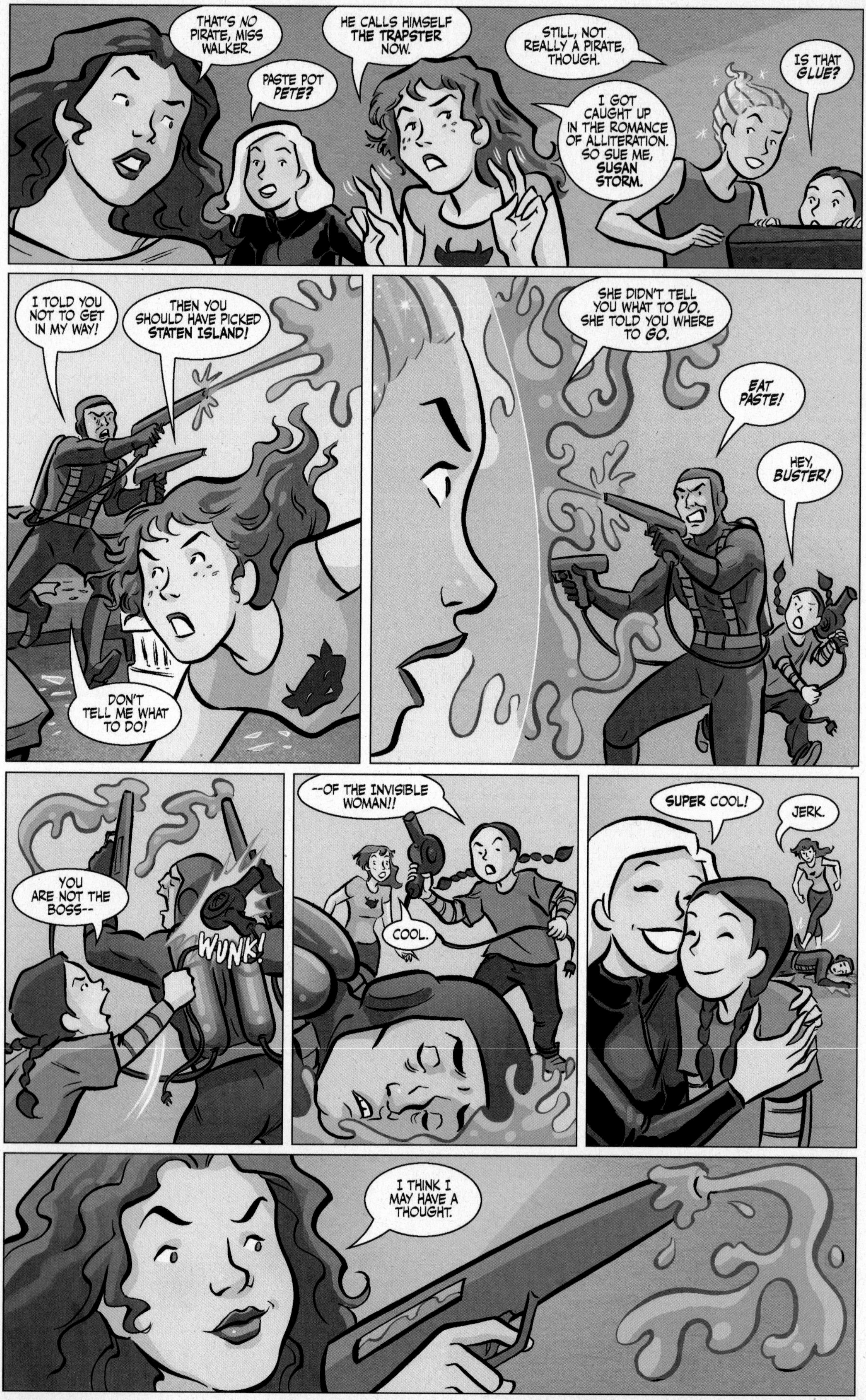
THAT'S NO PIRATE, MISS WALKER.
PASTE POT PETE?
HE CALLS HIMSELF THE TRAPSTER NOW.
STILL, NOT REALLY A PIRATE, THOUGH.
I GOT CAUGHT UP IN THE ROMANCE OF ALLITERATION. SO SUE ME, SUSAN STORM.
IS THAT GLUE?
I TOLD YOU NOT TO GET IN MY WAY!
THEN YOU SHOULD HAVE PICKED STATEN ISLAND!
DON'T TELL ME WHAT TO DO!
SHE DIDN'T TELL YOU WHAT TO DO. SHE TOLD YOU WHERE TO GO.
EAT PASTE!
HEY, BUSTER!
YOU ARE NOT THE BOSS--
WUNK!
--OF THE INVISIBLE WOMAN!!
COOL.
SUPER COOL!
JERK.
I THINK I MAY HAVE A THOUGHT.

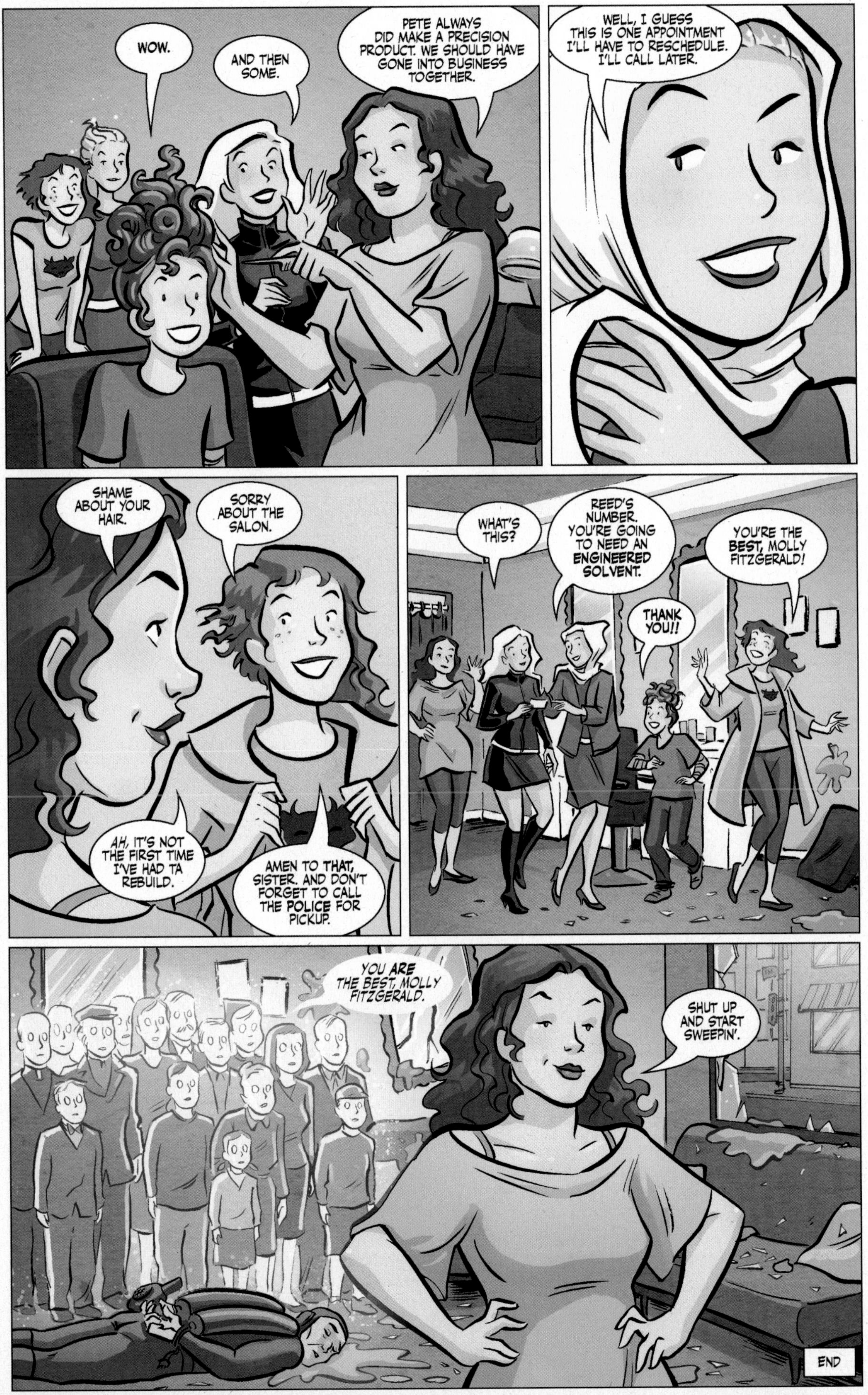
WOW.
AND THEN SOME.
PETE ALWAYS DID MAKE A PRECISION PRODUCT. WE SHOULD HAVE GONE INTO BUSINESS TOGETHER.
WELL, I GUESS THIS IS ONE APPOINTMENT I'LL HAVE TO RESCHEDULE. I'LL CALL LATER.
SHAME ABOUT YOUR HAIR.
SORRY ABOUT THE SALON.
AH, IT'S NOT THE FIRST TIME I'VE HAD TA REBUILD.
AMEN TO THAT, SISTER. AND DON'T FORGET TO CALL THE POLICE FOR PICKUP.
WHAT'S THIS?
REED'S NUMBER. YOU'RE GOING TO NEED AN ENGINEERED SOLVENT.
THANK YOU!!
YOU'RE THE BEST, MOLLY FITZGERALD!
YOU ARE THE BEST, MOLLY FITZGERALD.
SHUT UP AND START SWEEPIN'.
END

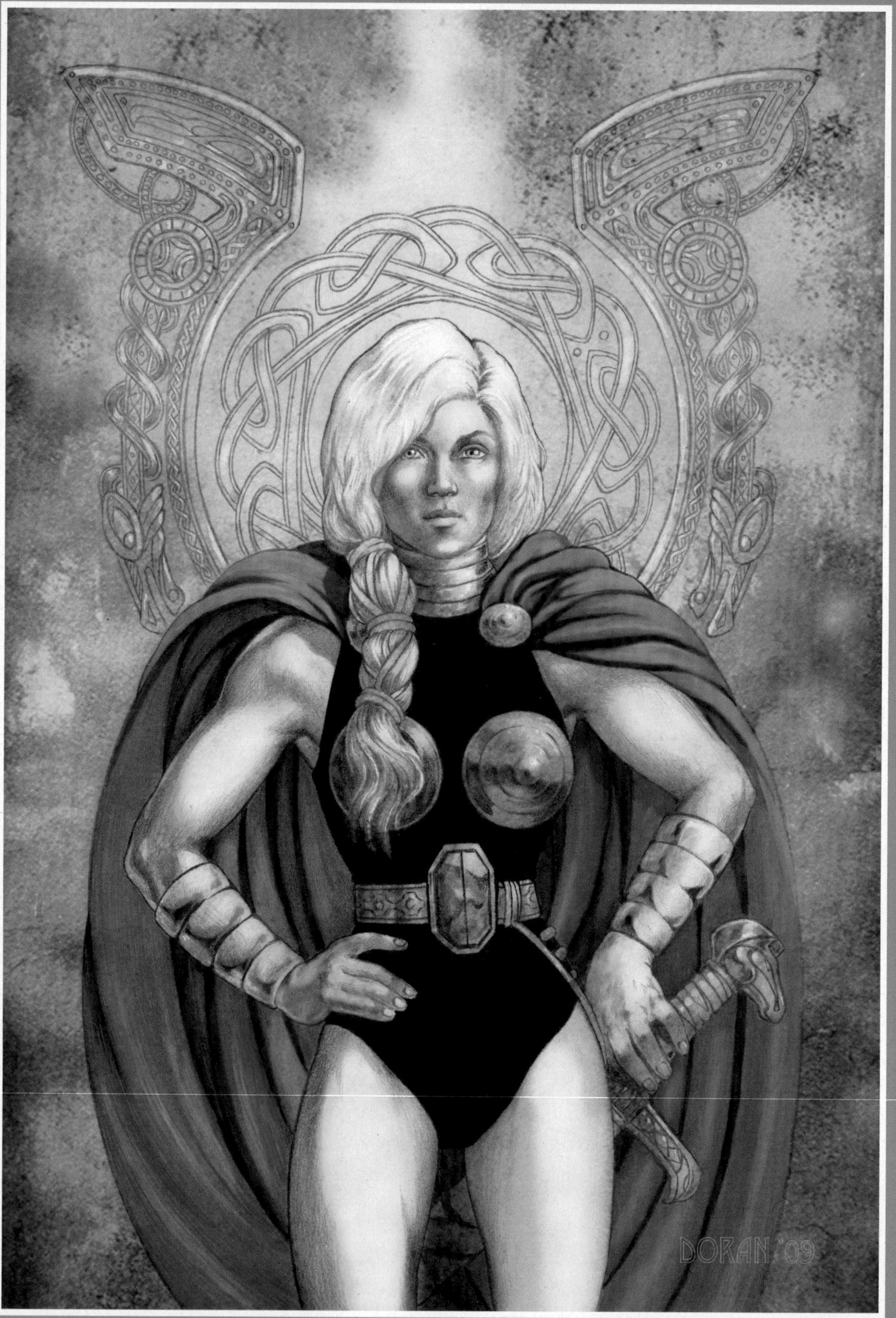
DORAN '09

VALKYRIE

Art by COLLEEN DORAN

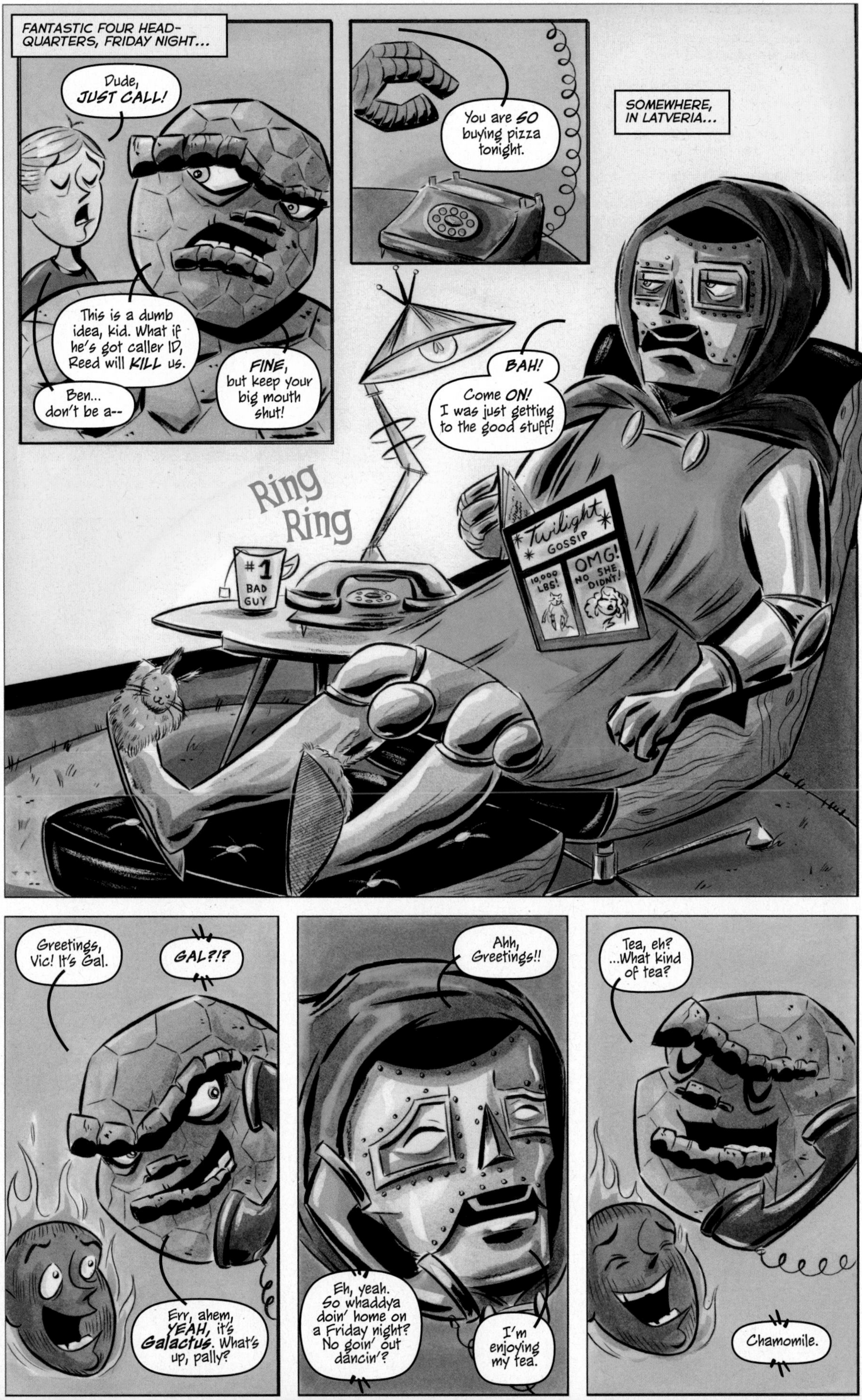
FANTASTIC FOUR HEAD-QUARTERS, FRIDAY NIGHT...
Dude, JUST CALL!
This is a dumb idea, kid. What if he's got caller ID, Reed will KILL us.
Ben... don't be a--
FINE, but keep your big mouth shut!
You are SO buying pizza tonight.
SOMEWHERE, IN LATVERIA...
Ring Ring
BAH!
Come ON! I was just getting to the good stuff!
#1 BAD GUY
Twilight GOSSIP
10,000 LBS!
OMG! NO SHE DIDNT!
Greetings, Vic! It's Gal.
GAL?!?
Err, ahem, YEAH, it's Galactus. What's up, pally?
Ahh, Greetings!!
Eh, yeah. So whaddya doin' home on a Friday night? No goin' out dancin'?
I'm enjoying my tea.
Tea, eh? ...What kind of tea?
Chamomile.

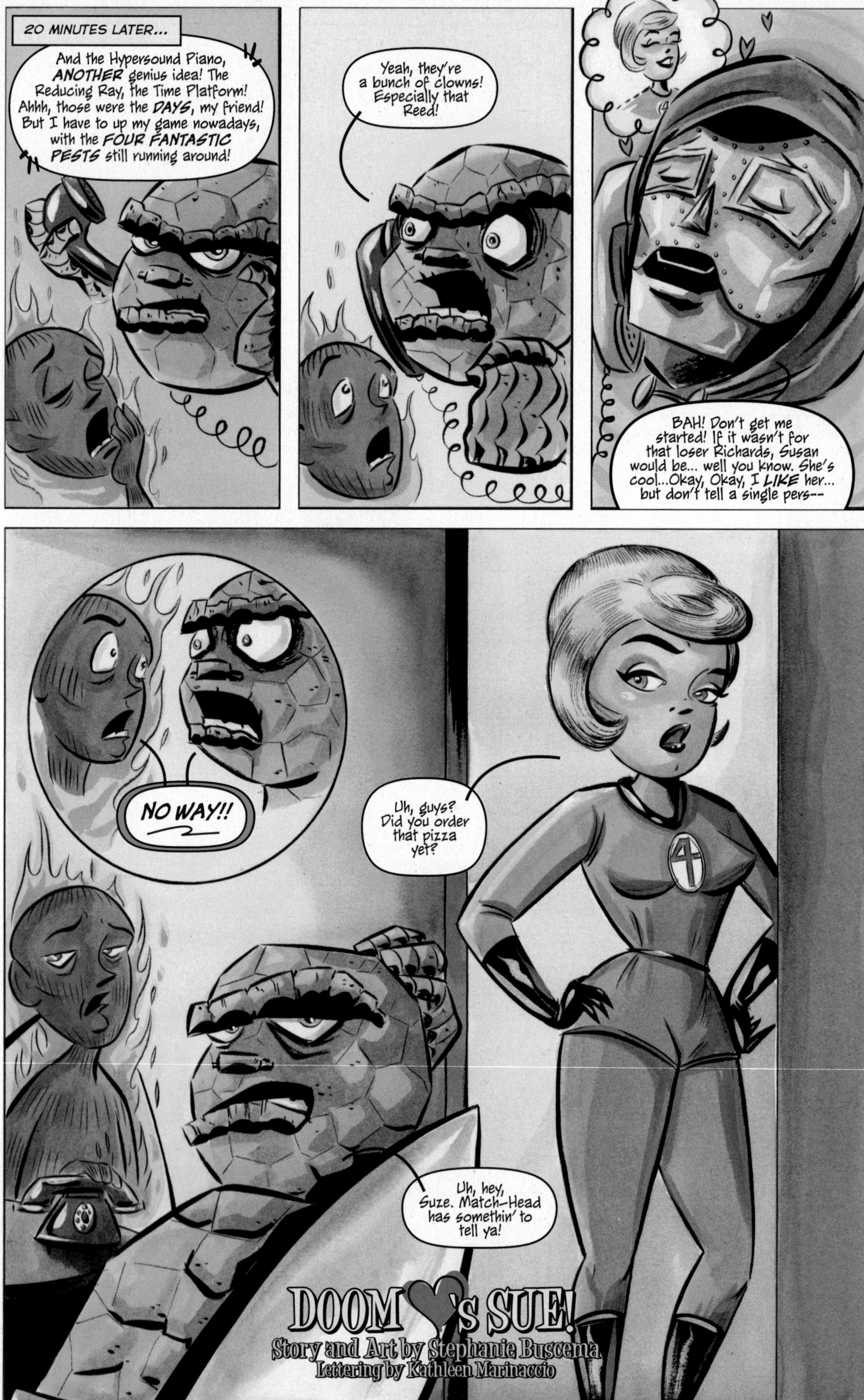
20 MINUTES LATER...
And the Hypersound Piano, ANOTHER genius idea! The Reducing Ray, the Time Platform! Ahhh, those were the DAYS, my friend! But I have to up my game nowadays, with the FOUR FANTASTIC PESTS still running around!
Yeah, they're a bunch of clowns! Especially that Reed!
BAH! Don't get me started! If it wasn't for that loser Richards, Susan would be... well you know. She's cool...Okay, Okay, I LIKE her... but don't tell a single pers--
NO WAY!!
Uh, guys? Did you order that pizza yet?
Uh, hey, Suze. Match-Head has somethin' to tell ya!
DOOM ♥'s SUE!
Story and Art by Stephanie Buscema
Lettering by Kathleen Marinaccio

TOSS

CHOP
SLASH
MM

PLOP

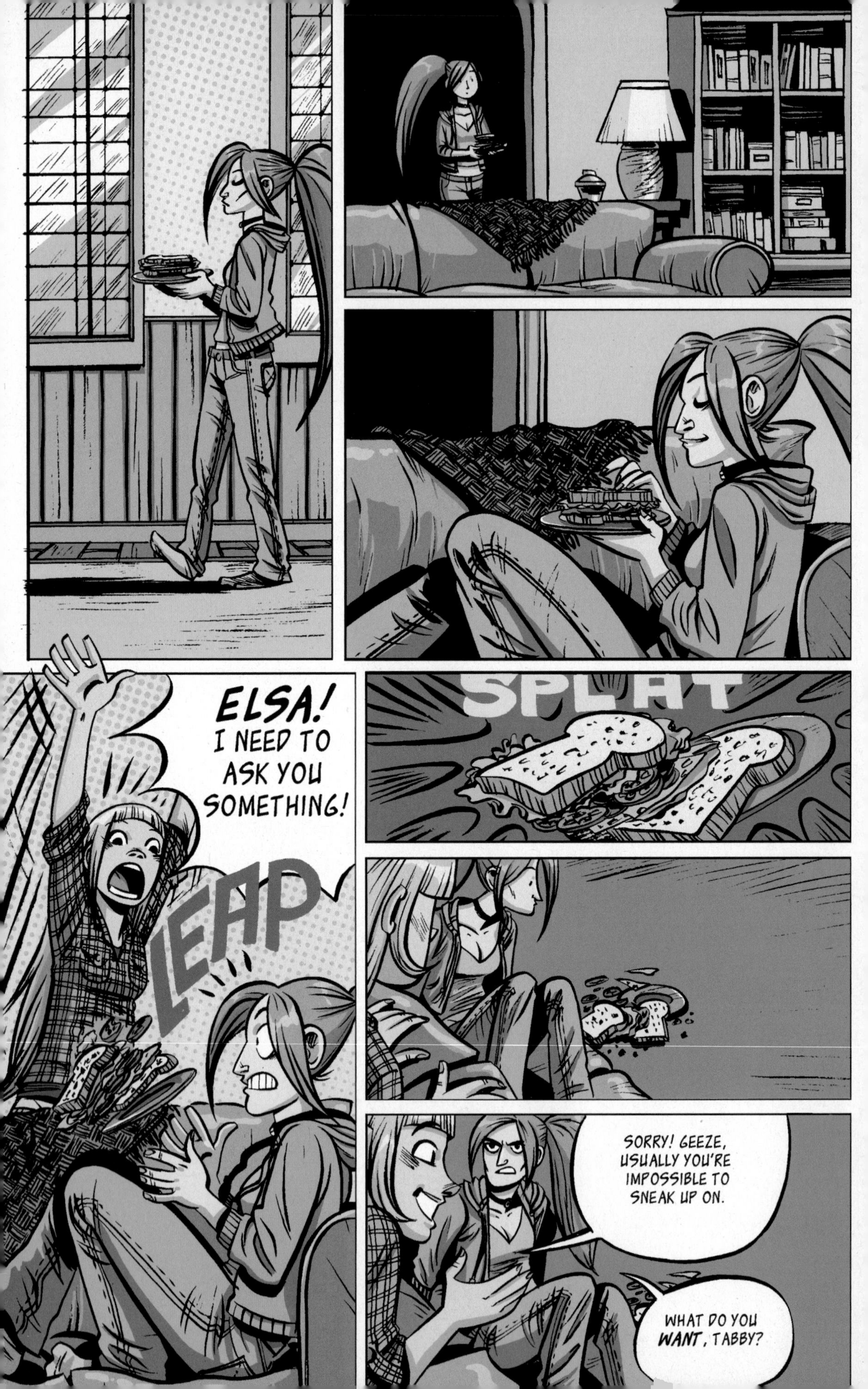
ELSA! I NEED TO ASK YOU SOMETHING!
LEAP
SPLAT
SORRY! GEEZE, USUALLY YOU'RE IMPOSSIBLE TO SNEAK UP ON.
WHAT DO YOU WANT, TABBY?

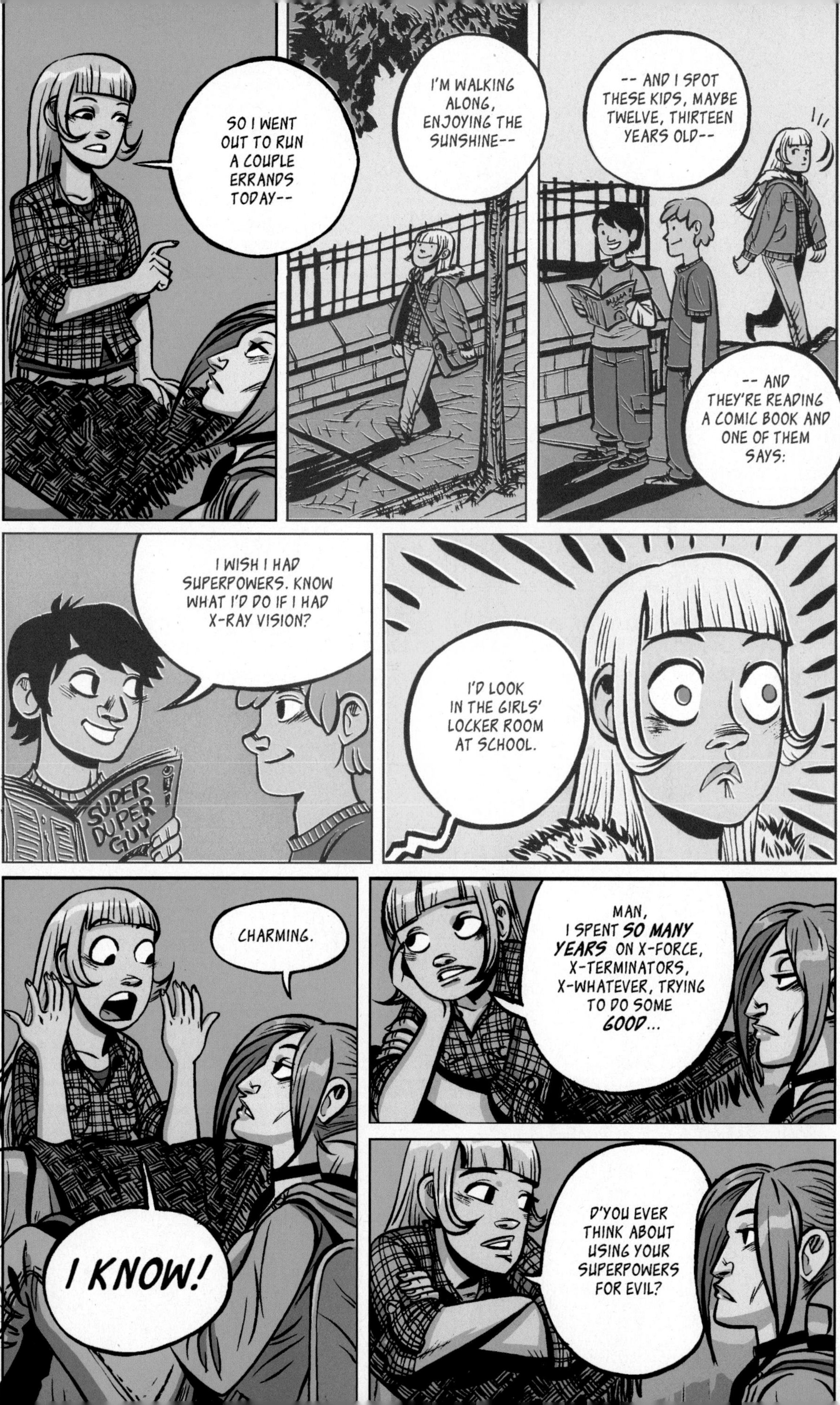
SO I WENT OUT TO RUN A COUPLE ERRANDS TODAY--
I'M WALKING ALONG, ENJOYING THE SUNSHINE--
-- AND I SPOT THESE KIDS, MAYBE TWELVE, THIRTEEN YEARS OLD--
-- AND THEY'RE READING A COMIC BOOK AND ONE OF THEM SAYS:
I WISH I HAD SUPERPOWERS. KNOW WHAT I'D DO IF I HAD X-RAY VISION?
SUPER DUPER GUY
I'D LOOK IN THE GIRLS' LOCKER ROOM AT SCHOOL.
CHARMING.
I KNOW!
MAN, I SPENT SO MANY YEARS ON X-FORCE, X-TERMINATORS, X-WHATEVER, TRYING TO DO SOME GOOD...
D'YOU EVER THINK ABOUT USING YOUR SUPERPOWERS FOR EVIL?

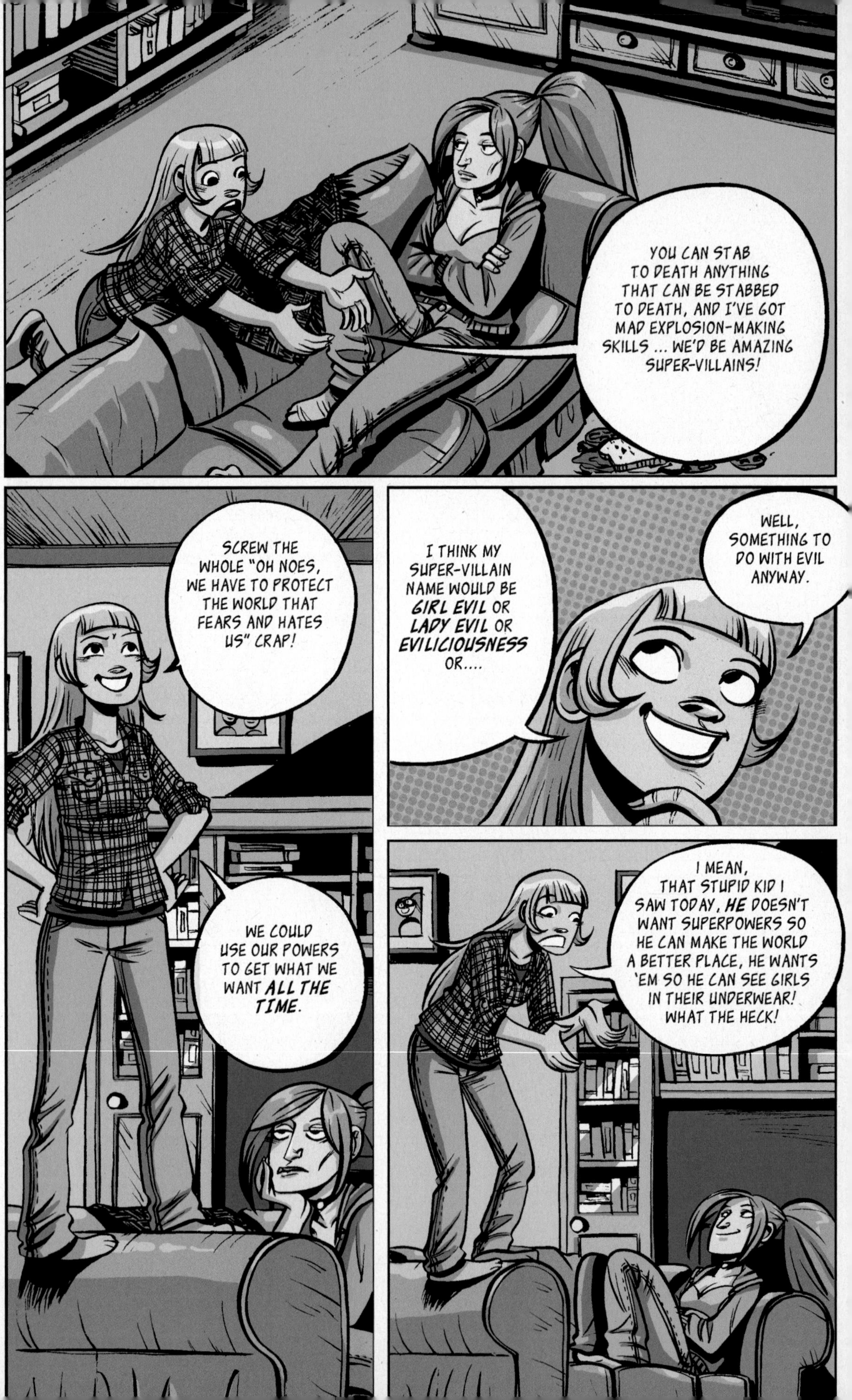
YOU CAN STAB TO DEATH ANYTHING THAT CAN BE STABBED TO DEATH, AND I'VE GOT MAD EXPLOSION-MAKING SKILLS ... WE'D BE AMAZING SUPER-VILLAINS!
SCREW THE WHOLE "OH NOES, WE HAVE TO PROTECT THE WORLD THAT FEARS AND HATES US" CRAP!
WE COULD USE OUR POWERS TO GET WHAT WE WANT **ALL THE TIME**.
I THINK MY SUPER-VILLAIN NAME WOULD BE **GIRL EVIL** OR **LADY EVIL** OR **EVILICIOUSNESS** OR....
WELL, SOMETHING TO DO WITH EVIL ANYWAY.
I MEAN, THAT STUPID KID I SAW TODAY, **HE** DOESN'T WANT SUPERPOWERS SO HE CAN MAKE THE WORLD A BETTER PLACE, HE WANTS 'EM SO HE CAN SEE GIRLS IN THEIR UNDERWEAR! WHAT THE HECK!

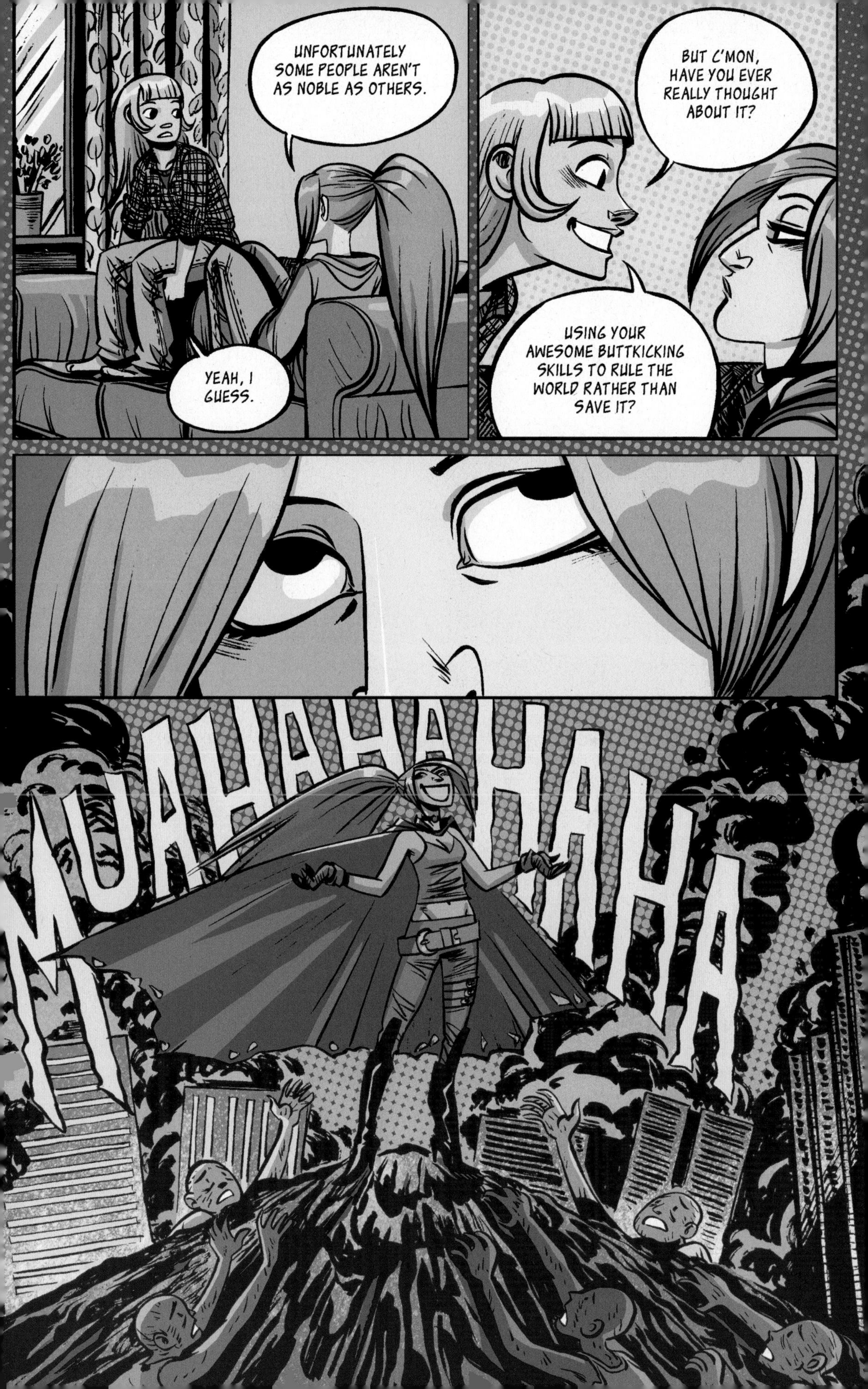
UNFORTUNATELY SOME PEOPLE AREN'T AS NOBLE AS OTHERS.
YEAH, I GUESS.
BUT C'MON, HAVE YOU EVER REALLY THOUGHT ABOUT IT?
USING YOUR AWESOME BUTTKICKING SKILLS TO RULE THE WORLD RATHER THAN SAVE IT?
MUAHAHAHAHAHAHA

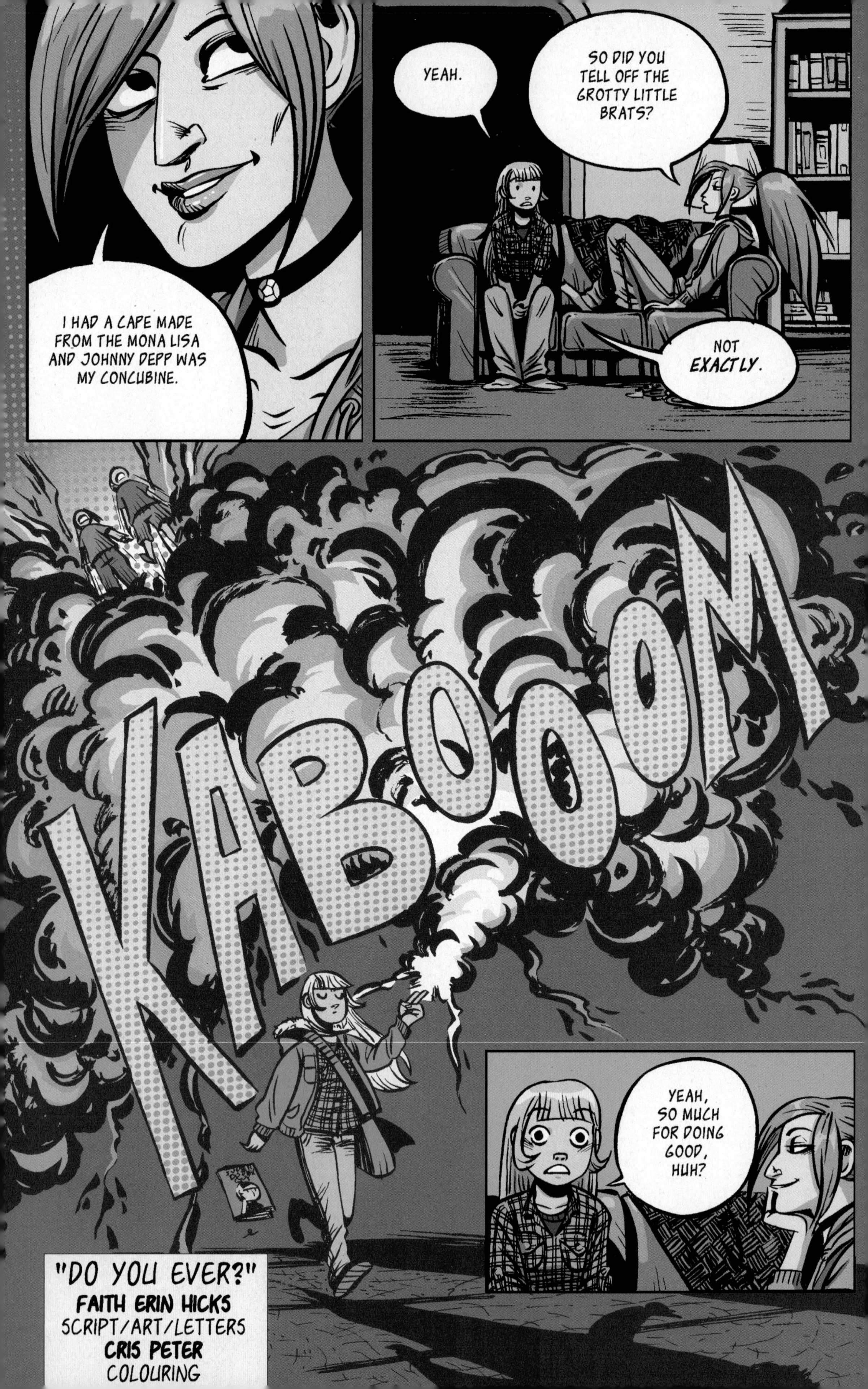
I HAD A CAPE MADE FROM THE MONA LISA AND JOHNNY DEPP WAS MY CONCUBINE.
YEAH.
SO DID YOU TELL OFF THE GROTTY LITTLE BRATS?
NOT *EXACTLY*.
KABOOOM!
YEAH, SO MUCH FOR DOING GOOD, HUH?
"DO YOU EVER?"
FAITH ERIN HICKS
SCRIPT/ART/LETTERS
CRIS PETER
COLOURING

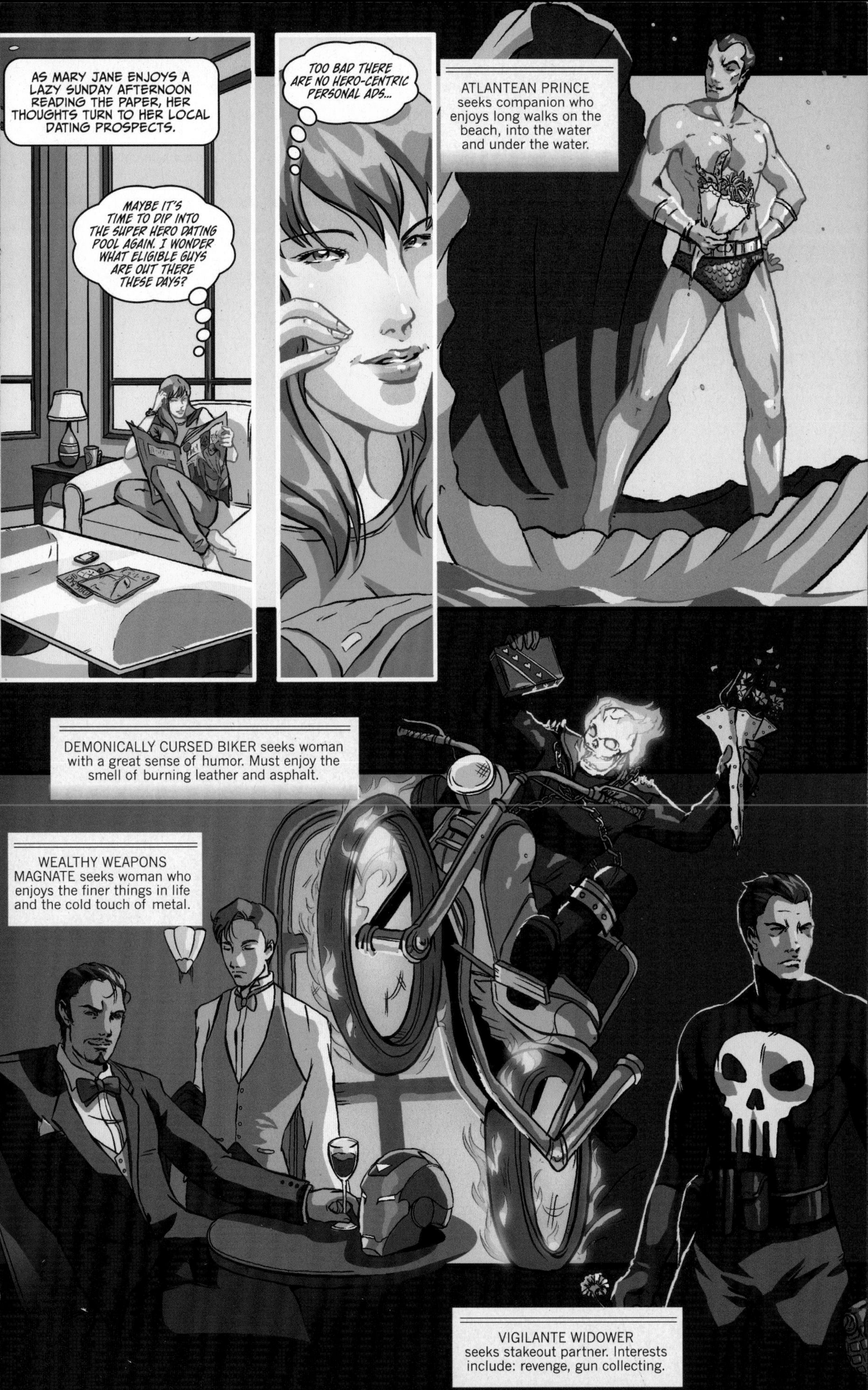

AS MARY JANE ENJOYS A LAZY SUNDAY AFTERNOON READING THE PAPER, HER THOUGHTS TURN TO HER LOCAL DATING PROSPECTS.
MAYBE IT'S TIME TO DIP INTO THE SUPER HERO DATING POOL AGAIN. I WONDER WHAT ELIGIBLE GUYS ARE OUT THERE THESE DAYS?
TOO BAD THERE ARE NO HERO-CENTRIC PERSONAL ADS...
ATLANTEAN PRINCE seeks companion who enjoys long walks on the beach, into the water and under the water.
DEMONICALLY CURSED BIKER seeks woman with a great sense of humor. Must enjoy the smell of burning leather and asphalt.
WEALTHY WEAPONS MAGNATE seeks woman who enjoys the finer things in life and the cold touch of metal.
VIGILANTE WIDOWER seeks stakeout partner. Interests include: revenge, gun collecting.

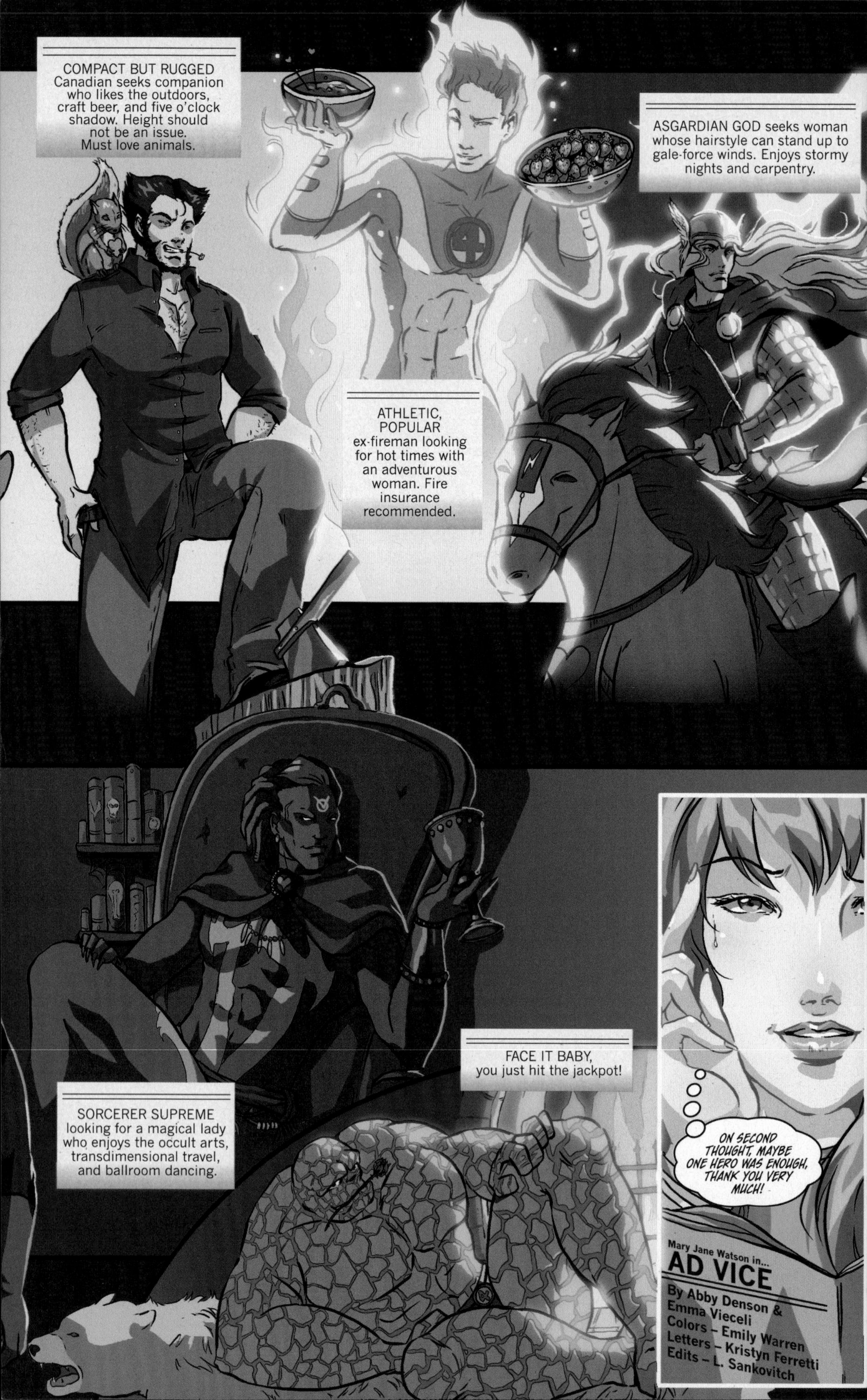
COMPACT BUT RUGGED Canadian seeks companion who likes the outdoors, craft beer, and five o'clock shadow. Height should not be an issue. Must love animals.
ASGARDIAN GOD seeks woman whose hairstyle can stand up to gale-force winds. Enjoys stormy nights and carpentry.
ATHLETIC, POPULAR ex-fireman looking for hot times with an adventurous woman. Fire insurance recommended.
FACE IT BABY, you just hit the jackpot!
SORCERER SUPREME looking for a magical lady who enjoys the occult arts, transdimensional travel, and ballroom dancing.
ON SECOND THOUGHT, MAYBE ONE HERO WAS ENOUGH, THANK YOU VERY MUCH!
Mary Jane Watson in...
AD VICE
By Abby Denson & Emma Vieceli
Colors – Emily Warren
Letters – Kristyn Ferretti
Edits – L. Sankovitch

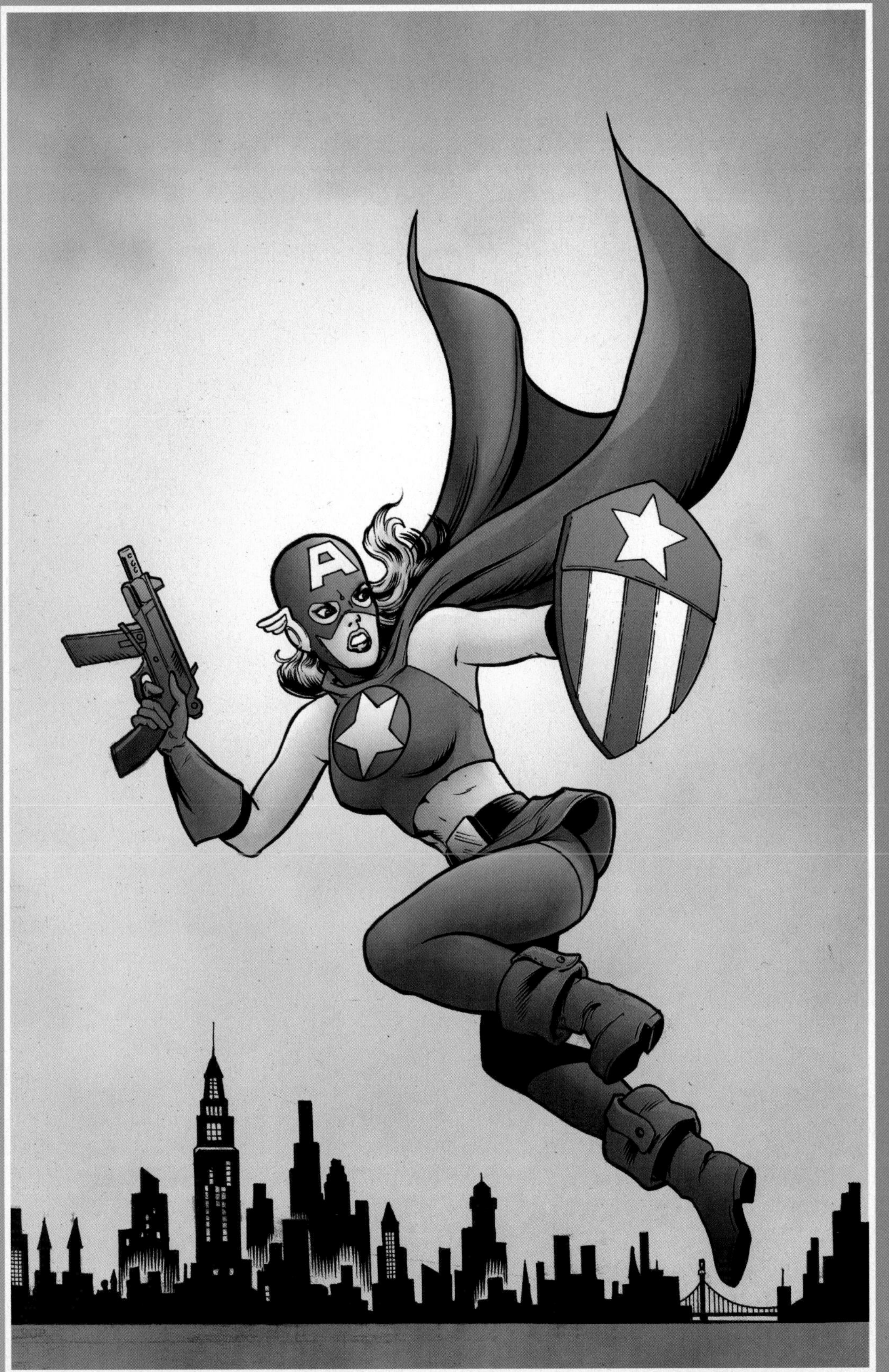

MISS AMERICA

Pencils by RAMONA FRADON Inks by REBECCA BUCHMAN Colors by JUNE CHUNG

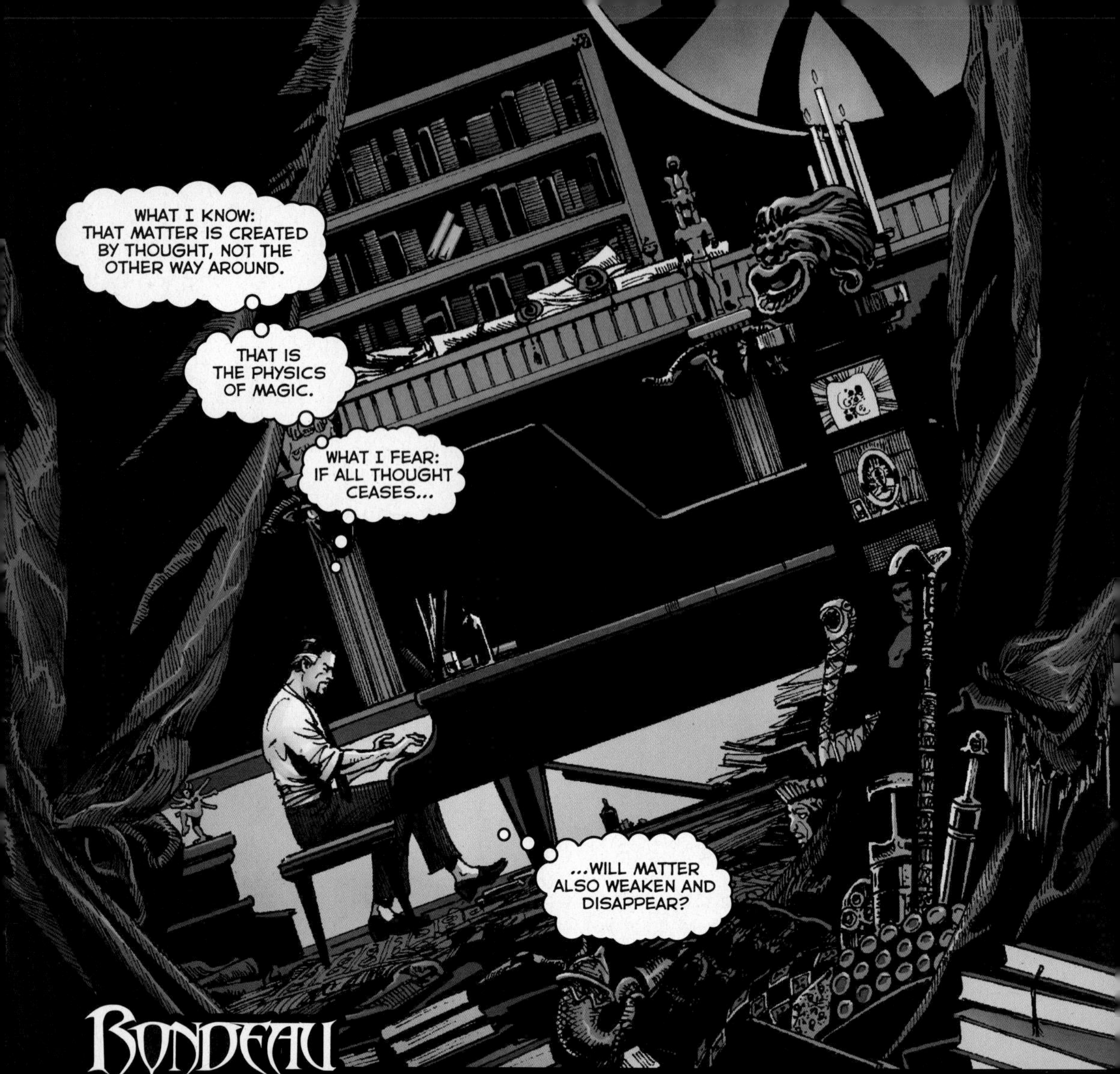
WHAT I KNOW: THAT MATTER IS CREATED BY THOUGHT, NOT THE OTHER WAY AROUND.
THAT IS THE PHYSICS OF MAGIC.
WHAT I FEAR: IF ALL THOUGHT CEASES...
...WILL MATTER ALSO WEAKEN AND DISAPPEAR?

RONDEAU

Script by Christine Boylan · Art by Cynthia Martin · Color Art by June Chung · Letters by Kathleen Marinaccio

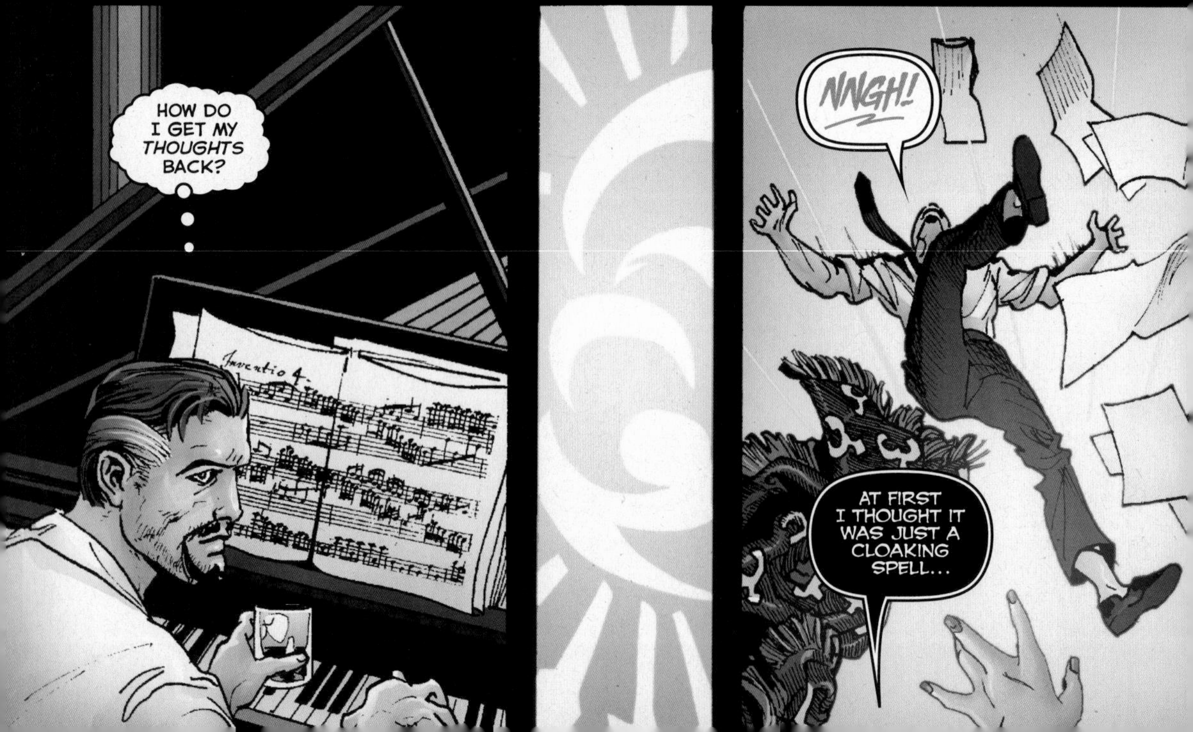
HOW DO I GET MY *THOUGHTS* BACK?
Inventio 4.
NNGH!
AT FIRST I THOUGHT IT WAS JUST A CLOAKING SPELL...

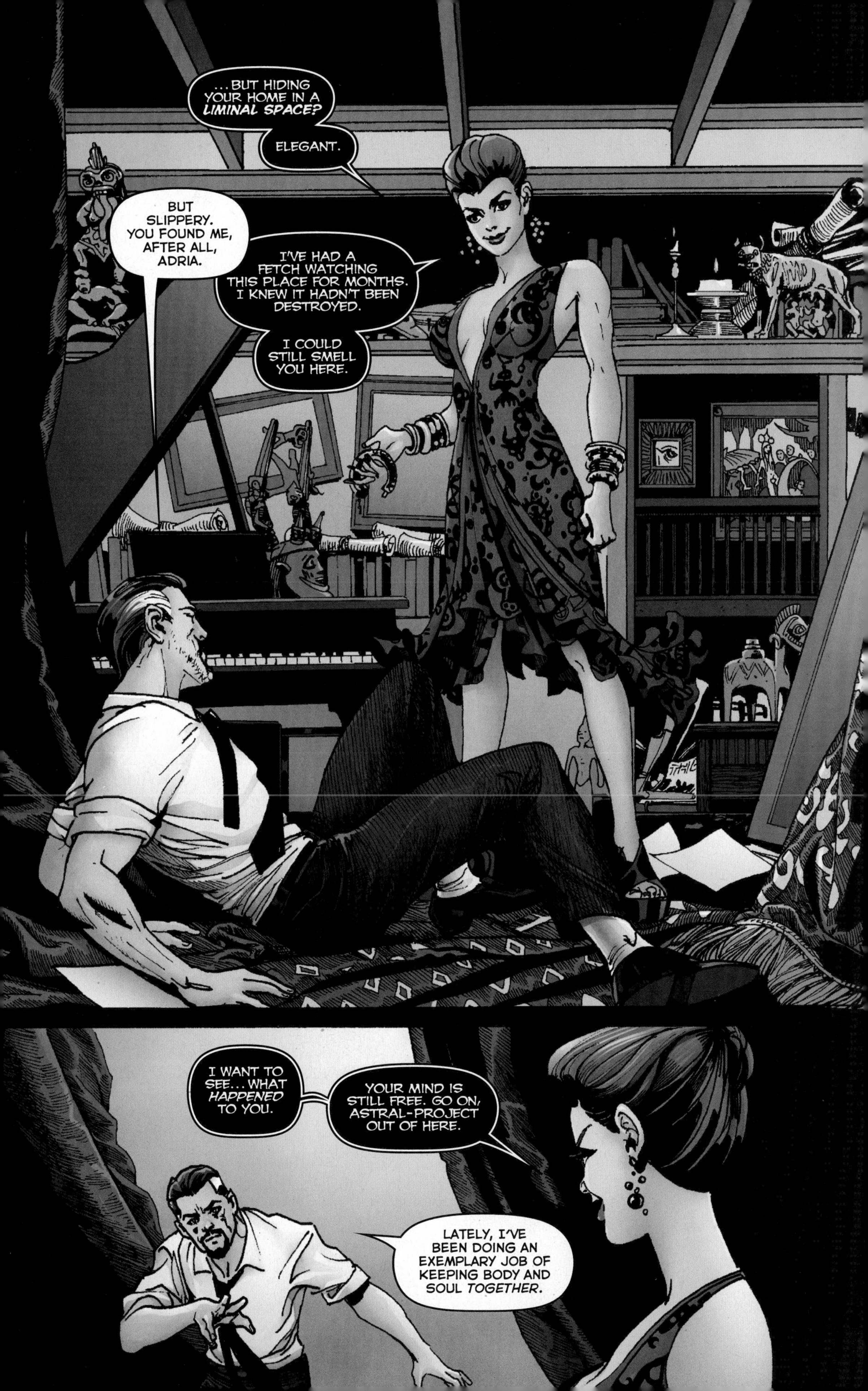
...BUT HIDING YOUR HOME IN A LIMINAL SPACE?
ELEGANT.
BUT SLIPPERY. YOU FOUND ME, AFTER ALL, ADRIA.
I'VE HAD A FETCH WATCHING THIS PLACE FOR MONTHS. I KNEW IT HADN'T BEEN DESTROYED.
I COULD STILL SMELL YOU HERE.
I WANT TO SEE... WHAT HAPPENED TO YOU.
YOUR MIND IS STILL FREE. GO ON, ASTRAL-PROJECT OUT OF HERE.
LATELY, I'VE BEEN DOING AN EXEMPLARY JOB OF KEEPING BODY AND SOUL TOGETHER.

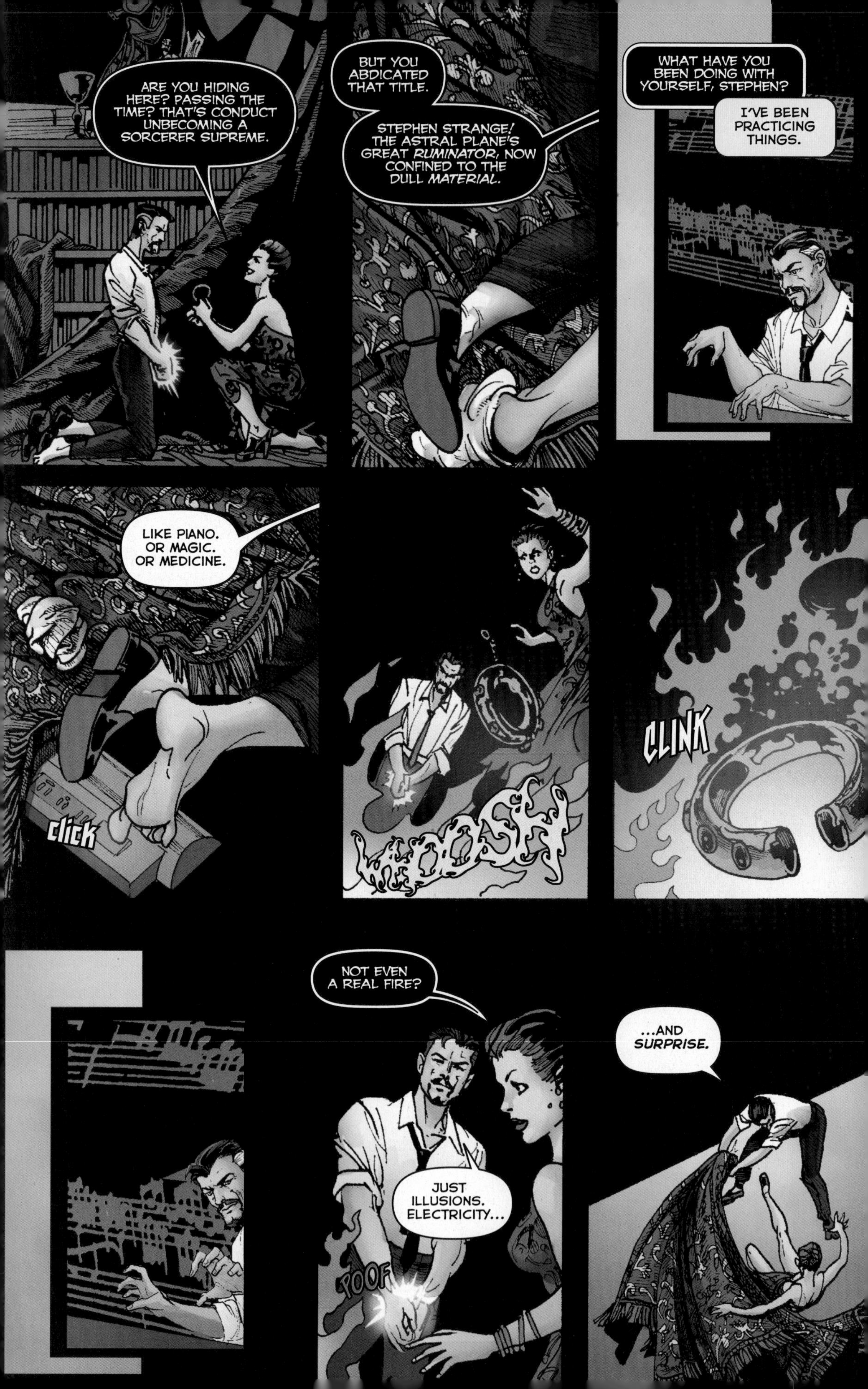
ARE YOU HIDING HERE? PASSING THE TIME? THAT'S CONDUCT UNBECOMING A SORCERER SUPREME.
BUT YOU ABDICATED THAT TITLE.
STEPHEN STRANGE! THE ASTRAL PLANE'S GREAT RUMINATOR, NOW CONFINED TO THE DULL MATERIAL.
WHAT HAVE YOU BEEN DOING WITH YOURSELF, STEPHEN?
I'VE BEEN PRACTICING THINGS.
LIKE PIANO. OR MAGIC. OR MEDICINE.
CLICK
WHOOSH
CLINK
NOT EVEN A REAL FIRE?
JUST ILLUSIONS. ELECTRICITY...
POOF
...AND SURPRISE.

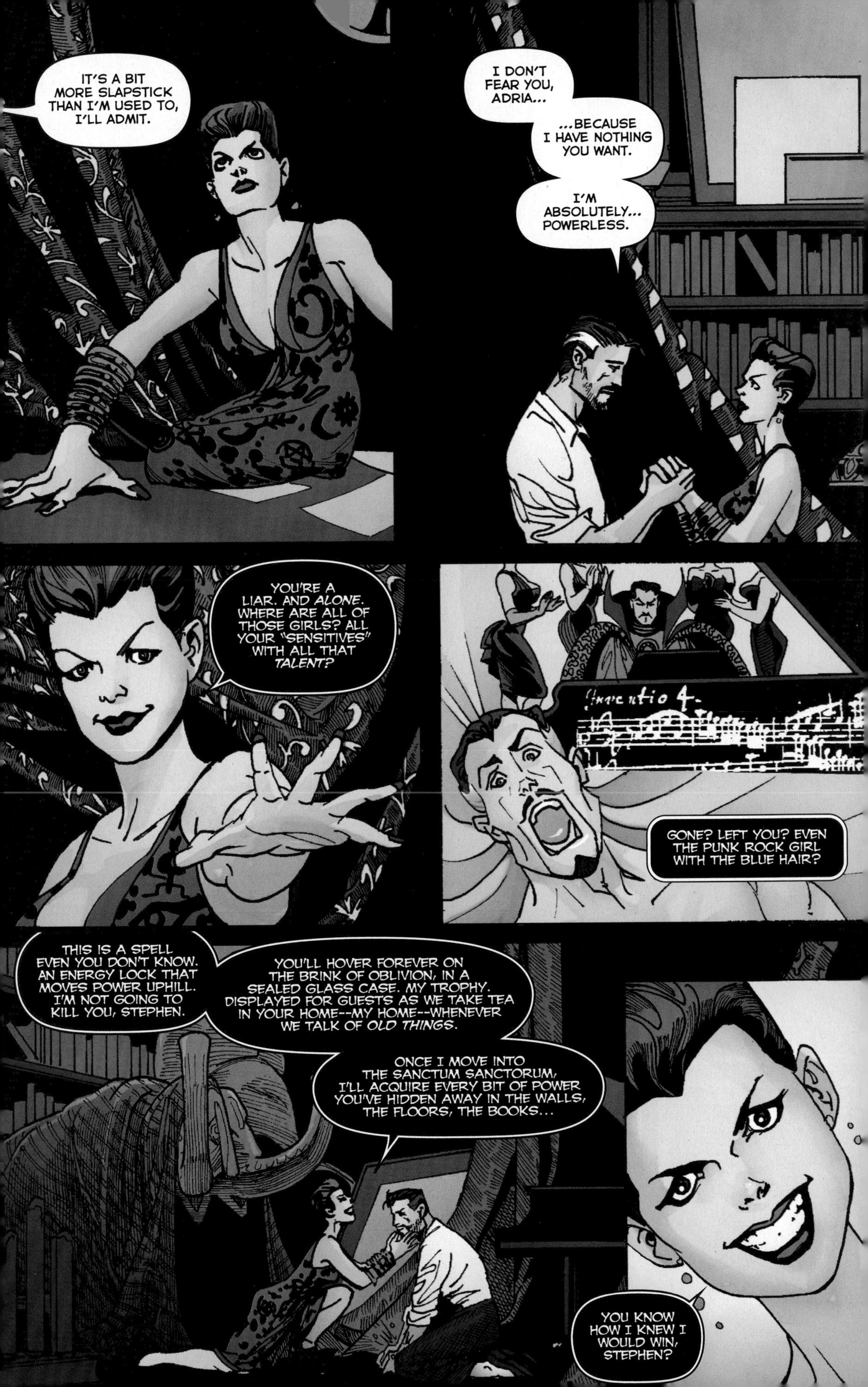
IT'S A BIT MORE SLAPSTICK THAN I'M USED TO, I'LL ADMIT.
I DON'T FEAR YOU, ADRIA...
...BECAUSE I HAVE NOTHING YOU WANT.
I'M ABSOLUTELY... POWERLESS.
YOU'RE A LIAR. AND *ALONE.* WHERE ARE ALL OF THOSE GIRLS? ALL YOUR "SENSITIVES" WITH ALL THAT *TALENT?*
GONE? LEFT YOU? EVEN THE PUNK ROCK GIRL WITH THE BLUE HAIR?
THIS IS A SPELL EVEN YOU DON'T KNOW. AN ENERGY LOCK THAT MOVES POWER UPHILL. I'M NOT GOING TO KILL YOU, STEPHEN.
YOU'LL HOVER FOREVER ON THE BRINK OF OBLIVION, IN A SEALED GLASS CASE. MY TROPHY. DISPLAYED FOR GUESTS AS WE TAKE TEA IN YOUR HOME--MY HOME--WHENEVER WE TALK OF *OLD THINGS.*
ONCE I MOVE INTO THE SANCTUM SANCTORUM, I'LL ACQUIRE EVERY BIT OF POWER YOU'VE HIDDEN AWAY IN THE WALLS, THE FLOORS, THE BOOKS...
YOU KNOW HOW I KNEW I WOULD WIN, STEPHEN?

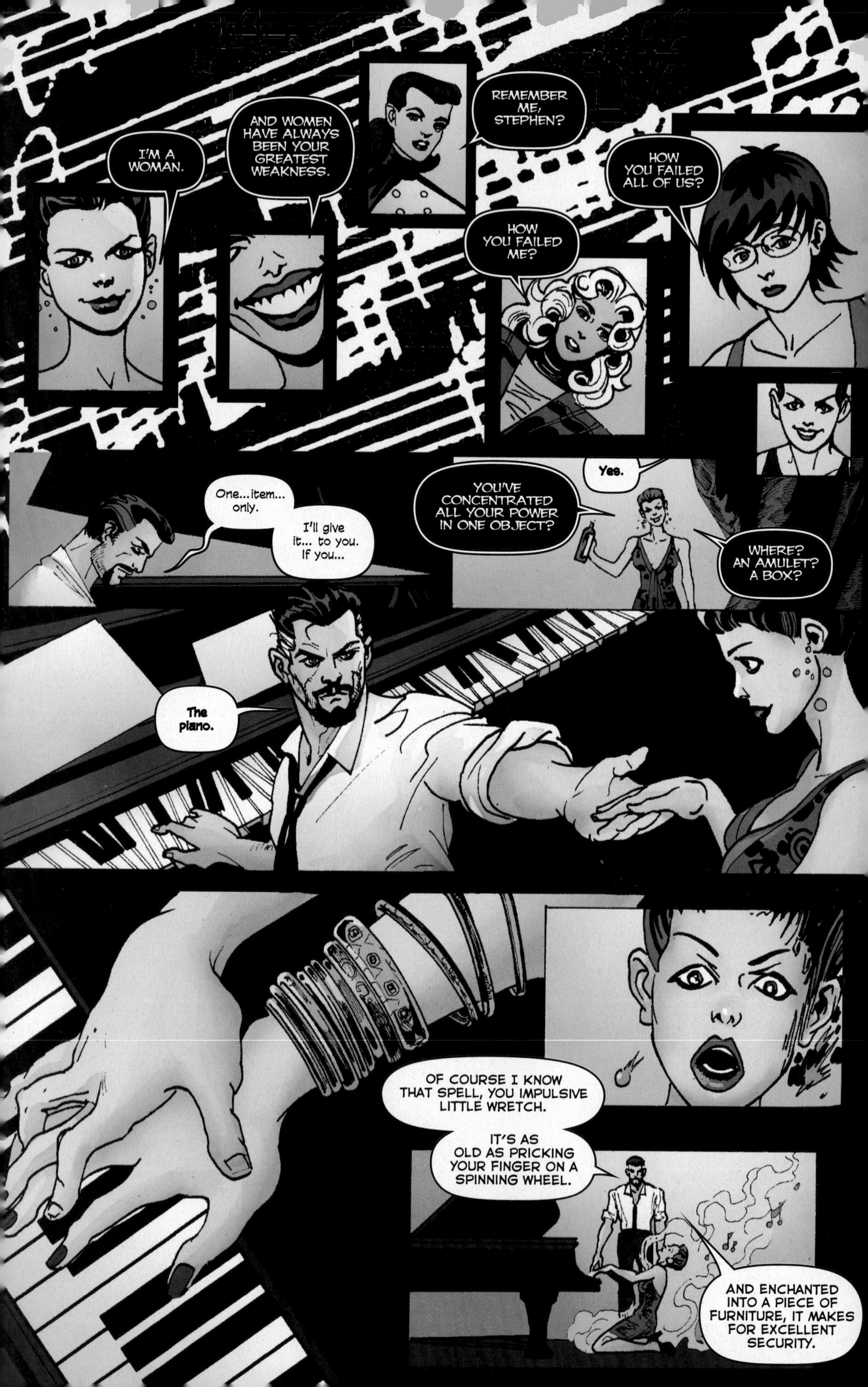
I'M A WOMAN.
AND WOMEN HAVE ALWAYS BEEN YOUR GREATEST WEAKNESS.
REMEMBER ME, STEPHEN?
HOW YOU FAILED ME?
HOW YOU FAILED ALL OF US?
One...item... only.
I'll give it... to you. If you...
Yes.
YOU'VE CONCENTRATED ALL YOUR POWER IN ONE OBJECT?
WHERE? AN AMULET? A BOX?
The piano.
OF COURSE I KNOW THAT SPELL, YOU IMPULSIVE LITTLE WRETCH.
IT'S AS OLD AS PRICKING YOUR FINGER ON A SPINNING WHEEL.
AND ENCHANTED INTO A PIECE OF FURNITURE, IT MAKES FOR EXCELLENT SECURITY.

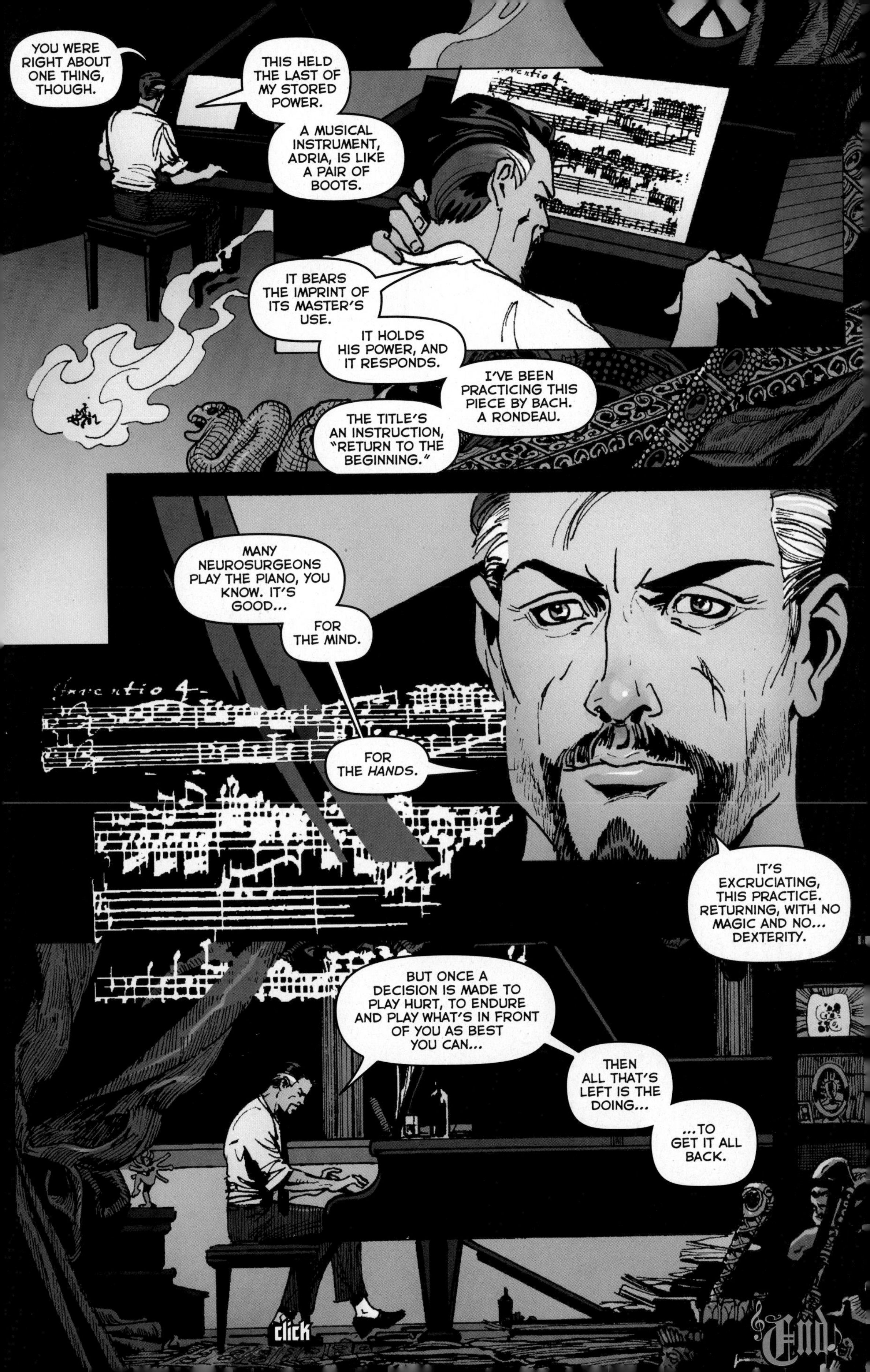
YOU WERE RIGHT ABOUT ONE THING, THOUGH.
THIS HELD THE LAST OF MY STORED POWER.
A MUSICAL INSTRUMENT, ADRIA, IS LIKE A PAIR OF BOOTS.
IT BEARS THE IMPRINT OF ITS MASTER'S USE.
IT HOLDS HIS POWER, AND IT RESPONDS.
I'VE BEEN PRACTICING THIS PIECE BY BACH. A RONDEAU.
THE TITLE'S AN INSTRUCTION, "RETURN TO THE BEGINNING."
MANY NEUROSURGEONS PLAY THE PIANO, YOU KNOW. IT'S GOOD...
FOR THE MIND.
FOR THE *HANDS*.
IT'S EXCRUCIATING, THIS PRACTICE. RETURNING, WITH NO MAGIC AND NO... DEXTERITY.
BUT ONCE A DECISION IS MADE TO PLAY HURT, TO ENDURE AND PLAY WHAT'S IN FRONT OF YOU AS BEST YOU CAN...
THEN ALL THAT'S LEFT IS THE DOING...
...TO GET IT ALL BACK.
click
End

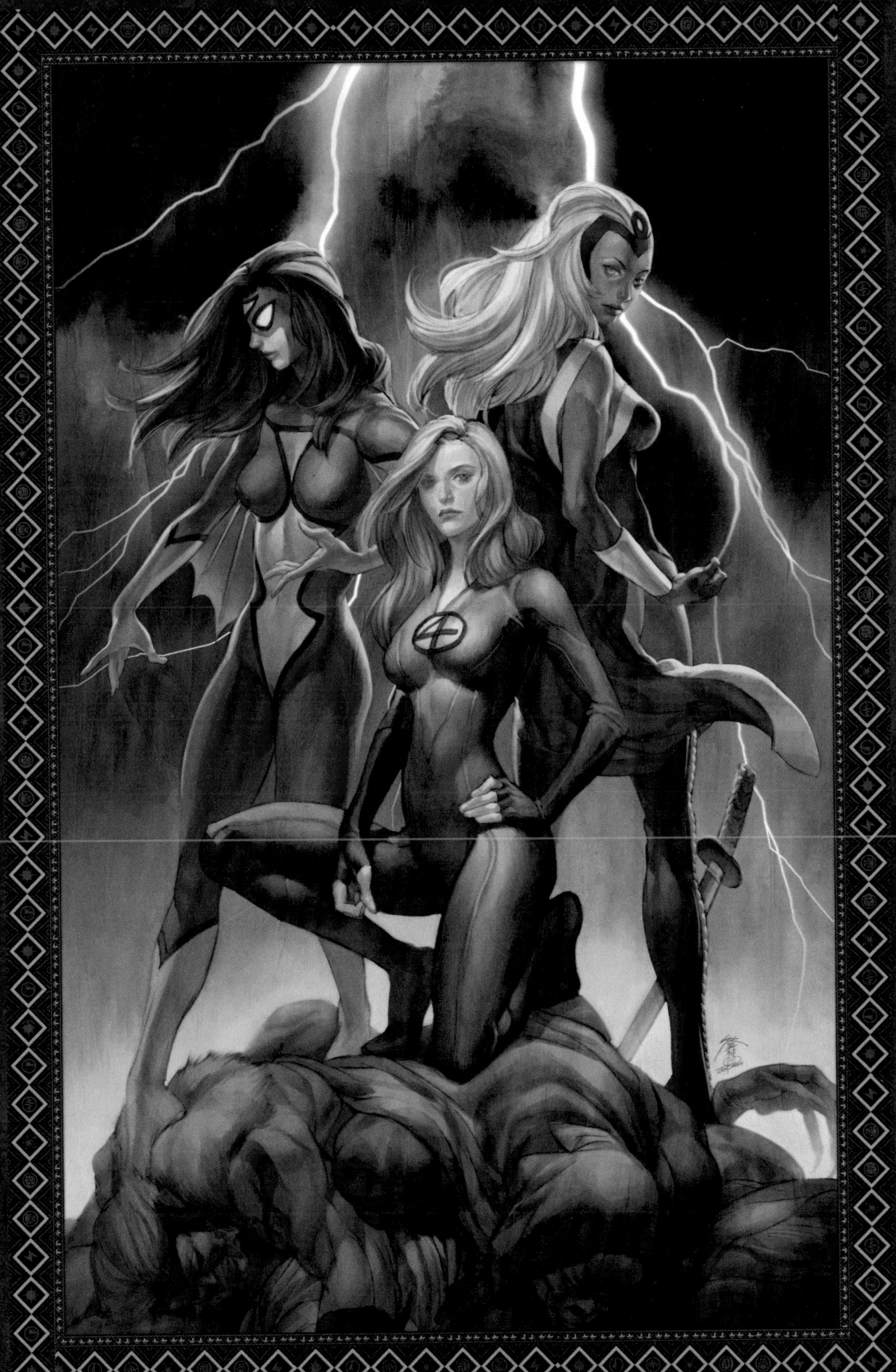

GIRL COMICS #3

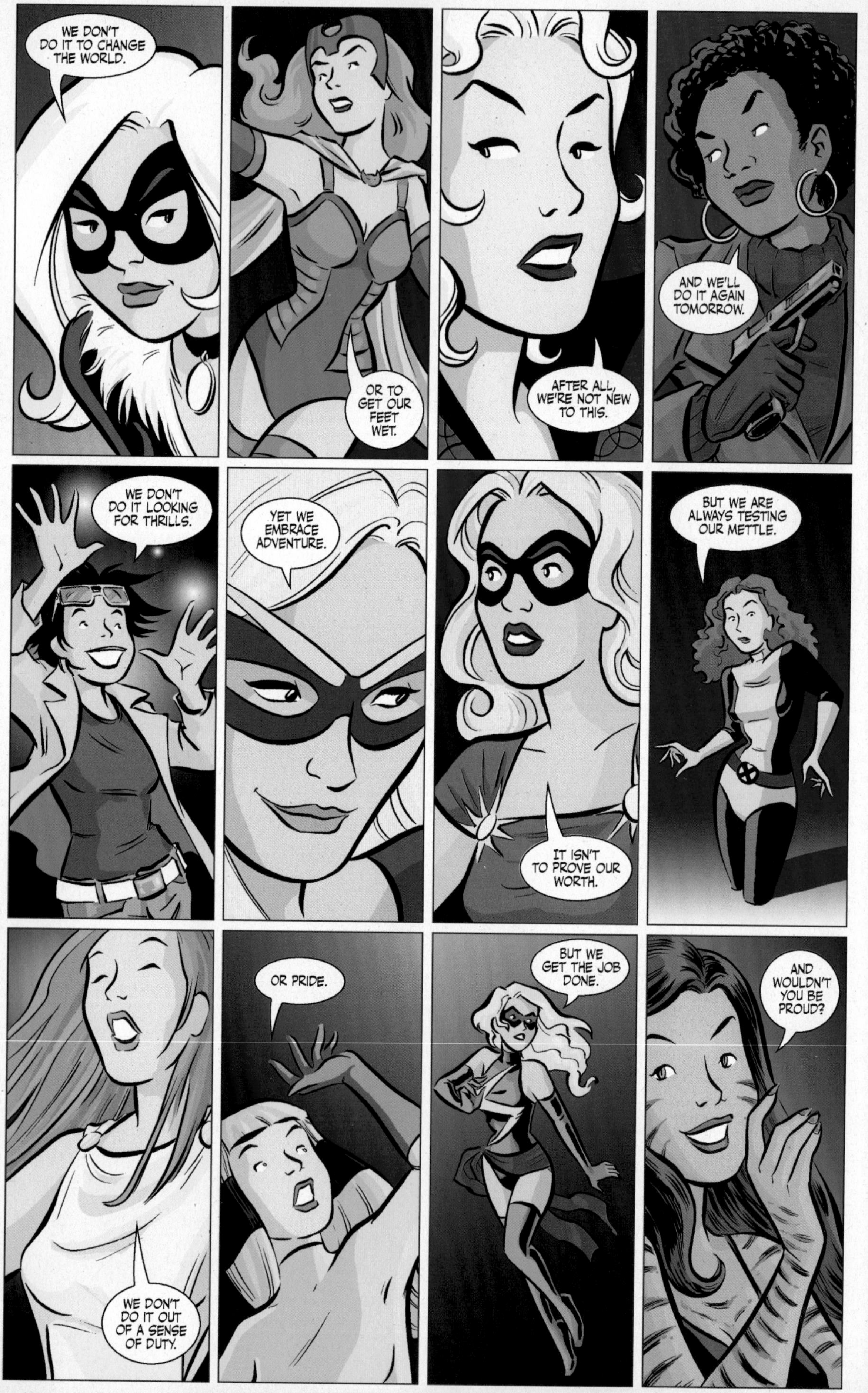
WE DON'T DO IT TO CHANGE THE WORLD.
OR TO GET OUR FEET WET.
AFTER ALL, WE'RE NOT NEW TO THIS.
AND WE'LL DO IT AGAIN TOMORROW.
WE DON'T DO IT LOOKING FOR THRILLS.
YET WE EMBRACE ADVENTURE.
IT ISN'T TO PROVE OUR WORTH.
BUT WE ARE ALWAYS TESTING OUR METTLE.
WE DON'T DO IT OUT OF A SENSE OF DUTY.
OR PRIDE.
BUT WE GET THE JOB DONE.
AND WOULDN'T YOU BE PROUD?

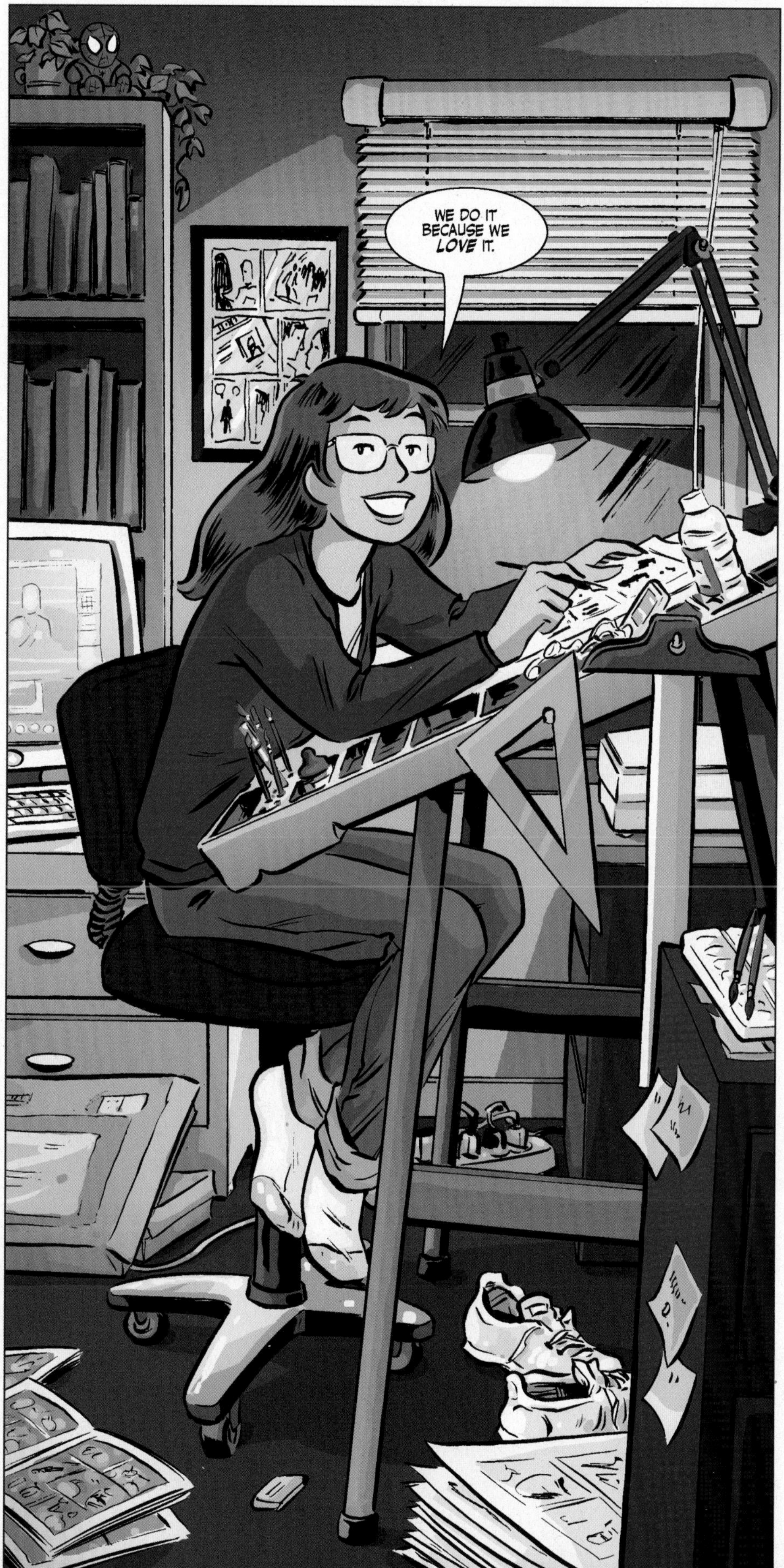
WE DO IT BECAUSE WE LOVE IT.

GIRL COMICS

Part Three of Three

INTRODUCTION:
COLLEEN COOVER

COVER ART:
JO CHEN

PRODUCTION:
IRENE LEE

ASSISTANT EDITORS:
SANA AMANAT
& RACHEL PINNELAS

ASSOCIATE EDITOR:
LAUREN SANKOVITCH

EDITOR:
JEANINE SCHAEFER

EDITOR IN CHIEF:
JOE QUESADA

PUBLISHER:
DAN BUCKLEY

EXEC. PRODUCER:
ALAN FINE

SPECIAL THANKS:
SPRING HOTELING

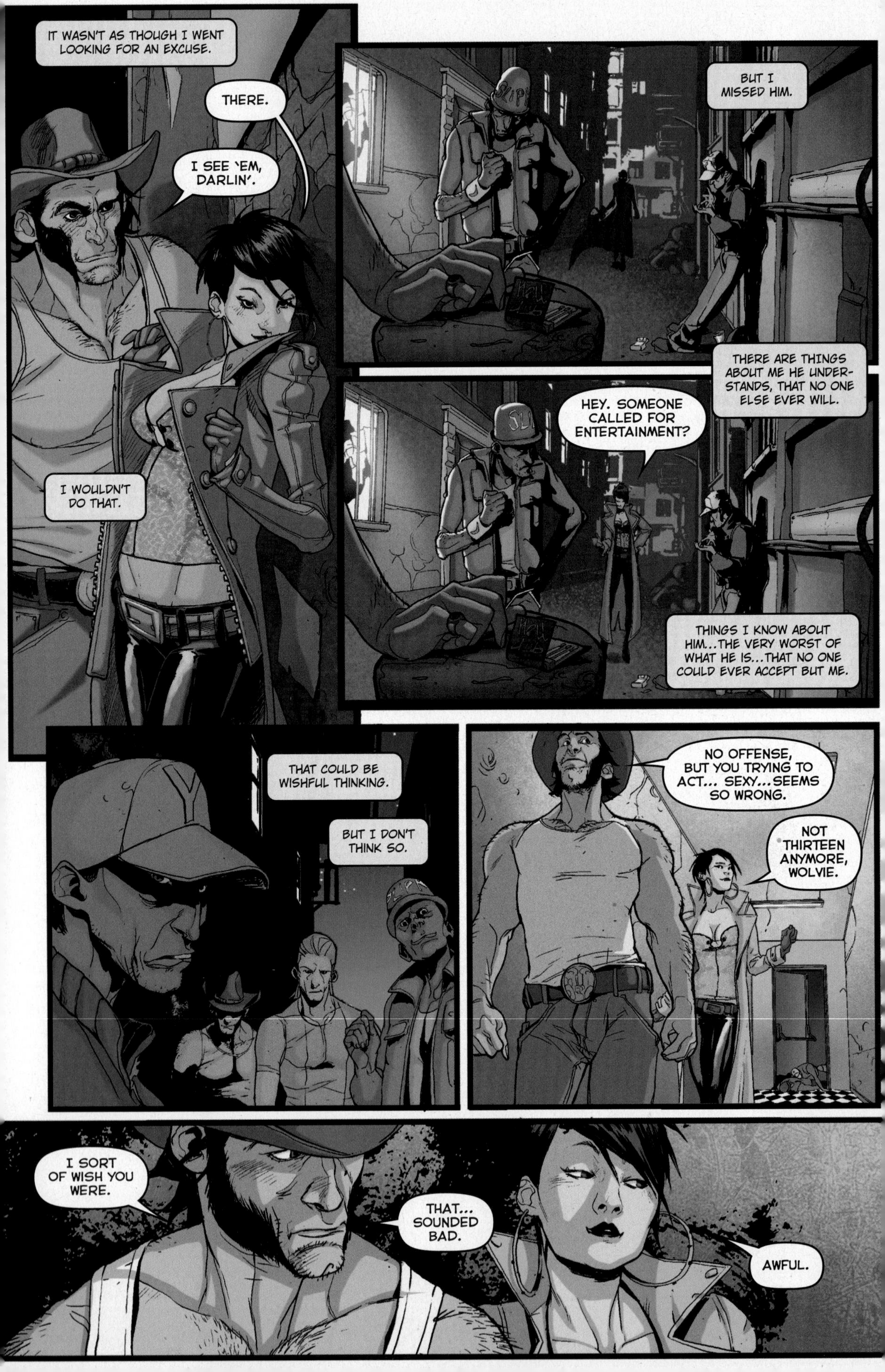

IT WASN'T AS THOUGH I WENT LOOKING FOR AN EXCUSE.
THERE.
I SEE 'EM, DARLIN'.
I WOULDN'T DO THAT.
BUT I MISSED HIM.
THERE ARE THINGS ABOUT ME HE UNDER-STANDS, THAT NO ONE ELSE EVER WILL.
HEY. SOMEONE CALLED FOR ENTERTAINMENT?
THINGS I KNOW ABOUT HIM...THE VERY WORST OF WHAT HE IS...THAT NO ONE COULD EVER ACCEPT BUT ME.
THAT COULD BE WISHFUL THINKING.
BUT I DON'T THINK SO.
NO OFFENSE, BUT YOU TRYING TO ACT... SEXY...SEEMS SO WRONG.
NOT THIRTEEN ANYMORE, WOLVIE.
I SORT OF WISH YOU WERE.
THAT... SOUNDED BAD.
AWFUL.

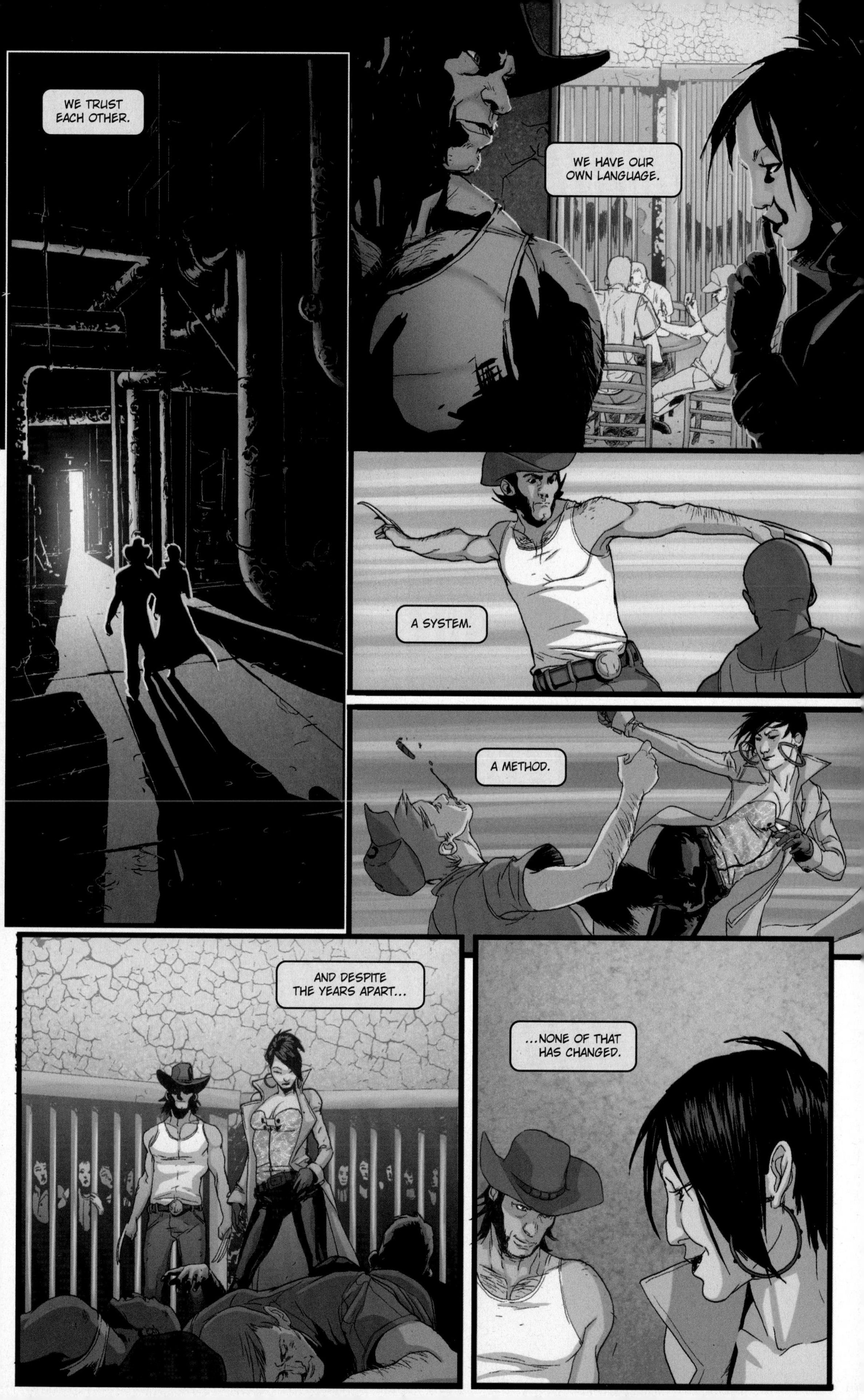
WE TRUST EACH OTHER.
WE HAVE OUR OWN LANGUAGE.
A SYSTEM.
A METHOD.
AND DESPITE THE YEARS APART...
...NONE OF THAT HAS CHANGED.

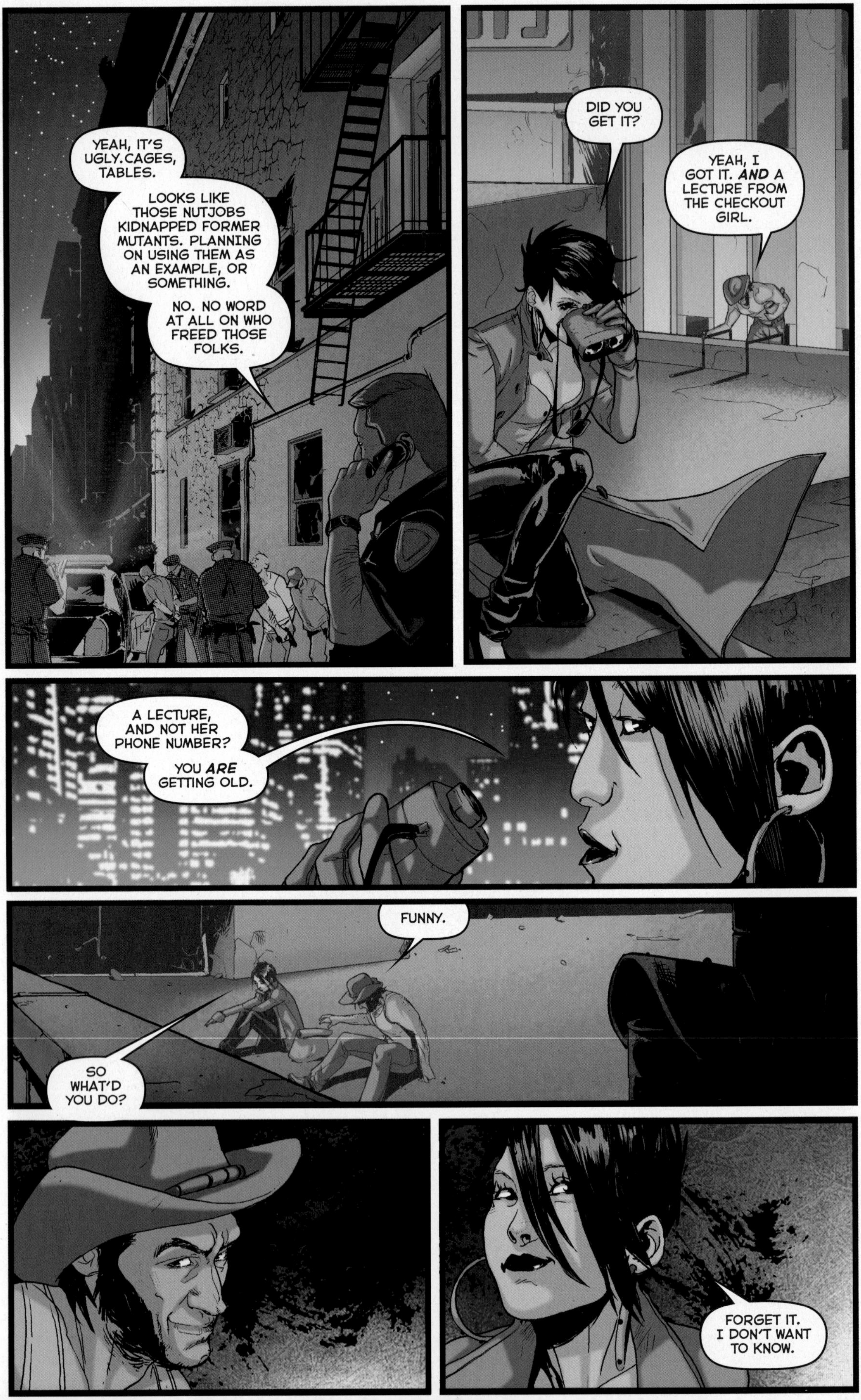
YEAH, IT'S UGLY.CAGES, TABLES.
LOOKS LIKE THOSE NUTJOBS KIDNAPPED FORMER MUTANTS. PLANNING ON USING THEM AS AN EXAMPLE, OR SOMETHING.
NO. NO WORD AT ALL ON WHO FREED THOSE FOLKS.
DID YOU GET IT?
YEAH, I GOT IT. ***AND*** A LECTURE FROM THE CHECKOUT GIRL.
A LECTURE, AND NOT HER PHONE NUMBER?
YOU ***ARE*** GETTING OLD.
FUNNY.
SO WHAT'D YOU DO?
FORGET IT. I DON'T WANT TO KNOW.

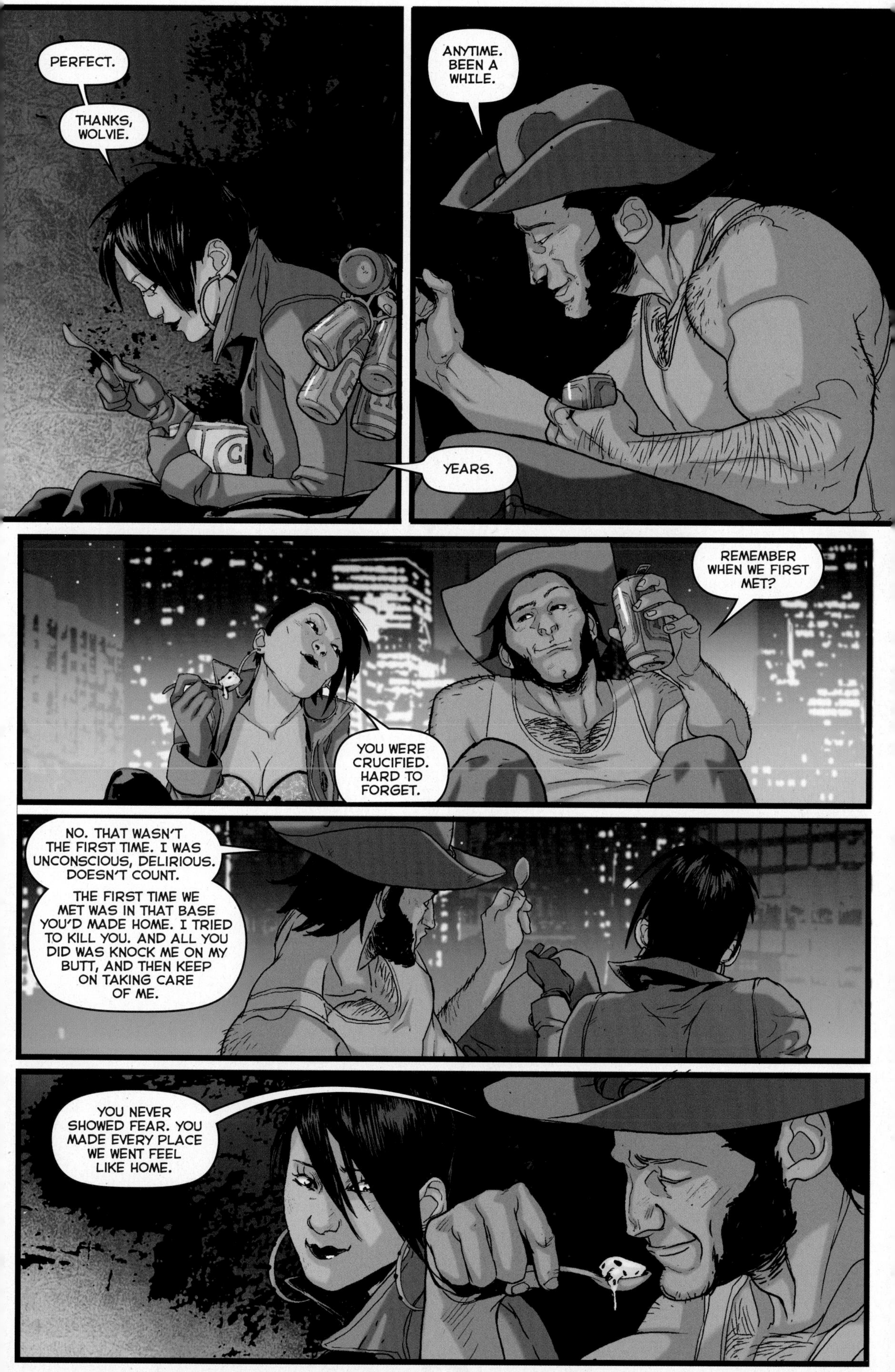
PERFECT.
THANKS, WOLVIE.
ANYTIME. BEEN A WHILE.
YEARS.
REMEMBER WHEN WE FIRST MET?
YOU WERE CRUCIFIED. HARD TO FORGET.
NO. THAT WASN'T THE FIRST TIME. I WAS UNCONSCIOUS, DELIRIOUS. DOESN'T COUNT.
THE FIRST TIME WE MET WAS IN THAT BASE YOU'D MADE HOME. I TRIED TO KILL YOU. AND ALL YOU DID WAS KNOCK ME ON MY BUTT, AND THEN KEEP ON TAKING CARE OF ME.
YOU NEVER SHOWED FEAR. YOU MADE EVERY PLACE WE WENT FEEL LIKE HOME.

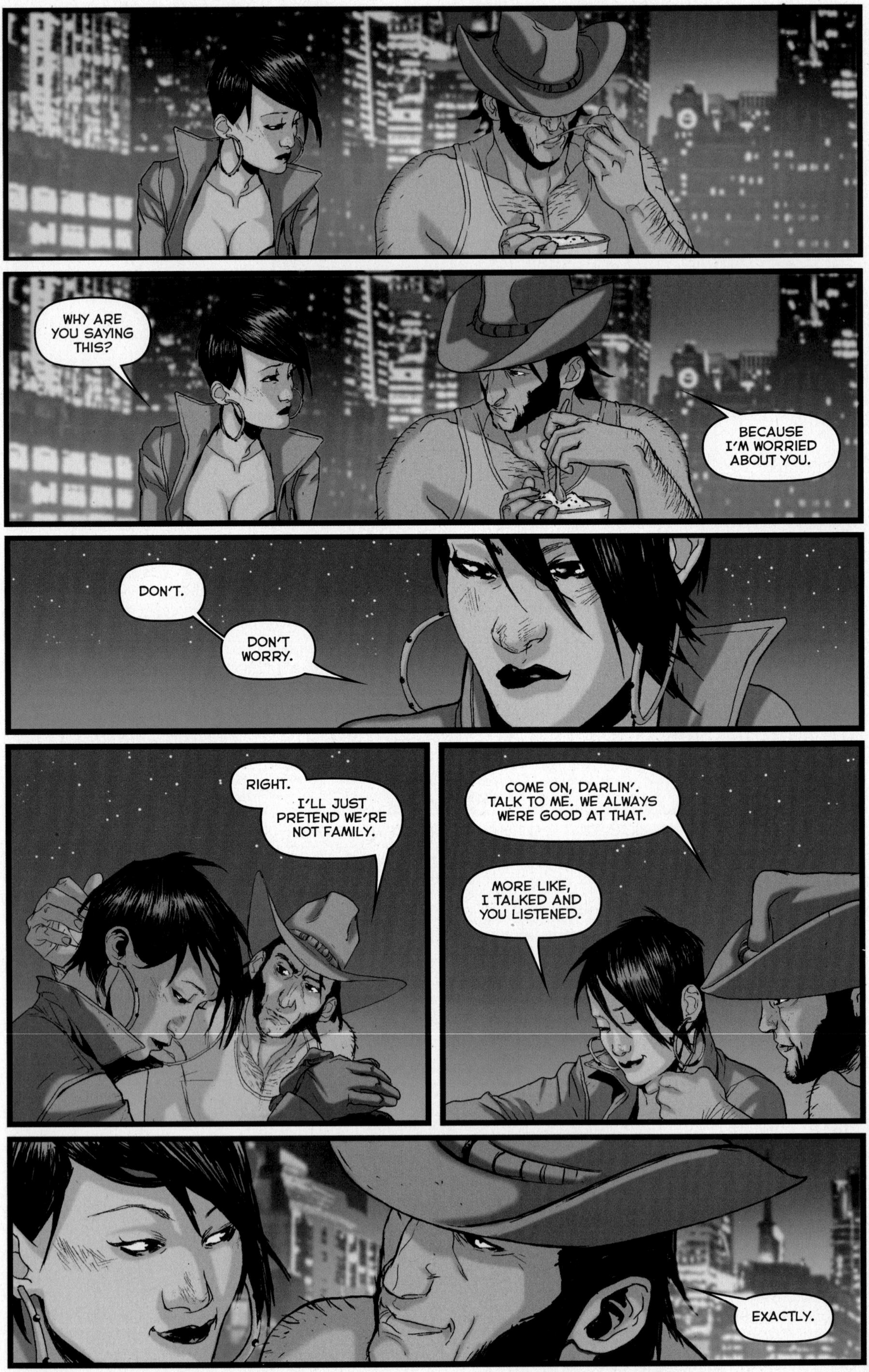
WHY ARE YOU SAYING THIS?
BECAUSE I'M WORRIED ABOUT YOU.
DON'T.
DON'T WORRY.
RIGHT.
I'LL JUST PRETEND WE'RE NOT FAMILY.
COME ON, DARLIN'. TALK TO ME. WE ALWAYS WERE GOOD AT THAT.
MORE LIKE, I TALKED AND YOU LISTENED.
EXACTLY.

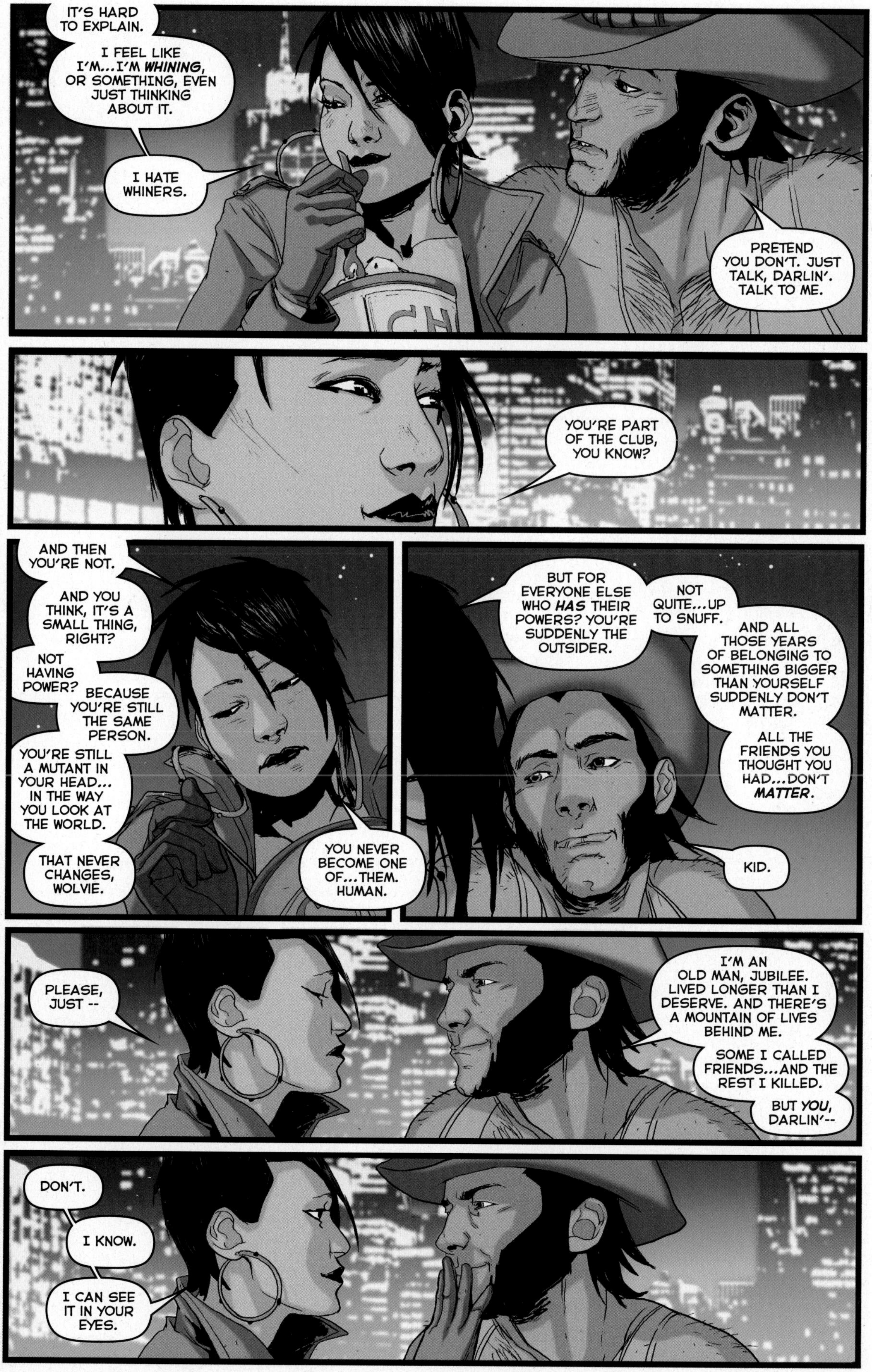
IT'S HARD TO EXPLAIN.
I FEEL LIKE I'M...I'M WHINING, OR SOMETHING, EVEN JUST THINKING ABOUT IT.
I HATE WHINERS.
PRETEND YOU DON'T. JUST TALK, DARLIN'. TALK TO ME.
YOU'RE PART OF THE CLUB, YOU KNOW?
AND THEN YOU'RE NOT.
AND YOU THINK, IT'S A SMALL THING, RIGHT?
NOT HAVING POWER?
BECAUSE YOU'RE STILL THE SAME PERSON.
YOU'RE STILL A MUTANT IN YOUR HEAD... IN THE WAY YOU LOOK AT THE WORLD.
THAT NEVER CHANGES, WOLVIE.
YOU NEVER BECOME ONE OF...THEM. HUMAN.
BUT FOR EVERYONE ELSE WHO HAS THEIR POWERS? YOU'RE SUDDENLY THE OUTSIDER.
NOT QUITE...UP TO SNUFF.
AND ALL THOSE YEARS OF BELONGING TO SOMETHING BIGGER THAN YOURSELF SUDDENLY DON'T MATTER.
ALL THE FRIENDS YOU THOUGHT YOU HAD...DON'T MATTER.
KID.
PLEASE, JUST --
I'M AN OLD MAN, JUBILEE. LIVED LONGER THAN I DESERVE. AND THERE'S A MOUNTAIN OF LIVES BEHIND ME.
SOME I CALLED FRIENDS...AND THE REST I KILLED.
BUT YOU, DARLIN'--
DON'T.
I KNOW.
I CAN SEE IT IN YOUR EYES.

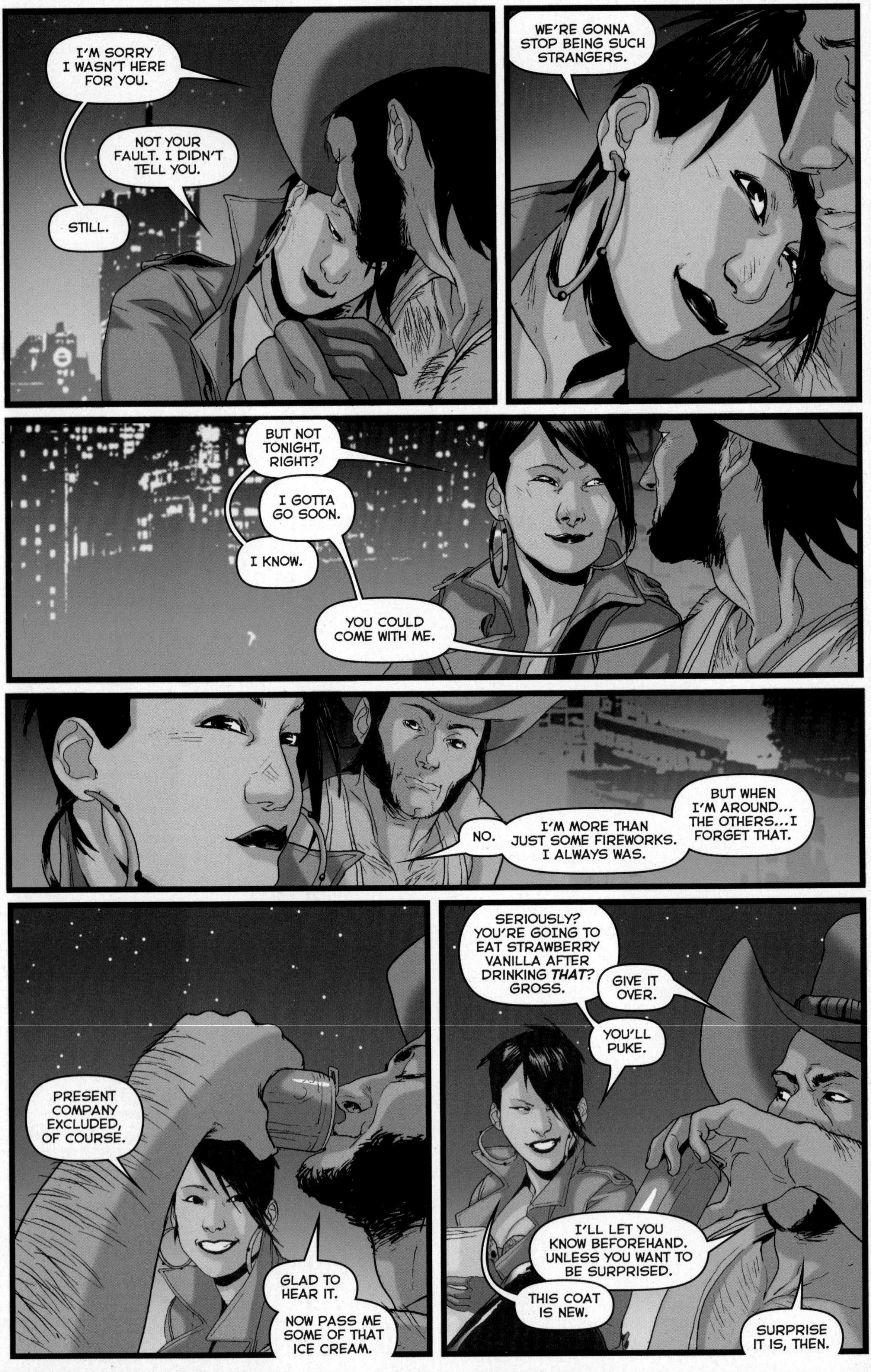
I'M SORRY I WASN'T HERE FOR YOU.
NOT YOUR FAULT. I DIDN'T TELL YOU.
STILL.
WE'RE GONNA STOP BEING SUCH STRANGERS.
BUT NOT TONIGHT, RIGHT?
I GOTTA GO SOON.
I KNOW.
YOU COULD COME WITH ME.
NO.
I'M MORE THAN JUST SOME FIREWORKS. I ALWAYS WAS.
BUT WHEN I'M AROUND... THE OTHERS...I FORGET THAT.
PRESENT COMPANY EXCLUDED, OF COURSE.
GLAD TO HEAR IT.
NOW PASS ME SOME OF THAT ICE CREAM.
SERIOUSLY? YOU'RE GOING TO EAT STRAWBERRY VANILLA AFTER DRINKING *THAT*? GROSS.
GIVE IT OVER.
YOU'LL PUKE.
I'LL LET YOU KNOW BEFOREHAND. UNLESS YOU WANT TO BE SURPRISED.
THIS COAT IS NEW.
SURPRISE IT IS, THEN.

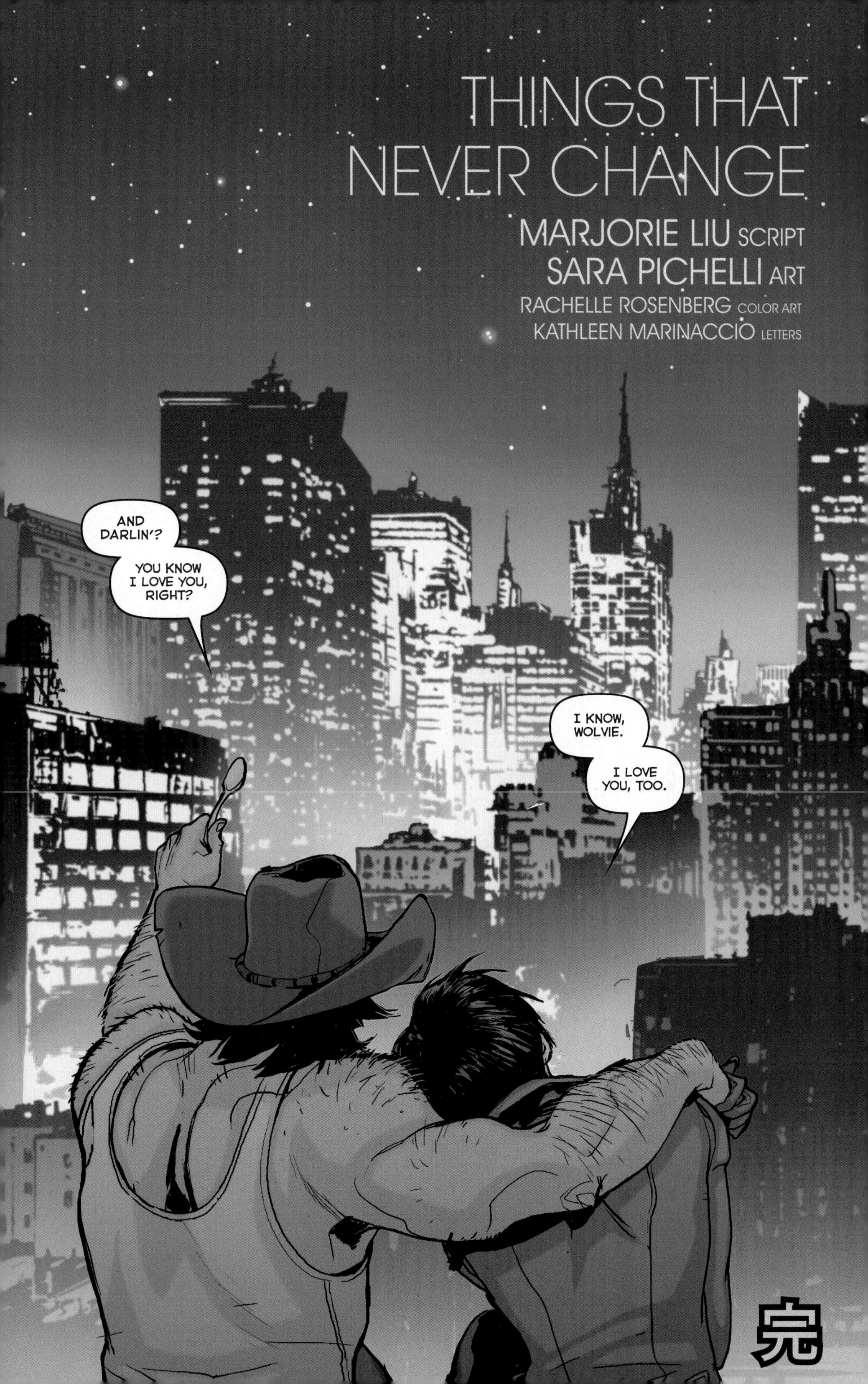
THINGS THAT NEVER CHANGE
MARJORIE LIU SCRIPT
SARA PICHELLI ART
RACHELLE ROSENBERG COLOR ART
KATHLEEN MARINACCIO LETTERS
AND DARLIN'?
YOU KNOW I LOVE YOU, RIGHT?
I KNOW, WOLVIE.
I LOVE YOU, TOO.
完

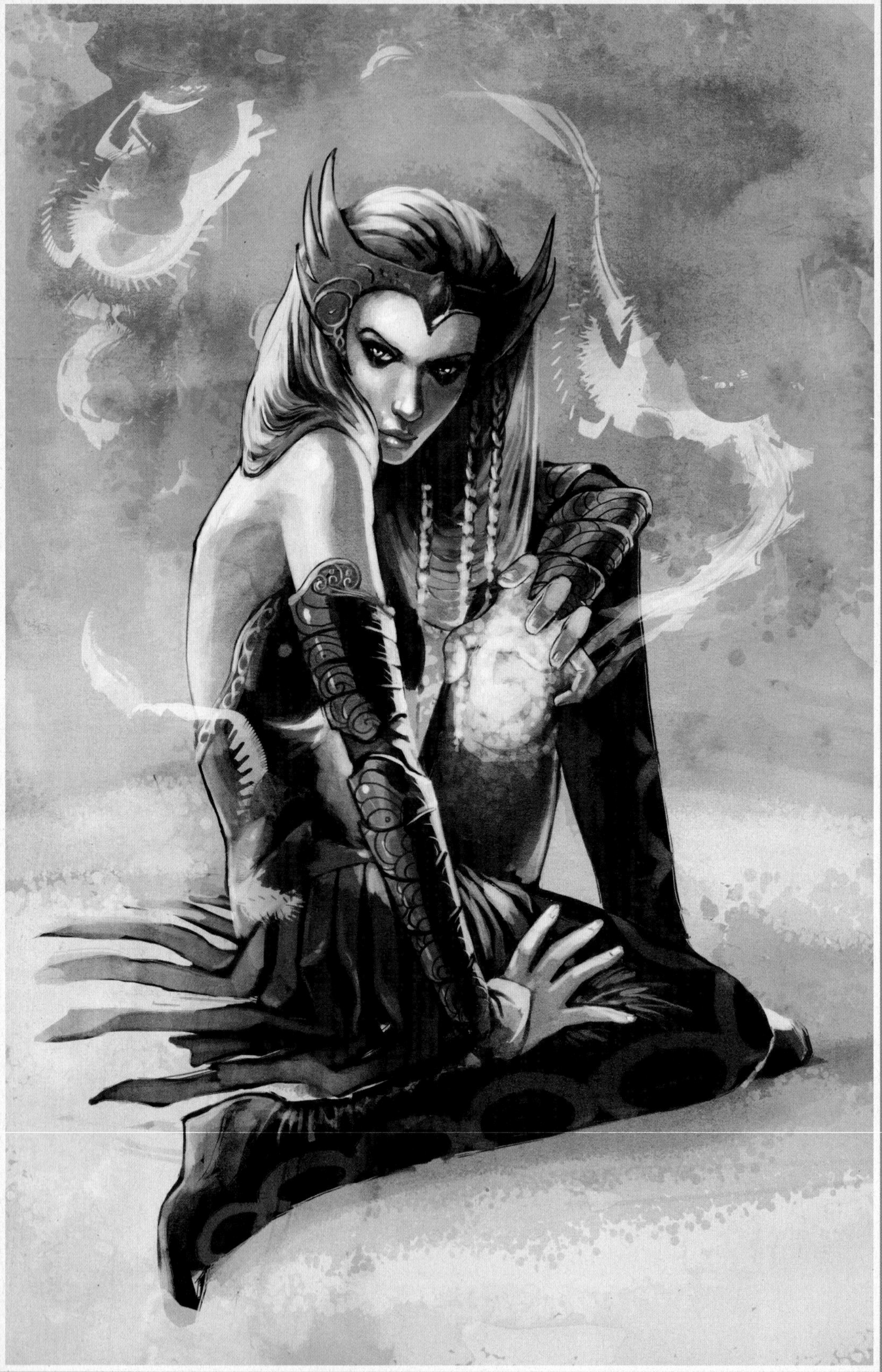

AMORA THE ENCHANTRESS

By STEPHANIE HANS

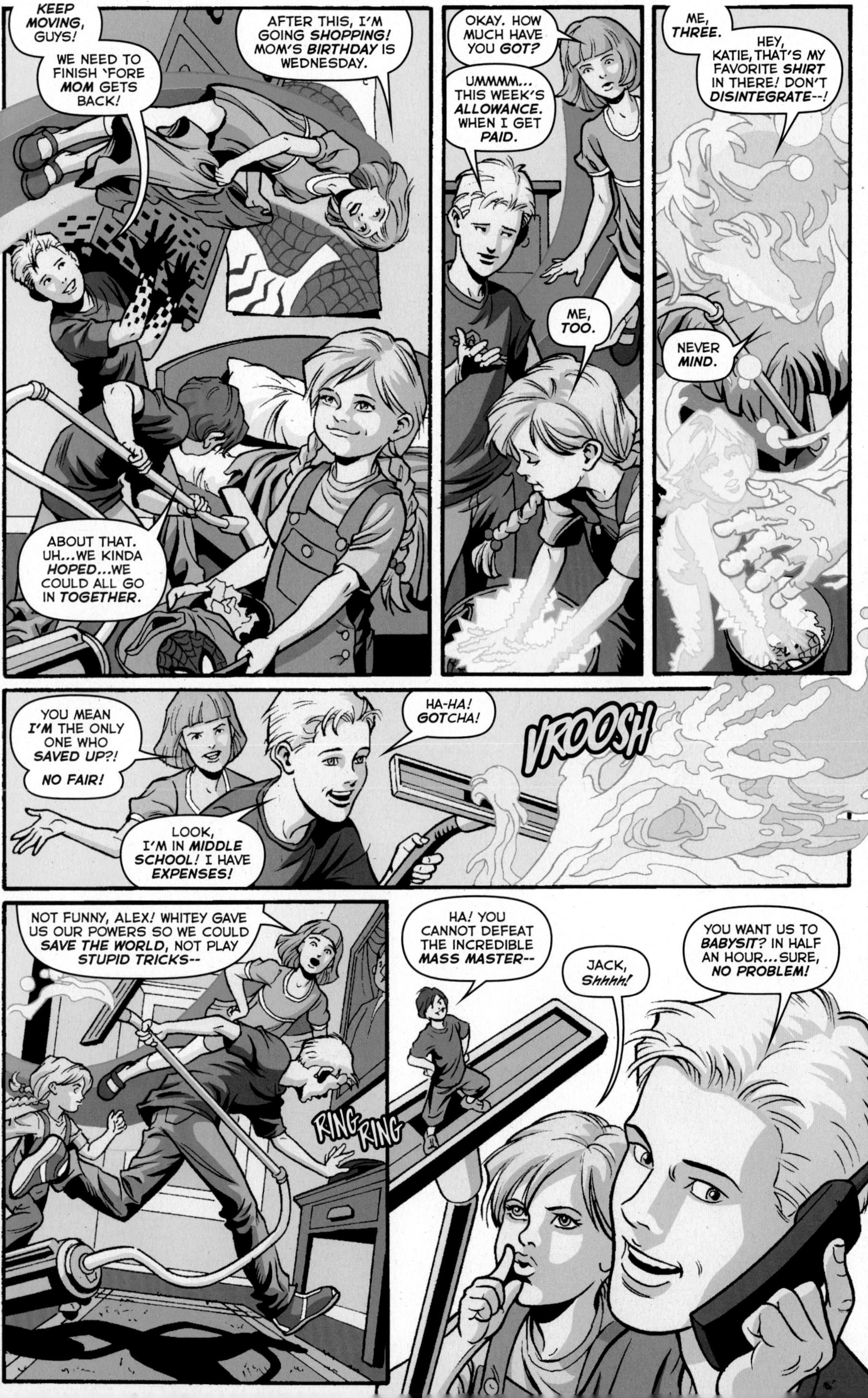

KEEP MOVING, GUYS!
WE NEED TO FINISH 'FORE MOM GETS BACK!
AFTER THIS, I'M GOING SHOPPING! MOM'S BIRTHDAY IS WEDNESDAY.
ABOUT THAT. UH...WE KINDA HOPED...WE COULD ALL GO IN TOGETHER.
OKAY. HOW MUCH HAVE YOU GOT?
UMMMM... THIS WEEK'S ALLOWANCE. WHEN I GET PAID.
ME, TOO.
ME, THREE.
HEY, KATIE, THAT'S MY FAVORITE SHIRT IN THERE! DON'T DISINTEGRATE--!
NEVER MIND.
YOU MEAN I'M THE ONLY ONE WHO SAVED UP?!
NO FAIR!
HA-HA! GOTCHA!
VROOSH
LOOK, I'M IN MIDDLE SCHOOL! I HAVE EXPENSES!
NOT FUNNY, ALEX! WHITEY GAVE US OUR POWERS SO WE COULD SAVE THE WORLD, NOT PLAY STUPID TRICKS--
RING RING
HA! YOU CANNOT DEFEAT THE INCREDIBLE MASS MASTER--
JACK, Shhhh!
YOU WANT US TO BABYSIT? IN HALF AN HOUR...SURE, NO PROBLEM!

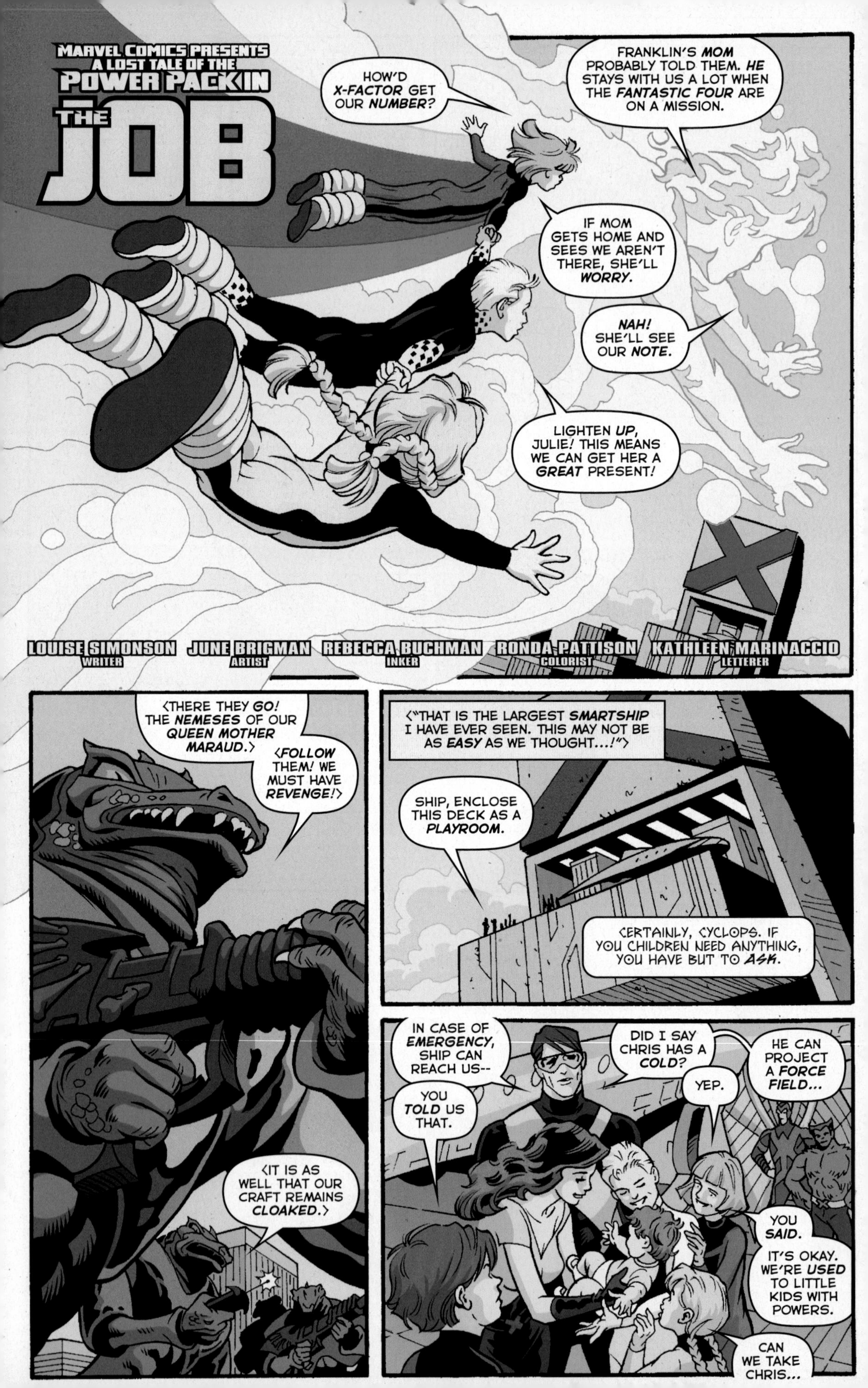
MARVEL COMICS PRESENTS
A LOST TALE OF THE
POWER PACK IN
THE JOB
HOW'D X-FACTOR GET OUR NUMBER?
FRANKLIN'S MOM PROBABLY TOLD THEM. HE STAYS WITH US A LOT WHEN THE FANTASTIC FOUR ARE ON A MISSION.
IF MOM GETS HOME AND SEES WE AREN'T THERE, SHE'LL WORRY.
NAH! SHE'LL SEE OUR NOTE.
LIGHTEN UP, JULIE! THIS MEANS WE CAN GET HER A GREAT PRESENT!
LOUISE SIMONSON WRITER
JUNE BRIGMAN ARTIST
REBECCA BUCHMAN INKER
RONDA PATTISON COLORIST
KATHLEEN MARINACCIO LETTERER
<THERE THEY GO! THE NEMESES OF OUR QUEEN MOTHER MARAUD.>
<FOLLOW THEM! WE MUST HAVE REVENGE!>
<IT IS AS WELL THAT OUR CRAFT REMAINS CLOAKED.>
<"THAT IS THE LARGEST SMARTSHIP I HAVE EVER SEEN. THIS MAY NOT BE AS EASY AS WE THOUGHT...!">
SHIP, ENCLOSE THIS DECK AS A PLAYROOM.
CERTAINLY, CYCLOPS. IF YOU CHILDREN NEED ANYTHING, YOU HAVE BUT TO ASK.
IN CASE OF EMERGENCY, SHIP CAN REACH US--
YOU TOLD US THAT.
DID I SAY CHRIS HAS A COLD?
YEP.
HE CAN PROJECT A FORCE FIELD...
YOU SAID.
IT'S OKAY. WE'RE USED TO LITTLE KIDS WITH POWERS.
CAN WE TAKE CHRIS...

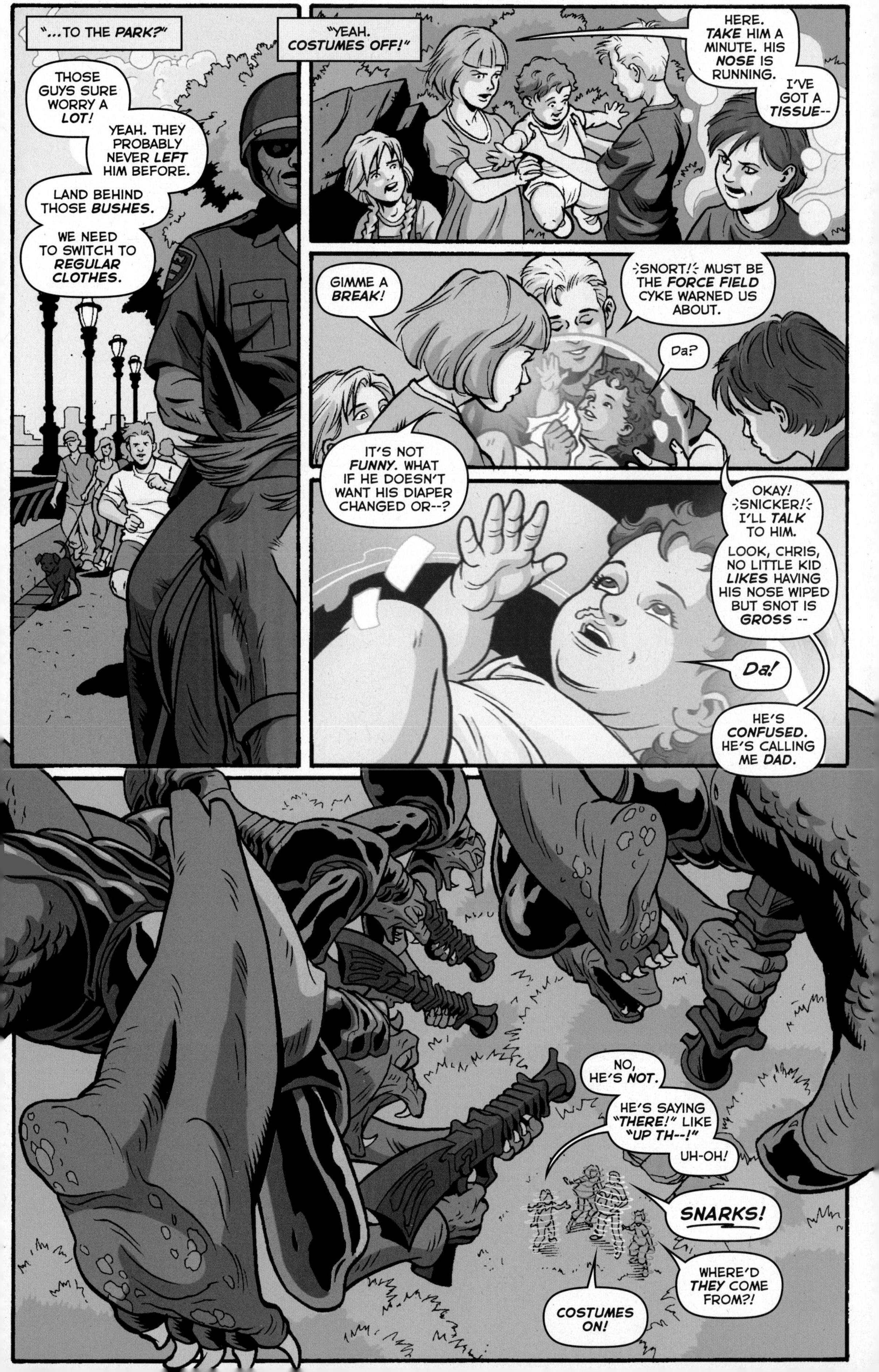

"...TO THE PARK?"
THOSE GUYS SURE WORRY A LOT!
YEAH. THEY PROBABLY NEVER LEFT HIM BEFORE.
LAND BEHIND THOSE BUSHES.
WE NEED TO SWITCH TO REGULAR CLOTHES.
"YEAH. COSTUMES OFF!"
HERE. TAKE HIM A MINUTE. HIS NOSE IS RUNNING.
I'VE GOT A TISSUE--
GIMME A BREAK!
SNORT! MUST BE THE FORCE FIELD CYKE WARNED US ABOUT.
Da?
IT'S NOT FUNNY. WHAT IF HE DOESN'T WANT HIS DIAPER CHANGED OR--?
OKAY! SNICKER! I'LL TALK TO HIM.
LOOK, CHRIS, NO LITTLE KID LIKES HAVING HIS NOSE WIPED BUT SNOT IS GROSS --
Da!
HE'S CONFUSED. HE'S CALLING ME DAD.
NO, HE'S NOT.
HE'S SAYING "THERE!" LIKE "UP TH--!"
UH-OH!
SNARKS!
WHERE'D THEY COME FROM?!
COSTUMES ON!

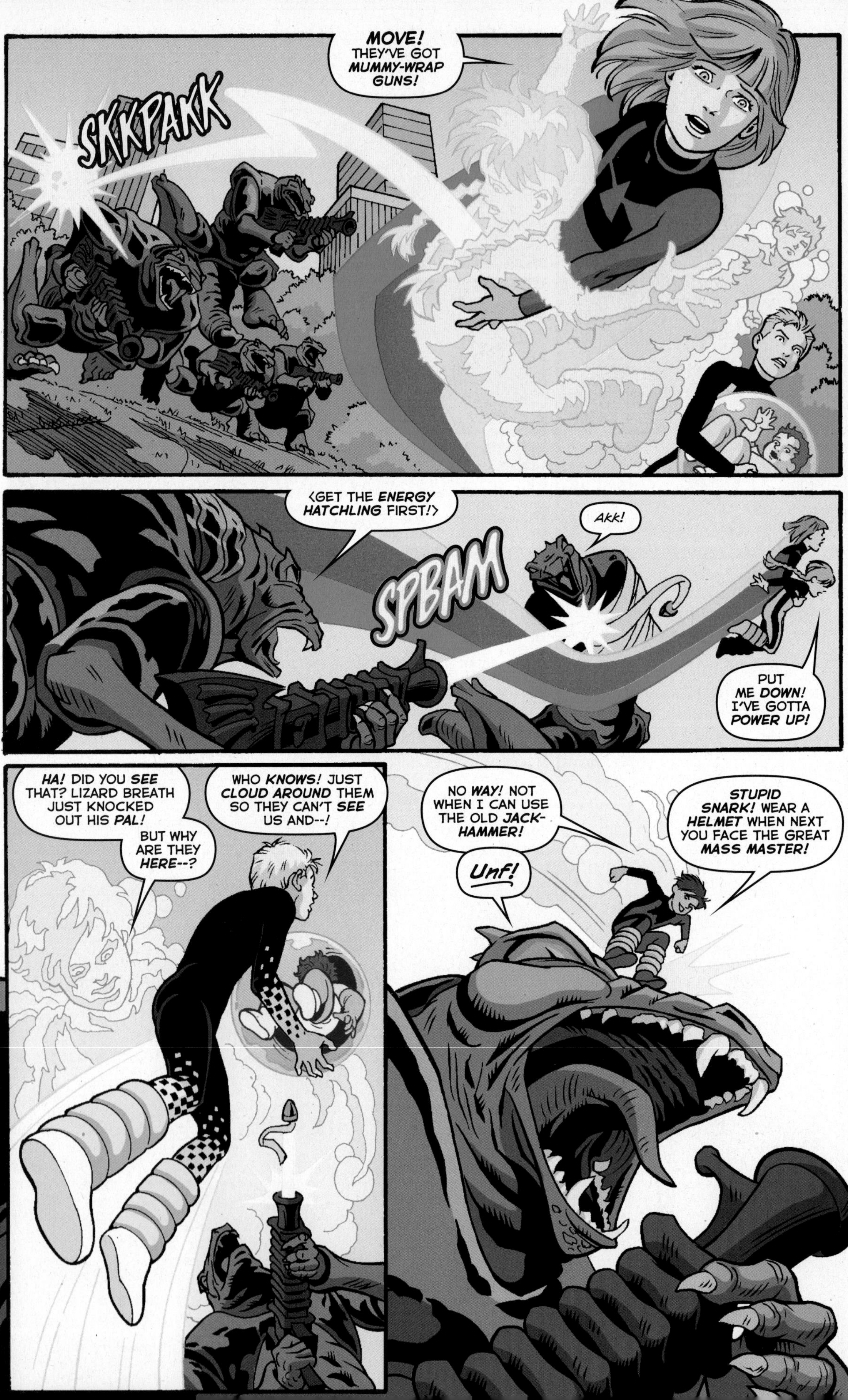
MOVE! THEY'VE GOT MUMMY-WRAP GUNS!
SKKPAKK
<GET THE ENERGY HATCHLING FIRST!>
AKK!
SPBAM
PUT ME DOWN! I'VE GOTTA POWER UP!
HA! DID YOU SEE THAT? LIZARD BREATH JUST KNOCKED OUT HIS PAL!
BUT WHY ARE THEY HERE--?
WHO KNOWS! JUST CLOUD AROUND THEM SO THEY CAN'T SEE US AND--!
NO WAY! NOT WHEN I CAN USE THE OLD JACK-HAMMER!
UNF!
STUPID SNARK! WEAR A HELMET WHEN NEXT YOU FACE THE GREAT MASS MASTER!

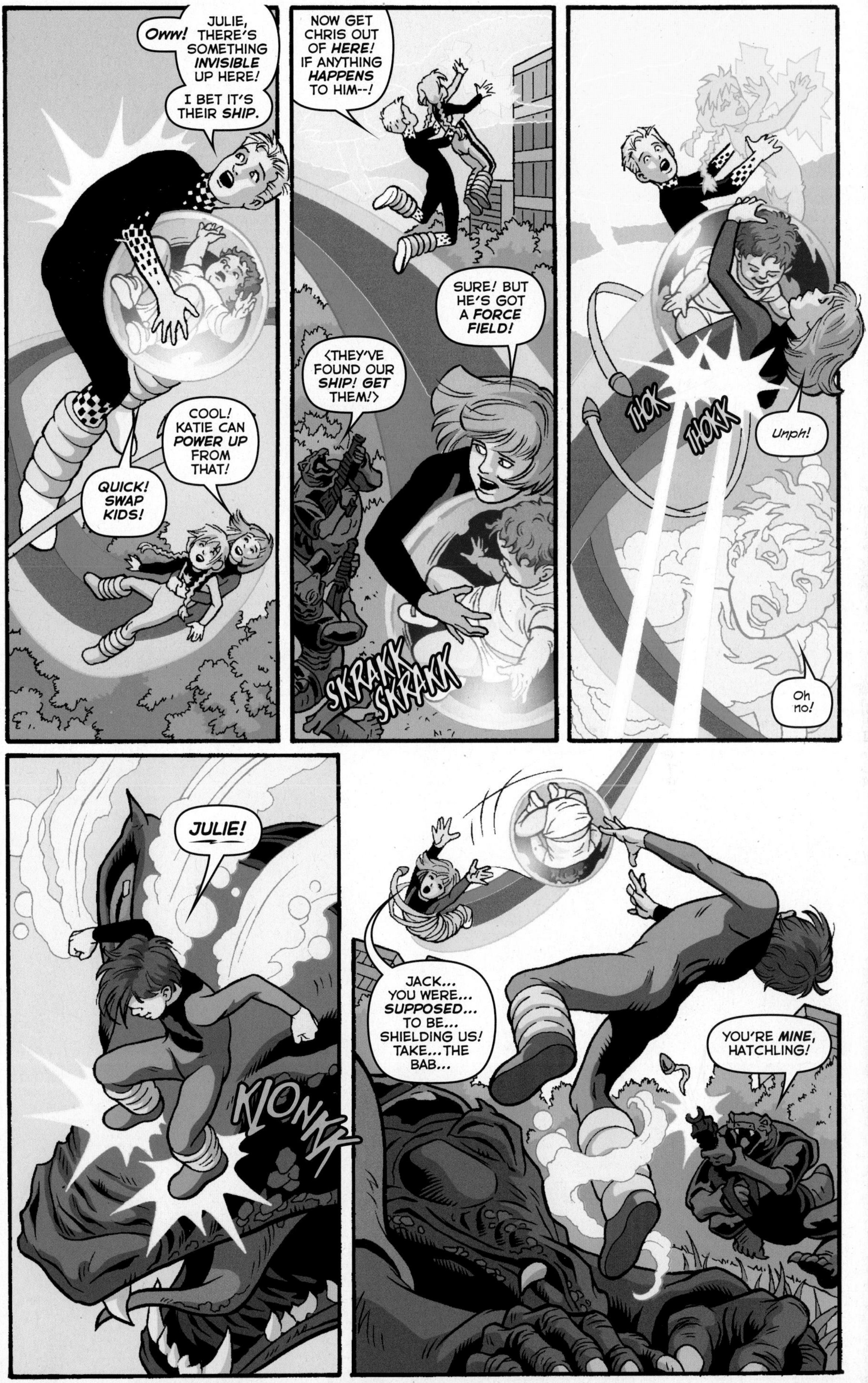
Oww!
JULIE, THERE'S SOMETHING INVISIBLE UP HERE!
I BET IT'S THEIR SHIP.
COOL! KATIE CAN POWER UP FROM THAT!
QUICK! SWAP KIDS!
NOW GET CHRIS OUT OF HERE! IF ANYTHING HAPPENS TO HIM--!
SURE! BUT HE'S GOT A FORCE FIELD!
<THEY'VE FOUND OUR SHIP! GET THEM!>
SKRAKK SKRAKK
THOK
THOKK
Unph!
Oh no!
JULIE!
KLONKK
JACK... YOU WERE... SUPPOSED... TO BE... SHIELDING US! TAKE... THE BAB...
YOU'RE MINE, HATCHLING!

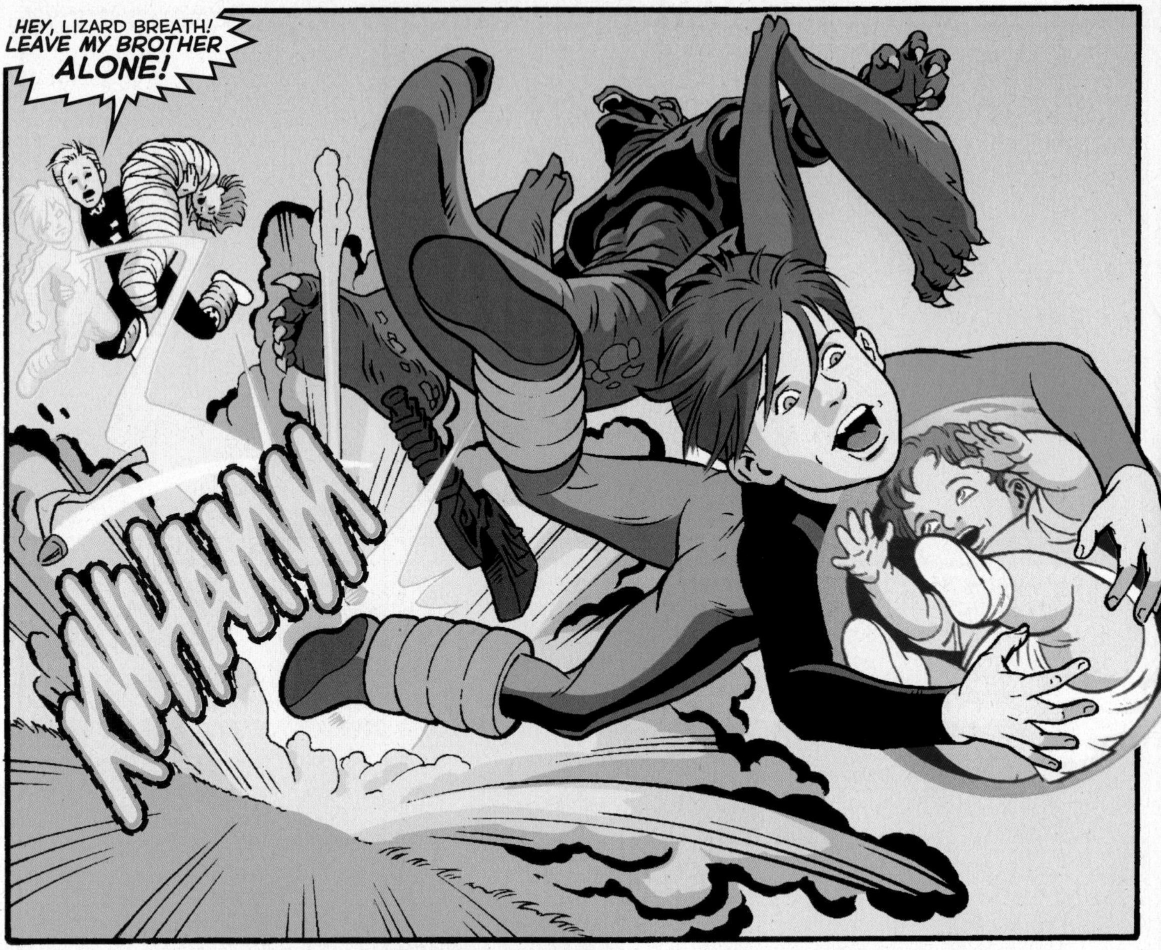
HEY, LIZARD BREATH! LEAVE MY BROTHER ALONE!
KWHAMM

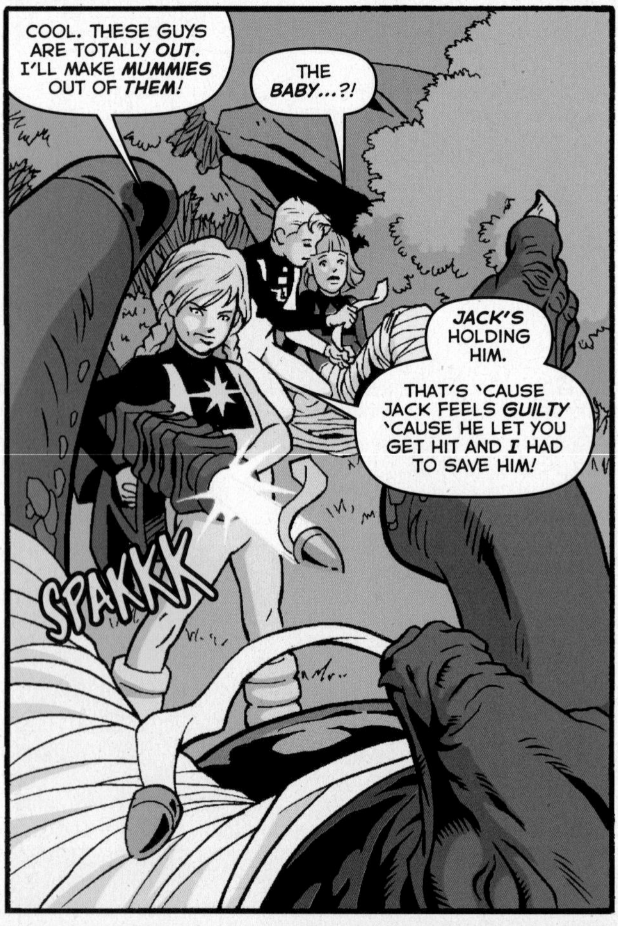
COOL. THESE GUYS ARE TOTALLY OUT. I'LL MAKE MUMMIES OUT OF THEM!
THE BABY...?!
JACK'S HOLDING HIM.
THAT'S 'CAUSE JACK FEELS GUILTY 'CAUSE HE LET YOU GET HIT AND I HAD TO SAVE HIM!
SPAKKK

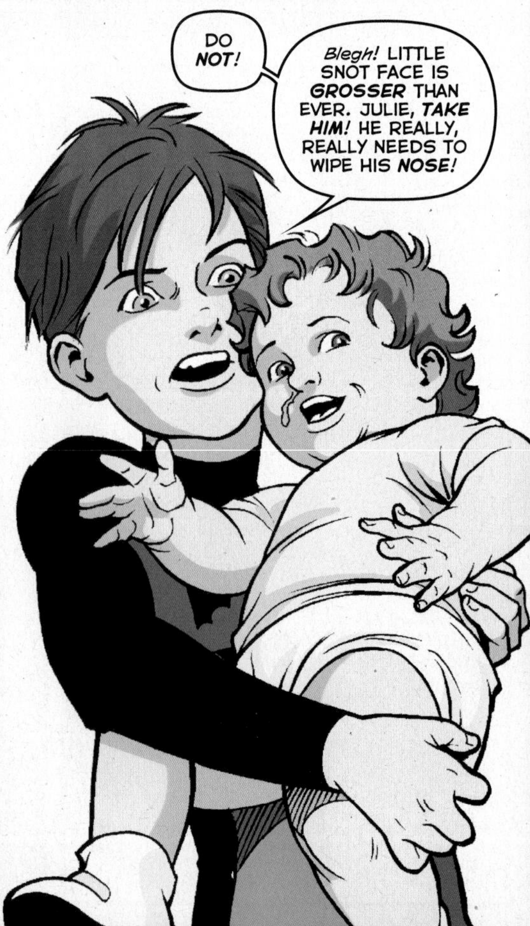
DO NOT!
Blegh! LITTLE SNOT FACE IS GROSSER THAN EVER. JULIE, TAKE HIM! HE REALLY, REALLY NEEDS TO WIPE HIS NOSE!

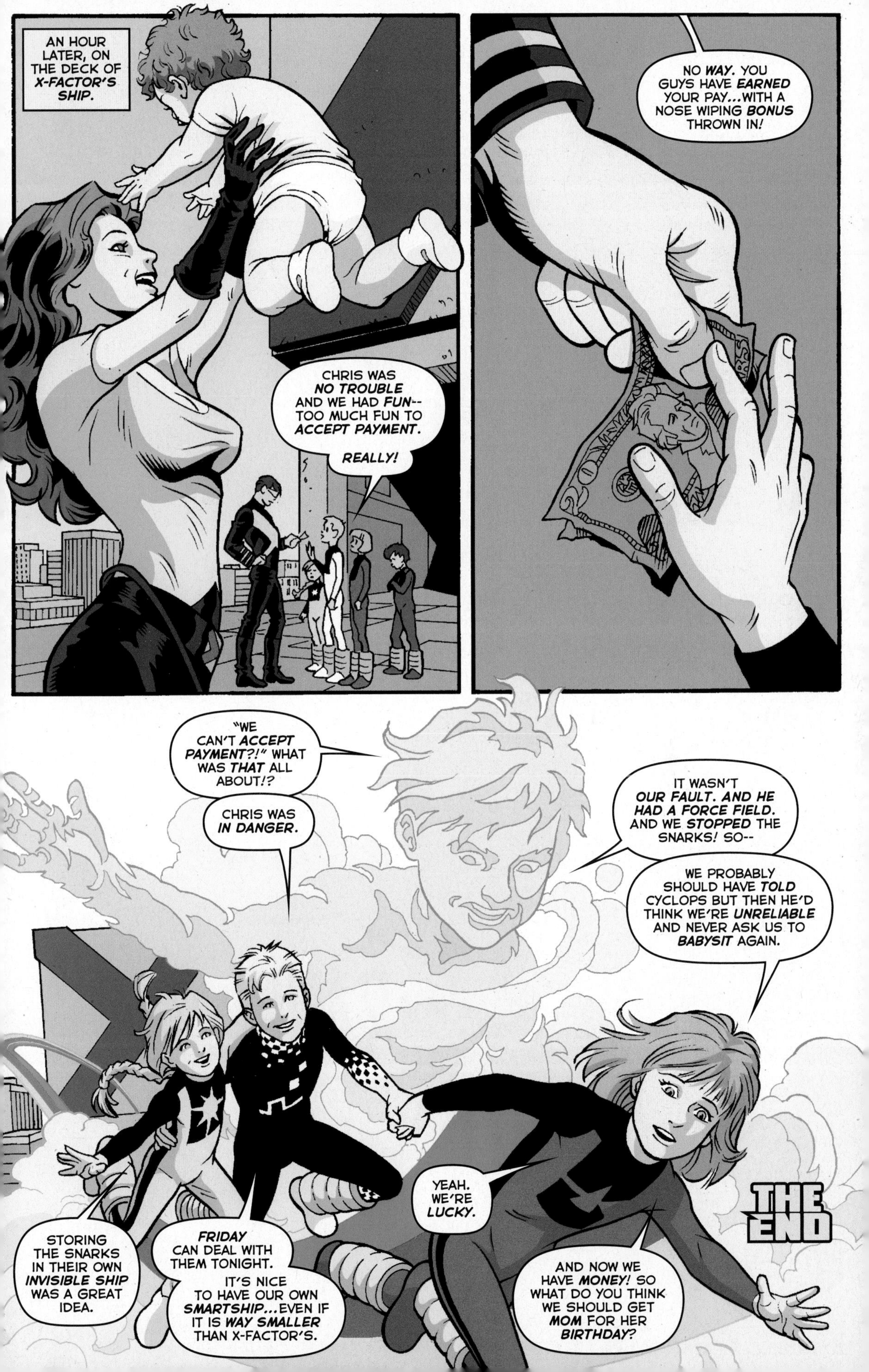
AN HOUR LATER, ON THE DECK OF X-FACTOR'S SHIP.
CHRIS WAS NO TROUBLE AND WE HAD FUN-- TOO MUCH FUN TO ACCEPT PAYMENT.
REALLY!
NO WAY. YOU GUYS HAVE EARNED YOUR PAY...WITH A NOSE WIPING BONUS THROWN IN!
"WE CAN'T ACCEPT PAYMENT?!" WHAT WAS THAT ALL ABOUT!?
CHRIS WAS IN DANGER.
IT WASN'T OUR FAULT. AND HE HAD A FORCE FIELD. AND WE STOPPED THE SNARKS! SO--
WE PROBABLY SHOULD HAVE TOLD CYCLOPS BUT THEN HE'D THINK WE'RE UNRELIABLE AND NEVER ASK US TO BABYSIT AGAIN.
STORING THE SNARKS IN THEIR OWN INVISIBLE SHIP WAS A GREAT IDEA.
FRIDAY CAN DEAL WITH THEM TONIGHT.
IT'S NICE TO HAVE OUR OWN SMARTSHIP...EVEN IF IT IS WAY SMALLER THAN X-FACTOR'S.
YEAH. WE'RE LUCKY.
AND NOW WE HAVE MONEY! SO WHAT DO YOU THINK WE SHOULD GET MOM FOR HER BIRTHDAY?
THE END

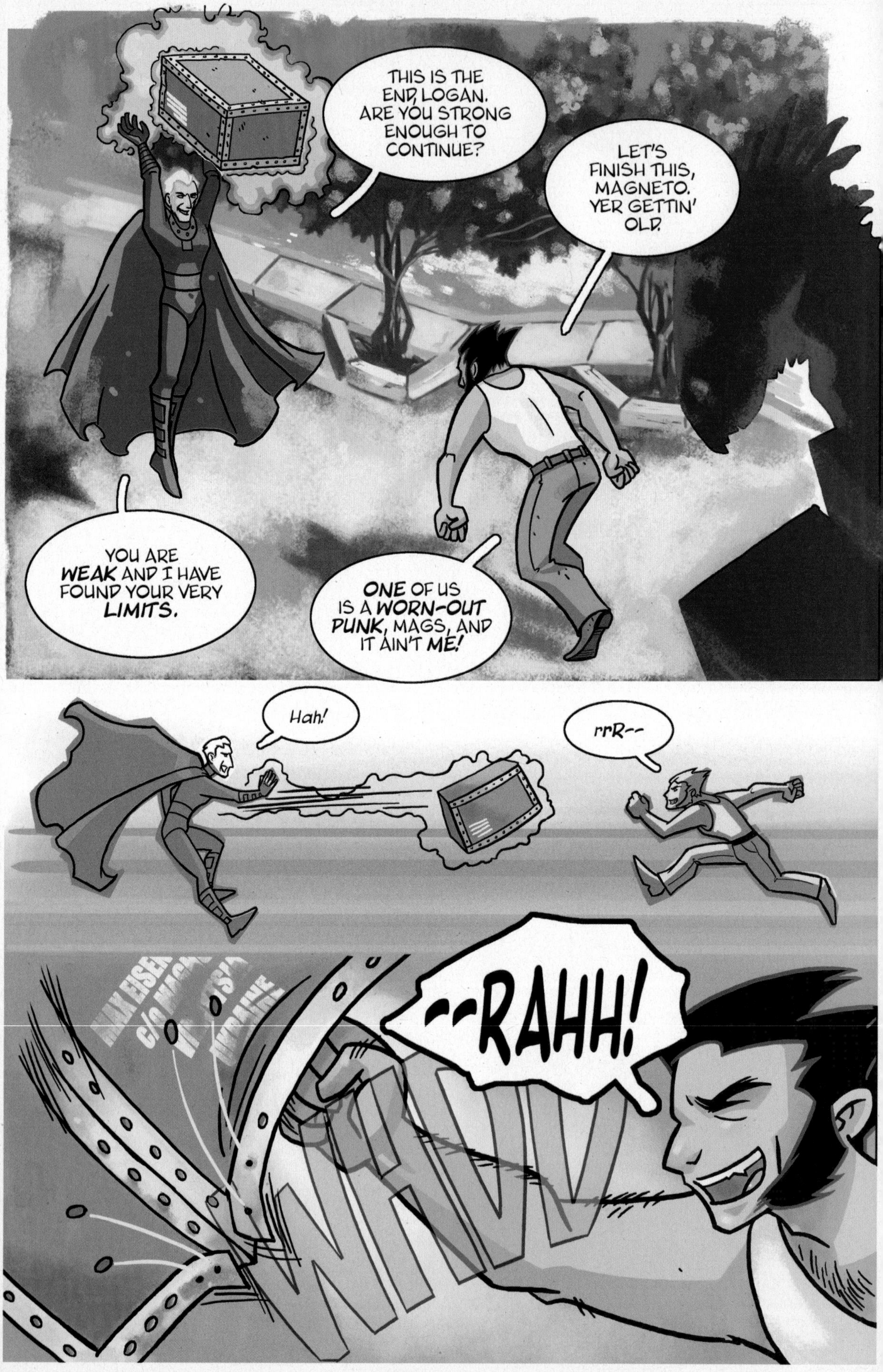
THIS IS THE END, LOGAN. ARE YOU STRONG ENOUGH TO CONTINUE?
LET'S FINISH THIS, MAGNETO. YER GETTIN' OLD.
YOU ARE **WEAK** AND I HAVE FOUND YOUR VERY **LIMITS.**
ONE OF US IS A **WORN-OUT PUNK,** MAGS, AND IT AIN'T **ME!**
Hah!
rrR--
--RAHH!

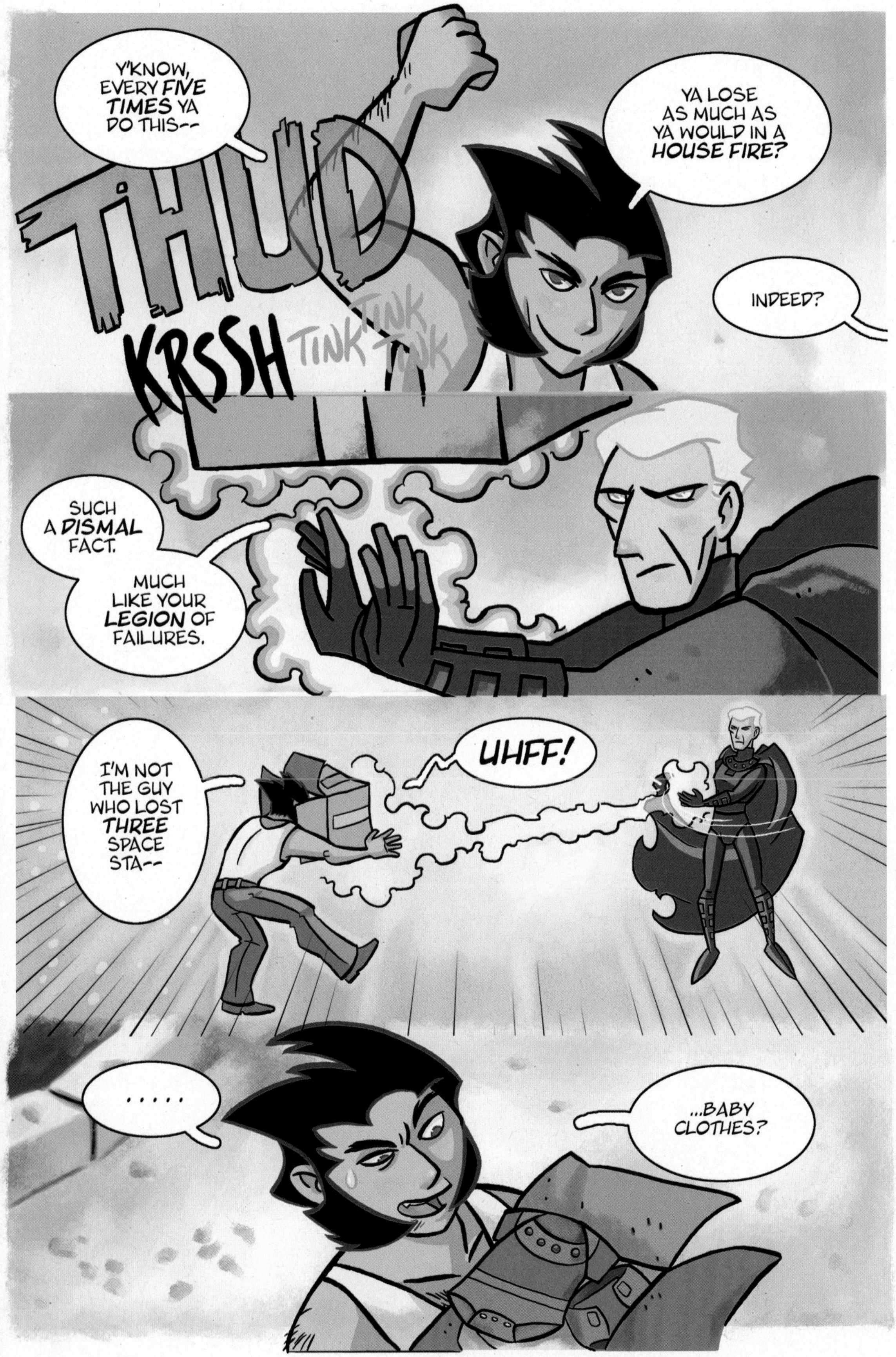
Y'KNOW, EVERY FIVE TIMES YA DO THIS--
YA LOSE AS MUCH AS YA WOULD IN A HOUSE FIRE?
THUD
KRSSH
TINK TINK TINK
INDEED?
SUCH A DISMAL FACT.
MUCH LIKE YOUR LEGION OF FAILURES.
I'M NOT THE GUY WHO LOST THREE SPACE STA--
UHFF!
.....
...BABY CLOTHES?

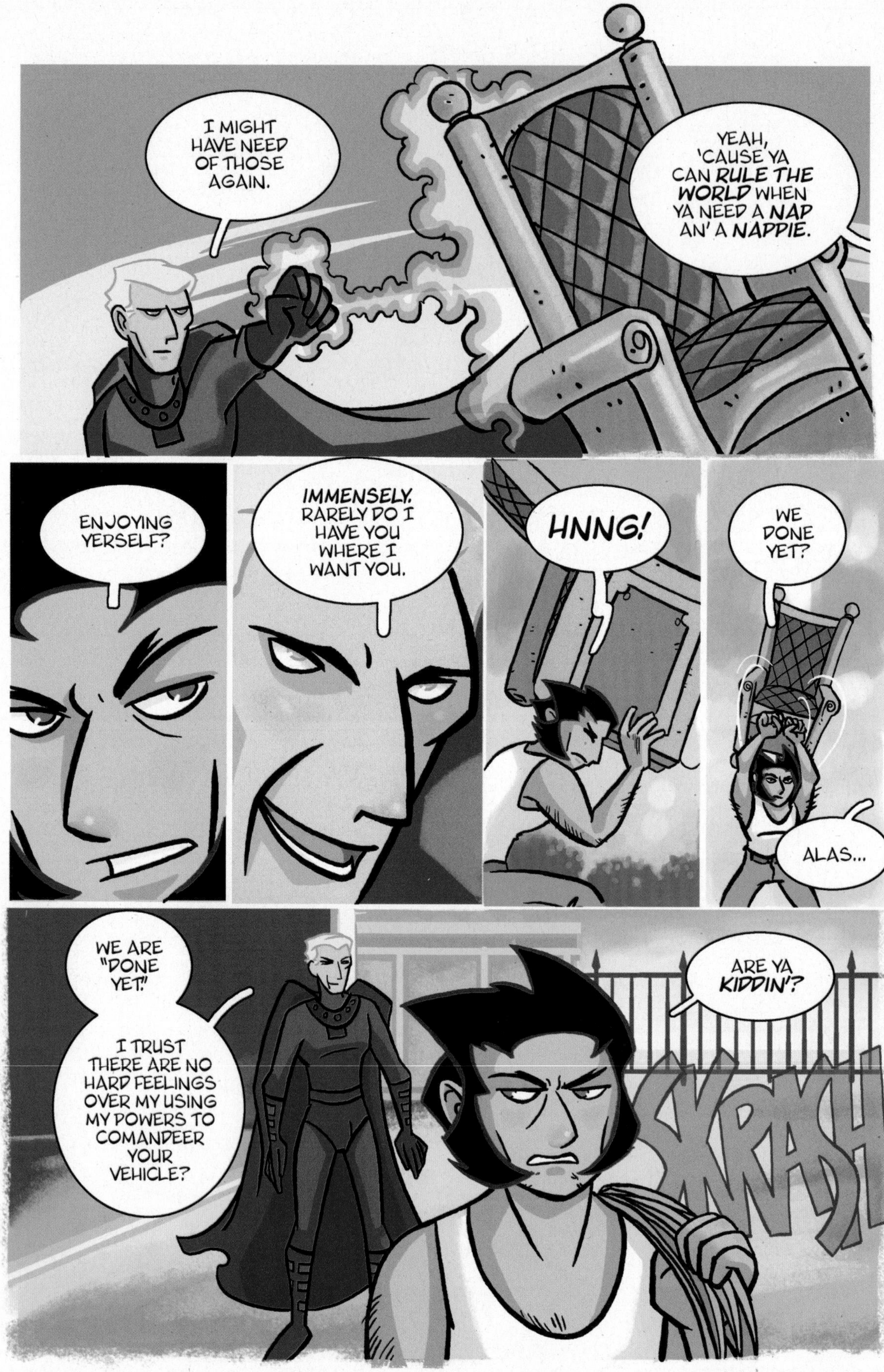
I MIGHT HAVE NEED OF THOSE AGAIN.
YEAH, 'CAUSE YA CAN RULE THE WORLD WHEN YA NEED A NAP AN' A NAPPIE.
ENJOYING YERSELF?
IMMENSELY. RARELY DO I HAVE YOU WHERE I WANT YOU.
HNNG!
WE DONE YET?
ALAS...
WE ARE "DONE YET."
I TRUST THERE ARE NO HARD FEELINGS OVER MY USING MY POWERS TO COMANDEER YOUR VEHICLE?
ARE YA KIDDIN'?
SKRASH

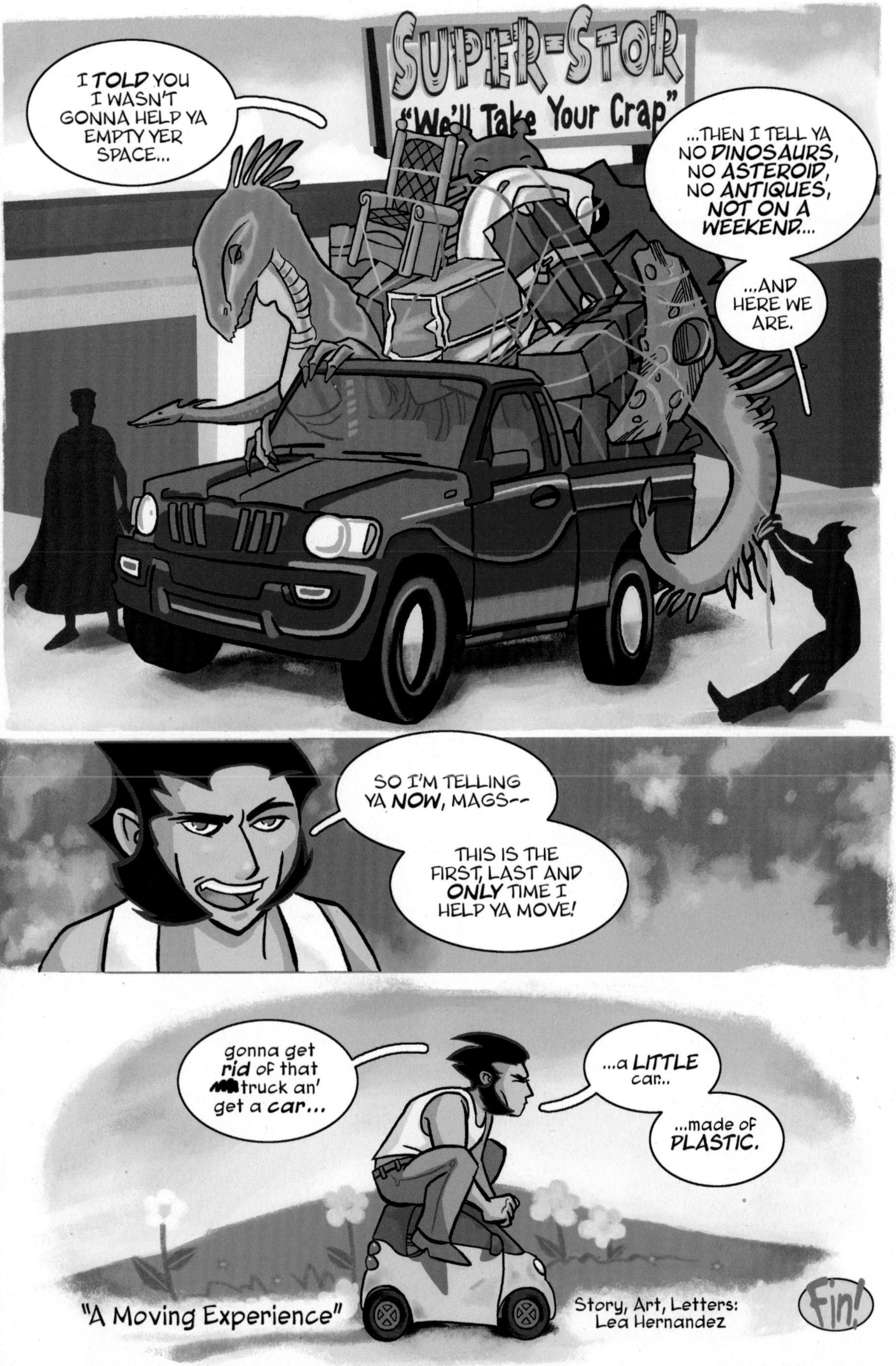
SUPER-STOR
"We'll Take Your Crap"
I TOLD YOU I WASN'T GONNA HELP YA EMPTY YER SPACE...
...THEN I TELL YA NO DINOSAURS, NO ASTEROID, NO ANTIQUES, NOT ON A WEEKEND....
...AND HERE WE ARE.
SO I'M TELLING YA NOW, MAGS--
THIS IS THE FIRST, LAST AND ONLY TIME I HELP YA MOVE!
gonna get rid of that [redacted] truck an' get a car...
...a LITTLE car...
...made of PLASTIC.
"A Moving Experience"
Story, Art, Letters: Lea Hernandez
Fin!

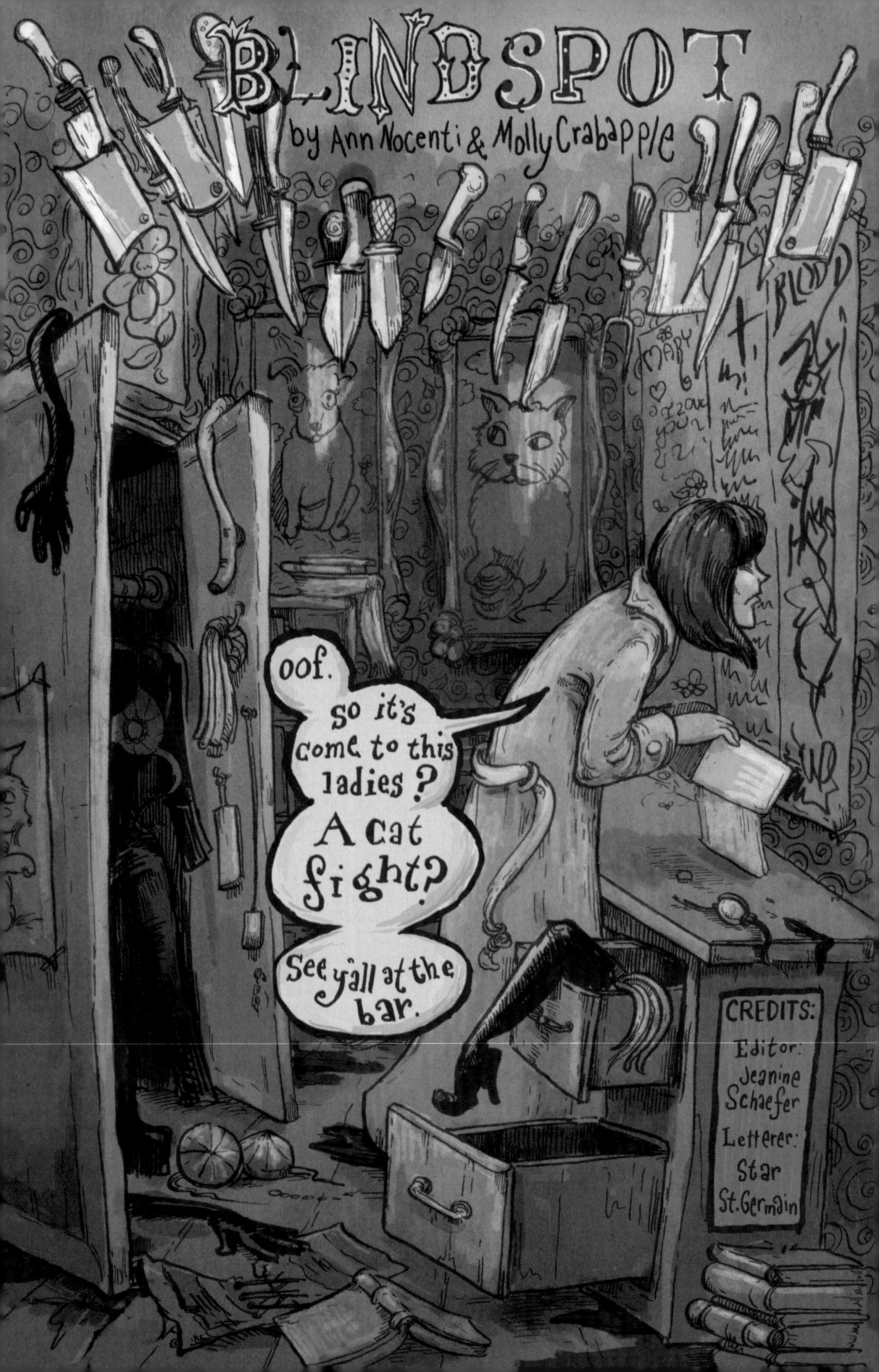
BLINDSPOT
by Ann Nocenti & Molly Crabapple
oof.
so it's come to this ladies? A cat fight?
See y'all at the bar.
CREDITS:
Editor: Jeanine Schaefer
Letterer: Star St. Germain

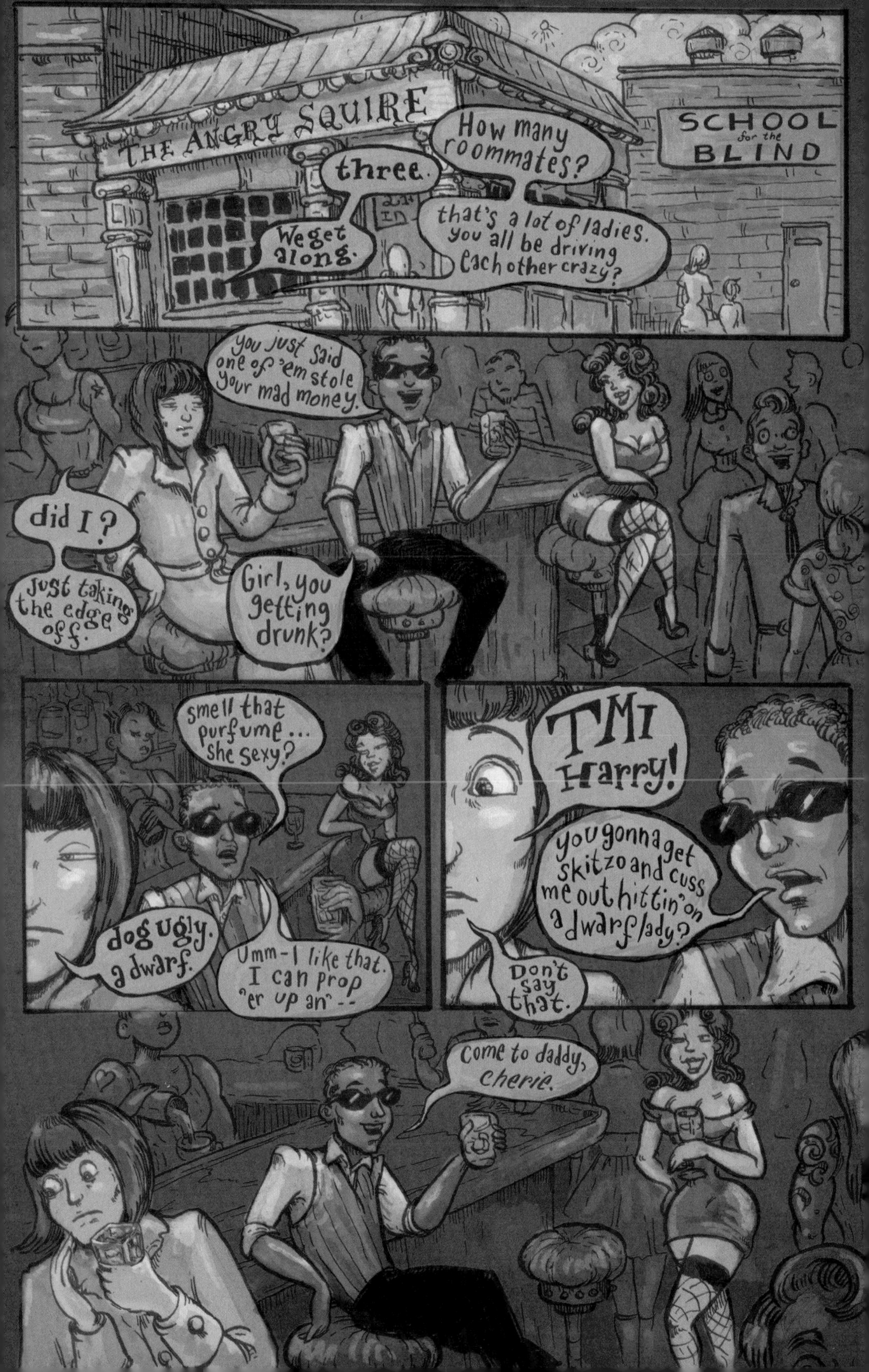
THE ANGRY SQUIRE
SCHOOL for the BLIND
How many roommates?
three.
We get along.
that's a lot of ladies. you all be driving each other crazy?
you just said one of 'em stole your mad money.
did I?
just taking the edge off.
Girl, you getting drunk?
smell that purfume... she sexy?
dog ugly. a dwarf.
Umm-I like that. I can prop 'er up an'--
TMI Harry!
you gonna get skitzo and cuss me out hittin' on a dwarf lady?
Don't say that.
Come to daddy, cherie.

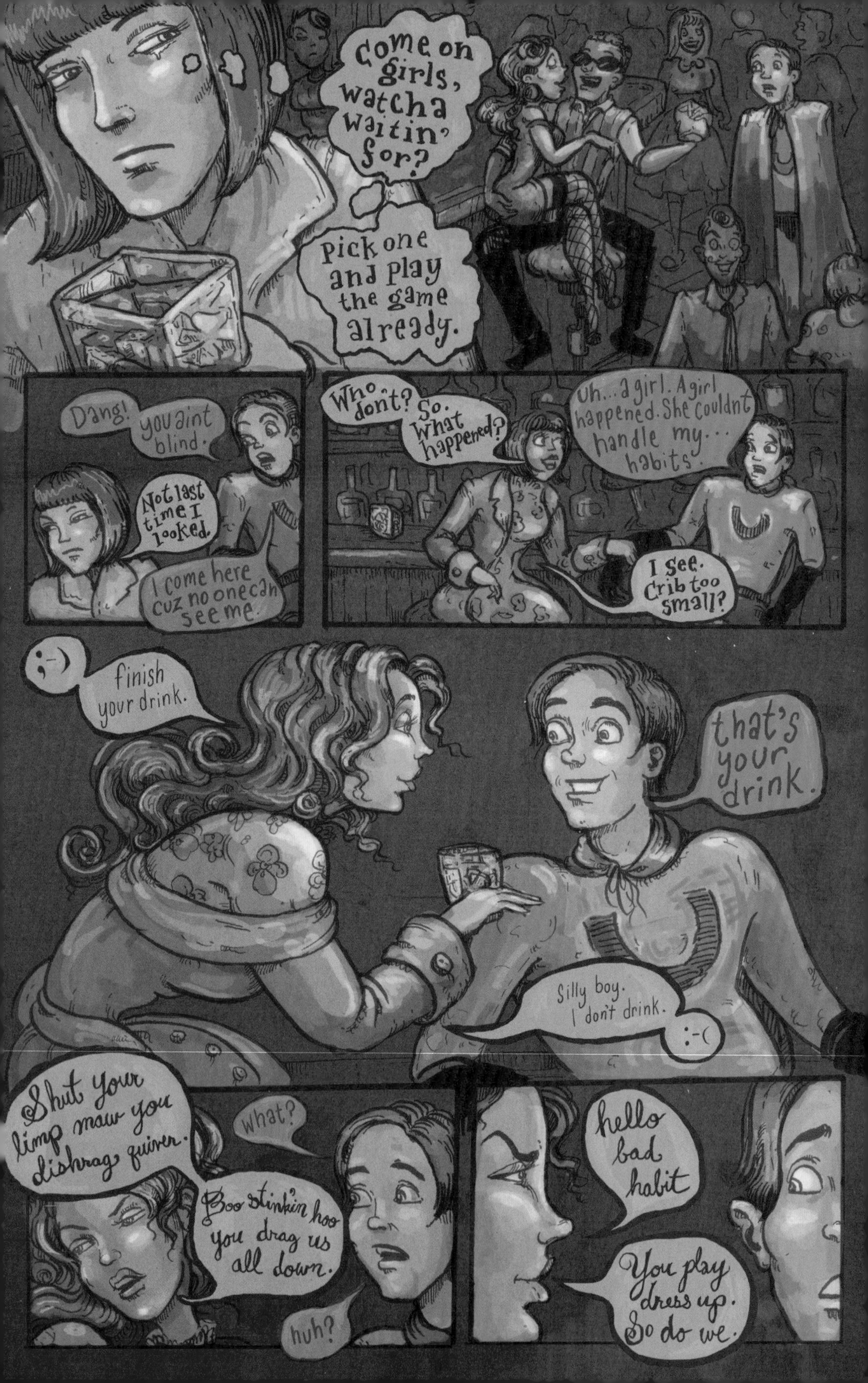
Come on girls, watcha waitin' for?
Pick one and play the game already.
Dang!
you aint blind.
Not last time I looked.
I come here cuz no one can see me.
Who don't?
So. What happened?
Uh... a girl. A girl happened. She couldnt handle my... habits.
I see. Crib too small?
:-)
finish your drink.
that's your drink.
Silly boy. I don't drink.
:-(
Shut your limp maw you dishrag quiver.
what?
Boo stinkin hoo you drag us all down.
huh?
hello bad habit
You play dress up. So do we.

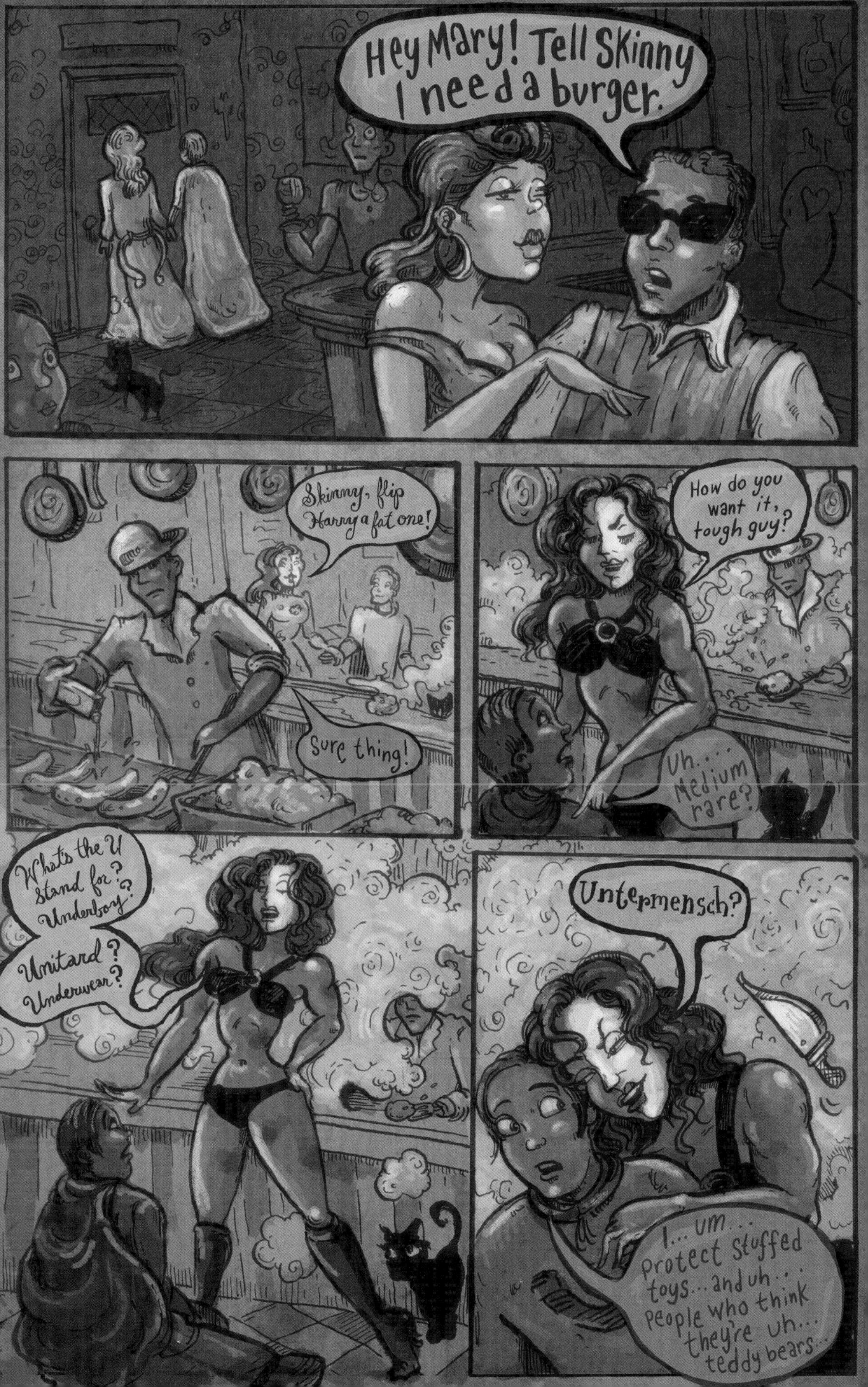
Hey Mary! Tell Skinny I need a burger.
Skinny, flip Harry a fat one!
Sure thing!
How do you want it, tough guy?
Uh... Medium rare?
What's the U stand for? Underboy?
Unitard? Underwear?
Untermensch?
I... um... protect stuffed toys... and uh... people who think they're uh... teddy bears...

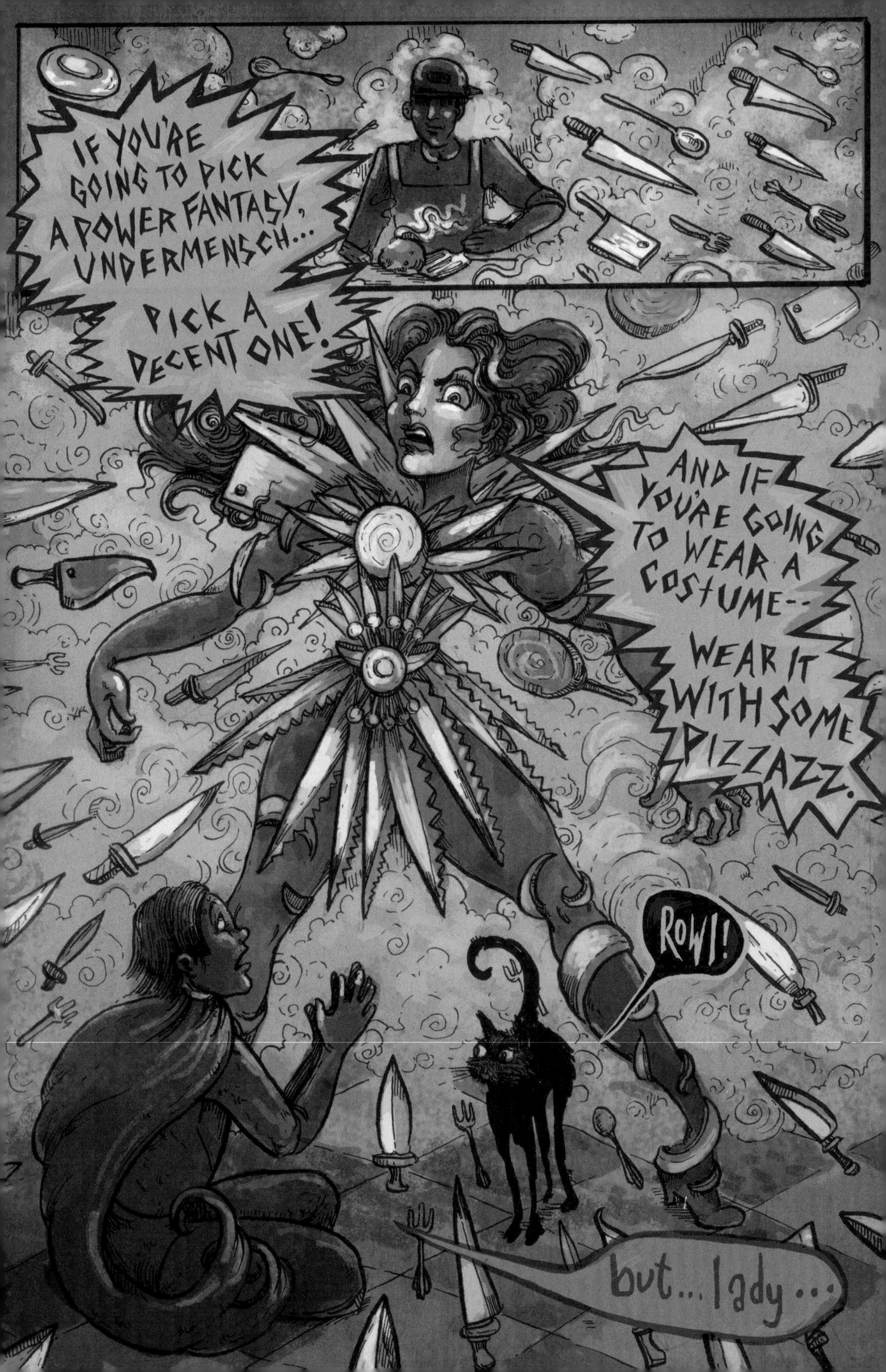
IF YOU'RE GOING TO PICK A POWER FANTASY, UNDERMENSCH...
PICK A DECENT ONE!
AND IF YOU'RE GOING TO WEAR A COSTUME--
WEAR IT WITH SOME PIZZAZZ.
ROWI!
but... lady...

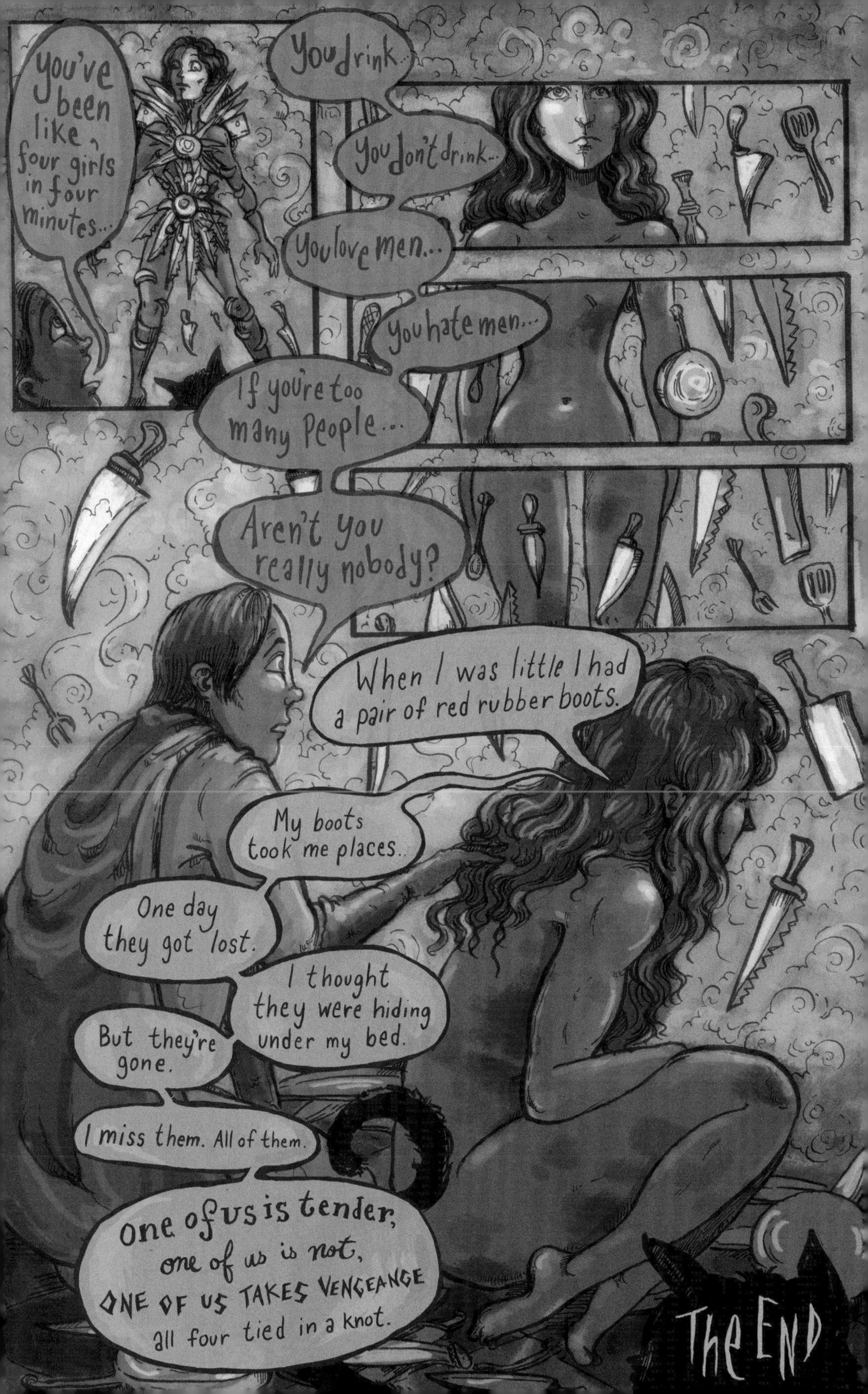
You've been like four girls in four minutes...
You drink...
You don't drink...
You love men...
You hate men...
If you're too many people...
Aren't you really nobody?
When I was little I had a pair of red rubber boots.
My boots took me places..
One day they got lost.
I thought they were hiding under my bed.
But they're gone.
I miss them. All of them.
One of us is tender, one of us is not, ONE OF US TAKES VENGEANCE all four tied in a knot.
The End

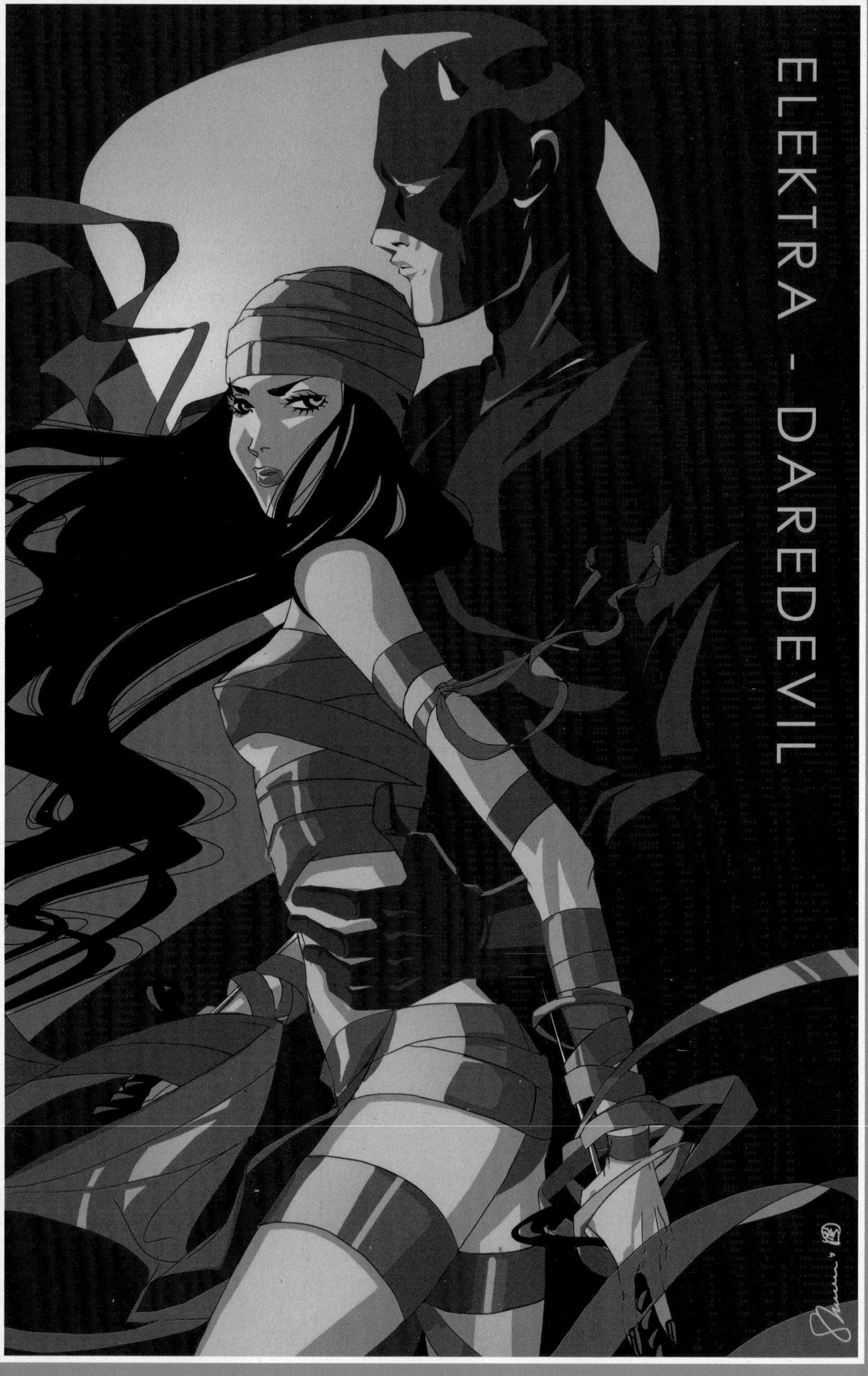
ELEKTRA - DAREDEVIL

ELEKTRA AND DAREDEVIL

By SHO MURASE

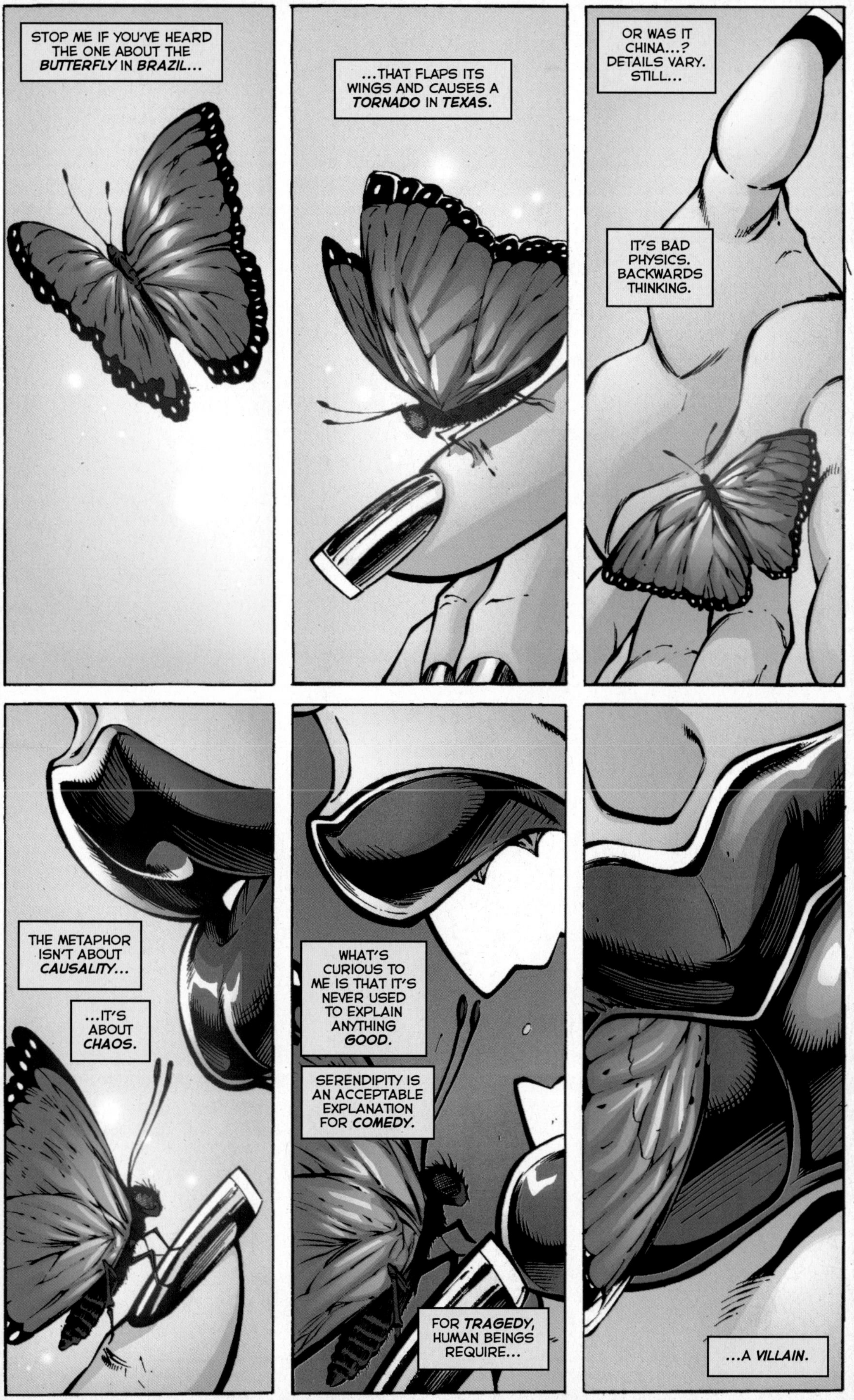
STOP ME IF YOU'VE HEARD THE ONE ABOUT THE *BUTTERFLY* IN *BRAZIL*...
...THAT FLAPS ITS WINGS AND CAUSES A *TORNADO* IN *TEXAS*.
OR WAS IT CHINA...? DETAILS VARY. STILL...
IT'S BAD PHYSICS. BACKWARDS THINKING.
THE METAPHOR ISN'T ABOUT *CAUSALITY*...
...IT'S ABOUT *CHAOS*.
WHAT'S CURIOUS TO ME IS THAT IT'S NEVER USED TO EXPLAIN ANYTHING *GOOD*.
SERENDIPITY IS AN ACCEPTABLE EXPLANATION FOR *COMEDY*.
FOR *TRAGEDY*, HUMAN BEINGS REQUIRE...
...A *VILLAIN*.

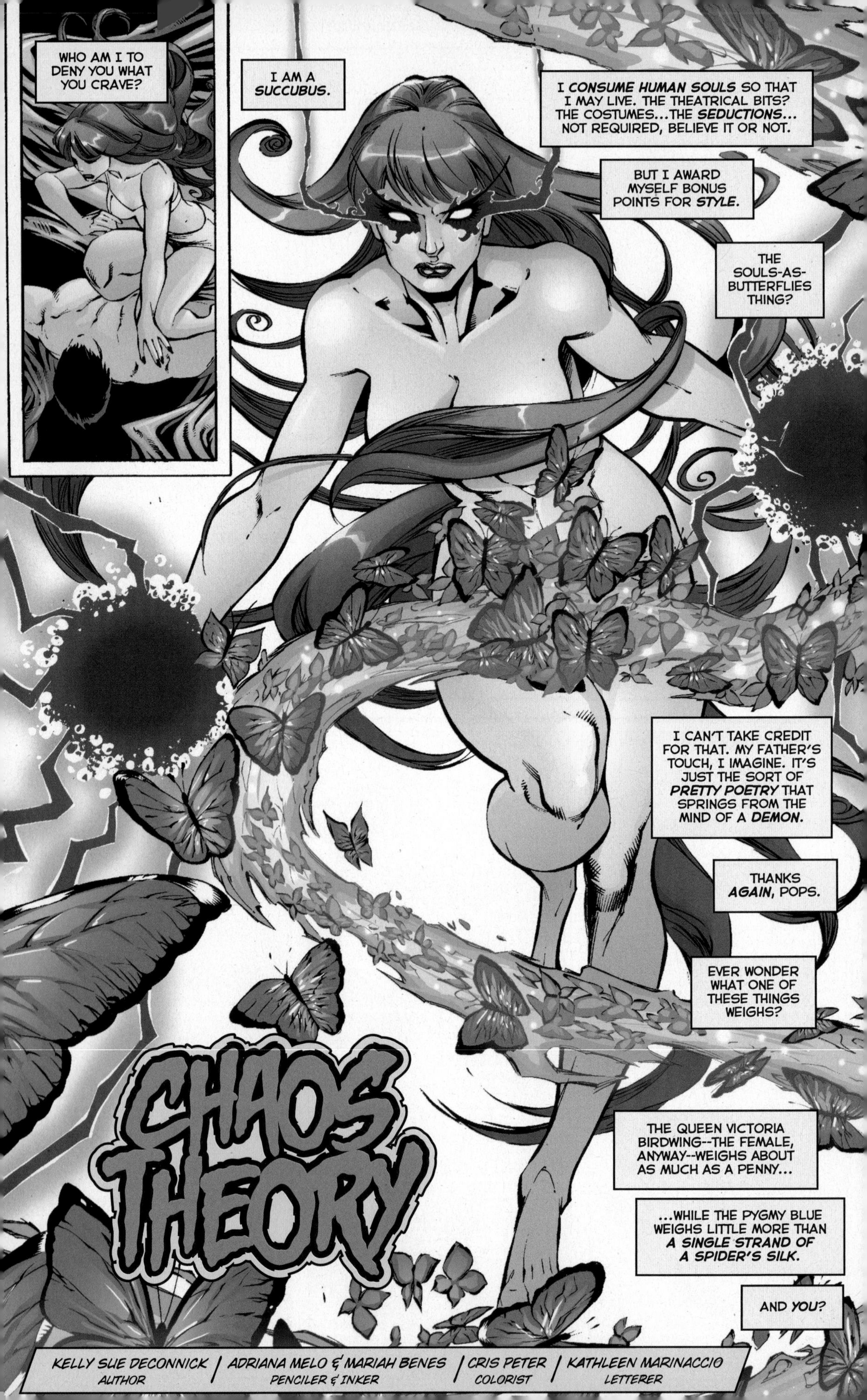
WHO AM I TO DENY YOU WHAT YOU CRAVE?
I AM A *SUCCUBUS*.
I *CONSUME HUMAN SOULS* SO THAT I MAY LIVE. THE THEATRICAL BITS? THE COSTUMES...THE *SEDUCTIONS*... NOT REQUIRED, BELIEVE IT OR NOT.
BUT I AWARD MYSELF BONUS POINTS FOR *STYLE*.
THE SOULS-AS-BUTTERFLIES THING?
I CAN'T TAKE CREDIT FOR THAT. MY FATHER'S TOUCH, I IMAGINE. IT'S JUST THE SORT OF *PRETTY POETRY* THAT SPRINGS FROM THE MIND OF A *DEMON*.
THANKS *AGAIN*, POPS.
EVER WONDER WHAT ONE OF THESE THINGS WEIGHS?
THE QUEEN VICTORIA BIRDWING--THE FEMALE, ANYWAY--WEIGHS ABOUT AS MUCH AS A PENNY...
...WHILE THE PYGMY BLUE WEIGHS LITTLE MORE THAN *A SINGLE STRAND OF A SPIDER'S SILK*.
AND *YOU*?
CHAOS THEORY
KELLY SUE DECONNICK AUTHOR
ADRIANA MELO & MARIAH BENES PENCILER & INKER
CRIS PETER COLORIST
KATHLEEN MARINACCIO LETTERER

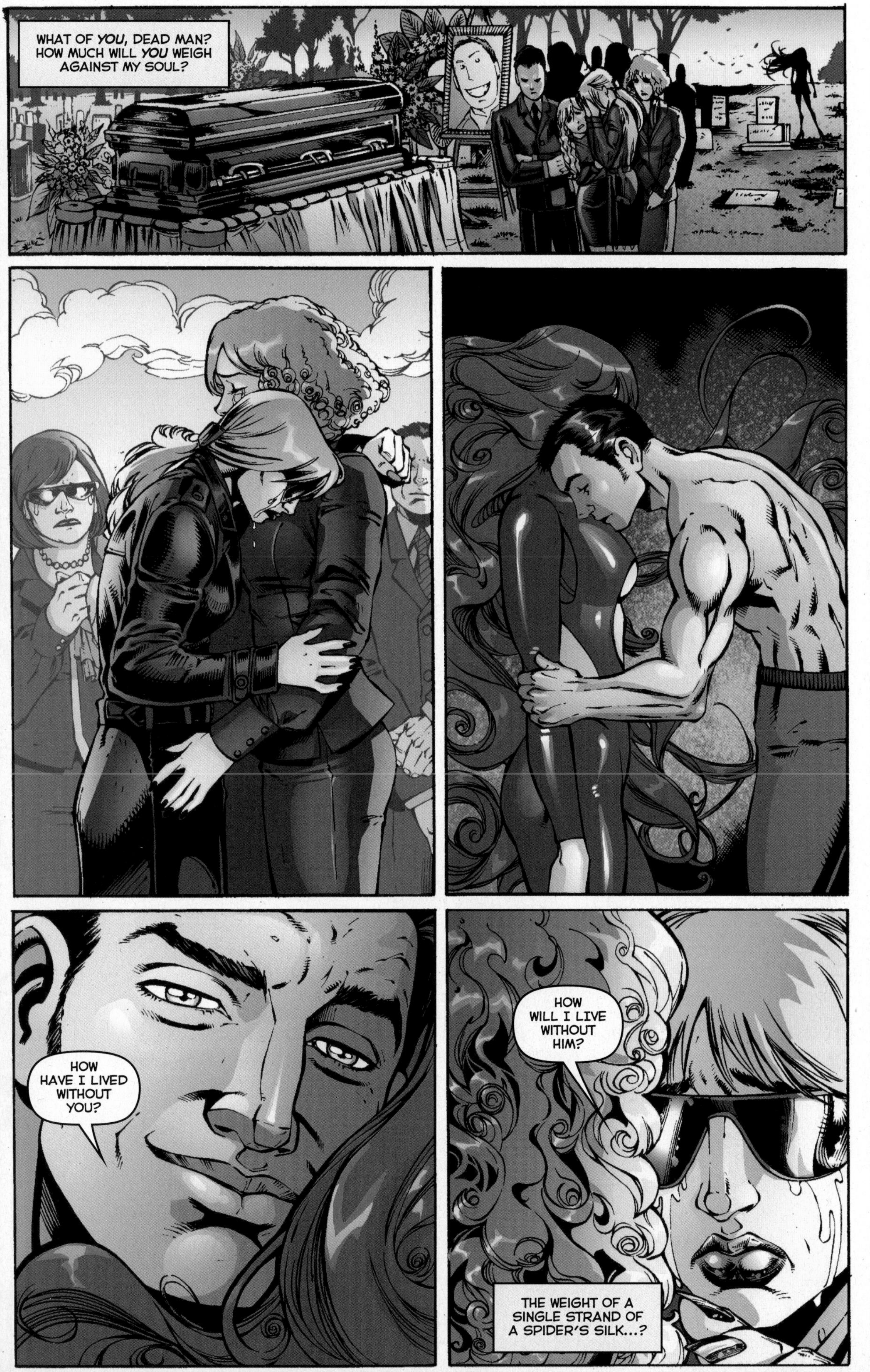
WHAT OF YOU, DEAD MAN? HOW MUCH WILL YOU WEIGH AGAINST MY SOUL?
HOW HAVE I LIVED WITHOUT YOU?
HOW WILL I LIVE WITHOUT HIM?
THE WEIGHT OF A SINGLE STRAND OF A SPIDER'S SILK...?

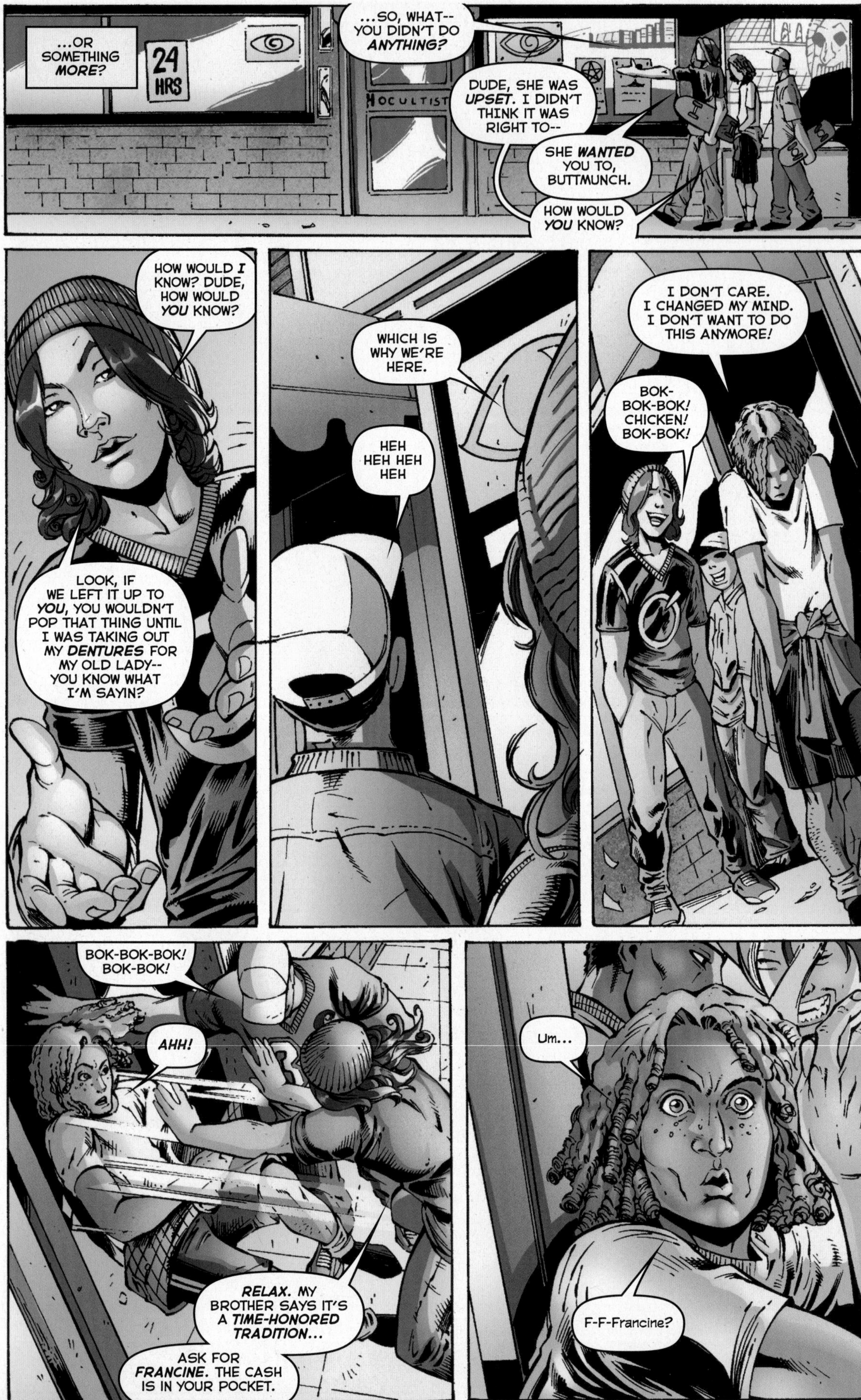
...OR SOMETHING MORE?
24 HRS
OCULTIST
...SO, WHAT-- YOU DIDN'T DO ANYTHING?
DUDE, SHE WAS UPSET. I DIDN'T THINK IT WAS RIGHT TO--
SHE WANTED YOU TO, BUTTMUNCH.
HOW WOULD YOU KNOW?
HOW WOULD I KNOW? DUDE, HOW WOULD YOU KNOW?
LOOK, IF WE LEFT IT UP TO YOU, YOU WOULDN'T POP THAT THING UNTIL I WAS TAKING OUT MY DENTURES FOR MY OLD LADY-- YOU KNOW WHAT I'M SAYIN?
WHICH IS WHY WE'RE HERE.
HEH HEH HEH HEH
I DON'T CARE. I CHANGED MY MIND. I DON'T WANT TO DO THIS ANYMORE!
BOK-BOK-BOK! CHICKEN! BOK-BOK!
BOK-BOK-BOK! BOK-BOK!
AHH!
RELAX. MY BROTHER SAYS IT'S A TIME-HONORED TRADITION...
ASK FOR FRANCINE. THE CASH IS IN YOUR POCKET.
Um...
F-F-Francine?

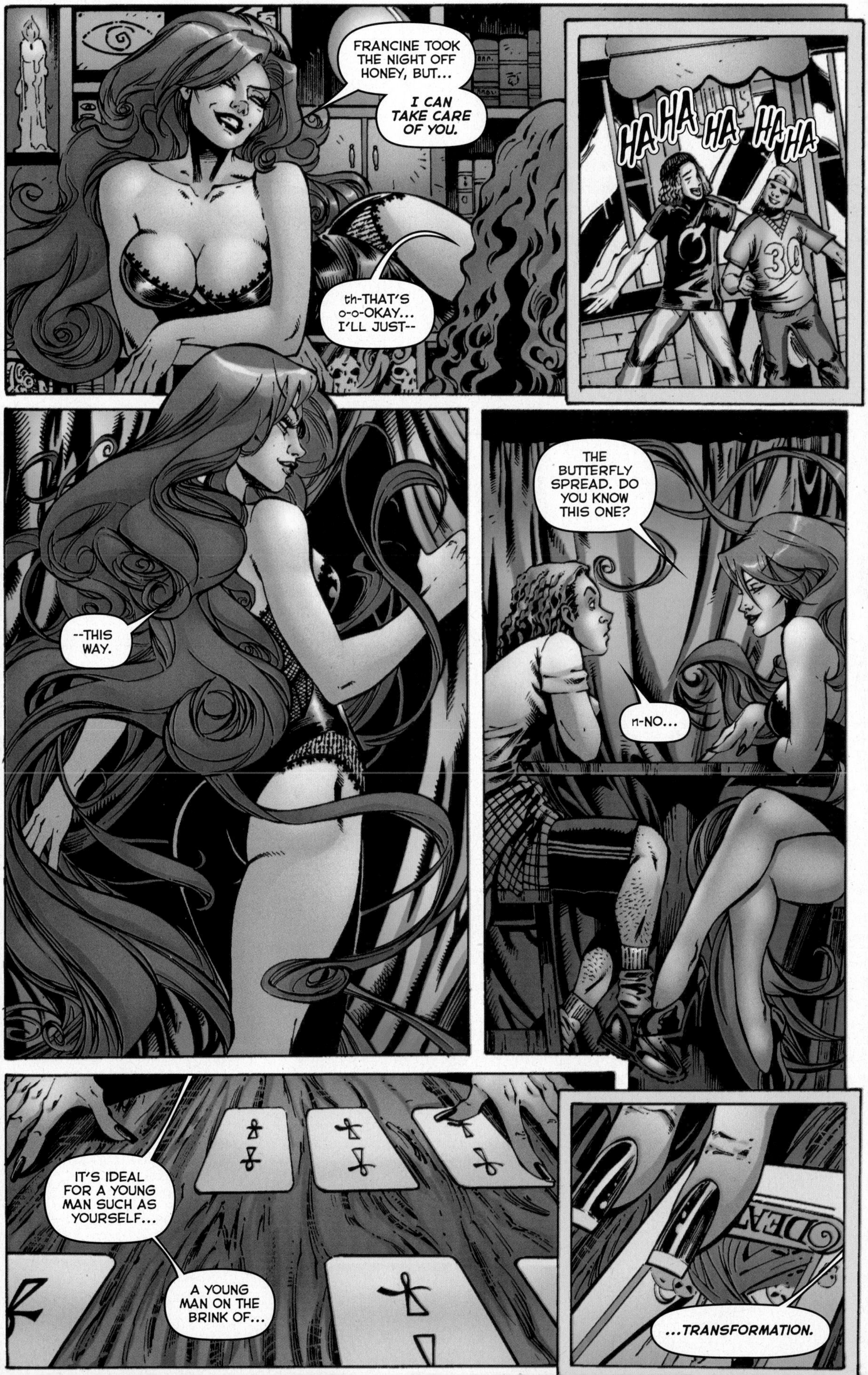
FRANCINE TOOK THE NIGHT OFF HONEY, BUT...
I CAN TAKE CARE OF YOU.
th-THAT'S o-o-OKAY... I'LL JUST--
HA HA HA HA HA
--THIS WAY.
THE BUTTERFLY SPREAD. DO YOU KNOW THIS ONE?
n-NO...
IT'S IDEAL FOR A YOUNG MAN SUCH AS YOURSELF...
A YOUNG MAN ON THE BRINK OF...
...TRANSFORMATION.

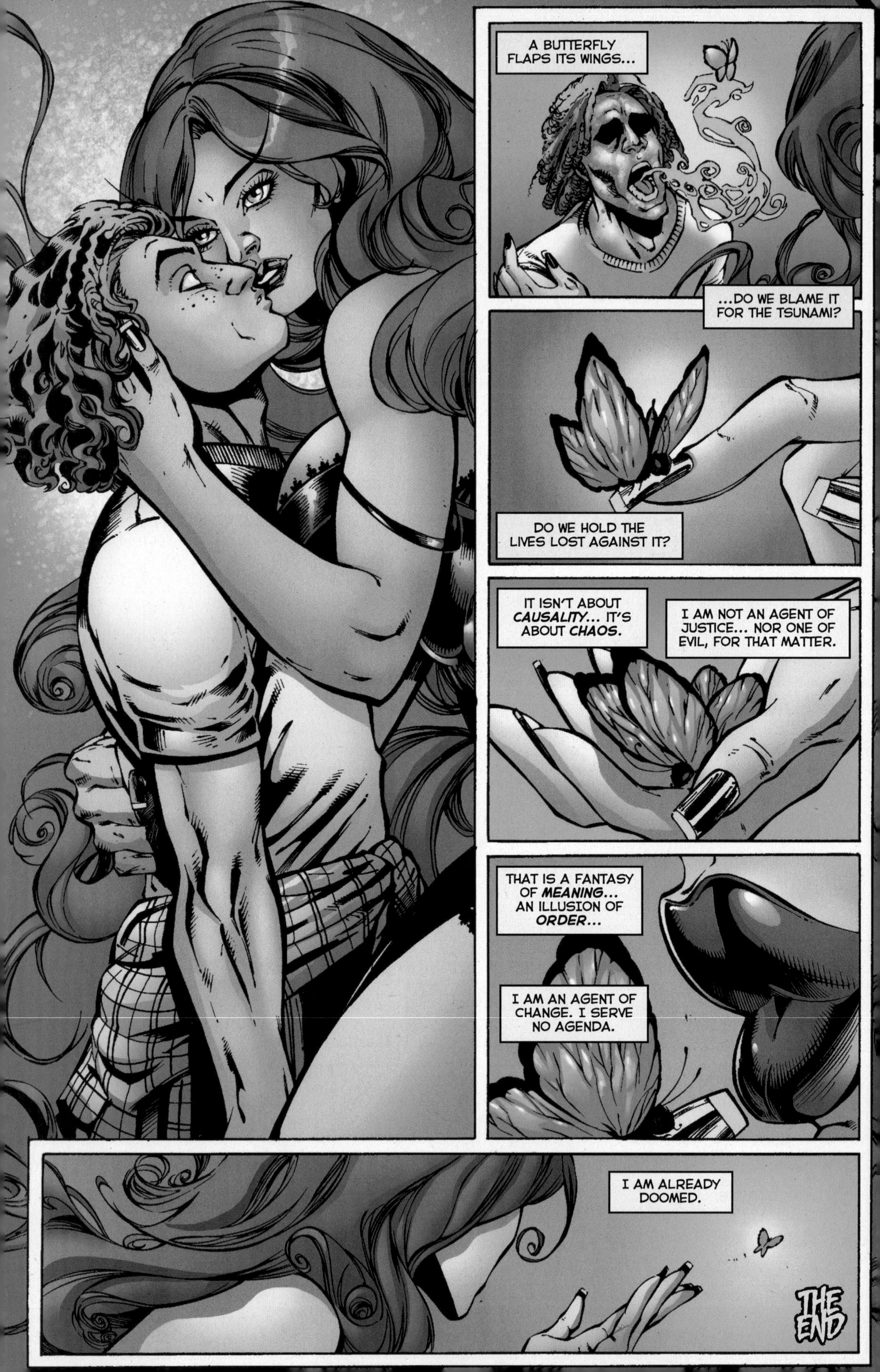
A BUTTERFLY FLAPS ITS WINGS...
...DO WE BLAME IT FOR THE TSUNAMI?
DO WE HOLD THE LIVES LOST AGAINST IT?
IT ISN'T ABOUT *CAUSALITY*... IT'S ABOUT *CHAOS*.
I AM NOT AN AGENT OF JUSTICE... NOR ONE OF EVIL, FOR THAT MATTER.
THAT IS A FANTASY OF *MEANING*... AN ILLUSION OF *ORDER*...
I AM AN AGENT OF CHANGE. I SERVE NO AGENDA.
I AM ALREADY DOOMED.
THE END

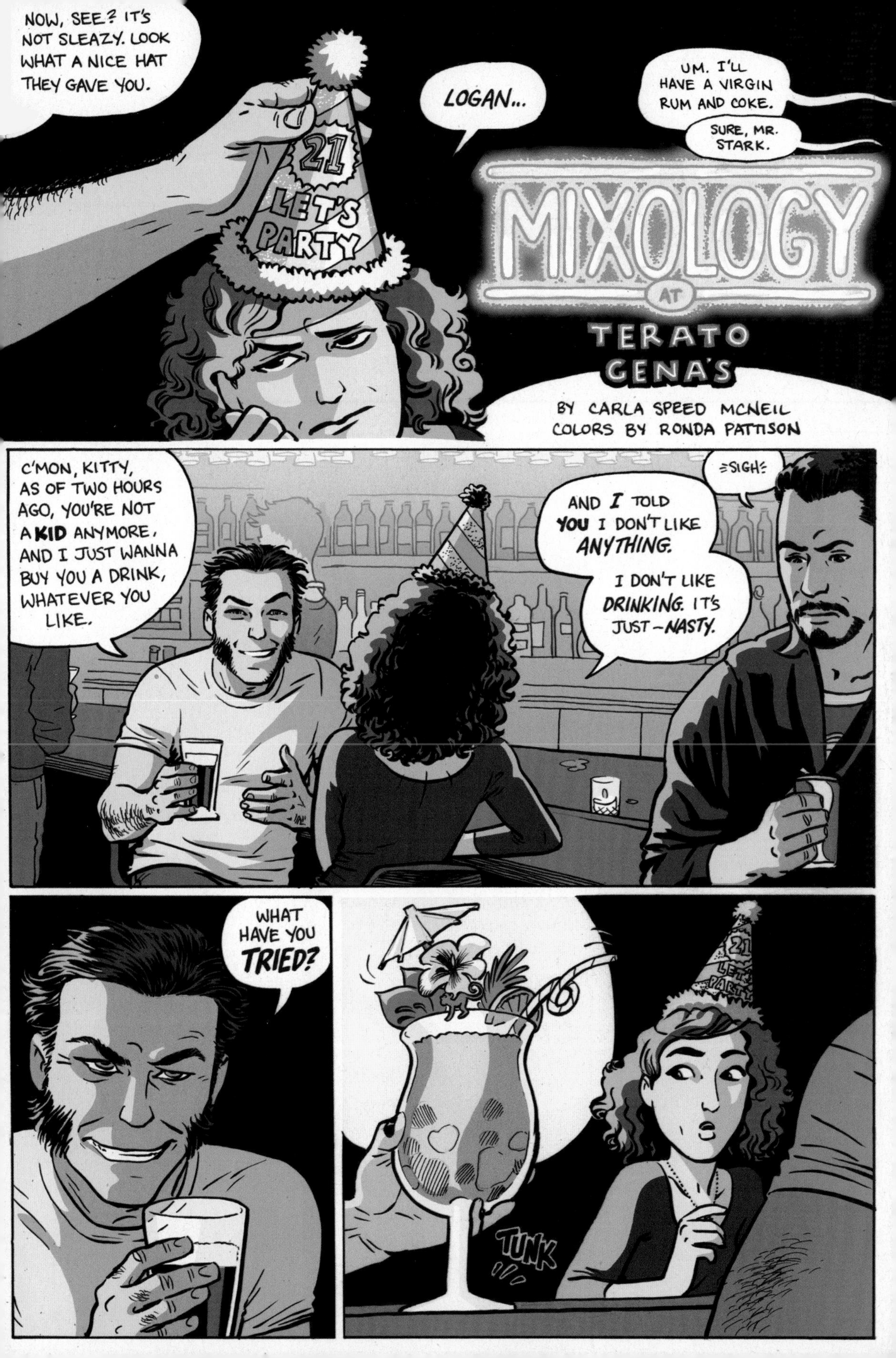
NOW, SEE? IT'S NOT SLEAZY. LOOK WHAT A NICE HAT THEY GAVE YOU.
LOGAN...
UM. I'LL HAVE A VIRGIN RUM AND COKE.
SURE, MR. STARK.
21 LET'S PARTY
MIXOLOGY AT TERATO GENA'S
BY CARLA SPEED MCNEIL
COLORS BY RONDA PATTISON
C'MON, KITTY, AS OF TWO HOURS AGO, YOU'RE NOT A KID ANYMORE, AND I JUST WANNA BUY YOU A DRINK, WHATEVER YOU LIKE.
AND I TOLD YOU I DON'T LIKE ANYTHING.
I DON'T LIKE DRINKING. IT'S JUST—NASTY.
SIGH
WHAT HAVE YOU TRIED?
TUNK
21 LET'S PARTY

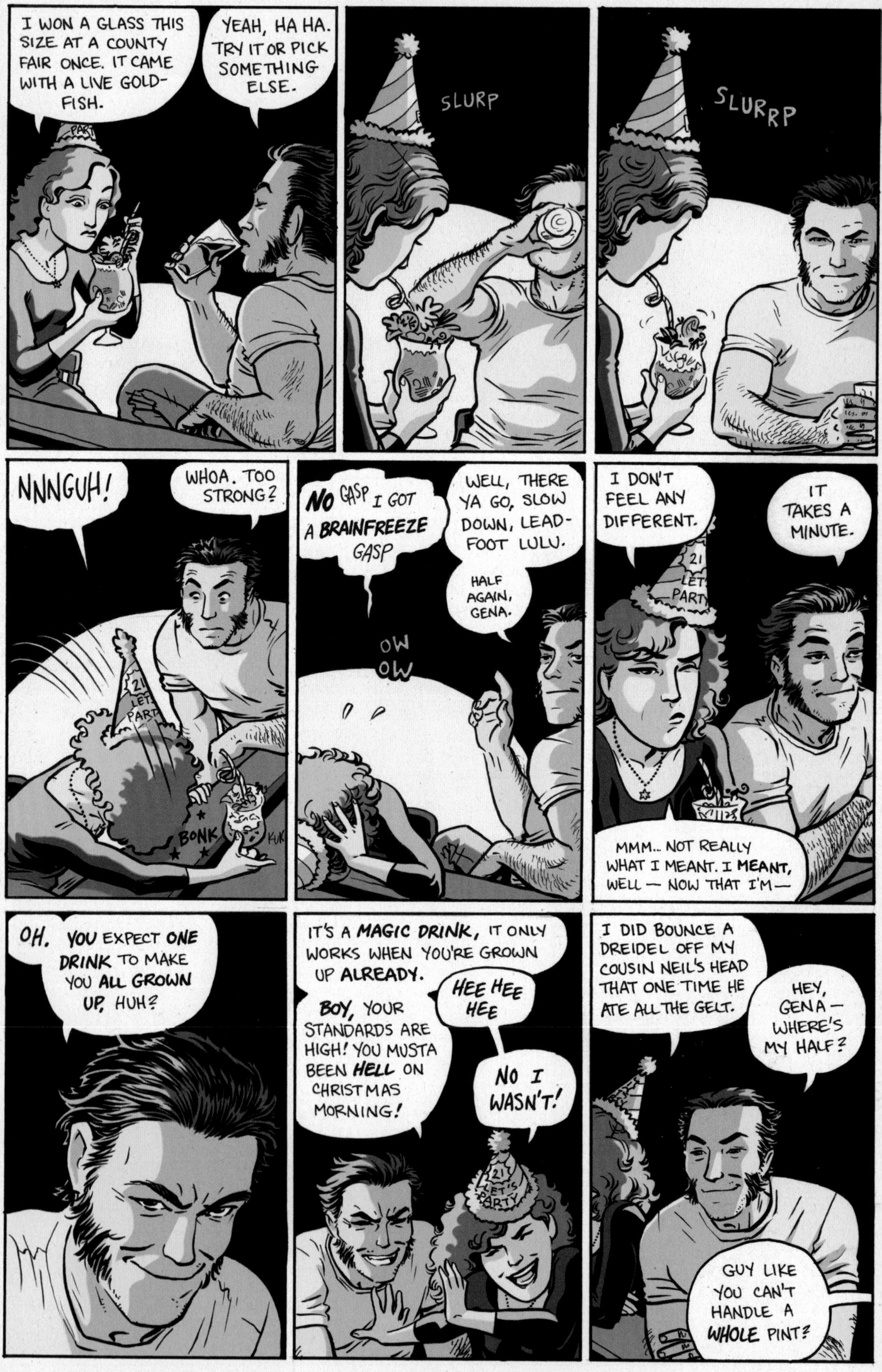
I WON A GLASS THIS SIZE AT A COUNTY FAIR ONCE. IT CAME WITH A LIVE GOLD-FISH.
YEAH, HA HA. TRY IT OR PICK SOMETHING ELSE.
SLURP
SLURRP
NNNGUH!
WHOA. TOO STRONG?
BONK
NO GASP I GOT A BRAINFREEZE GASP
WELL, THERE YA GO, SLOW DOWN, LEAD-FOOT LULU.
HALF AGAIN, GENA.
OW OW
I DON'T FEEL ANY DIFFERENT.
IT TAKES A MINUTE.
MMM... NOT REALLY WHAT I MEANT. I MEANT, WELL — NOW THAT I'M—
OH. YOU EXPECT ONE DRINK TO MAKE YOU ALL GROWN UP, HUH?
IT'S A MAGIC DRINK, IT ONLY WORKS WHEN YOU'RE GROWN UP ALREADY.
BOY, YOUR STANDARDS ARE HIGH! YOU MUSTA BEEN HELL ON CHRISTMAS MORNING!
HEE HEE HEE
NO I WASN'T!
I DID BOUNCE A DREIDEL OFF MY COUSIN NEIL'S HEAD THAT ONE TIME HE ATE ALL THE GELT.
HEY, GENA— WHERE'S MY HALF?
GUY LIKE YOU CAN'T HANDLE A WHOLE PINT?

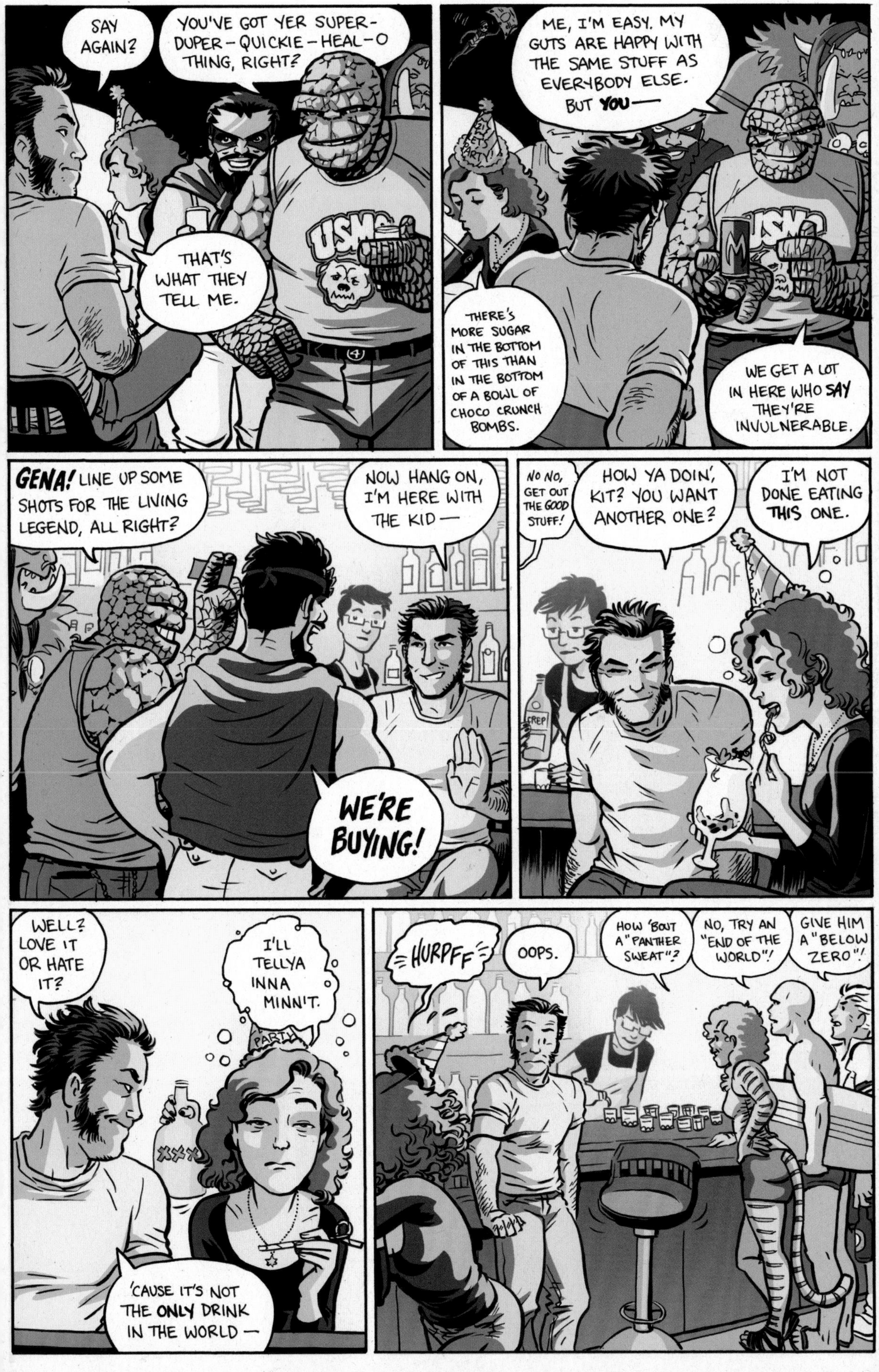
SAY AGAIN?
YOU'VE GOT YER SUPER-DUPER-QUICKIE-HEAL-O THING, RIGHT?
THAT'S WHAT THEY TELL ME.
ME, I'M EASY. MY GUTS ARE HAPPY WITH THE SAME STUFF AS EVERYBODY ELSE. BUT YOU—
THERE'S MORE SUGAR IN THE BOTTOM OF THIS THAN IN THE BOTTOM OF A BOWL OF CHOCO CRUNCH BOMBS.
WE GET A LOT IN HERE WHO SAY THEY'RE INVULNERABLE.
GENA! LINE UP SOME SHOTS FOR THE LIVING LEGEND, ALL RIGHT?
NOW HANG ON, I'M HERE WITH THE KID—
WE'RE BUYING!
NO NO, GET OUT THE GOOD STUFF!
HOW YA DOIN', KIT? YOU WANT ANOTHER ONE?
I'M NOT DONE EATING THIS ONE.
WELL? LOVE IT OR HATE IT?
I'LL TELLYA INNA MINNIT.
'CAUSE IT'S NOT THE ONLY DRINK IN THE WORLD—
HURPFF
OOPS.
HOW 'BOUT A "PANTHER SWEAT"?
NO, TRY AN "END OF THE WORLD"!
GIVE HIM A "BELOW ZERO"!

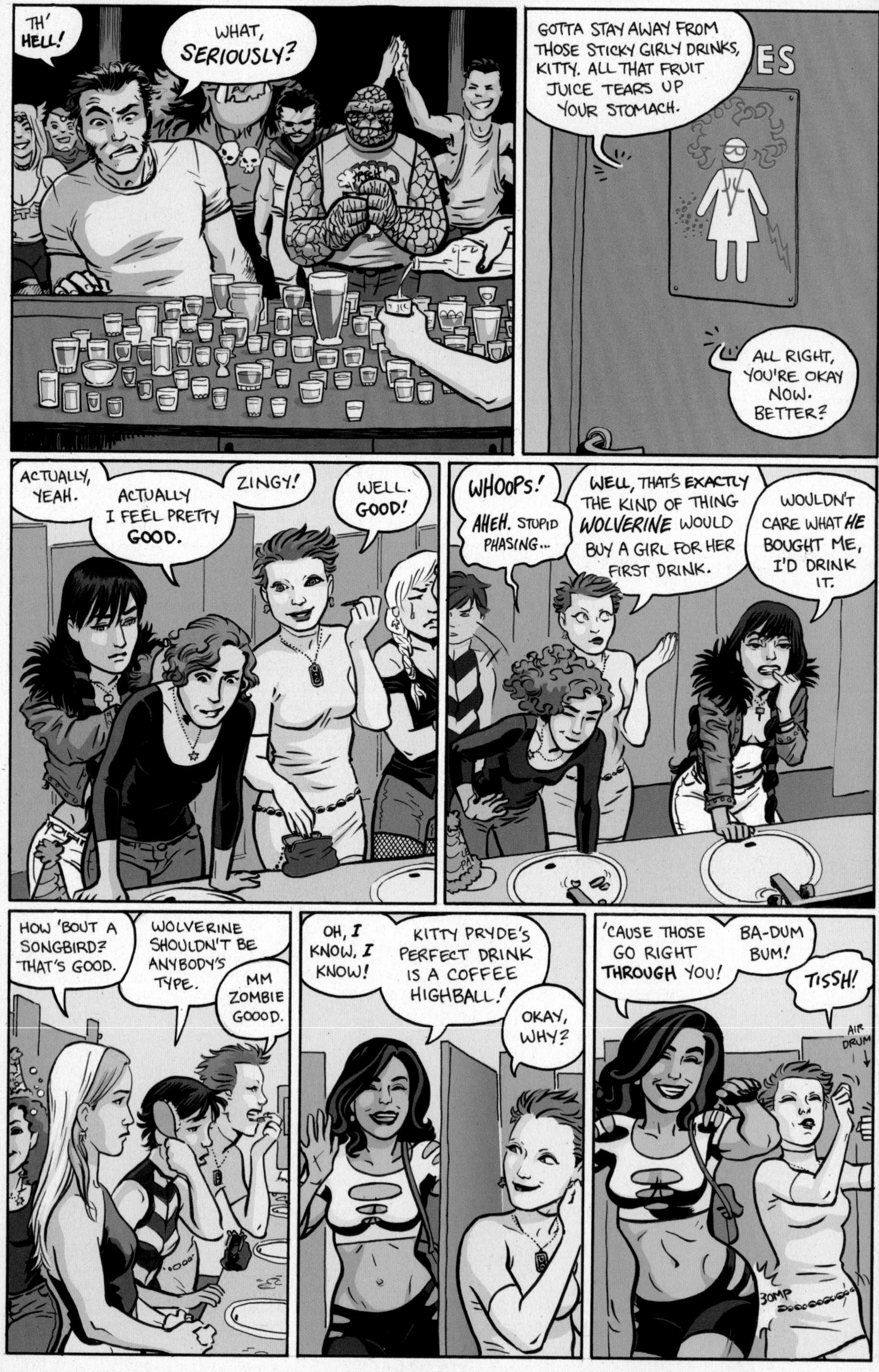

TH' HELL!
WHAT, SERIOUSLY?
GOTTA STAY AWAY FROM THOSE STICKY GIRLY DRINKS, KITTY. ALL THAT FRUIT JUICE TEARS UP YOUR STOMACH.
ALL RIGHT, YOU'RE OKAY NOW. BETTER?
ACTUALLY, YEAH.
ACTUALLY I FEEL PRETTY GOOD.
ZINGY!
WELL. GOOD!
WHOOPS!
AHEH. STUPID PHASING...
WELL, THAT'S EXACTLY THE KIND OF THING WOLVERINE WOULD BUY A GIRL FOR HER FIRST DRINK.
WOULDN'T CARE WHAT HE BOUGHT ME, I'D DRINK IT.
HOW 'BOUT A SONGBIRD? THAT'S GOOD.
WOLVERINE SHOULDN'T BE ANYBODY'S TYPE.
MM ZOMBIE GOOOD.
OH, I KNOW. I KNOW!
KITTY PRYDE'S PERFECT DRINK IS A COFFEE HIGHBALL!
OKAY, WHY?
'CAUSE THOSE GO RIGHT THROUGH YOU!
BA-DUM BUM!
TISSH!
AIR DRUM

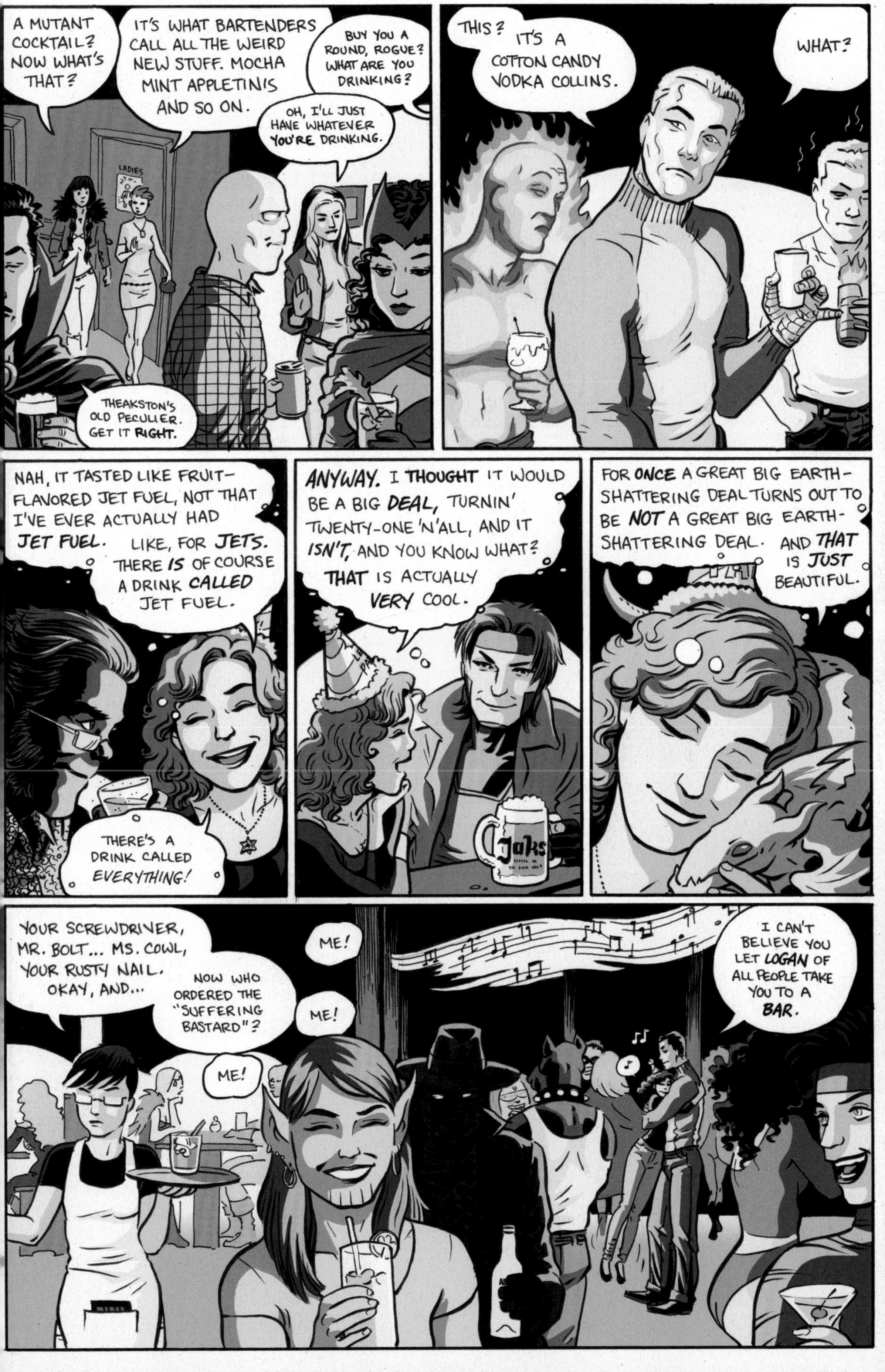
A MUTANT COCKTAIL? NOW WHAT'S THAT?
IT'S WHAT BARTENDERS CALL ALL THE WEIRD NEW STUFF. MOCHA MINT APPLETINIS AND SO ON.
BUY YOU A ROUND, ROGUE? WHAT ARE YOU DRINKING?
OH, I'LL JUST HAVE WHATEVER YOU'RE DRINKING.
THEAKSTON'S OLD PECULIER. GET IT RIGHT.
LADIES
THIS? IT'S A COTTON CANDY VODKA COLLINS.
WHAT?
NAH, IT TASTED LIKE FRUIT-FLAVORED JET FUEL, NOT THAT I'VE EVER ACTUALLY HAD JET FUEL. LIKE, FOR JETS. THERE IS OF COURSE A DRINK CALLED JET FUEL.
THERE'S A DRINK CALLED EVERYTHING!
ANYWAY. I THOUGHT IT WOULD BE A BIG DEAL, TURNIN' TWENTY-ONE 'N'ALL, AND IT ISN'T, AND YOU KNOW WHAT? THAT IS ACTUALLY VERY COOL.
Jaks
FOR ONCE A GREAT BIG EARTH-SHATTERING DEAL TURNS OUT TO BE NOT A GREAT BIG EARTH-SHATTERING DEAL. AND THAT IS JUST BEAUTIFUL.
YOUR SCREWDRIVER, MR. BOLT... MS. COWL, YOUR RUSTY NAIL. OKAY, AND...
NOW WHO ORDERED THE "SUFFERING BASTARD"?
ME!
ME!
ME!
I CAN'T BELIEVE YOU LET LOGAN OF ALL PEOPLE TAKE YOU TO A BAR.

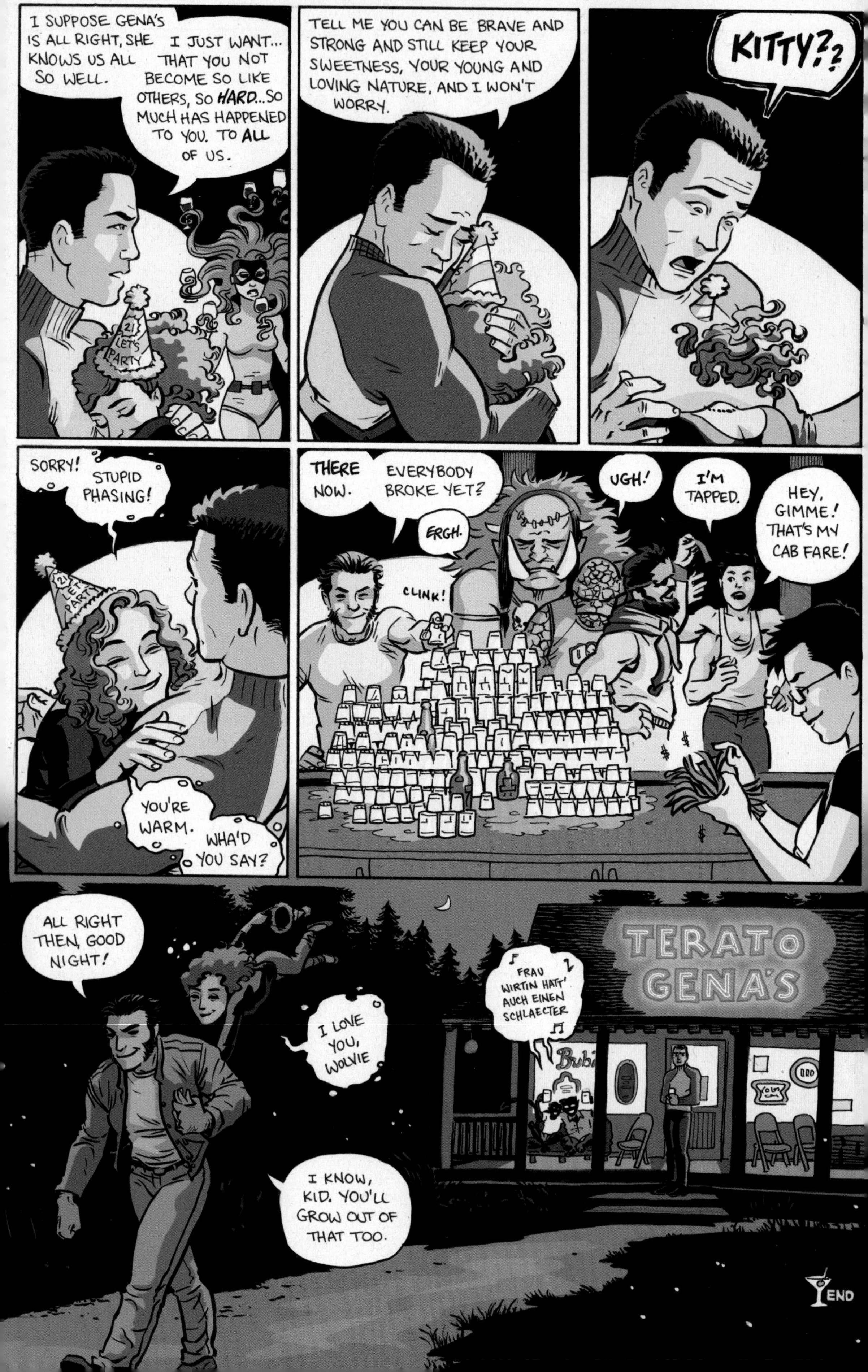
I SUPPOSE GENA'S IS ALL RIGHT, SHE KNOWS US ALL SO WELL.
I JUST WANT... THAT YOU NOT BECOME SO LIKE OTHERS, SO HARD...SO MUCH HAS HAPPENED TO YOU. TO ALL OF US.
21 LET'S PARTY
TELL ME YOU CAN BE BRAVE AND STRONG AND STILL KEEP YOUR SWEETNESS, YOUR YOUNG AND LOVING NATURE, AND I WON'T WORRY.
KITTY??
SORRY!
STUPID PHASING!
21 LET'S PARTY
YOU'RE WARM.
WHA'D YOU SAY?
THERE NOW.
EVERYBODY BROKE YET?
ERGH.
CLINK!
UGH!
I'M TAPPED.
HEY, GIMME! THAT'S MY CAB FARE!
ALL RIGHT THEN, GOOD NIGHT!
I LOVE YOU, WOLVIE
I KNOW, KID. YOU'LL GROW OUT OF THAT TOO.
FRAU WIRTIN HATT' AUCH EINEN SCHLAECTER
TERATO GENA'S
END

FINDING MYSELF AMONG THE PANELS

by **LORRAINE CINK**

Marvel Comics changed me, my life, and my future.

Before I was the author of Marvel books, host of Marvel video series and podcasts, or Director of Creative Content for Marvel Entertainment, I was raised to be someone else.

My upbringing was filled with the echoes of the traditional conventions:

"Children should be seen and not heard."
— Adults

"Little girls are sugar and spice and everything nice."
— Kids around the schoolyard

"Lorraine, put your dress down. I can see your underwear."
— My mother

Every day was a reminder that little girls were supposed to be lovely, quiet creatures full of patience and kindness who most definitely didn't mind wearing scratchy dresses all day. We were being shaped to be future wives or mothers — titles in relation to those we are supposed to serve. Needless to say, this mold wasn't an easy fit.

I was born "a wild thing." I arrived screaming into the world, full of curiosity, a little too loud, feeling too much, ready to fight, to laugh, to cry, to love. Over the years, like so many of us "wild things," the world tried to domesticate me and quiet my voice. I learned ballet, how to share, and when to be quiet (which I struggled with most). But I still couldn't escape scabby knees from riding cardboard boxes down dusty dirt hills or getting motor oil on my good shirt. Though my wildness was unavoidable, I also worried, "Is who or what I am bad? Is it dangerous to be wild?"

I followed around my big brother, hoping to find an answer or perhaps a bit of adventure. What I found was his comic book stash. It wasn't the adventure I was looking for, but it was more than I could have asked for. Encountering the characters of the Marvel Universe was my introduction to loud, angry, tough, funny, and courageous women who were allowed to exist just the way they were. No one told them that they were weak, incapable things that needed protection — they were strong, adept, and above all, wonderfully dangerous.

That was especially true for some of my favorite characters. While Jean Grey was, in many ways, the bygone feminine ideal, she was also fire, death, and rebirth incarnate as the Phoenix. Yes, Storm was regal and stoic, but she also was a weather goddess who could electrocute anyone who crossed her path. Even Mary Jane Watson, who caught every man's eye, never cared much for relationships, putting herself and her

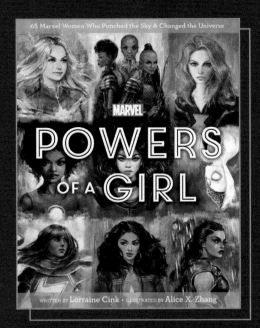

65 Marvel Women Who Punched the Sky & Changed the Universe

MARVEL

POWERS OF A GIRL

WRITTEN BY Lorraine Cink • ILLUSTRATED BY Alice X. Zhang

Marvel: Powers of a Girl cover by Alice X. Zhang

dreams ahead of any Romeo, even Peter Parker. And the blue-skinned, gray-moraled Mystique, who could shape-shift into anyone, was beautiful but terrifying. When I read their stories, I knew they were like me; these women were wild things too.

We were dangerous.

In comics, mutants try to survive in a world that hates and fears them because they are different. Being a young person who felt strange, untamed, questioning my sexuality, my purpose, and my innermost self felt much the same. Not fitting the mold felt dangerous. I was different, and if I didn't comply, I might face an inhospitable world.

But when I turned to the pages and cartoons of the X-Men and other Marvel super heroes, I saw a different path. If they could be heroes and their true selves, perhaps I too could remain untamed and still do good things. I realized my worth was not determined by how well I fit the mold, but rather by my good works.

I didn't know I'd grow up to write books like *Marvel: Powers of a Girl*, which not

only tells the stories of the women in the Marvel Universe but of the powers that make them heroes. Spoiler alert: It isn't just their super-powers. What I did know, thanks to these stories, was that anyone can be a hero by choosing to do good things with the power they have. And above all, that we can be a wild, powerful woman or girl, and do amazing things by simply choosing to do them.

Because of comics, my life has been indelibly changed for the better. Today, one of my great joys is encountering women and girls on *their* journeys. I live for telling little girls dressed up as Captain Marvel, Ghost-Spider, Squirrel Girl, and Black Widow that they look powerful (not just pretty). It is an honor hugging weepy teens who explain how their favorite hero helped them find their voice. And it's been a thrill seeing women blossom from fans to fan-favorite creators. Just like me, so many of these women and girls have learned through their love of these incredible characters and stories that they too are wonderfully dangerous, and the world is better for it.

LORRAINE CINK is author of *Marvel: Powers of a Girl*, and co-author of *Marvel Absolutely Everything You Need to Know* and *Ultimate Marvel*. She is Director of Creative Content for Marvel Entertainment and can be heard on *This Week in Marvel* and as a guest contributor on the *Women of Marvel* podcast.

THE WOMEN OF MARVEL LOCKER ROOM

by MacKENZIE CADENHEAD

In my Marvel job interview, I was told that there was a bit of a "locker-room mentality" in the office and was asked if I could handle it. Like so many women faced with similar questions, I deflected, telling a slightly off-color joke. I made the interviewer laugh and was hired. On my first day, I was the new "girl in the Ultimates office." The former "girl in the Ultimates office" had only lasted a few weeks, and I got the distinct impression that some of my co-workers wanted to give it a couple days before committing my actual name to memory. Though the interview question and my epithet probably bother me more now than either did at the time, they certainly didn't surprise me.

I was used to entering worlds where I wasn't the core demographic. That was part of the appeal — establishing my place in environments that I wanted to be a part of even if others didn't see where I fit in... YET. And while it's a good skill to be able to acclimate quickly to your surroundings, you run the risk of losing yourself. Things could have gone that way for me at Marvel. Thankfully they didn't.

In part that's because comics, as a medium, requires collaboration. As an editor, I love taking dissonant personalities and guiding them into harmony. But that only works when there's trust, which starts with the editor being their authentic self. For me, there was another crucial ingredient to finding and feeling confident in my voice at Marvel — the women I worked with.

In my first week, Editor Jennifer Lee let me know she had my back and that her door was always open. That may not seem like a big thing, but when you enter a space knowing you're different, the offer of allyship is huge. That small gesture sets you up to succeed, offering a respite from every other moment of your workday spent trying to prove your worth. True to her word, Jenny's support was unyielding, her feedback honest, and to this day, she is one of my most trusted confidants.

Then there was the late, great Flo Steinberg, who cheered me on from the start. It's safe to say Flo had seen it all by the time I met her. Beginning with her tenure as Stan Lee's assistant in the 1960s and through her many different roles over the decades, no one knew Marvel better. With the warmest smiles and greatest hugs, Flo let every woman know we belonged. Who were we, or anyone else, to argue?

When I was an editor, Flo was Marvel's proofreader, and every time she returned one of my books, she would tell me how good my work was and how important my voice was. I can't overstate how her kindness and affirmation turned around the most challenging days.

I also had support from many incredible male colleagues, but the psychic importance of seeing someone like you in the room is impossible to quantify. And while we may all have identified as women, we certainly didn't have the same opinions or experiences. Our differences shaped us and strengthened our work — be they differences of cultural background, race, ethnicity, sexual orientation, religious beliefs, etc. Still, being able to share a knowing glance with Jenny, Flo, Editor Jennifer Grünwald, Production Manager Susan Crespi or any of the other women I worked with was bolstering.

Growing up, media wanted me to believe that women in the workplace were catty backstabbers out for each other's jobs. We were taught there was only room for one. The women at Marvel debunked that narrative with our everyday actions. When (now) Marvel executive Sana Amanat entered my life as an assistant editor with a natural ability to art direct and story instincts that sharpened with every script, I, like Jenny (perhaps *because* of Jenny), didn't think, "Uh-oh, competition." I thought, "Here's someone I can support, who can challenge me." She was someone with whom I could have a meaningful creative relationship — a relationship that's now sixteen years strong.

Since I started in comics, the women at Marvel have multiplied. Not just within the office walls but beyond, expanding into an incredible international community of creators and fans through the Women of Marvel convention panels, a podcast, and comics. That expansion also includes a series that Sana and I, along with Marvel.com Editor

Christine Dinh, created to shine a light on amazing women and nonbinary creators in our industry called *Asked & Answered with the Women of Marvel.*

On its surface, *Asked & Answered* is a fun Q&A column. But go a little deeper, and it's an invitation for our daughters and nonbinary kids to see themselves in these creators, and perhaps discover a previously unconsidered path. And, for our sons, to normalize seeing women and nonbinary people in these roles and as role models.

Upon reflection, maybe that interviewer was right. Maybe there is a locker-room mentality at Marvel. Mine is just a different locker room — and mentality — than the one he meant. My Women of Marvel locker room is filled with battle-ready and battle-worn teammates. We celebrate each other's victories and bandage each other's wounds. We acknowledge our scars and cheer each other on to the next match. We tell some excellent jokes too. We don't always agree, but we do try to listen because we know the importance of our teammates' voices.

MacKENZIE CADENHEAD is a writer and editor based in New York. She is the author of the middle-grade fantasy novel *Sally's Bones*, the YA science fiction thriller *Sleeper*, and co-author of the *Marvel Super Hero Adventures* series of chapter books for young readers. She currently writes the column *Asked & Answered with the Women of Marvel* on Marvel.com. Favorite past employment includes pizza delivery person, dramaturg, and comic book editor for Marvel comics (not in that order).

ASKED & ANSWERED
WOMEN OF MARVEL

KRISTEN ANDERSON-LOPEZ
by MacKENZIE CADENHEAD

She's written some of the most beloved musical showstoppers of the last decade (*Frozen*'s "Let it Go," *Coco*'s "Remember Me"). She's won multiple awards, including Oscars and Grammys. Now Kristen Anderson-Lopez has made hers Marvel by penning the nostalgic and super-catchy theme songs for Marvel Studios' *WandaVision* — surely, I can't be the only one playing "Agatha All Along" on repeat!

Anderson-Lopez's songs are funny, smart and often leave you with a lump in your throat. To say that we comics-loving theater nerds are psyched to claim her as a Woman of Marvel is an understatement. We had some questions for her.

We asked, she answered.

What is the first thing you do when you wake up?
Check the time and maybe glance at the *NY Times* app.

Super-power of choice?
Wanda's — she's got mind control but can also float which would come in handy on the NYC sidewalks.

The key to collaboration is…?
Safe, honest communication.

Developed any new skills over the last few months at home?
We've been doing these Hello Fresh meals for our family which is like getting a LEGO set for dinner. The step-by-step instruction and ingredients kit are everything I need to learn how to cook.

Favorite TV theme song?
Gilmore Girls — Carole King and daughter duet, yes please!!

When humans live on Mars, what one food item must we bring with us?
My husband's unbelievably delicious homemade smashburgers.

In an alternate universe, what would your alternate job be?
Psychologist. Preferably a couples or family counselor — a good one can transform so much pain into love by helping a family listen and communicate.

What's on your desert island mix tape?
"Tiny Dancer" (Elton John)
"Penny Lane" (Beatles)
"Get Out the Map" (Indigo Girls)
"Rainbow" (Kacey Musgraves)
"Make Your Own Kind of Music" (Mama Cass version)
"Sir Duke" (Stevie Wonder)
"Kyoto" (Phoebe Bridgers)
"Feelin' Alright" (Joe Cocker)
"Can't We Be Friends?" (Ella Fitzgerald)

"Graceland" (Paul Simon)
"The Lazarus Heart" (Sting)
"What a Wonderful World" (Louis Armstrong version)
"In My Life" (Beatles)
"Both Sides Now" (Joni Mitchell)
"Bitter Sweet Symphony" (The Verve)

What was your favorite book, movie, or TV show as a kid?

Anne of Green Gables. I truly relate to her wild imagination and the way her "extraness" creates the highs and lows in her life. We named our second daughter after Anne.

What is your favorite book, movie, or TV show now?

Oh, wow. There are so many. Currently obsessed with *Minari*, a beautiful movie that will definitely win multiple Oscars. I also really love *Ted Lasso*. I love stories that celebrate good people just trying to do their best.

Best advice you've gotten?

Oprah had an article with the pull quote, "You are not your thoughts. You are the thinker of those thoughts." It's good to make sure your thoughts know who is in control so they don't take over.

Musical or show-stopping number that still knocks your socks off?

I'm sorry if this is lame, but I know how hard it is to sing "Let It Go." So I have extreme respect for the actresses who bring down the Act 1 curtain in the *Frozen* live-action musical. They are singing their faces off while also initiating and executing very complicated stage magic. They are pulling off the impossible and it's breathtaking.

What or who makes you laugh?

My husband is hysterically funny and makes me laugh out loud at least a dozen times a day.

What was 13-year-old Kristen's jam?

EVITA. I did a one-woman version in my walk-in closet on my Mr. Microphone. Like, every day of eighth grade, this happened.

Other than Wanda and Vision, Marvel character(s) most deserving of their own theme song?

He's Tony!
He's Tony Stark!
Fighting crime is his walk in the park!
Servin' up justice with a side of snark!
He's our Tony Stark!

Board games or video games?

Board games. Definitely board games. We are very into "The Game of Things" at the moment. I DID just try an Oculus game where you get to drum beat by hitting cubes in the air. It made me feel like a badass, but I looked insane and felt like I was going to hurt someone.

Stage or screen?

I love both for different reasons. I love stage for the one-of-a-kind spiritual experience we can all share in one space together. I love screen because I can stay home in my sweatpants, I don't have to take a long car ride or subway to an overly crowded place, and I don't have to stand in a long ladies' room line to go to the bathroom. But having experienced ONLY the screen for ten months now, I'm VERY excited to experience the transcendence that can only be found through live theater.

Times Square — where dreams are made or just a place to get a selfie with an unauthorized Spidey?

See the above answer! Times Square can be tough to navigate if I'm exhausted and burnt out as sometimes can happen if I have a new show in the unique form of hell that is called "Previews." That said, there have been some incredible moments looking up at the buildings on a breezy spring evening and seeing a big billboard for something I've created up there. That is pretty darn magic and I'm so grateful to have had that feeling.

Favorite lyric you've written?

Oh, I can't possibly answer that. Once they are out in the world, they don't belong to me anymore. I'm excited about some of the things I am writing for our new projects!

Mantra or quote that keeps you going?

"Nothing in the world can take the place of persistence. Talent will not; nothing is more common than unsuccessful men with talent. Genius will not; unrewarded genius is almost a proverb. Education will not; the world is full of educated derelicts. Persistence and determination alone are omnipotent." — Calvin Coolidge

Best thing about being a Woman of Marvel?

Wow! I didn't realize I was a Woman of Marvel!!! Well, the best thing is the incredible fan base. It has been an honor to create and feel myself in conversation with this global, diverse, intelligent audience.

ASKED & ANSWERED
WOMEN OF MARVEL

PEACH MOMOKO
by MacKENZIE CADENHEAD

Peach Momoko's work is simply breathtaking. The Marvel Stormbreaker's variant covers are total must-haves, and she continues to reimagine the Marvel Universe with her DEMON DAYS saga. She had her writing and interior art debut with DEMON DAYS: X-MEN #1, and the next installment of the prestige series, DEMON DAYS: MARIKO #1, arrives on June 16!

Her talent is only matched by her generosity (seriously — look what she illustrated just for us, below!). Her answers made me hungry. I want to meet her dog. She's a Woman of Marvel and we had some questions for her.

We asked. She answered.

What is the first thing you do when you wake up?
When I wake up, first thing I do is tickle my dog, Momo. (And sometimes fall back to sleep because of it.)

Favorite food to eat?
My favorite food is anything noodle (ramen, soba, udon, pasta, anything).

Favorite food to illustrate?
I usually like to paint soul food. Food that represents daily meal. So after realizing I haven't painted food lately, I decided to paint what I ate today — Nabeyaki Udon.

What are you totally in to right now?
Right now I have been into playing video games (specifically Apex Legends and *The Binding of Isaac*), the smell of sandalwood, and eating "yogurt scotch Chelsea."

Of all the Marvel characters you've illustrated, which one would you like to be for a day and why?
I always think about this whenever I watch a movie or read a comic. But right now, the first character that came to mind was Scarlet Witch. She can fly...move objects...mind-control... Everything I want do.

Better to ask permission or forgiveness?
I prefer to ask permission.

Who is your dream collaborator (living or dead)?
My dream is to collaborate with Takashi Nakamura's anime, doing character design and/or image board/storyboard. And also to go on Toshio Suzuki's radio show as a guest (producer of Ghibli Studio).

Must have items when working?
I need my iPad. I can stream music, videos and search for references.

What music can you not stop listening to right now?
It really depends on my mood. (Do I want to paint an action-packed scene? Do I want to paint a

sad and depressing scene? Do I want to paint an aggressive scene?)

But this week (end of May 2021), I have been listening to:
"Machi" (Quruli)
"Jishaku" (Aiko)
"Tsuyogari Mashita" (Aimyon)
"Strawberry Moon" (Daoko)
"Ai No Kotodama ~Spiritual Message~" (Southern All-Stars)
"Suna No Wakusei" (Yuuming Matsutoya)
"Kisui" (Yuusari)

Fantastic Four #32
variant cover by **Peach Momoko**

What was your favorite book, movie, or TV show as a kid?
When I was about 6 years old, I loved reading Takashi Nakamura's *Peter Pan*. I remember looking at Tinkerbell when my mom was cooking.

What is your favorite book, movie, or TV show now?
Nothing currently off the top of my head. I love watching movies and shows but nothing is ringing a bell that is a "favorite" now.

What item would you save from a burning building?
In a burning building, I would grab my I.D. (Assuming we are only talking "item.")

What's your most vivid childhood memory?
I ate too much peanut butter and puked in my bathtub.
I was eating a bowl of sugar under the dining table (hiding from my mom).
I told my mom I wanted a KEROKEROKEROPPI (Sanrio character) purse, then when my mom bought it, I told her, "I don't want it anymore." She got mad at me and kicked me out of the house for a while.

Story or folktale you heard as a child that still influences you today?
A Japanese folktale called Mottainai Obake. It is about wasting food (leftovers), and at night the wasted food becomes ghosts and kidnaps you.

How awesome is your dog?!
Momo is awesome as usual!

Fortune teller — "Tell me everything" or "No thanks, I'll be surprised"?
No thanks, I like surprises.

Who makes you laugh?
My husband and partner, Yo. And Momo.

Mantra or quote that keeps you going?
I love all the quotes by Little My from the book Moomin Valley [by Tove Jansson]. The one that is really special to me is:

"ひま、やることがない。
なんて間抜けなセリフだこと。
春は花を見て、
夏は太陽を浴びて、
秋は落ち葉を踏んで、
冬は静かに春を待つの。
やることがないんじゃないわ。
やることをわかってないのよ"

which translates to:

"Bored, there is nothing to do?
What a pointless way of thinking.
In spring, you look at flowers.
In summer, you bathe in sun.
In autumn, you step off foliage.
In winter, you quietly wait for spring.
It's not that you are bored and have nothing to do;
You just don't understand what you are doing."

Best thing about being a Woman of Marvel?
I'm simply honored that I am amongst one of the woman artists working in this industry.

ASKED & ANSWERED

WOMEN OF MARVEL

GUGU MBATHA-RAW AND WUNMI MOSAKU
by MacKENZIE CADENHEAD

Gugu Mbatha-Raw and Wunmi Mosaku are two stellar actresses whose work I just love (check out Mbatha-Raw in *Black Mirror: San Junipero* and Mosaku in *Lovecraft Country*). Watching them together on everyone's new favorite series, Marvel Studios' *Loki* is delectable.

Getting to know them better through our quirky questions has been the icing on the cake. They've got good advice to share. They know what to put on a mixtape. They are timeless Women of Marvel. And we had some questions for them.

We asked. She answered.

What is the first thing you do when you wake up?
Wunmi: Check my phone.
Gugu: Stretch.

What makes a great day?
Wunmi: Quiet. Peace and quiet. Good food. Cuddles. And then I would say hanging out with my niece and nephew.
Gugu: A chocolate brownie.

What gets you up at 3:00 A.M.?
Wunmi: Anxiety.

Gugu: Oh, God, I would never get up at 3:00 A.M.! I had to get up at 3:00 A.M., actually, to come to Canada for this job. So I guess work occasionally gets me up at 3:00 A.M.

In an alternate timeline, what would your alternate job be?
Wunmi: I would have been a math professor.

Gugu: I'd probably love to be a painter, like an artist.

Super-power of choice?
Wunmi: Being in one place and then another place. I want to be in bed, just being in bed. Go to my mum's house, go to my mum's house. Go home. No travel, just be there.
Gugu: I'd love to be able to fly or be invisible. I think those are pretty cool, useful ones. Or just teleport somewhere, not having to worry about quarantine.

Best advice you've gotten?
Wunmi: Leave every room a bit nicer than you found it.
Gugu: Follow your instincts.

What's on your "Transcends All Timelines" mixtape?
Wunmi: Erykah Badu, Jill Scott, Red Hot Chili Peppers, Sia, All Saints, Incubus, Destiny's Child.
Gugu: It's got to be some Prince. He's on there. Definitely some Nina Simone. Timeless, timeless artists like Otis Redding. I love those old school kind of soulful singers, so they'd be up there for me.

What's the best thing about your best friend?
Wunmi: That she understands me.
Gugu: Actually I've got two best friends. They both make me feel like I can do anything.

If you could go anywhere in time, when would you visit and why?
Wunmi: I'd go back to see my parents as kids. I would like to see them as children and my grandparents' interaction with them.

Gugu: I really would love to go to ancient Egypt, because I've always been obsessed with Cleopatra, and I would just love to meet her and see what she was really like.

Who would you road trip with (dead or alive, someone you know or wish you knew, fictional or real)?
Wunmi: I'm going to say my husband. He likes to drive. He loves a road trip, and I can sleep the whole way.
Gugu: I'm planning a road trip with one of my best girlfriends, so it would have to be one of my best friends.
Truth or dare?
Wunmi: Truth.
Gugu: Truth.

What do you always make time for?
Wunmi: I always make time for my friends.
Gugu: My mom, my dad, and my friends.

What's your go-to karaoke song?
Wunmi: "Sitting on the Dock of the Bay."

Mantra or quote that keeps you going?
Wunmi: Blessed are the flexible, for they never lose their shape.
Gugu: This too shall pass. Keep calm and carry on. Carpe diem. Those are probably my most used ones.

Best thing about being a Woman of Marvel?
Gugu: The strength and the excitement from the fans, and also getting to do amazing fight sequences. And also getting to be the boss.

ASKED & ANSWERED

WOMEN OF MARVEL

CATE SHORTLAND

by MacKENZIE CADENHEAD

In Marvel Studios' *Black Widow*, director Cate Shortland gives the enigmatic Avenger Natasha Romanoff an epic send-off. With thrilling fight sequences, family drama to rival any at my holiday dinner table, and a deeply human protagonist, Shortland's film gives Scarlett Johansson's Natasha her due while introducing us to a new hero-to-watch, Yelena Belova (Florence Pugh).

She makes fascinating films about complex women. She tells us the truth about Vegemite. She's a Woman of Marvel. And we had some questions for her.

We asked. She answered.

What is the first thing you do when you wake up?
Cuddle my dogs. I've got three dogs.

The key to collaboration is…?
Trust.

If you could swap jobs with one member of the crew, who would it be?
The cinematographer.

Best advice you've gotten?
Listen.

Who starts the dinner table food fight — Natasha, Yelena or Red Guardian?
Alexei.

Must-have item when writing?
Sleep.

Must-have item when directing?
Coffee.

What gets you up at 3:00 A.M.?
My daughter. Thinking about my daughter. Thinking about my work. I'm an insomniac. Everything.

Who would you road trip with (dead or alive, someone you know or wish you knew, fictional or real)?
My mother.

What do you always make time for?
My daughter.

Vegemite — the best or as unappetizing as it looks?
The best.

Mantra or quote that keeps you going?
Thank you. Just two words, really.

Best thing about being a Woman of Marvel?
The sisterhood.

SUPER VISIBLE Q&A
WITH MARGARET STOHL & JUDITH STEPHENS
by **ANGÉLIQUE ROCHÉ**

Last year, *New York Times* best-selling author and Marvel creator Margaret "Margie" Stohl and producer, co-host and co-creator of the *Women of Marvel (WOM)* podcast, Judith "Judy" Stephens, set out to tell the story of the women of the "House of Ideas." Their upcoming book, *Super Visible*, provides a never before seen look at this history from 1939 through today including the stories and experiences of the historically invisible women of the comics industry.

Packed with biographies and illustrations of creators, graphic reprints and excerpts of historic Marvel comics and exclusive interviews with award-winning actors, *Super Visible* is set to hit bookshelves this year! I had a chance to sit down with both of these amazing Women of Marvel to discuss their careers, the process of writing *Super Visible*, and — of course — their love of all things Marvel.

AR: Please introduce yourselves.

MS: I'm a storyteller, a world builder, and a nerdy creator. Truly a Jill of a bunch of trades. I've worked in video games at places like Activision and Bungie. I've made video games for Marvel and work on some currently. I've also written fifteen books, but I'm best known for a Southern Gothic romance series, *Beautiful Creatures*. I got into comics for Marvel after my career as a Young Adult Fiction (YA) novelist.

JS: I spent fifteen years at Marvel, predominantly producing. I produced short-form content focusing on fan interactions. I've also done a lot of cosplay work and I'm fairly well-known within the cosplay community as

"Captain Marvel." I'm currently a freelance producer and co-host for the *WOM* podcast.

AR: How did you get introduced to Marvel personally and professionally?

MS: I had brothers. [My] brothers [were] a gateway to comics, action figures and TV. My first interaction with Marvel professionally was making the *Fantastic Four* video game, when I had my own game company, Seven Studios. We did *Silver Surfer* as well and I worked on *Spider-Man* at Activision for the original PlayStation. I re-met Marvel when I wrote *Black Widow: Forever Red*. Sana Amanat then recruited me to write the series *The Life of Captain Marvel*.

JS: I grew up with the original *X-Men Animated Series*. My parents would also leave out the Sunday cartoons and there was always a *Spider-Man* strip in there. I didn't actually start reading comic books until college. In my junior year of college, I applied for an internship at Marvel. I started as an intern in February 2006. A lot of what I did was help panel the digital comics. I read a lot of comics that way.

AR: Can you give a little insight into how *WOM* got started?

JS: It was really an accident. Back then, Marvel was looking to fill a panel slot on Sunday. At the time, there was an all-women [comic book] team. Marvel wanted to market that book but also advocate for women. We were in this weird moment of time back then. The conversations we are having now didn't exist yet. #MeToo hadn't happened. 2020 hadn't happened. [The] George Floyd [protests] hadn't happened. The conversations weren't there yet. People would ask questions during the panels like, "Why do we still need this panel? Isn't comics equal?" Somewhere along the way, Jeanine Schaefer, Sana [Amanat] and I all saw that this was a platform for us to find a voice. We understood that we still didn't have a collective voice yet. In the beginning, it was a thing Marvel did. Along the way, it became this force.

AR: What was your entry point to *WOM*?

MS: My relationship with Marvel changed after my first WOM panel. I came to Marvel because Disney was looking for the top in the field in YA to bridge the two worlds. But for me to walk into Comic-Con and be so included and welcomed in [Marvel] fandom — in a defined space within it — was just so mind-blowing. I was just like, "sign me up." Women of Marvel became an important

thing. I didn't care if I was invited to be on any other panel except for this one. I cared about it.

AR: And now y'all are writing a book. How did that come about?

JS: Simon and Schuster approached Marvel about doing some nonfiction books. One of them was about women at Marvel. I pitched some ideas and in 2020, we had a big Zoom call with Margie to kick it off. Initially, we were going to do fifteen to twenty interviews and some history. The book would be done by April or May. Then we got on the phone with some of these women — especially the women from the '60s and '70s — and they'd mention a name we hadn't heard of. "Oh, they'll talk to you, here's their email." Then that person would connect to us to four more women. Suddenly, we were at fifty interviews with so many more to go. From February 2021 to June 2021, we interviewed over 160 women, men and nonbinary folks.

MS: It was like a mystery. One thread at a time that would unfold. We'd follow the threads through fifty and sixty years. We found out a lot about the evolution of women in the workplace in New York City. We also learned a lot about the evolution of Marvel as a family company and about the birth of Marvel for the masses as a four-quadrant universe. Those were really exciting threads to pull. We really got to see behind the scenes. So that was fun.

AR: So in short, what is *Super Visible*?

JS: It is the story of women and nonbinary folks who have worked at Marvel going all the way back to 1939. The story of them joining Marvel, being part of the Marvel family, and it is the story of the future. It's not just the women who worked in the office like Flo Steinberg or Marie Severin, but it's also the creators that would go on to become prominent names like Tini Howard and Vita Ayala. It is the story of how women have, at every step of the way, been the catalyst for the content that we have now.

AR: Why is this book important?

MS: The book is one of those rare books that does not yet exist on the shelf but that needs to. We spoke to women who no one will ever speak to in another context. Women's history and content history is not chronicled the same way that men's is. We spoke to women who didn't realize they were the senior woman at the company or that they were the first writer or creator or any of these firsts at Marvel. So part of it is to establish that women have been in the building the whole time. That is critically important.

AR: Margie — how did this project differ from your other work to date?

MS: At first, I was scared of this project. I'd never done anything like this before. I've worked broadly and some of the things I value the most came about in the same way. Where I had a passionate interest but no experience. It is like scratching an itch and filling a need that nothing else is filling. We needed to do this. We didn't necessarily know how to do this, but we were going to. We knew we had to deliver for a bunch of women and nonbinary folk. We approached it knowing it was about more than us.

AR: Judy, what did you think was important to highlight in this book?

JS: To me it's always about women whose names have not been in lights, right? I spent fifteen years at Marvel hearing about the great work of Stan Lee, Jack Kirby, and Steve Ditko, but we seldom heard about Marie Severin or so many of the women who did such fabulous, amazing work at Marvel over the years. Their names were never in lights. For me, that was always the most important thing. It was always about the unsung heroes. I think that that's why, initially, we started the podcast. We wanted a space for us to be able to talk to other women, have a conversation, and advocate for all the women doing these great things.

Because, back when we first started, there were very few women and no [out] nonbinary creators working at Marvel at the time. Now it's much better. We still have, like, loads to go, but, for me, it's about the women.

It's about every woman we talk to having their moment, their mention. Like Susan Crespi, whose father was Danny Crespi, a huge element of the bullpen in the 1970s and 1980s. She came to Marvel after he passed and is still at Marvel today making sure the books go out to print on time. It's those women, it's those creators, it's those people that make this shine. I really hope what readers will get out of this is that they too can work at Marvel. That they too can join the [multitude] of people who have worked at Marvel. And maybe get their names in lights too.

AR: Do you have a favorite story, interview or essay from the book?

MARVEL
STOHL
PACHECO
FONTERIZ
MENYZ
SAUVAGE

"This book is relevant,
insightful and so
incredibly important."
—comicosity

THE LIFE OF
CAPTAIN
MARVEL

The Life of Captain Marvel cover by **InHyuk Lee**

JS: One of my favorites was this woman who worked in comics, both at Marvel and DC, in the 1970s. Her name is Irene Vartanoff. And she actually became fairly well-known within the very small comic community in the 1960s. Because she used to write letters to the editors, specifically to DC. And she had many of them published. And there was this huge community in the 1960s of people because they would print, like, where they were from. And so they would connect that way. And

so she went to some of the first comic book conventions, in New York City, in the 1960s. And she told us about them.

MS: Victoria Alonso. I would follow her into the sun, you know what I mean? She's this badass model of acceptance. She's worked in a male-dominated world a long time and doesn't want to be the only woman in the room. Time and again, we heard from so many people she'd mentored and paved the way for. I think she unlocked a bunch of doors for us after that conversation. So that was sort of a turning point for me.

AR: Any last words about the book?

JS: I feel like the thing that I want everyone to remember is that this is not the end of this story. That this is just the beginning of the story. I hope what comes after this is that there are many more books telling the history of women working within these industries. That maybe there's a continuation of this story, where we really dive into every one of these women and tell more of their individual stories.

MS: Yeah, this is a conversation between 160 women and nonbinary creators. And by far the most comprehensive, well-supported project on the history of women in comics, period. So we're pretty excited about that.

Super Visible releases this year and is currently available for pre-order. You can listen to my full interview and other amazing conversations on the upcoming seasons of the Women of Marvel podcast on Apple Podcasts or wherever you listen to podcasts.

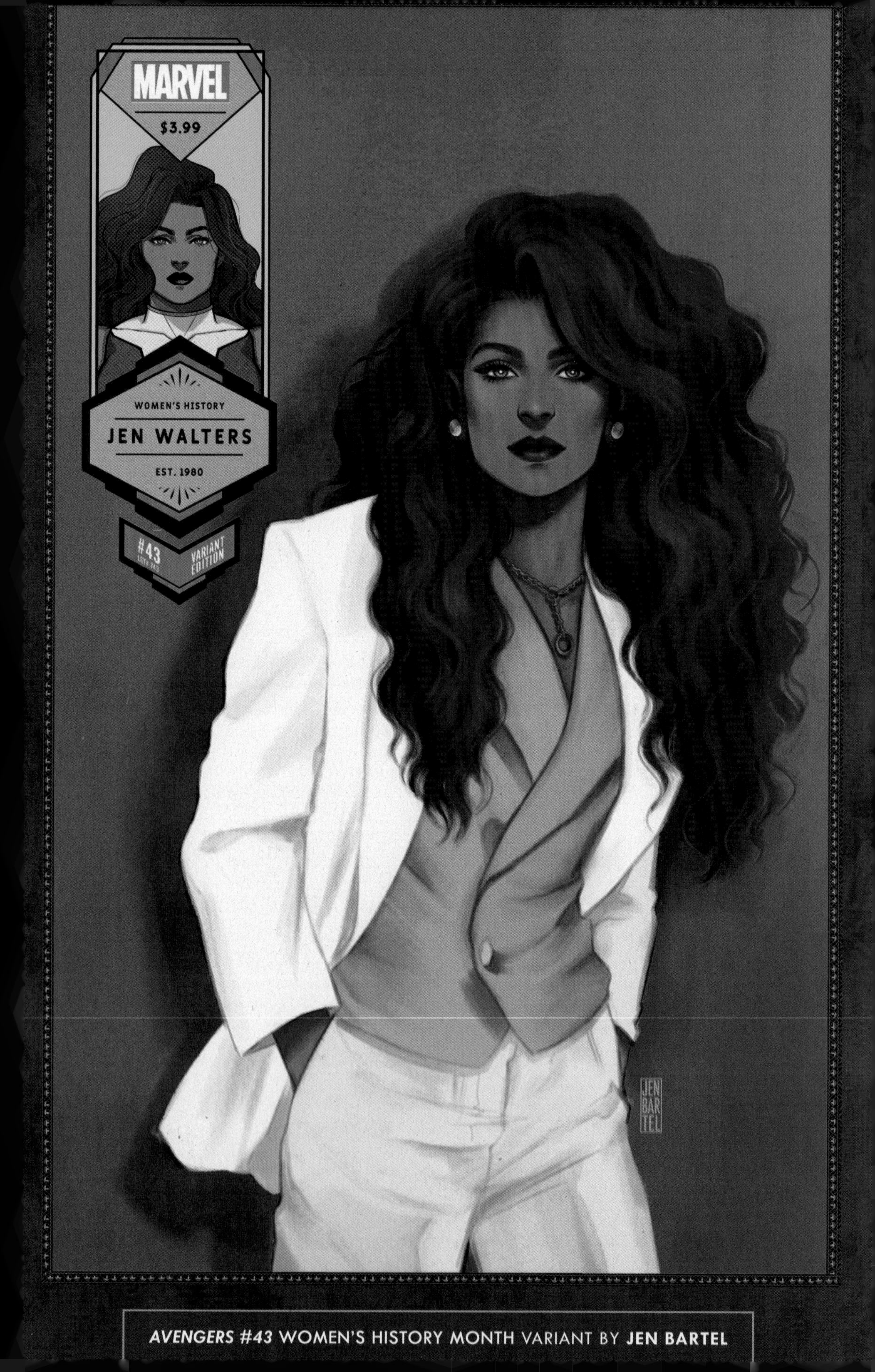
MARVEL
$3.99
WOMEN'S HISTORY
JEN WALTERS
EST. 1980
#43
VARIANT EDITION
JEN BARTEL

AVENGERS #43 WOMEN'S HISTORY MONTH VARIANT BY **JEN BARTEL**

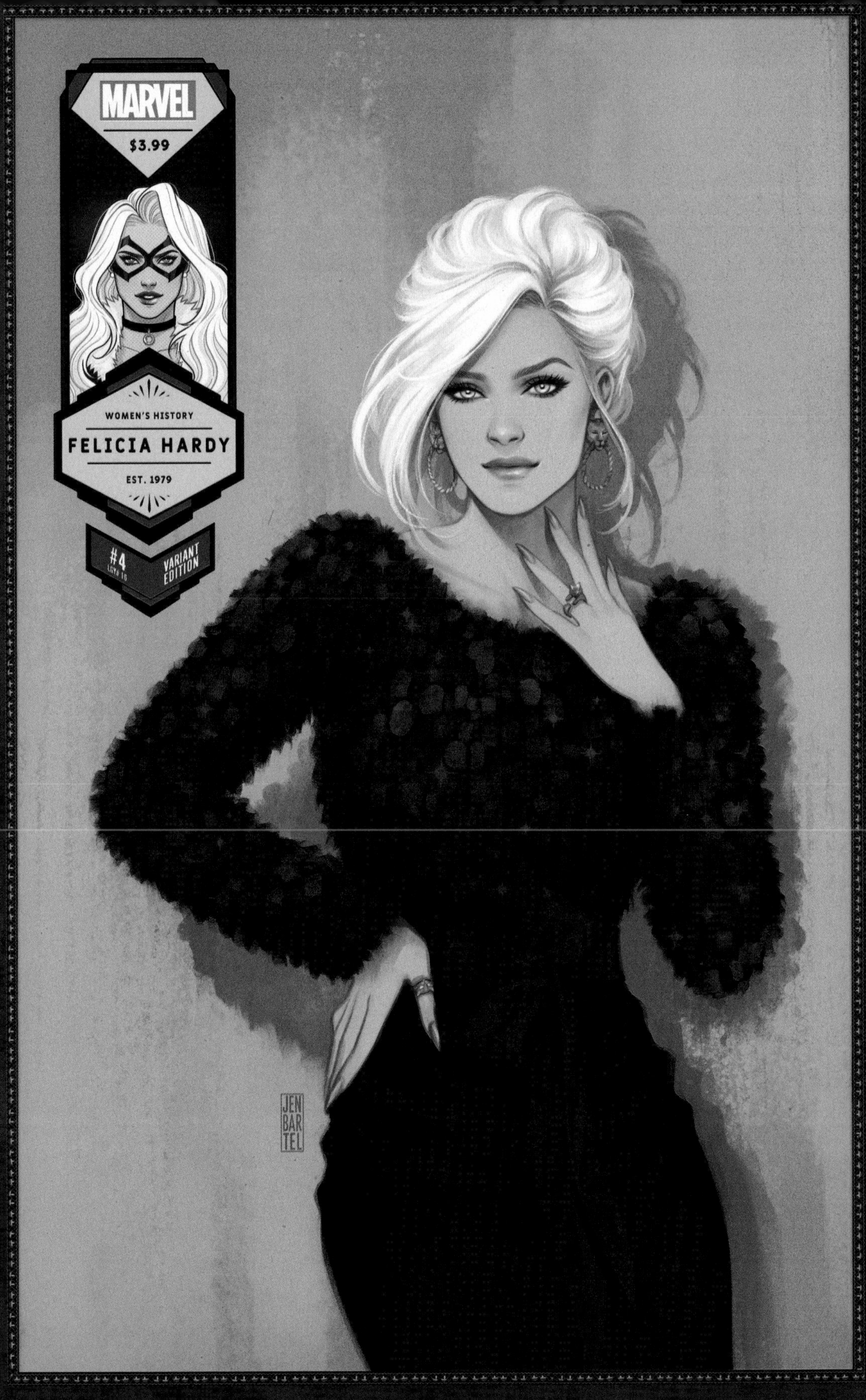
MARVEL
$3.99
WOMEN'S HISTORY
FELICIA HARDY
EST. 1979
#4
VARIANT EDITION
JEN BARTEL

BLACK CAT #4 WOMEN'S HISTORY MONTH VARIANT BY **JEN BARTEL**

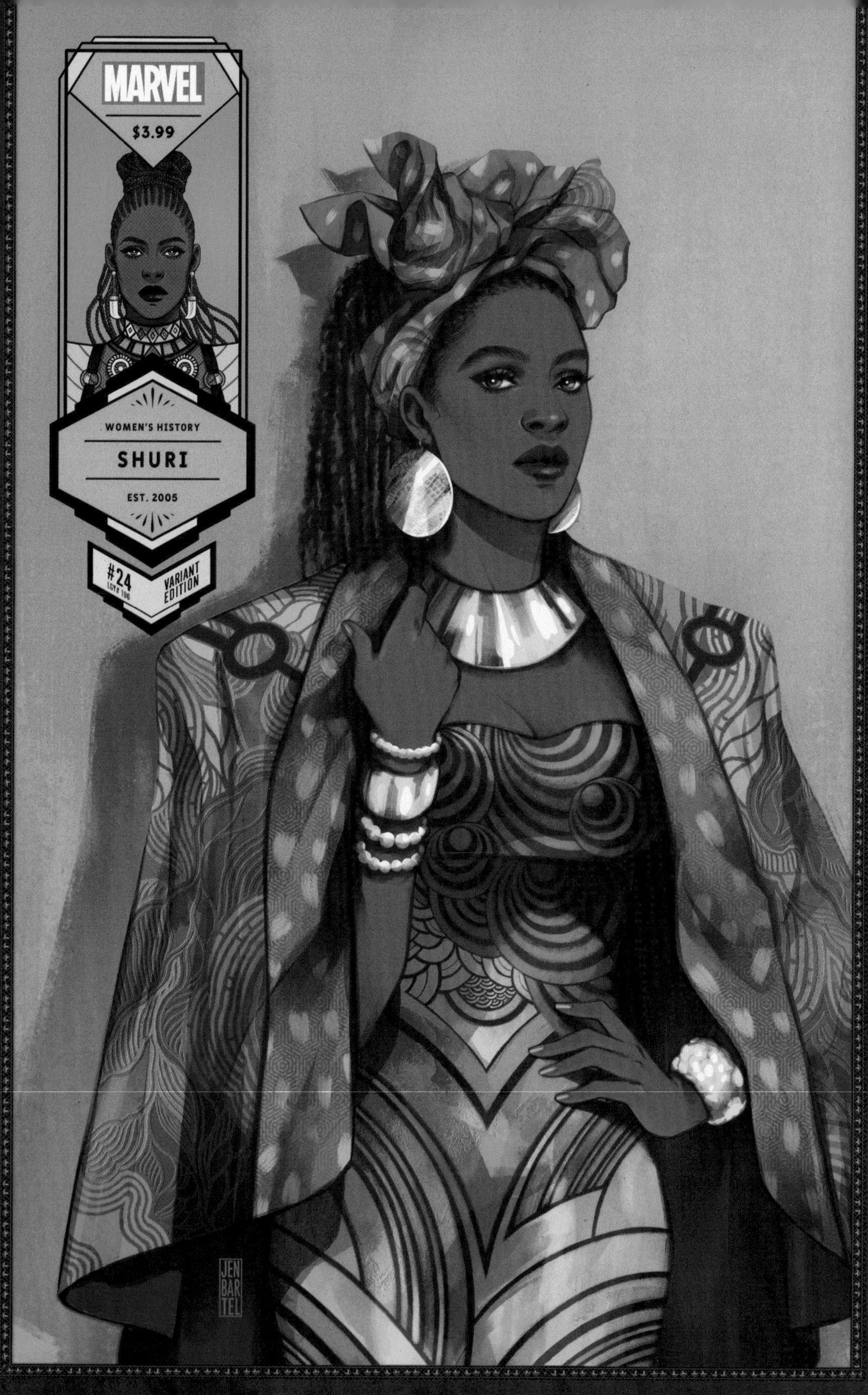
MARVEL
$3.99
WOMEN'S HISTORY
SHURI
EST. 2005
#24
VARIANT EDITION
JEN BARTEL

***BLACK PANTHER* #24** WOMEN'S HISTORY MONTH VARIANT BY **JEN BARTEL**

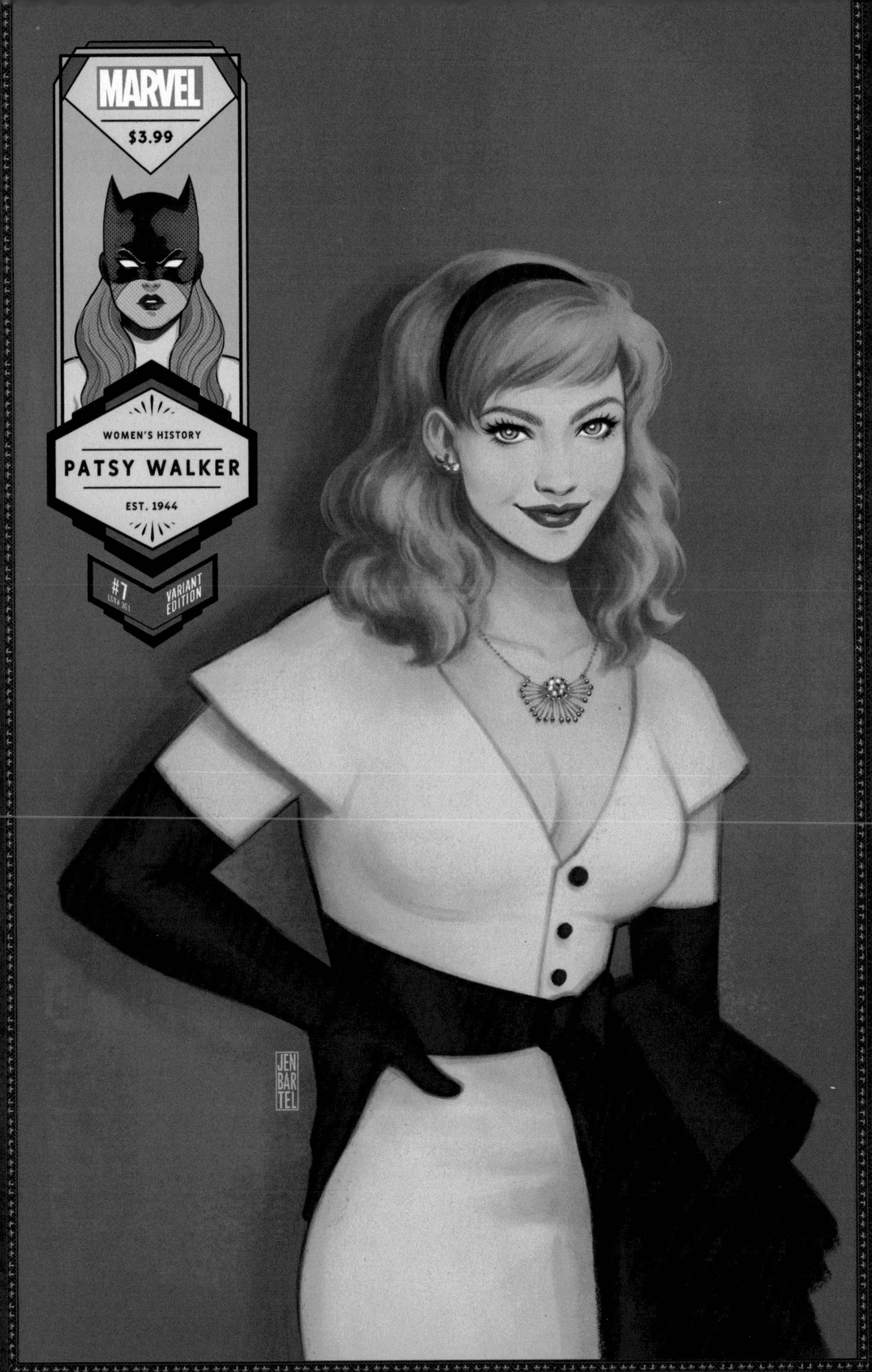
MARVEL
$3.99
WOMEN'S HISTORY
PATSY WALKER
EST. 1944
#7
VARIANT EDITION
JEN BAR TEL

IRON MAN #7 WOMEN'S HISTORY MONTH VARIANT BY **JEN BARTEL**

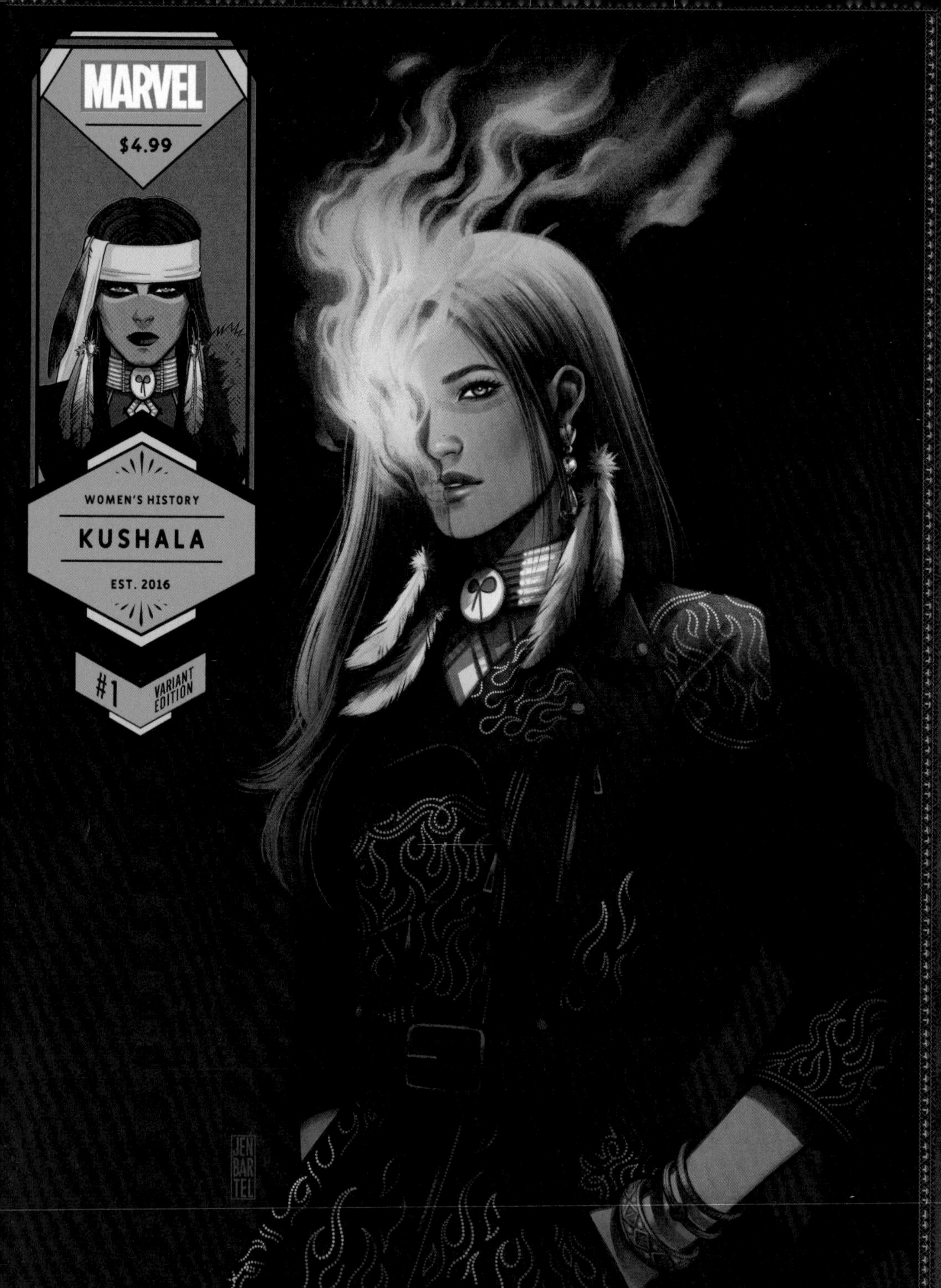
MARVEL
$4.99
WOMEN'S HISTORY
KUSHALA
EST. 2016
#1
VARIANT EDITION
JEN BARTEL

KING IN BLACK: GHOST RIDER #1 WOMEN'S HISTORY MONTH VARIANT BY **JEN BARTEL**

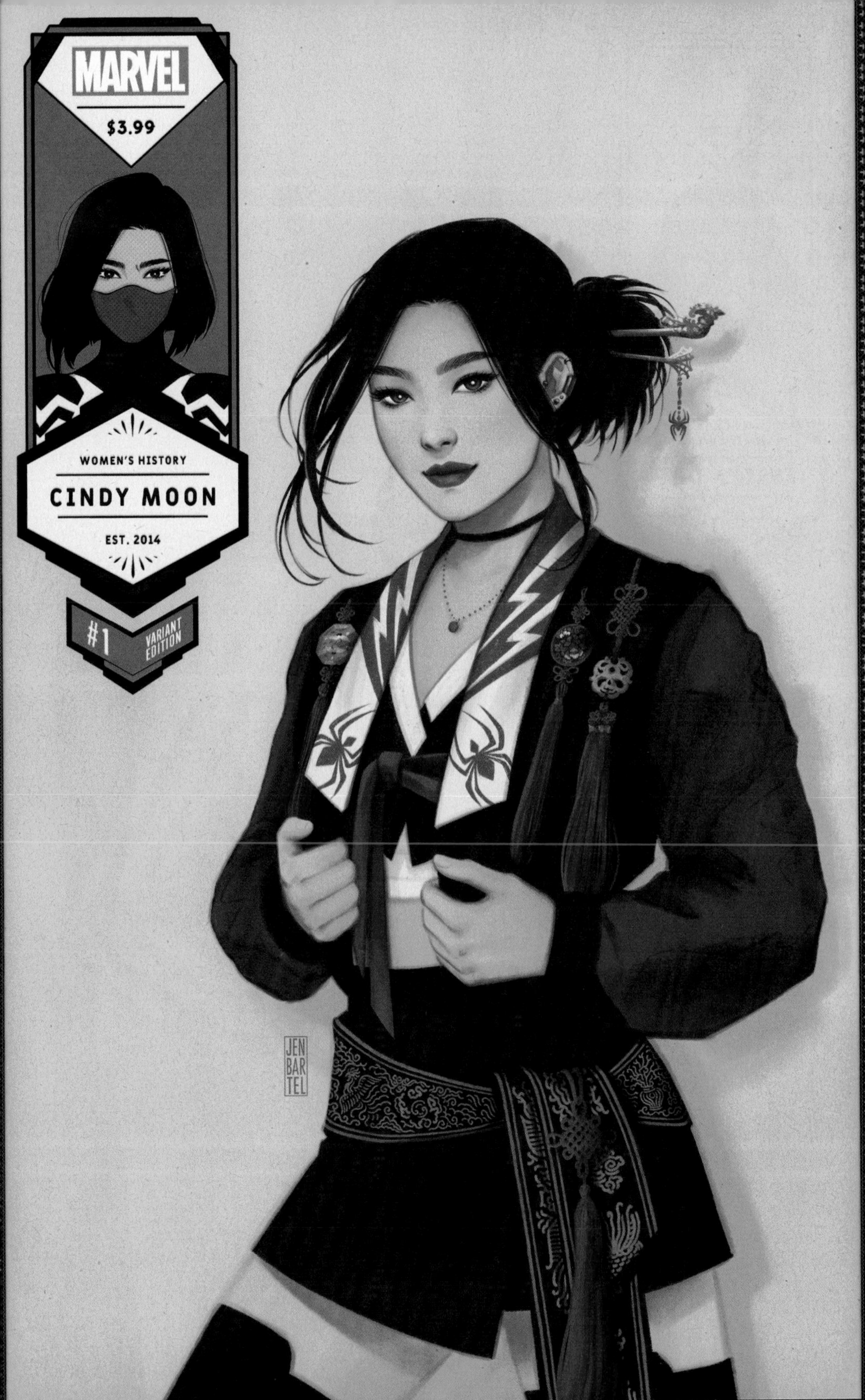
MARVEL
$3.99
WOMEN'S HISTORY
CINDY MOON
EST. 2014
#1
VARIANT EDITION
JEN BAR TEL

SILK #1 WOMEN'S HISTORY MONTH VARIANT BY **JEN BARTEL**

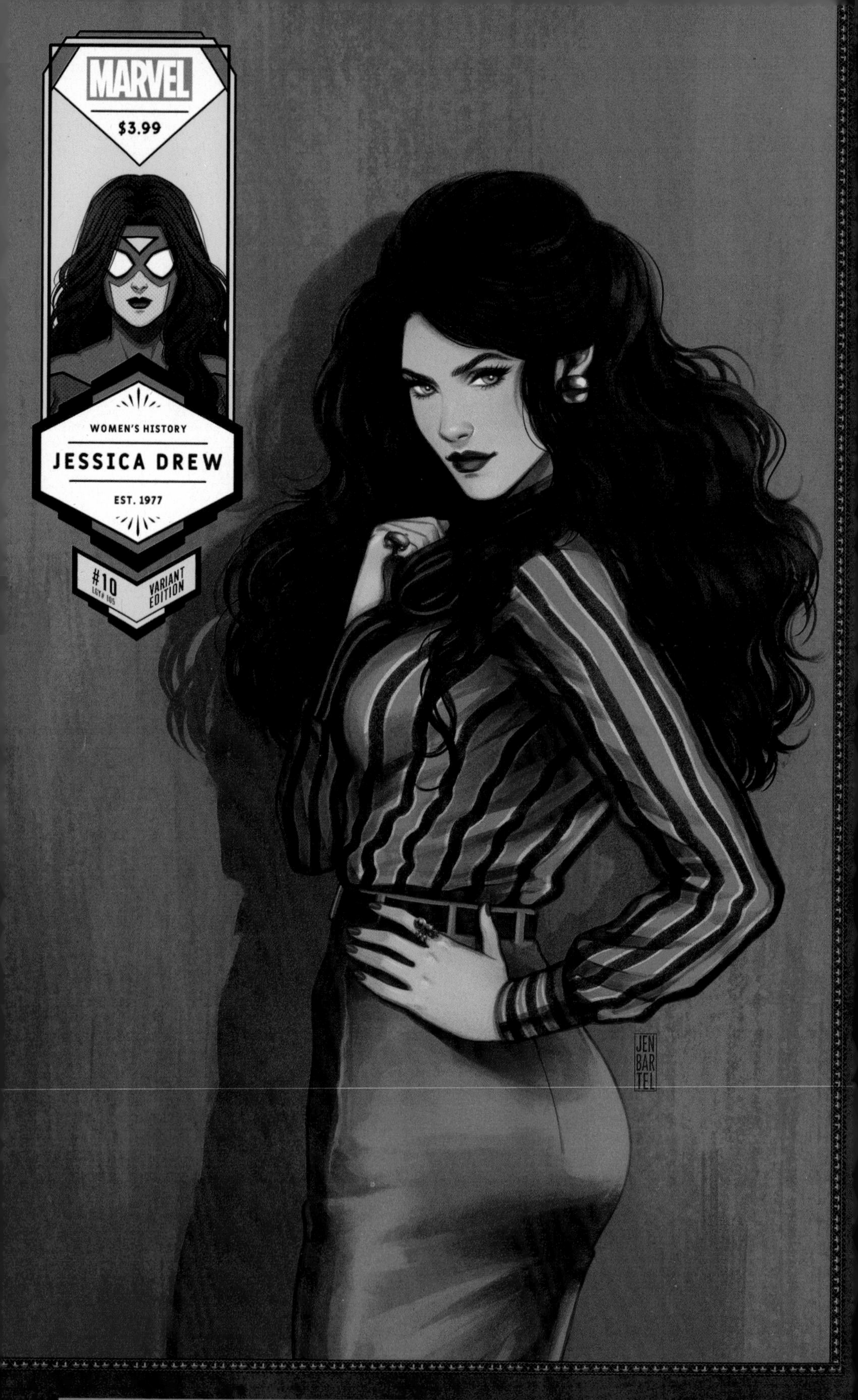
MARVEL
$3.99
WOMEN'S HISTORY
JESSICA DREW
EST. 1977
#10
LGY# 105
VARIANT EDITION
JEN BARTEL

SPIDER-WOMAN #10 WOMEN'S HISTORY MONTH VARIANT BY **JEN BARTEL**

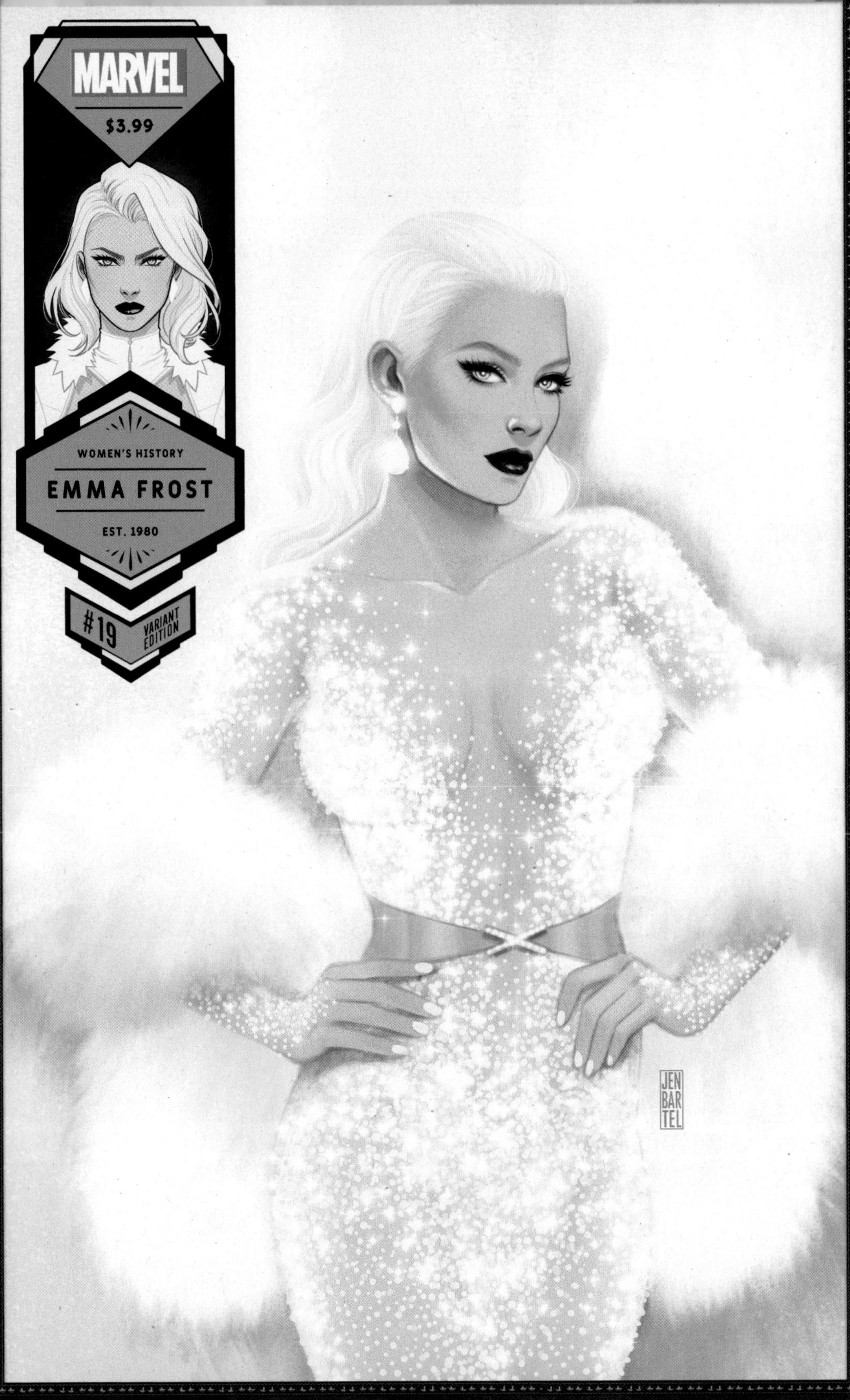

MARVEL
$3.99
WOMEN'S HISTORY
EMMA FROST
EST. 1980
#19
VARIANT EDITION
JEN BARTEL

X-MEN #19 WOMEN'S HISTORY MONTH VARIANT BY JEN BARTEL

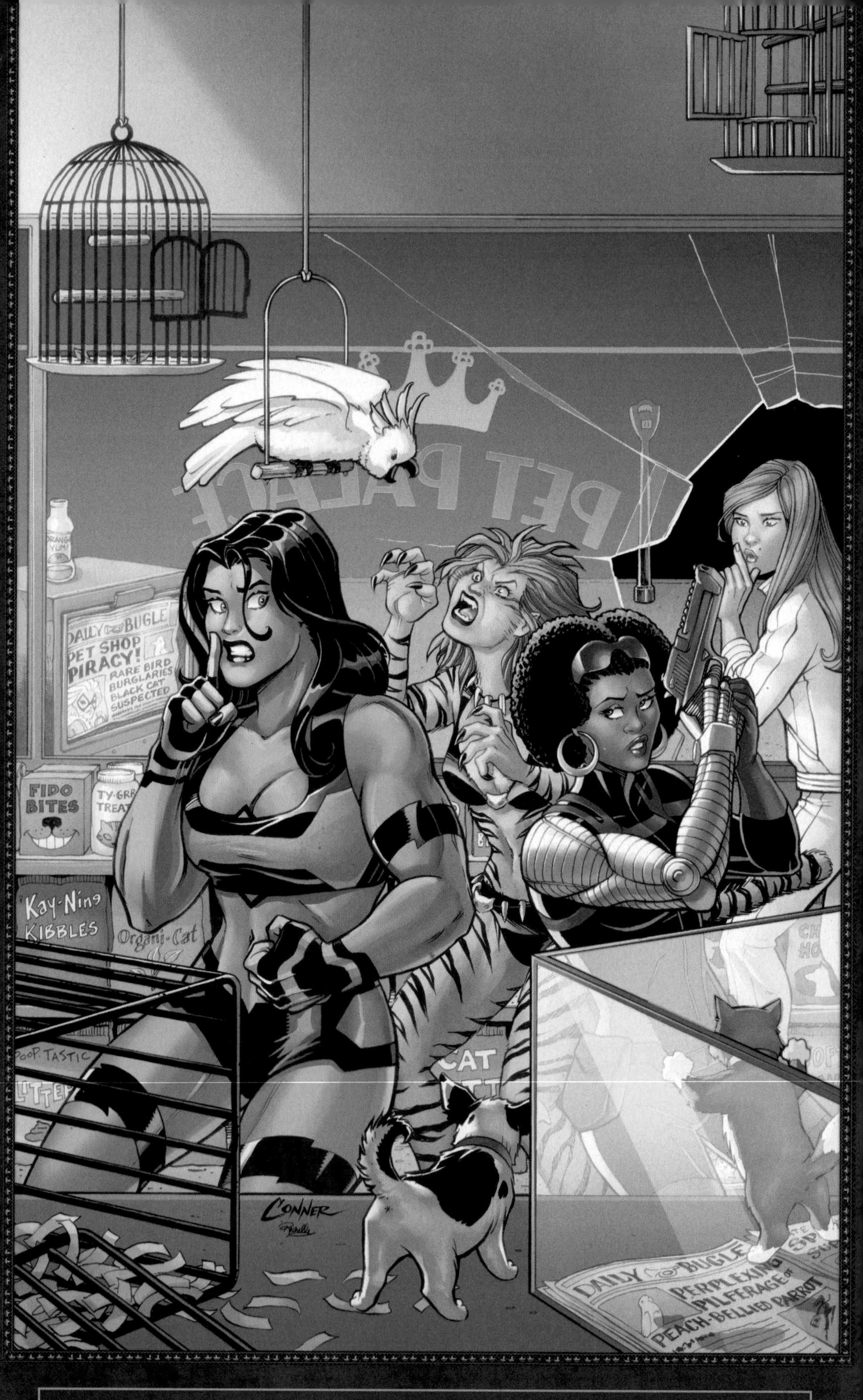
DAILY BUGLE
PET SHOP PIRACY!
RARE BIRD BURGLARIES BLACK CAT SUSPECTED
FIDO BITES
Kay-Nine KIBBLES
Organi-Cat
POOP-TASTIC
CONNER
DAILY BUGLE
PERPLEXING PILFERAGE OF PEACH-BELLIED PARROT

WOMEN OF MARVEL #1 VARIANT BY AMANDA CONNER & RACHELLE ROSENBERG

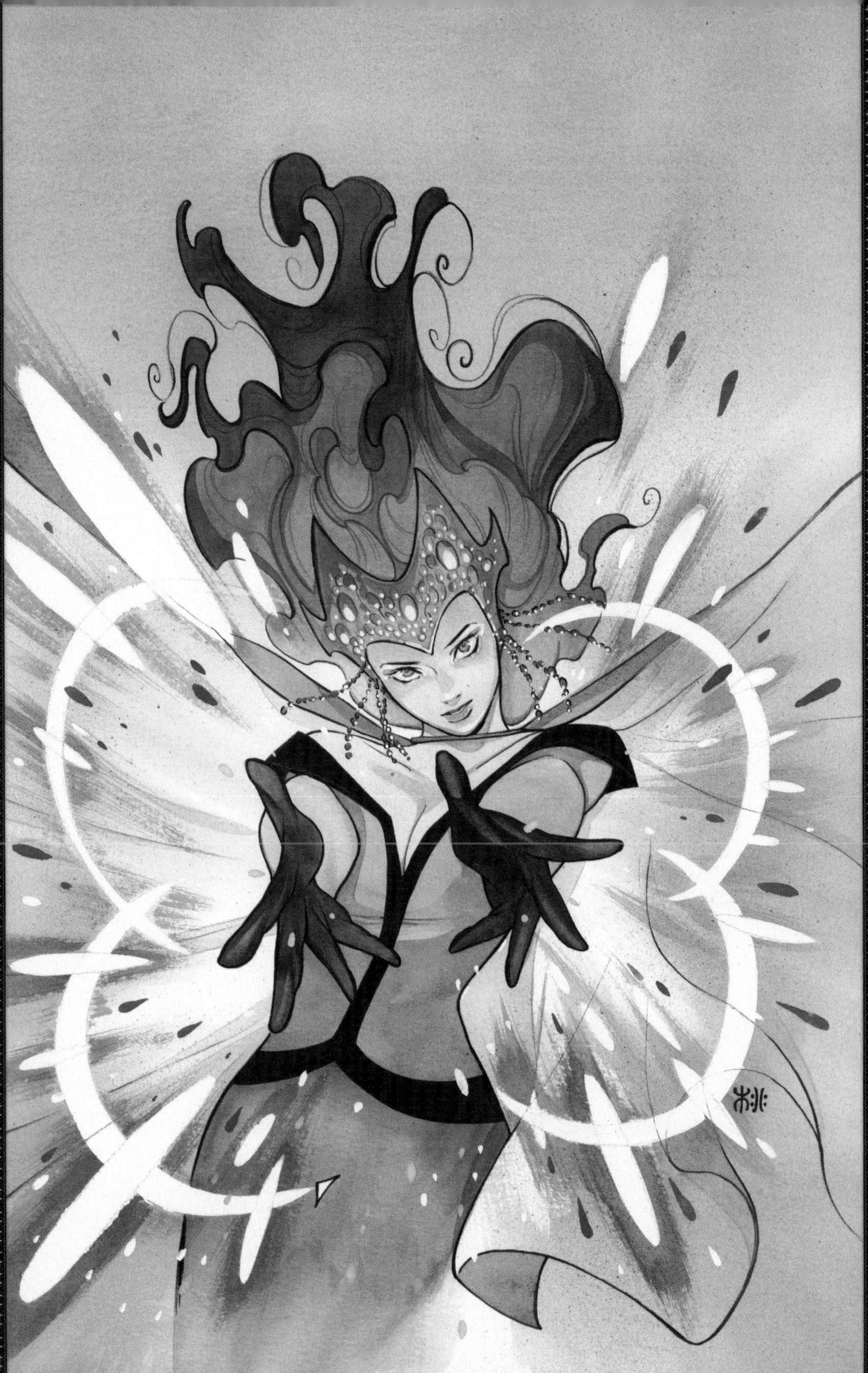

WOMEN OF MARVEL #1 VARIANT BY **PEACH MOMOKO**

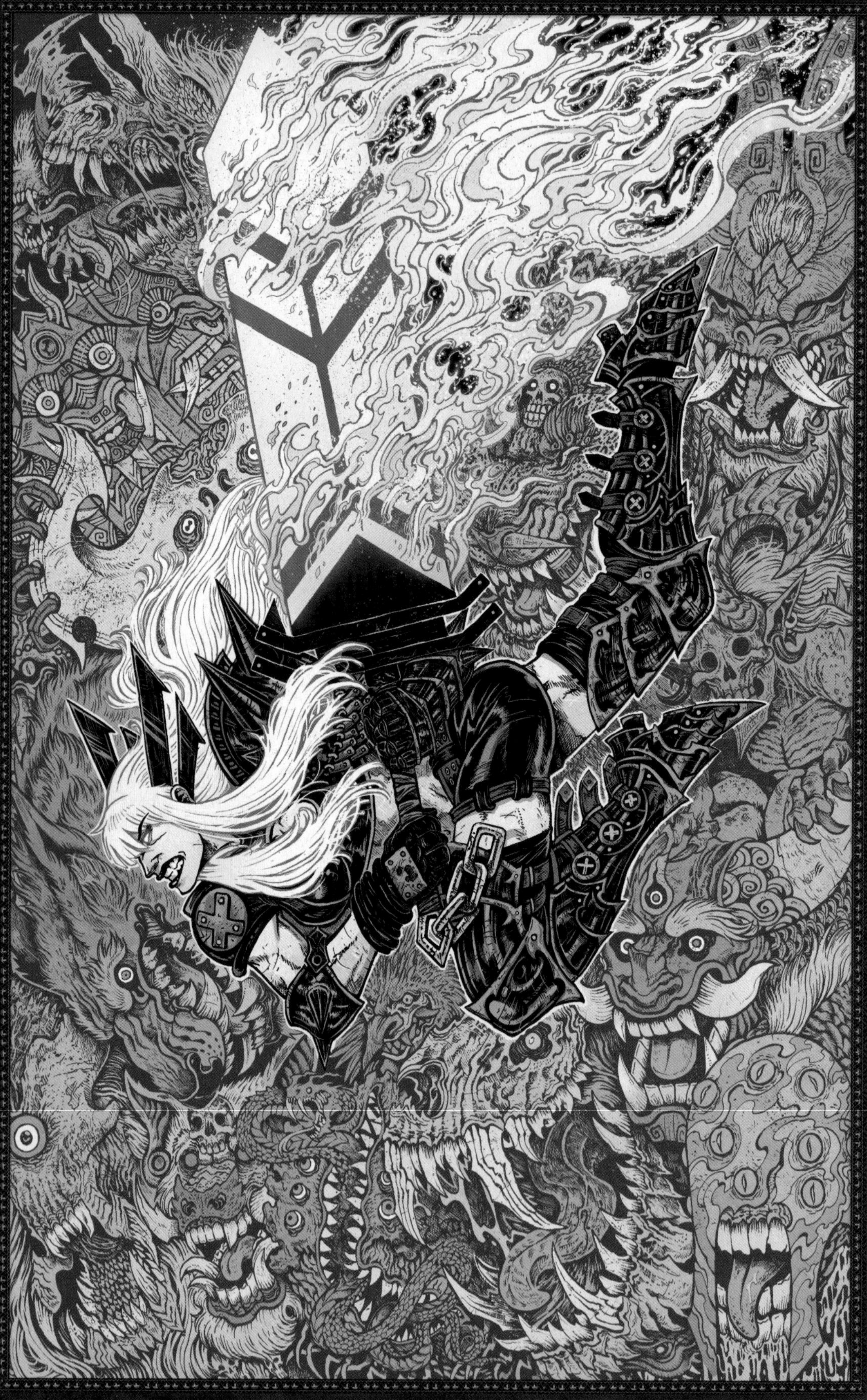

WOMEN OF MARVEL #1 VARIANT BY **MARIA WOLF** & **MIKE SPICER**